Oracle JRockit

The Definitive Guide

Develop and manage robust Java applications with
Oracle's high-performance Java Virtual Machine

Marcus Hirt

Marcus Lagergren

[PACKT] enterprise

PUBLISHING   professional expertise distilled

BIRMINGHAM - MUMBAI

Oracle JRockit
The Definitive Guide

First published: June 2010

Production Reference: 1260510

Published by Packt Publishing Ltd.
32 Lincoln Road
Olton
Birmingham, B27 6PA, UK.

ISBN 978-1-847198-06-8

www.packtpub.com

Cover Image by Mark Holland (MJH767@bham.ac.uk)

Credits

Authors

Marcus Hirt

Marcus Lagergren

Reviewers

Anders Åstrand

Staffan Friberg

Markus Grönlund

Daniel Källander

Bengt Rutisson

Henrik Ståhl

Acquisition Editor

James Lumsden

Development Editor

Rakesh Shejwal

Technical Editor

Sandesh Modhe

Indexer

Rekha Nair

Editorial Team Leader

Gagandeep Singh

Project Team Leader

Priya Mukherji

Project Coordinator

Ashwin Shetty

Proofreader

Andie Scothern

Graphics

Geetanjali Sawant

Production Coordinator

Melwyn D'sa

Cover Work

Melwyn D'sa

Foreword

I remember quite clearly the first time I met the JRockit team. It was JavaOne 1999 and I was there representing WebLogic. Here were these Swedish college kids in black T-shirts describing how they would build the world's best server VM. I was interested in hearing their story as the 1.2 release of HotSpot had been delayed again and we'd been running into no end of scalability problems with the Classic VM. However I walked away from the booth thinking that, while these guys were smart, they had no idea what they were biting off.

Fast-forward a few years. BEA buys JRockit and I become the technical liaison between the WebLogic and JRockit teams. By now JRockit has developed into an excellent offering—providing great scalability and performance on server-side systems. As we begin working together I have the distinct pleasure of getting to know the authors of this book: Marcus Lagergren and Marcus Hirt.

Lagergren is a remarkably prolific developer, who at the time was working on the compiler. He and I spent several sessions together examining optimizations of WebLogic code and deciphering why this method or that wasn't getting inlined or devirtualized. In the process we, along with the rest of the WebLogic and JRockit teams, were able to produce several SPECjAppServer world records and cement JRockit's reputation for performance.

Hirt, on the other hand, is extremely focused on profiling and diagnostics. It was natural, therefore, that he should lead the nascent tooling effort that would become JRockit Mission Control. This was an extension of an early observation we had, that in order to scale the JRockit engineering team, we would have to invest in tooling to make support and debugging easier.

Fast-forward a few more years. I'm now at Oracle when it acquires BEA. I have the distinct pleasure of again welcoming the JRockit team into a new company as they joined my team at Oracle. The core of the JRockit team is still the same and they now have a place among the small group of the world's experts in virtual machines.

Lagergren is still working on internals—now on JRockit Virtual Edition—and is as productive as ever. Under Hirt's leadership, Mission Control has evolved from an internal developer's tool into one of the JRockit features most appreciated by customers. With this combination of long experience and expertise in all layers of JRockit, it is difficult for me to imagine a better combination of authors to write this book.

Therefore, as has been the case many times before, I'm proud to be associated in some small way with the JRockit team. I trust that you will enjoy reading this book and hope that you will find the topic to be as satisfying as I have found it to be over the years.

Adam Messinger
Vice President of Development, Oracle Fusion Middleware group
February 14, 2010
San Francisco, CA

About the Authors

Marcus Hirt is one of the founders of Appeal Virtual Machines, the company that created the JRockit Java Virtual Machine. He is currently working as Architect, Team Lead, and Engineering Manager for the JRockit Mission Control team. In his spare time he enjoys coding on his many pet projects, composing music, and scuba diving. Marcus has contributed JRockit related articles, whitepapers, tutorials, and webinars to the JRockit community, and has been an appreciated speaker at Oracle Open World, eWorld, BEAWorld, EclipseCon, Nordev, and Expert Zone Developer Summit. He received his M.Sc. education in Computer Science at the Royal Institute of Technology in Stockholm. Marcus Hirt lives in Stockholm with his wife and two children.

Marcus Lagergren has an M.Sc. in Computer Science from the Royal Institute of Technology in Stockholm, Sweden. He majored in theoretical computer science and complexity theory since it was way more manly than, for example, database systems. He has a background in computer security but has worked with runtimes since 1999. Marcus was one of the founding members of Appeal Virtual Machines, the company that developed the JRockit JVM. Marcus has been Team Lead and Architect for the JRockit code generators and has been involved in pretty much every other aspect of the JRockit JVM internals over the years. He has presented at various conferences, such as JavaOne, BEAWorld, and eWorld and holds several patents on runtime technology. Since 2008, he works for Oracle on a fast virtualization platform. Marcus likes power tools, heavy metal, and scuba diving. Marcus Lagergren lives in Stockholm with his wife and two daughters.

Acknowledgement

We'd like to thank all the people who have been creative with us throughout the years, especially the other Appeal guys who have been a part of our lives for quite some time now. The authors cannot think of a finer and more competent group of people to have shared this journey with.

Furthermore, a great thank you is in order to our families who have been extremely patient with us during the writing of this book.

About the Reviewers

Anders Åstrand has a Master's degree in Computer Science from the Royal Institute of Technology, Sweden. He has worked at Oracle (formerly BEA Systems) since 2007, in the JRockit performance team.

Staffan Friberg leads the JRockit Performance Team at Oracle, with seven years of experience in QA and Performance Engineering for the JVM.

Markus Grönlund is a Senior Software Engineer with Oracle Corporation and has worked extensively in the Oracle JRockit Virtual Machine development and support arena for the past three years. Markus has been supporting Oracle JRockit VMs the largest mission critical JRockit customers, providing expertise in debugging, configuration, and training.

Prior to joining Oracle Corporation, Markus worked for seven years as a Senior Technical Architect for Intel Corporation, driving early adoption of next-generation Intel Architectures.

> I would like to thank the entire Oracle JRockit Virtual Machine team in Stockholm, Sweden. It is a true privilege to be part of such an amazing group of talented people. Thank you all!

Daniel Källander is Development Manager for JRockit and has been with the JRockit team since 2005. Since 1996, he has been a founding member of three IT companies. Before entering the IT industry he completed a Ph.D. in Theoretical Physics, and later also an MBA in International Business.

Bengt Rutisson is Development Manager at Oracle focusing on JRockit garbage collection and memory management. He joined the JRockit team in 2006 and has been working with garbage collection and memory management since then.

Prior to working with JRockit, Bengt has been responsible for several products in Java (for example, the Appear Context Engine) and in Component Pascal (for example, the BlackBox Component Builder).

Henrik Ståhl is Senior Director of Product Management at Oracle, responsible for product strategy for JRockit. In this position, he is constantly looking for new ways to make the Java Virtual Machine more useful. He has been working with the JRockit team since 2004, starting out as Team Lead for the JVM performance team before moving to a product management role. Prior to Oracle, he was Co-Founder and CTO of the Swedish IT consultancy Omegapoint, lead developer for the core part of the Swedish BankID service and Senior Consultant at Icon Medialab. Henrik holds an M.Sc. in Engineering Physics from the Royal Institute of Technology and lives outside of Stockholm, Sweden with his family.

For my family, who endured me being inaccessible for nights and weekends both working on the new major release and writing this book: Malin, Alexander, and little Natalie.

– Marcus Hirt

For my family: Klara, Alice, and Ylva. Especially for my lovely wife Klara, who ended up having to singlehandedly juggle two children too often and who, more than once, expressed her desire to purchase a copy of this book and burn it.

– Marcus Lagergren

Table of Contents

Preface

This book is the result of an amazing series of events.

In high school, back in the pre-Internet era, the authors used to hang out at the same bulletin board systems and found each other in a particularly geeky thread about math problems. Bulletin board friendship led to friendship in real life, as well as several collaborative software projects. Eventually, both authors went on to study at the Royal Institute of Technology (KTH) in Stockholm.

More friends were made at KTH, and a course in database systems in our third year brought enough people with a similar mindset together to achieve critical mass. The decision was made to form a consulting business named Appeal Software Solutions (the acronym A.S.S. seemed like a perfectly valid choice at the time). Several of us started to work alongside our studies and a certain percentage of our earnings was put away so that the business could be bootstrapped into a full-time occupation when everyone was out of university. Our long-term goal was always to work with product development, not consulting. However, at the time we did not know what the products would turn out to be.

In 1997, Joakim Dahlstedt, Fredrik Stridsman and Mattias Joëlson won a trip to one of the first JavaOne conferences by out-coding everyone in a Sun sponsored competition for university students. For fun, they did it again the next year with the same result.

It all started when our three heroes noticed that between the two JavaOne conferences in 1997 and 1998, the presentation of Sun's adaptive virtual machine HotSpot remained virtually unchanged. HotSpot, it seemed at the time, was the answer to the Java performance problem. Java back then was mostly an interpreted language and several static compilers for Java were on the market, producing code that ran faster than bytecode, but that usually violated the language semantics in some fundamental way. As this book will stress again and again, the potential power of an adaptive runtime approach exceeds, by far, that of any ahead-of-time solution, but is harder to achieve.

Since there were no news about HotSpot in 1998, youthful hubris caused us to ask ourselves "How hard can it be? Let's make a better adaptive VM, and faster!" We had the right academic backgrounds and thought we knew in which direction to go. Even though it definitely was more of a challenge than we expected, we would still like to remind the reader that in 1998, Java on the server side was only just beginning to take off, J2EE hardly existed and no one had ever heard of a JSP. The problem domain was indeed a lot smaller in 1998.

The original plan was to have a proof of concept implementation of our own JVM finished in a year, while running the consulting business at the same time to finance the JVM development. The JVM was originally christened "RockIT", being both rock 'n' roll, rock solid and IT. A leading "J" was later added for trademark reasons.

Naturally, after a few false starts, we needed to bring in venture capital. Explaining how to capitalize on an adaptive runtime (that the competitors gave away their own free versions of) provided quite a challenge. Not just because this was 1998, and investors had trouble understanding any venture not ultimately designed to either (1) send text messages with advertisements to cell phones or (2) start up a web-based mail order company.

Eventually, venture capital was secured and in early 2000, the first prototype of JRockit 1.0 went public. JRockit 1.0, besides being, as someone on the Internet put it "very 1.0", made some headlines by being extremely fast at things like multi-threaded server applications. Further venture capital was acquired using this as leverage. The consulting business was broken out into a separate corporation and Appeal Software Solutions was renamed Appeal Virtual Machines. Sales people were hired and we started negotiations with Sun for a Java license.

Thus, JRockit started taking up more and more of our time. In 2001, the remaining engineers working in the consulting business, which had also grown, were all finally absorbed into the full-time JVM project and the consulting company was mothballed. At this time we realized that we both knew exactly how to take JRockit to the next level and that our burn rate was too high. Management started looking for a suitor in the form of a larger company to marry.

In February 2002, BEA Systems acquired Appeal Virtual Machines, letting nervous venture capitalists sleep at night, and finally securing us the resources that we needed for a proper research and development lab. A good-sized server hall for testing was built, requiring reinforced floors and more electricity than was available in our building. For quite a while, there was a huge cable from a junction box on the street outside coming in through the server room window. After some time, we outgrew that lab as well and had to rent another site to host some of our servers.

As part of the BEA platform, JRockit matured considerably. The first two years at BEA, plenty of the value-adds and key differentiators between JRockit and other Java solutions were invented, for example the framework that was later to become JRockit Mission Control. Several press releases, world-beating benchmark scores, and a virtualization platform quickly followed. With JRockit, BEA turned into one of the "big three" JVM vendors on the market, along with Sun and IBM, and a customer base of thousands of users developed. A celebration was in order when JRockit started generating revenue, first from the tools suite and later from the unparalleled GC performance provided by the JRockit Real Time product.

In 2008, BEA was acquired by Oracle, which caused some initial concerns, but JRockit and the JRockit team ended up getting a lot of attention and appreciation.

For many years now, JRockit has been running mission-critical applications all over the world. We are proud to have been part of the making of a piece of software with that kind of market penetration and importance. We are equally proud to have gone from a pre-alpha designed by six guys in a cramped office in the Old Town of Stockholm to a world-class product with a world-class product organization.

The contents of this book stems from more than a decade of our experience with adaptive runtimes in general, and with JRockit in particular. Plenty of the information in this book has, to our knowledge, never been published anywhere before.

We hope you will find it both useful and educational!

What this book covers

Chapter 1: *Getting Started*. This chapter introduces the JRockit JVM and JRockit Mission Control. Explains how to obtain the software and what the support matrix is for different platforms. We point out things to watch out for when migrating between JVMs from different vendors, and explain the versioning scheme for JRockit and JRockit Mission control. We also give pointers to resources where further information and assistance can be found.

Chapter 2: *Adaptive Code Generation*. Code generation in an adaptive runtime is introduced. We explain why adaptive code generation is both harder to do in a JVM than in a static environment as well as why it is potentially much more powerful. The concept of "gambling" for performance is introduced. We examine the JRockit code generation and optimization pipeline and walk through it with an example. Adaptive and classic code optimizations are discussed. Finally, we introduce various flags and directive files that can be used to control code generation in JRockit.

Chapter 3: Adaptive Memory Management. Memory management in an adaptive runtime is introduced. We explain how a garbage collector works, both by looking at the concept of automatic memory management as well as at specific algorithms. Object allocation in a JVM is covered in some detail, as well as the meta-info needed for a garbage collector to do its work. The latter part of the chapter is dedicated to the most important Java APIs for controlling memory management. We also introduce the JRockit Real Time product, which can produce deterministic latencies in a Java application. Finally, flags for controlling the JRockit JVM memory management system are introduced.

Chapter 4: Threads and Synchronization. Threads and synchronization are very important building blocks in Java and a JVM. We explain how these concepts work in the Java language and how they are implemented in the JVM. We talk about the need for a Java Memory Model and the intrinsic complexity it brings. Adaptive optimization based on runtime feedback is done here as well as in all other areas of the JVM. A few important anti-patterns such as double-checked locking are introduced, along with common pitfalls in parallel programming. Finally we discuss how to do lock profiling in JRockit and introduce flags that control the thread system.

Chapter 5: Benchmarking and Tuning. The relevance of benchmarking and the importance of performance goals and metrics is discussed. We explain how to create an appropriate benchmark for a particular problem set. Some industrial benchmarks for Java are introduced. Finally, we discuss in detail how to modify application and JVM behavior based on benchmark feedback. Extensive examples of useful command-line flags for the JRockit JVM are given.

Chapter 6: JRockit Mission Control. The JRockit Mission Control tools suite is introduced. Startup and configuration details for different setups are given. We explain how to run JRockit Mission Control in Eclipse, along with tips on how to configure JRockit to run Eclipse itself. The different tools are introduced and common terminology is established. Various ways to enable JRockit Mission Control to access a remotely running JRockit, together with trouble-shooting tips, are provided.

Chapter 7: The Management Console. This chapter is about the Management Console component in JRockit Mission Control. We introduce the concept of diagnostic commands and online monitoring of a JVM instance. We explain how trigger rules can be set, so that notifications can be given upon certain events. Finally, we show how to extend the Management Console with custom components.

Chapter 8: The Runtime Analyzer. The JRockit Runtime Analyzer (JRA) is introduced. The JRockit Runtime Analyzer is an on-demand profiling framework that produces detailed recordings about the JVM and the application it is running. The recorded profile can later be analyzed offline, using the JRA Mission Control plugin. Recorded data includes profiling of methods and locks, as well as garbage collection information, optimization decisions, object statistics, and latency events. You will learn how to detect some common problems in a JRA recording and how the latency analyzer works.

Chapter 9: The Flight Recorder. The JRockit Flight Recorder has superseded JRA in newer versions of the JRockit Mission Control suite. This chapter explains the features that have been added that facilitate even more verbose runtime recordings. Differences in functionality and GUI are covered.

Chapter 10: The Memory Leak Detector. This chapter introduces the JRockit Memory Leak Detector, the final tool in the JRockit Mission Control tools suite. We explain the concept of a memory leak in a garbage collected language and discuss several use cases for the Memory Leak Detector. Not only can it be used to find unintentional object retention in a Java application, but it also works as a generic heap analyzer. Some of the internal implementation details are given, explaining why this tool also runs with a very low overhead.

Chapter 11: JRCMD. The command-line tool JRCMD is introduced. JRCMD enables a user to interact with all JVMs that are running on a particular machine and to issue them diagnostic commands. The chapter has the form of a reference guide and explains the most important available diagnostic commands. A diagnostic command can be used to examine or modify the state of a running JRockit JVM

Chapter 12: Using the JRockit Management APIs. This chapter explains how to programmatically access some of the functionality in the JRockit JVM. This is the way the JRockit Mission Control suite does it. The APIs JMAPI and JMXMAPI are introduced. While they are not fully officially supported, several insights can be gained about the inner mechanisms of the JVM by understanding how they work. We encourage you to experiment with your own setup.

Chapter 13: JRockit Virtual Edition. We explain virtualization in a modern "cloud-based" environment. We introduce the product JRockit Virtual Edition. Removing the OS layer from a virtualized Java setup is less problematic than one might think. It can also help getting rid of some of the runtime overhead that is typically associated with virtualization. We go on to explain how potentially this can even reduce Java virtualization overhead to levels not possible even on physical hardware.

What you need for this book

You will need a correctly installed JRockit JVM and runtime environment. To get full benefits from this book, a JRockit version of R28 or later is recommended. However, an R27 version will also work. Also, a correctly installed Eclipse for RCP/Plug-in Developers is useful, especially if trying out the different ways to extend JRockit Mission Control and for working with the programs in the code bundle.

Who this book is for

This book is for anyone with a working knowledge of Java, such as developers or administrators with experience from a few years of professional Java development or from managing larger Java installations. The book is divided into three parts.

The first part is focused on what a Java Virtual Machine, and to some extent any adaptive runtime, does and how it works. It will bring up strengths and weaknesses of runtimes in general and of JRockit more specifically, attempting to explain good Java coding practices where appropriate. Peeking inside the "black box" that is the JVM will hopefully provide key insights into what happens when a Java system runs. The information in the first part of the book will help developers and architects understand the consequences of certain design decisions and help them make better ones. This part might also work as study material in a university-level course on adaptive runtimes.

The second part of the book focuses on using the JRockit Mission Control to make Java applications run more optimally. This part of the book is useful for administrators and developers who want to tune JRockit to run their particular applications with maximum performance. It is also useful for developers who want to tune their Java applications for better resource utilization and performance. It should be realized, however, that there is only so much that can be done by tuning the JVM—sometimes there are simple or complex issues in the actual applications, that, if resolved, will lead to massive performance increases. We teach you how the JRockit Mission Control suite suite assists you in finding such bottlenecks and helps you cut hardware and processing costs.

The final part of the book deals with important JRockit-related technologies that have recently, or will soon, be released. This chapter is for anyone interested in how the Java landscape is transforming over the next few years and why. The emphasis is on virtualization.

Finally, there is a bibliography and a glossary of all technical terms used in the book.

Conventions

This book will, at times, show Java source code and command lines. Java code is formatted with a fixed width font with standard Java formatting. Command-line utilities and parameters are also be printed with a fixed width font. Likewise, references to file names, code fragments, and Java packages in sentences will use a fixed width font.

Short and important information, or anecdotes, relevant to the current section of text is placed in information boxes.

 The contents of an information box – this is important!

Technical terms and fundamental concepts are highlighted as **keywords**. Keywords also often appear in the glossary for quick reference.

Throughout the book, the capitalized tags `JROCKIT_HOME` and `JAVA_HOME` should be expanded to the full path of your JRockit JDK/JRE installation. For example, if you have installed JRockit so that your `java` executable is located in:

```
C:\jrockits\jrockit-jdk1.5.0_17\bin\java.exe
```

the `JROCKIT_HOME` and `JAVA_HOME` variables should be expanded to:

```
C:\jrockits\jrockit-jdk1.5.0_17\
```

The JRockit JVM has its own version number. The latest major version of JRockit is R28. Minor revisions of JRockit are annotated with point release numbers after the major version number. For example R27.1 and R27.2. We will, throughout the book, assume R27.x to mean any R27-based version of the JRockit JVM, and R28.x to mean any R28-based version of the JRockit JVM.

 This book assumes that R28 is the JRockit JVM being used, where no other context is supplied. Information relevant only to earlier versions of JRockit is specifically tagged.

JRockit Mission Control clients use more standard revision numbers, for example 4.0. Any reference to 3.x and 4.0 in the context of tools mean the corresponding versions of the JRockit Mission Control clients. At the time of this writing, 4.0 is the latest version of the Mission Control client, and is, unless explicitly stated otherwise, assumed to be the version in use in the examples in this book.

We will sometimes refer to third-party products. No deeper familiarity with them is required to get full benefits from this book. The products mentioned are:

Oracle WebLogic Server — the Oracle J2EE application server.

`http://www.oracle.com/weblogicserver`

Oracle Coherence — the Oracle in-memory distributed cache technology.

`http://www.oracle.com/technology/products/coherence/index.html`

Oracle Enterprise Manager — the Oracle application management suite.

`http://www.oracle.com/us/products/enterprise-manager/index.htm`

Eclipse — the Integrated Development Environment for Java (and other languages).

`http://www.eclipse.org`

HotSpot™ — the HotSpot™ virtual machine.

`http://java.sun.com/products/hotspot`

See the link associated with each product for further information.

Reader feedback

Feedback from our readers is always welcome. Let us know what you think about this book — what you liked or may have disliked. Reader feedback is important for us to develop titles that you really get the most out of.

To send us general feedback, simply send an e-mail to `feedback@packtpub.com`, and mention the book title via the subject of your message.

If there is a book that you need and would like to see us publish, please send us a note in the **SUGGEST A TITLE** form on `www.packtpub.com` or e-mail `suggest@packtpub.com`.

If there is a topic that you have expertise in and you are interested in either writing or contributing to a book on, see our author guide on `www.packtpub.com/authors`.

Customer support

Now that you are the proud owner of a Packt book, we have a number of things to help you to get the most from your purchase.

> **Downloading the example code for the book**
>
> Visit http://www.packtpub.com/site/default/ files/8068_Code.zip to directly download the example code.
>
> The downloadable files contain instructions on how to use them.

Errata

Although we have taken every care to ensure the accuracy of our content, mistakes do happen. If you find a mistake in one of our books—maybe a mistake in the text or the code—we would be grateful if you would report this to us. By doing so, you can save other readers from frustration and help us improve subsequent versions of this book. If you find any errata, please report them by visiting http://www. packtpub.com/support, selecting your book, clicking on the **let us know** link, and entering the details of your errata. Once your errata are verified, your submission will be accepted and the errata will be uploaded on our website, or added to any list of existing errata, under the Errata section of that title. Any existing errata can be viewed by selecting your title from http://www.packtpub.com/support.

Piracy

Piracy of copyright material on the Internet is an ongoing problem across all media. At Packt, we take the protection of our copyright and licenses very seriously. If you come across any illegal copies of our works, in any form, on the Internet, please provide us with the location address or website name immediately so that we can pursue a remedy.

Please contact us at copyright@packtpub.com with a link to the suspected pirated material.

We appreciate your help in protecting our authors, and our ability to bring you valuable content.

Questions

You can contact us at questions@packtpub.com if you are having a problem with any aspect of the book, and we will do our best to address it.

1
Getting Started

While parts of this book, mainly the first part, contain generic information on the inner workings of all adaptive runtimes, the examples and in-depth information still assume that the JRockit JVM is used. This chapter briefly explains how to obtain the JRockit JVM and covers porting issues that may arise while deploying your Java application on JRockit.

In this chapter, you will learn:

- How to obtain JRockit
- The platforms supported by JRockit
- How to migrate to JRockit
- About the command-line options to JRockit
- How to interpret JRockit version numbers
- Where to get help if you run into trouble

Obtaining the JRockit JVM

To get the most out of this book, the latest version of the JRockit JVM is required. For JRockit versions prior to R27.5, a license key was required to access some of the more advanced features in JRockit. As part of the Oracle acquisition of BEA Systems, the license system was removed and it is now possible to access all features in JRockit without any license key at all. This makes it much easier to evaluate JRockit and to use JRockit in development. To use JRockit in production, a license must still be purchased. For Oracle customers, this is rarely an issue, as JRockit is included with most application suites, for example, any suite that includes WebLogic Server will also include JRockit.

At the time of writing, the easiest way to get a JRockit JVM is to download and install JRockit Mission Control—the diagnostics and profiling tools suite for JRockit. The folder layout of the Mission Control distribution is nearly identical to that of any JDK and can readily be used as a JDK. The authors would very much like to be able to provide a self-contained JVM-only JDK for JRockit, but this is currently beyond our control. We anticipate this will change in the near future.

Before JRockit Mission Control is downloaded, ensure that a supported platform is used. The server part of Mission Control is supported on all platforms for which JRockit is supported.

Following is the platform matrix for JRockit Mission Control 3.1.x:

Platform	Java 1.4.2	Java 5.0	Java 6
Linux x86	X	X	X
Linux x86-64	N/A	X	X
Linux Itanium	X (server only)	X (server only)	N/A
Solaris SPARC (64-bit)	X (server only)	X (server only)	X (server only)
Windows x86	X	X	X
Windows x86-64	N/A	X (server only)	X (server only)
Windows Itanium	X (server only)	X (server only)	N/A

Following is the platform matrix for JRockit Mission Control 4.0.0:

Platform	Java 5.0	Java 6
Linux x86	X	X
Linux x86-64	X	X
Solaris SPARC (64-bit)	X (server only)	X (server only)
Windows x86	X	X
Windows x86-64	X	X

Note that the JRockit Mission Control client is not (yet) supported on Solaris, but that 64-bit Windows support has been added in 4.0.0.

 When running JRockit Mission Control on Windows, ensure that the system's temporary directory is on a file system that supports per-user file access rights. In other words, make sure it is not on a FAT formatted disk. On a FAT formatted disk, essential features such as automatic discovery of local JVMs will be disabled.

The easiest way to get to the JRockit home page is to go to your favorite search engine and type in "**download JRockit**". You should end up on a page on the **Oracle Technology Network** from which the JVM and the Mission Control suite can be downloaded. The installation process varies between platforms, but should be rather self explanatory.

Migrating to JRockit

Throughout this book, we will refer to the directory where the JRockit JVM is installed as JROCKIT_HOME. It might simplify things to make JROCKIT_HOME a system variable pointing to that particular path. After the installation has completed, it is a good idea to put the JROCKIT_HOME/bin directory on the path and to update the scripts for any Java applications that should be migrated to JRockit. Setting the JAVA_HOME environment variable to JROCKIT_HOME is also recommended. In most respects JRockit is a direct drop in replacement for other JVMs, but some startup arguments, for example arguments that control specific garbage collection behavior, typically differ between JVMs from different vendors. Common arguments, however, such as arguments for setting a maximum heap size, tend to be standardized between JVMs.

For more information about specific migration details, see the *Migrating Applications to the Oracle JRockit JDK* Chapter in the online documentation for JRockit.

Command-line options

There are three main types of command-line options to JRockit—system properties, standardized options (-X flags), and non-standard ones (-XX flags).

System properties

Startup arguments to a JVM come in many different flavors. Arguments starting with –D are interpreted as a directive to set a system property. Such system properties can provide configuration settings for various parts of the Java class libraries, for example RMI. JRockit Mission Control provides debugging information if started with –Dcom.jrockit.mc.debug=true. In JRockit versions post R28, the use of system properties to provide parameters to the JVM has been mostly deprecated. Instead, most options to the JVM are provided through non-standard options and the new HotSpot style VM flags.

Standardized options

Configuration settings for the JVM typically start with -x for settings that are commonly supported across vendors. For example, the option for setting the maximum heap size, -Xmx, is the same on most JVMs, JRockit included. There are a few exceptions here. The JRockit flag –Xverbose provides logging with optional sub modules. The similar (but more limited) flag in HotSpot is called just –verbose.

Non-standard options

Vendor-specific configuration options are usually prefixed with -XX. These options should be treated as potentially unsupported and subject to change without notice. If any JVM setup depends on -XX-prefixed options, those flags should be removed or ported before an application is started on a JVM from a different vendor.

Once the JVM options have been determined, the user application can be started. Typically, moving an existing application to JRockit leads to an increase in runtime performance and a slight increase in memory consumption.

The JVM documentation should always be consulted to determine if non-standard command-line options have the same semantics between different JVMs and JVM versions.

VM flags

In JRockit versions post R28, there is also a subset of the non-standard options called VM flags. The VM flags use the -XX:<flag>=<value> syntax. These flags can also be read and, depending on the particular flag, written using the command-line utility JRCMD after the JVM has been started. For more information on JRCMD, see Chapter 11.

Changes in behavior

Sometimes there is a change of runtime behavior when moving from one JVM to another. Usually it boils down to different JVMs interpreting the Java Language Specification or Java Virtual Machine Specification differently, but correctly. In several places there is some leeway in the specification that allows different vendors to implement the functionality in a way that best suits the vendor's architecture. If an application relies too much on a particular implementation of the specification, the application will almost certainly fail when switching to another implementation.

For example, during the milestone testing for an older version of Eclipse, some of the tests started failing when running on JRockit. This was due to the tests having inter-test dependencies, and this particular set of tests were relying on the test harness running the tests in a particular order. The JRockit implementation of the reflective listing of methods (`Class#getDeclaredMethods`) did not return the methods in the same order as other JVMs, which according to the specification is fine. It was later decided by the Eclipse development team that relying on a particular method ordering was a bug, and the tests were consequently corrected.

If an application has not been written to the specification, but rather to the behavior of the JVM from a certain vendor, it can fail. It can even fail when running with a more recent version of the JVM from the same vendor. When in doubt, consult the Java Language Specification and the documentation for the JDK.

Differences in performance may also be an issue when switching JVMs for an application. Latent bugs that weren't an issue with one JVM may well be an issue with another, if for example, performance differences cause events to trigger earlier or later than before. These things tend to generate support issues but are rarely the fault of the JVM.

For example, a customer reported that JRockit crashed after only a day. Investigation concluded that the application also crashed with a JVM from another vendor, but it took a few more days for the application to crash. It was found that the crashing program ran faster in JRockit, and that the problem; a memory leak, simply came to light much more quickly.

Naturally, any JVM, JRockit included, can have bugs. In order to brand itself "Java", a Java Virtual Machine implementation has to pass an extensive test suite—the **Java Compatibility Kit (JCK)**.

JRockit is continuously subjected to a battery of tests using a distributed test system. Large test suites, of which the JCK is one component, are run to ensure that JRockit can be released as a stable, Java compatible, and certified JVM. Large test suites from various high profile products, such as Eclipse and WebLogic Server, as well as specially designed stress tests, are run on all supported platforms before a release can take place. Continuous testing against performance regressions is also done as a fundamental part of our QA infrastructure. Even so, bugs do happen. If JRockit does crash, it should always be reported to Oracle support engineers.

A note on JRockit versioning

The way JRockit is versioned can be a little confusing. There are at least three version numbers of interest for each JRockit release:

1. The JRockit JVM version.
2. The JDK version.
3. The Mission Control version.

One way to obtain the version number of the JVM is to run `java -version` from the command prompt. This would typically result in something like the following lines being printed to the console:

```
java version "1.6.0_14"
   Java(TM) SE Runtime Environment (build 1.6.0_14-b08)
   Oracle JRockit(R) (build R28.0.0-582-123273-1.6.0_
      14-20091029-2121-windows-ia32, compiled mode)
```

The first version number is the JDK version being bundled with the JVM. This number is in sync with the standard JDK versions, for the JDK shipped with HotSpot. From the example, we can gather that Java 1.6 is supported and that it is bundled with the JDK classes from update 14-b08. If you, for example, are looking to see what JDK class-level security fixes are included in a certain release, this would be the version number to check.

The JRockit version is the version number starting with an 'R'. In the above example this would be R28.0.0. Each version of the JRockit JVM is built for several different JDKs. The R27.6.5, for instance, exists in versions for Java 1.4, 1.5 (5.0) and 1.6 (6.0). With the R28 version of JRockit, the support for Java 1.4 was phased out.

The number following the version number is the build number, and the number after that is the change number from the versioning system. In the example, the build number was 582 and the change number 123273. The two numbers after the change number are the date (in compact ISO 8601 format) and time (CET) the build was made. After that comes the operating system and CPU architecture that the JVM was built for.

The version number for JRockit Mission Control can be gathered by executing `jrmc -version` or `jrmc -version | more` from the command line.

On Windows, the JRockit Mission Control launcher (`jrmc`) is based on the `javaw` launcher to avoid opening a console window. Console output will not show unless explicitly redirected, for example to `more`.

The output should look like this:

```
Oracle JRockit(R) Mission Control(TM) 4.0 (for JRockit R28.0.0)
  java.vm.version = R28.0.0-582-123273-1.6.0
   _14-20091029-2121-windows-ia32
  build = R28.0.0-582
  chno = 123217
  jrmc.fullversion = 4.0.0
  jrmc.version = 4.0
  jrockit.version = R28.0.0
  year = 2009
```

The first line tells us what version of Mission Control this is and what version of JRockit it was created for. The `java.vm.version` line tells us what JVM Mission Control is actually running on. If Mission Control has been launched too "creatively", for example by directly invoking its main class, there may be differences between the JVM information in the two lines. If this is the case, some functionality in JRockit Mission Control, such as automatic local JVM discovery, may be disabled.

Getting help

There are plenty of helpful resources on JRockit and JRockit Mission Control available on the **Oracle Technology Network**, such as blogs, articles, and forums. JRockit developers and support staff are continuously monitoring the forums, so if an answer to a particular question cannot be found in the forums already, it is usually answered within a few days. Some questions are asked more frequently than others and have been made into "stickies"—forum posts that will stay at the top of the topic listings. There is, for example, a "sticky" available on how to acquire license files for older versions of JRockit.

The JRockit Forum can, at the time of writing, be found here:

`http://forums.oracle.com/forums/forum.jspa?forumID=561`

Here are the locations of some popular JRockit blogs:

`http://blogs.oracle.com/jrockit/`

`http://blogs.oracle.com/hirt/`

`http://blogs.oracle.com/staffan/`

Summary

This chapter provided a short guide for getting started with the JRockit JVM and for migrating existing applications to the JRockit JVM. We covered installing JRockit and provided insights into common pitfalls when migrating a Java application from one JVM to another.

The different categories of command-line flags that JRockit supports were explained, and we showed examples of how to find the version numbers for the different components of the JRockit JDK.

Finally, we provided pointers to additional help.

2
Adaptive Code Generation

This chapter covers code generation and code optimization in a JVM runtime environment, both as a general concept as well as taking a closer look at the JRockit code generation internals. We start by discussing the Java bytecode format, and how a JIT compiler works, making a case for the power of adaptive runtimes. After that, we drill down into the JRockit JVM. Finally, the reader learns how to control code generation and optimization in JRockit.

You will learn the following from this chapter:

- The benefits of a portable platform-independent language such as Java.
- The structure of the Java bytecode format and key details of the Java Virtual Machine specification.
- How the JVM interprets bytecode in order to execute a Java program.
- Adaptive optimizations at runtime versus static ahead-of-time compilation. Why the former is better but harder to do. The "gambling on performance" metaphor.
- Why code generation in an adaptive runtime is potentially very powerful.
- How Java can be compiled to native code, and what the main problems are. Where should optimizations be done—by the Java programmer, by the JVM, or at the bytecode level?
- How the JRockit code pipeline works and its design rationales.
- How to control the code generator in JRockit.

Platform independence

The main selling point for Java when it first came out, and the main contributor to its success as a mainstream language, was the write once/run everywhere concept. Java programs compile into platform-independent, compact Java bytecode (`.class` files). There is no need to recompile a Java application for different architectures, since all Java programs run on a platform-specific Java Virtual Machine that takes care of the final transition to native code.

This widely enhanced portability is a good thing. An application, such as a C++ program, that compiles to a platform-dependent format, has a lot less flexibility. The C++ compiler may compile and heavily optimize the program, for example for the x86 architecture. Then x86 will be the only architecture on which the program can run. We can't readily move the program, optimizations and all, to SPARC. It has to be recompiled, perhaps by a weaker compiler that doesn't optimize as well as for x86. Also if the x86 architecture is upgraded with new instructions, the program will not be able to take advantage of these without being recompiled. Portability can of course be achieved by distributing source code, but that may instead be subject to various license restrictions. In Java, the portability problem is moved to the JVM, and thus becomes third-party responsibility for the programmer.

In the Java world, all platforms on which a JVM exists can execute Java. Platform-independent bytecode is not a new concept per se, and has been used in several languages in the past, for example Pascal and Smalltalk. However, Java was the first language where it was a major factor in its widespread adoption.

When Java was new, its applications were mainly in the form of **Applets**, designed for embedded execution in a web browser. Applets are typical examples of client side programs. However, Java is not only platform-independent, but it also has several other nice intrinsic language properties such as built-in memory management and protection against buffer overruns. The JVM also provides the application with a secure sandboxed platform model. All of these things make Java ideal not only for client applications, but also for complex server side logic.

It took a few years before the benefits of Java as a server-side language were fully acknowledged. Its inherent robustness led to rapidly shorter application development times compared to C++, and to widespread server adoption. Shorter development cycles matter a lot when the application being developed is fairly complex, such as is typically the case for the server side.

The Java Virtual Machine

While platform-independent bytecode provides complete portability between different hardware platforms, a physical CPU still can't execute it. The CPU only knows to execute its particular flavor of native code.

 Throughout this text, we will refer to code that is specific to a certain hardware architecture as **native code.** For example, x86 assembly language or x86 machine code is native code for the x86 platform. Machine code should be taken to mean code in binary platform-dependent format. Assembly language should be taken to mean machine code in human-readable form.

Thus, the JVM is required to turn the bytecodes into native code for the CPU on which the Java application executes. This can be done in one of the following two ways (or a combination of both):

- The Java Virtual Machine specification fully describes the JVM as a state machine, so there is no need to actually translate bytecode to native code. The JVM can emulate the entire execution state of the Java program, including emulating each bytecode instruction as a function of the JVM state. This is referred to as **bytecode interpretation**. The only native code (barring JNI) that executes directly here is the JVM itself.
- The Java Virtual Machine compiles the bytecode that is to be executed to native code for a particular platform and then calls the native code. When bytecode programs are compiled to native code, this is typically done one method at the time, just before the method in question is to be executed for the first time. This is known as **Just-In-Time compilation (JIT)**.

Naturally, a native code version of a program executes orders of magnitude faster than an interpreted one. The tradeoff is, as we shall see, bookkeeping and compilation time overhead.

Stack machine

The Java Virtual Machine is a stack machine. All bytecode operations, with few exceptions, are computed on an evaluation stack by popping operands from the stack, executing the operation and pushing the result back to the stack. For example, an addition is performed by pushing the two terms to the stack, executing an add instruction that consumes the operands and produces a sum, which is placed on the stack. The party interested in the result of the addition then pops the result.

In addition to the stack, the bytecode format specifies up to 65,536 registers or **local variables**.

An operation in bytecode is encoded by just one byte, so Java supports up to 256 **opcodes**, from which most available values are claimed. Each operation has a unique byte value and a human-readable **mnemonic**.

> The only new bytecode value that has been assigned throughout the history of the Java Virtual Machine specification is 0xba—previously reserved, but about to be used for the new operation invokedynamic. This operation can be used to implement dynamic dispatch when a dynamic language (such as Ruby) has been compiled to Java bytecode. For more information about using Java bytecode for dynamic languages, please refer to *Java Specification Request (JSR) 292* on the Internet.

Bytecode format

Consider the following example of an add method in Java source code and then in Java bytecode format:

```java
public int add(int a, int b) {
   return a + b;
}
```

```
public int add(int, int);
   Code:
      0:    iload_1    // stack: a
      1:    iload_2    // stack: a, b
      2:    iadd       // stack: (a+b)
      3:    ireturn    // stack:
}
```

The input parameters to the add method, a and b, are passed in local variable slots 1 and 2 (Slot 0 in an instance method is reserved for this, according to the JVM specification, and this particular example is an instance method). The first two operations, with opcodes iload_1 and iload_2, push the contents of these local variables onto the evaluation stack. The third operation, iadd, pops the two values from the stack, adds them and pushes the resulting sum. The fourth and final operation, ireturn, pops the sum from the bytecode stack and terminates the method using the sum as return value. The bytecode in the previous example has been annotated with the contents of the evaluation stack after each operation has been executed.

> Bytecode for a class can be dumped using the javap command with the -c command-line switch. The command javap is part of the JDK.

Operations and operands

As we see, Java bytecode is a relatively compact format, the previous method only being four bytes in length (a fraction of the source code mass). Operations are always encoded with one byte for the opcode, followed by an optional number of operands of variable length. Typically, a bytecode instruction complete with operands is just one to three bytes.

Here is another small example, a method that determines if a number is even or not. The bytecode has been annotated with the hexadecimal values corresponding to the opcodes and operand data.

```
public boolean even(int number) {
   return (number & 1) == 0;
}

public boolean even(int);
   Code:
      0:   iload_1      // 0x1b                number
      1:   iconst_1     // 0x04                number, 1
      2:   iand         // 0x7e                (number & 1)
      3:   ifne    10   // 0x9a 0x00 0x07
      6:   iconst_1     // 0x03                1
      7:   goto    11   // 0xa7 0x00 0x04
      10:  iconst_0     // 0x03                0
      11:  ireturn      // 0xac
}
```

The program pushes its in-parameter, `number` and the constant 1 onto the evaluation stack. The values are then popped, ANDed together, and the result is pushed on the stack. The `ifne` instruction is a conditional branch that pops its operand from the stack and branches if it is not zero. The `iconst_0` operation pushes the constant 0 onto the evaluation stack. It has the opcode value `0x3` in bytecode and takes no operands. In a similar fashion `iconst_1` pushes the constant 1. The constants are used for the `boolean` return value.

Compare and jump instructions, for example `ifne` (branch on not equal, bytecode `0x9a`), generally take two bytes of operand data (enough for a 16 bit jump offset).

> For example, if a conditional jump should move the instruction pointer 10,000 bytes forward in the case of a `true` condition, the operation would be encoded as `0x9a 0x27 0x10` (`0x2710` is 10,000 in hexadecimal. All values in bytecode are big-endian).

Other more complex constructs such as table switches also exist in bytecode with an entire jump table of offsets following the opcode in the bytecode.

The constant pool

A program requires data as well as code. Data is used for operands. The operand data for a bytecode program can, as we have seen, be kept in the bytecode instruction itself. But this is only true when the data is small enough, or commonly used (such as the constant 0).

Larger chunks of data, such as string constants or large numbers, are stored in a **constant pool** at the beginning of the `.class` file. Indexes to the data in the pool are used as operands instead of the actual data itself. If the string `aVeryLongFunctionName` had to be separately encoded in a compiled method each time it was operated on, bytecode would not be compact at all.

Furthermore, references to other parts of the Java program in the form of method, field, and class metadata are also part of the `.class` file and stored in the constant pool.

Code generation strategies

There are several ways of executing bytecode in a JVM, from just emulating the bytecode in a pure bytecode interpreter to converting everything to native code for a particular platform.

Pure bytecode interpretation

Early JVMs contained only simple bytecode interpreters as a means of executing Java code. To simplify this a little, a bytecode interpreter is just a main function with a large `switch` construct on the possible opcodes. The function is called with a state representing the contents of the Java evaluation stack and the local variables. Interpreting a bytecode operation uses this state as input and output. All in all, the fundamentals of a working interpreter shouldn't amount to more than a couple of thousand lines of code.

There are several simplicity benefits to using a pure interpreter. The code generator of an interpreting JVM just needs to be recompiled to support a new hardware architecture. No new native compiler needs to be written. Also, a native compiler for just one platform is probably much larger than our simple `switch` construct.

A pure bytecode interpreter also needs little bookkeeping. A JVM that compiles some or all methods to native code would need to keep track of all compiled code. If a method is changed at runtime, which Java allows, it needs to be scheduled for regeneration as the old code is obsolete. In a pure interpreter, its new bytecodes are simply interpreted again from the start the next time that we emulate a call to the method.

It follows that the amount of bookkeeping in a completely interpreted model is minimal. This lends itself well to being used in an adaptive runtime such as a JVM, where things change all the time.

Naturally, there is a significant performance penalty to a purely interpreted language when comparing the execution time of an interpreted method with a native code version of the same code. Sun Microsystems' Classic Virtual Machine started out as a pure bytecode interpreter.

Running our previous add method, with its four bytecode instructions, might easily require the execution of ten times as many native instructions in an interpreter written in C. Whereas, a native version of our add most likely would just be two assembly instructions (add and return).

```
int evaluate(int opcode, int* stack, int* localvars) {
  switch (opcode) {
    ...
    case iload_1:
    case iload_2:
      int lslot = opcode - iload_1;
      stack[sp++] = localvars[lslot];
      break;
    case iadd:
      int sum = stack[--sp] + stack[--sp];
      stack[sp++] = sum;
      break;
    case ireturn:
      return stack[--sp];
    ...
  }
}
```

The previous example shows simple pseudo code for a bytecode interpreter with just enough functionality to execute our add method. Even this simple code snippet amounts to tens of assembly instructions in the natively compiled JVM. Considering that a natively compiled version of the add method would just be two instructions, this illustrates the performance problem with pure bytecode interpretation.

JIT compiling the add method on x86 yields us:

```
add eax, edx   // eax = edx+eax
ret            // return eax
```

Note that this book will sometimes show assembly code examples in places, to illustrate points. No prior knowledge of assembly code on any platform is needed to reap the full benefits of the text. However, the concept of low level languages should be familiar to the reader. If you feel yourself breaking out in a cold sweat over the assembly listings that are displayed in a few places throughout the text, don't worry too much. They are not necessary to understand the big picture.

Static compilation

In the early days of Java, several simple "brute force" approaches to getting around the bytecode performance problem were made. These usually involved static compilation in some form. Usually, an entire Java program was compiled into native code before execution. This is known as **ahead-of-time compilation**. Basically, ahead-of-time compilation is what your average C++ compiler does all the time.

As a limited subset of the problem of static compilation for Java is easy to solve, a row of products appeared in the late nineties, using methodologies like turning bytecodes into naive C code and then passing it to a C compiler. Most of the time, the resulting code ran significantly faster than purely interpreted bytecode. However, these kinds of products rarely supported the full dynamic nature of the Java language and were unable to graciously handle things like code being replaced at runtime without large workarounds.

The obvious disadvantage of static compilation for Java is that the benefits of platform independence immediately disappear. The JVM is removed from the equation.

Another disadvantage is that the automatic memory management of Java has to be handled more or less explicitly, leading to limited implementations with scalability issues.

As Java gradually moved more and more towards server side applications, where its dynamic nature was put to even more use, static solutions became impractical. For example, an application server generating plenty of **Java Server Pages (JSPs)** on the fly reduces a static compiler to a JIT compiling JVM, only slower and less adaptive.

Note that static ahead-of-time solutions, while unsuitable for implementing Java, can be useful in certain other contexts, for example **ahead-of-time analysis**. Program analysis is a time consuming business. If some of it can be done offline, before program execution, and communicated to the JVM, there may be performance benefits to be had. For example, `.class` files may be annotated with offline profiling data, perhaps in the form of Java `Annotations`.

Total JIT compilation

Another way to speed up bytecode execution is to not use an interpreter at all, and JIT compile all Java methods to native code immediately when they are first encountered. The compilation takes place at runtime, inside the JVM, not ahead-of-time.

Unlike completely static ahead-of-time compilation, on the fly compilation fits better into the Java model with a mobile adaptive language.

Total JIT compilation has the advantage that we do not need to maintain an interpreter, but the disadvantage is that compile time becomes a factor in the total runtime. While we definitely see benefits in JIT compiling hot methods, we also unnecessarily spend expensive compile time on cold methods and methods that are run only once. Those methods might as well have been interpreted instead.

A frequently executed method is said to be **hot.** A method that is not frequently executed and doesn't contribute to the overall program performance regardless of its implementation is said to be **cold**.

This can be remedied by implementing different levels of compiler quality in the JIT compiler, starting out with every method as a quick and dirty version. When the JVM knows that a method is hot, for example if the number of invocations of the method reaches a certain threshold value, it can be queued for recompilation with more optimizations applied. This naturally takes longer.

The main disadvantage of total JIT compilation is still low code generation speed. In the same way that an interpreted method executes hundreds of times slower than a native one, a native method that has to be generated from Java bytecodes takes hundreds of times longer to get ready for execution than an interpreted method. When using total JIT compilation, it is extremely important to spend clock cycles on optimizing code only where it will pay off in better execution time. The mechanism that detects hot methods has to be very advanced, indeed. Even a quick and dirty JIT compiler is still significantly slower at getting code ready for execution than a pure interpreter. The interpreter never needs to translate bytecodes into anything else.

Another issue that becomes more important with total JIT compilation is the large amounts of throwaway code that is produced. If a method is regenerated, for example since assumptions made by the compiler are no longer valid, the old code takes up precious memory. The same is true for a method that has been optimized. Therefore, the JVM requires some kind of "garbage collection" for generated code or a system with large amounts of JIT compilation would slowly run out of native memory as code buffers grow.

JRockit is an example of a JVM that uses an advanced variant of total JIT compilation as its code generation strategy.

Mixed mode interpretation

The first workable solution that was proposed, that would both increase execution speed and not compromise the dynamic nature of Java, was **mixed mode interpretation**.

In a JVM using mixed mode interpretation, all methods start out as interpreted when they are first encountered. However, when a method is found to be hot, it is scheduled for JIT compilation and turned into more efficient native code. This adaptive approach is similar to that of keeping different code quality levels in the JIT, described in the previous section.

Detecting hot methods is a fundamental functionality of every modern JVM, regardless of code execution model, and it will be covered to a greater extent later in this chapter. Early mixed mode interpreters typically detected the hotness of a method by counting the number of times it was invoked. If this number was large enough, optimizing JIT compilation would be triggered for the method.

Similar to total JIT compilation, if the process of determining if a method is hot is good enough, the JVM spends compilation time only on the methods where it makes the most difference. If a method is seldom executed, the JVM would waste no time turning it into native code, but rather keep interpreting it each time that it is called.

Bookkeping JIT code is a simple problem with mixed mode interpretation. If a version of a compiled method needs to be regenerated or an assumption is invalidated, its code is thrown out. The next time the method is called, it will once again be interpreted. If the method is still hot, it will eventually be recompiled with the changed model of the world incorporated.

 Sun Microsystems was the first vendor to embrace mixed mode interpretation in the HotSpot compiler, available both in a client version and a server side version, the latter with more advanced code optimizations. HotSpot in turn, was based on technology acquired from Longview Technologies LLC (which started out as Animorphic).

Adaptive code generation

Java is dynamic in nature and certain code generation strategies fit less well than others. From the earlier discussion, the following conclusions can be drawn:

- Code generation should be done at runtime, not ahead of time.
- All methods cannot be treated equally by code generator. There needs to be a way to discern a hot method from a cold one. Otherwise unnecessary optimization effort is spent on cold methods, or worse, not enough optimization effort on hot methods.
- In a JIT compiler, bookkeeping needs to be in place in order to keep up with the adaptive runtime. This is because generated native code invalidated by changes to the running program must be thrown away and potentially regenerated.

Achieving code execution efficiency in an adaptive runtime, no matter what JIT or interpretation strategy it uses, all boils down to the equation:

Total Execution Time = Code Generation Time + Execution Time

In other words, if we spend lots of effort carefully generating and optimizing every method to make sure it turns into efficient native code, we contribute too much code generation time to the total execution time. We want the JVM to execute our Java code in every available clock cycle, not use the expensive cycles to garbage collect or generate code.

If we spend too little time preparing methods for execution, their runtime performance is likely to be bad and thus contribute too many "inefficient" cycles to the total execution time.

The JVM needs to know precisely which methods are worth the extra time spent on more elaborate code generation and optimization efforts.

There are, of course, other aspects of **total execution time**, such as time spent in garbage collection. This, however, is beyond the scope of this chapter and will be covered in more detail in the chapter on memory management. Here it is sufficient to mention that the code optimizer sometimes can help reduce garbage collection overhead by generating efficient code, that is less memory bound. One example would be by applying **escape analysis**, which is briefly covered later in this chapter.

Determining "hotness"

As we have seen, "one size fits all" code generation that interprets every method, or JIT compiling every method with a high optimization level, is a bad idea in an adaptive runtime. The former, because although it keeps code generation time down, execution time goes way up. The latter, because even though execution is fast, generating the highly optimized code takes up a significant part of the total runtime. We need to know if a method is hot or not in order to know if we should give it lots of code generator attention, as we can't treat all methods the same.

Profiling to determine "hotness" can, as was hinted at in the previous sections, be implemented in several different ways. The common denominator for all ways of profiling is that a number of **samples** of where code spends execution time is collected. These are used by the runtime to make optimization decisions—the more samples available, the better informed decisions are made. Just a few isolated samples in different methods won't really tell us much about the execution profile of a program. Naturally, collecting samples always incurs some overhead in itself, and there is a tradeoff between having enough samples and the overhead of collecting them.

Invocation counters

One way to sample hot methods is to use **invocation counters**. An invocation counter is typically associated with each method and is incremented when the method is called. This is done either by the bytecode interpreter or in the form of an extra add instruction compiled into the prologue of the native code version of the method.

Especially in the JIT compiled world, where code execution speed doesn't disappear into interpretation overhead, invocation counters may incur some visible runtime overhead, usually in the form of cache misses in the CPU. This is because a particular location in memory has to be frequently written to by the add at the start of each method.

Software-based thread sampling

Another, more cache friendly, way to determine hotness is by using thread sampling. This means periodically examining where in the program Java threads are currently executing and logging their instruction pointers. Thread sampling requires no code instrumentation.

Stopping threads, which is normally required in order to extract their contexts is, however, quite an expensive operation. Thus, getting a large amount of samples without disrupting anything at all requires a complete JVM-internal thread implementation, a custom operating system such as in Oracle JRockit Virtual Edition, or specialized hardware support.

Hardware-based sampling

Certain hardware platforms, such as Intel IA-64, provides hardware instrumentation mechanisms that may be used by an application. One example is the hardware IP sample buffer. While generating code for IA-64 is a rather complex business, at least the hardware architecture allows for collecting a large amount of samples cheaply, thus facilitating better optimization decisions.

Another benefit of hardware-based sampling is that it may provide other data, not just instruction pointers, cheaply. For example, hardware profilers may export data on how often a hardware branch predictor makes an incorrect assumption, or on how often the CPU caches miss in particular locations. The runtime can use this information to generate more optimal code. Inverting the condition of the jump instruction that caused the branch prediction miss and prefetching data ahead of the instruction that caused the cache miss would solve these issues. Thus, efficient hardware-based sampling can lay an excellent groundwork for further adaptive code optimizations in the runtime.

Optimizing a changing program

In assembly code, method calls typically end up as `call` instructions. Variants of these exist in all hardware architectures. Depending on the type of call, the format of the `call` instruction varies.

In object-oriented languages, virtual method dispatch is usually compiled as **indirect calls** (that is the destination has to be read from memory) to addresses in a **dispatch table**. This is because a virtual call can have several possible receivers depending on the class hierarchy. A dispatch table exists for every class and contains the receivers of its virtual calls. A static method or a virtual method that is known to have only one implementation can instead be turned into a **direct call** with a fixed destination. This is typically much faster to execute.

In native code, a static call would look something similar to:

`call 0x2345670` (a jump to a fixed location)

A virtual call would look something similar to:

`mov eax, [esi]`   (load type info from receiver in `esi`)

`call [eax+0x4c]`   (`eax` + `0x4c` is the dispatch table entry)

As we have to dereference memory twice for the virtual call, it is slower than just calling a fixed destination address.

Consider a static environment, such as a compiled C++ program. For the code generator, everything that can be known about the application is known at compile time. For example, we know that any given virtual method with a single implementation will never be overridden by another, simply because no other virtual method exists. New code cannot enter the system, so the overrider also *will* never exist. This not only removes the need for the extra bookkeeping required for throwing out old code, but it also allows for the C++ compiler to generate static calls to the virtual method.

Now, consider the same virtual method in a Java program. At the moment it exists only in one version, but Java allows that it can be overridden at any time during program execution. When the JIT compiler wants to generate a call to this method, it would prefer that the method remained a single implementation forever. Then, the previous C++ optimization can be used and the call can be generated as a fast fixed call instead of a slower virtual dispatch. However, if the method is not declared `final`, it can be overridden at any time. It looks like we don't dare use the direct call at all, even though it is highly unlikely that the method will ever be overridden.

There are several other situations in Java where the world looks good right now to the compiler, and optimizations can be applied, but if the world changes in the future, the optimizations would have to be immediately reverted. For compiled Java, in order to match compiled C++ in speed, there must be a way to do these kinds of optimizations anyway.

The JVM solves this by "gambling". It bases its code generation decisions on assumptions that the world will remain unchanged forever, which is usually the case. If it turns out not to be so, its bookkeeping system triggers callbacks if any assumption is violated. When this happens, the code containing the original assumption needs to be regenerated—in our example the static dispatch needs to be replaced by a virtual one. Having to revert code generated based on an assumption about a closed world is typically very costly, but if it happens rarely enough, the benefit of the original assumption will deliver a performance increase anyway.

Some typical assumptions that the JIT compiler and JVM, in general, might bet on are:

- A virtual method probably won't be overridden. As it only exists only in one version, it can always be called with a fixed destination address like a static method.

- A `float` will probably never be `NaN`. We can use hardware instructions instead of an expensive call to the native floating point library that is required for corner cases.

- The program probably won't throw an exception in a particular `try` block. Schedule the `catch` clause as cold code and give it less attention from the optimizer.

- The hardware instruction `fsin` probably has the right precision for most trigonometry. If it doesn't, cause an exception and call the native floating point library instead.

- A lock probably won't be too saturated and can start out as a fast **spinlock**.

- A lock will probably be repeatedly taken and released by the same thread, so the unlock operation and future reacquisitions of the lock can optimistically be treated as no-ops.

A static environment that was compiled ahead of time and runs in a closed world can not, in general, make these kinds of assumptions. An adaptive runtime, however, can revert its illegal decisions if the criteria they were based on are violated. In theory, it can make any crazy assumption that might pay off, as long as it can be reverted with small enough cost. Thus, an adaptive runtime is potentially far more powerful than a static environment given that the "gambling" pays off.

Getting the gambling right is a very difficult problem. If we assume that relatively rare events will occur frequently, in order to avoid regenerating code, we can never achieve anything near the performance of a static compiler. However, if very frequent events are assumed to be rare, we will instead have to pay the penalty in increased code generation time for reoptimizations or invalidations. There is a fine area of middle ground here of what kinds of assumptions can be made. There is a significant art to finding this middle ground, and this is where a high performance runtime can make its impact. Given that we find this area—and JRockit is based on runtime information feedback in all relevant areas to make the best decisions—an adaptive runtime has the potential to outperform a static environment every time.

Inside the JIT compiler

While it is one thing to compile bytecodes to native code and have it executed within the JVM, getting it to run as efficiently as possible is a different story. This is where 40 years of research into compilers is useful, along with some insight into the Java language. This section discusses how a JIT compiler can turn bytecode into efficient native code.

Working with bytecode

A compiler for a programming language typically starts out with source code, such as C++. A Java JIT compiler, in a JVM, is different in the way that it has to start out with Java bytecode, parts of which are quite low level and assembly-like. The JIT compiler frontend, similar to a C++ compiler frontend, can be reused on all architectures, as it's all about tokenizing and understanding a format that is platform-independent—bytecode.

While compiled bytecode may sound low level, it is still a well-defined format that keeps its code (operations) and data (operands and constant pool entries) strictly separated from each other. Parsing bytecode and turning it into a program description for the compiler frontend actually has a lot more in common with compiling Java or C++ source code, than trying to deconstruct a binary executable. Thus, it is easier to think of bytecode as just a different form of source code—a structured program description. The bytecode format adds no serious complexities to the compiler frontend compared to source code. In some ways, bytecode helps the compiler by being unambiguous. Types of variables, for instance, can always be easily inferred by the kind of bytecode instruction that operates on a variable.

However, bytecode also makes things more complex for the compiler writer. Compiling byte code to native code is, somewhat surprisingly, in some ways harder than compiling human-readable source code.

One of the problems that has to be solved is the evaluation stack metaphor that the Java Virtual Machine specification mandates. As we have seen, most bytecode operations pop operands from the stack and push results. No native platforms are stack machines, rather they rely on registers for storing intermediate values. Mapping a language that uses local variables to native registers is straightforward, but mapping an evaluation stack to registers is slightly more complex. Java also defines plenty of virtual registers, local variables, but uses an evaluation stack anyway. It is the authors' opinion that this is less than optimal. One might argue that it is strange that the virtual stack is there at all, when we have plenty of virtual registers. Why isn't an add operation implemented simply as "x = y+z" instead of "push y, push z, add, pop x". Clearly the former is simpler, given that we have an ample supply of registers.

It turns out that as one needs to compile bytecodes to a native code, the stack metaphor often adds extra complexity. In order to reconstruct an expression, such as add, the contents of the execution stack must be emulated at any given point in the program.

Another problem, that in rare cases may be a design advantage, is the ability of Java bytecodes to express more than Java source code. This sounds like a good thing when it comes to portability—Java bytecode is a mobile format executable by any JVM. Wouldn't it make sense to decouple the Java source code from the bytecode format so that one might write Java compilers for other languages that in turn can run on Java Virtual Machines? Of course it would, and it was probably argued that this would further help the spread and adoption of Java early in its design stage. However, for some reason or other, auto-generated bytecode from foreign environments is rarely encountered. A small number of products that turn other languages into Java bytecode exist, but they are rarely used. It seems that when the need for automatic bytecode generation exists, the industry prefers to convert the alien source code to Java and then compile the generated Java code. Also, when auto generated Java code exists, it tends to conform pretty much to the structure of compiled Java source code.

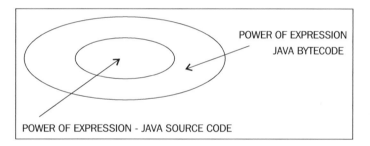

POWER OF EXPRESSION
JAVA BYTECODE

POWER OF EXPRESSION - JAVA SOURCE CODE

The problem that bytecode can express more than Java has led to the need for **bytecode verification** in the JVM, a requirement defined by the Java Virtual Machine specification. Each JVM implementation needs to check that the bytecode of an executing program does no apparently malicious tricks, such as jumping outside the method, overflowing the evaluation stack, or creating recursive subroutines.

Though bytecode portability and cross compiling several languages to bytecode is potentially a good thing, it also leads to problems. This is especially because bytecode allows **unstructured control flow**. Control flow with gotos to arbitrary labels is available in bytecode, which is not possible in the Java language. Therefore, it is possible to generate bytecodes that have no Java source code equivalent.

Allowing bytecodes that have no Java equivalent can lead to some other problems. For example, how would a Java source code debugger handle bytecode that cannot be decompiled into Java?

Consider the following examples:

- In bytecode, it is conceivable to create a `goto` that jumps into the body of a loop from before the loop header (irreducible flow graphs). This construct is not allowed in Java source code. Irreducible flow graphs are a classic obstacle for an optimizing compiler.

- It is possible to create a `try` block that is its own `catch` block. This is not allowed in Java source code.

- It is possible to take a lock in one method and release it in another method. This is not allowed in Java source code and will be discussed further in Chapter 4.

Bytecode obfuscation

The problem of bytecode expressing more than source code is even more complex. Through the years, various bytecode obfuscators have been sold with promises of "protecting your Java program from prying eyes". For Java bytecode this is mostly a futile exercise because, as we have already discussed, there is a strict separation between code and data. Classic anti-cracking techniques are designed to make it hard or impossible for adversaries to find a sensitive place in a program. Typically, this works best in something like a native binary executable, such as an `.exe` file, where distinctions between code and data are less clear. The same applies to an environment that allows self-modifying code. Java bytecode allows none of these. So, for a human adversary with enough determination, any compiled Java program is more vulnerable by design.

Bytecode obfuscators use different techniques to protect bytecode. Usually, it boils down to **name mangling** or **control flow obfuscation**.

Name mangling means that the obfuscator goes over all the variable info and field and method names in a Java program, changing them to short and inexplicable strings, such as a, a_, and a__ (or even more obscure Unicode strings) instead of `getPassword`, `setPassword`, and `decryptPassword`. This makes it harder for an adversary to crack your program, since no clues can be gleaned from method and field names. Name mangling isn't too much of a problem for the compiler writer, as no control flow has been changed from the Java source code.

It is more problematic if the bytecode obfuscator deliberately creates unstructured control flow not allowed in Java source code. This technique is used to prevent decompilers from reconstructing the original program. Sadly though, obfuscated control flow usually leads to the compiler having to do extra work, restructuring the lost control flow information that is needed for optimizations. Sometimes it isn't possible for the JVM to do a proper job at all, and the result is lowered performance. Thus control flow obfuscation should be avoided.

Bytecode "optimizers"

Various bytecode "optimizers" are also available in the market. They were especially popular in the early days of Java, but they are still encountered from time to time. Bytecode "optimizers" claim performance through restructuring bytecodes into more "efficient" forms. For example, divisions with powers of two can be replaced by shifts, or a loop can be inverted, potentially saving a `goto` instruction.

In modern JVMs, we have failed to find proof that "optimized" bytecodes are superior to unaltered ones straight out of `javac`. A modern JVM has a code generator well capable of doing a fine job optimizing code, and even though bytecode may look low level, it certainly isn't to the JVM. Any optimization done already at the bytecode level is likely to be retransformed into something else several times over on the long journey to native code.

We have never seen a case where a customer has been able to demonstrate a performance benefit from bytecode optimization. However, we have frequently run into customer cases where the program behavior isn't the expected one and varies between VMs because of failed bytecode optimization.

Our advice is to not use bytecode optimizers, ever!

Abstract syntax trees

As we have seen, Java bytecode has its advantages and disadvantages. The authors find it helpful just to think of bytecode as serialized source code, and not as some low level assembler that needs to run as fast as possible. In an interpreter, bytecode performance matters, but not to a great extent as the interpretation process is so slow anyway. Performance comes later in the code pipeline.

> While bytecode is both compact and extremely portable, it suffers from the strength of expression problem. It contains low-level constructs such as gotos and conditional jumps, and even the dreaded jsr (jump to subroutine, used for implementing finally clauses) instruction. As of Java 1.6, however, subroutines are inlined instead by javac and most other Java compilers.

A bytecode to native compiler can't simply assume that the given bytecode is compiled Java source code, but needs to cover all eventualities. A compiler whose frontend reads source code (be it Java, C++, or anything else) usually works by first tokenizing the source code into known constructs and building an **Abstract Syntax Tree (AST)**. Clean ASTs are possible only if control flow is structured and no arbitrary goto instructions exist, which is the case for Java source code. The AST represents code as sequences, expressions, or iterations (loop nodes). Doing an in-order traversal of the tree reconstructs the program. The AST representation has many advantages compared to bytecode.

For example, consider the following method that computes the sum of the elements in an array:

```
public int add(int [] series)  {
   int sum = 0;
   for (int i = 0; i < series.length; i++) {
     sum += series[i];
   }
   return sum;
}
```

When turning it to bytecode, the `javac` compiler most likely creates an abstract syntax tree that looks something like this:

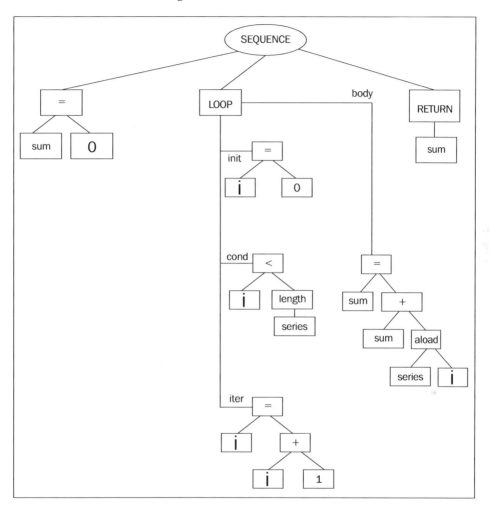

Several important prerequisites for code optimization, such as identifying loop invariants and loop bodies require expensive analysis in a control flow graph. Here, this comes very cheap, as loops are given implicitly by the representation.

However, in order to create the bytecode, the structured `for` loop, probably already represented as a loop node in the Java compiler's abstract syntax tree, needs to be broken up into conditional and unconditional jumps.

```
public int add(int[]);
  Code:
    0: iconst_0
    1: istore_2          //sum=0
    2: iconst_0
    3: istore_3          //i=0
    4: iload_3           //loop_header:
    5: aload_1
    6: arraylength
    7: if_icmpge 22      //if (i>=series.length) then goto 22
    10: iload_2
    11: aload_1
    12: iload_3
    13: iaload
    14: iadd
    15: istore_2         //sum += series[i]
    16: iinc     3, 1    //i++
    19: goto     4       //goto loop_header
    22: iload_2
    23: ireturn          //return sum
```

Now, without structured control flow information, the bytecode compiler has to spend expensive CPU cycles restructuring control flow information that has been lost, sometimes irretrievably.

Perhaps, in retrospect, it would have been a better design rationale to directly use an encoded version of the compiler's ASTs as bytecode format. Various academic papers have shown that ASTs are possible to represent in an equally compact or more compact way than Java bytecode, so space is not a problem. Interpreting an AST at runtime would also only be slightly more difficult than interpreting bytecode.

The earliest versions of the JRockit JIT used a decompiling frontend. Starting from byte code, it tried to recreate the ASTs present when `javac` turned source code into bytecode. If unsuccessful, the decompiler fell back to more naive JIT compilation. Reconstructing ASTs, however, turned out to be a very complex problem and the decompiler was scrapped in the early 2000s, to be replaced by a unified frontend that created control flow graphs, able to support arbitrary control flow directly from bytecode.

Where to optimize

Programmers tend to optimize their Java programs prematurely. This is completely understandable. How can you trust the black box, the JVM below your application, to do something optimal with such a high-level construct as Java source code? Of course this is partially true, but even though the JVM can't fully create an understanding of what your program does, it can still do a lot with what it gets.

It is sometimes surprising how much faster a program runs after automatic adaptive optimization, simply because the JVM is better at detecting patterns in a very large runtime environment than a human. On the other hand, some things lend themselves better to manual optimization. This book is in no way expressing the viewpoint that all code optimizations should be left to the JVM; however, as we have explained, explicit optimization on the bytecode level is probably a good thing to avoid.

There are plenty of opportunities for writing efficient programs in Java and situations where an adaptive runtime can't help. For example, a JVM can never turn a quadratic algorithm into a linear one, replacing your BubbleSort with a QuickSort. A JVM can never invent its own object cache where you should have written one yourself. These are the kinds of cases that matter in Java code. The JVM isn't magical. Adaptive optimization can never substitute bad algorithms with good ones. At most, it can make the bad ones run a little bit faster.

However, the JVM can easily deal with many constructs in standard object-oriented code. The programmer will probably gain very little by avoiding the declaration of an extra variable or by copying and pasting field loads and stores all over the place instead of calling a simple getter or setter. These are examples of micro-optimizations that make the Java code harder to read and that don't make the JIT compiled code execute any faster.

Sometimes, Java source code level optimizations are downright destructive. All too often people come up with hard-to-read Java code that they claim is optimal because some micro benchmark (where only the interpreter was active and not the optimizing JIT) told them so. An example from the real world is a server application where the programmer did a lot of iterations over elements in arrays. Believing it important to avoid using a loop condition, he surrounded the `for` loops with a `try` block and `catch` clause for the `ArrayIndexOutOfBoundsException`, that was thrown when the program tried to read outside the array. Not only was the source very hard to read, but once the runtime had optimized the method, it was also significantly slower than a standard loop would have been. This is because exceptions are very expensive operations and are assumed to be just that—exceptions. The "gambling" behavior of the JVM, thinking that exceptions are rare, became a bad fit.

It is all too easy to misunderstand what you are measuring when you are looking for a performance bottleneck. Not every problem can be stripped down into a small self contained benchmark. Not every benchmark accurately reflects the problem that is being examined. Chapter 5 will go into extensive detail on benchmarking and how to know what to look for in Java performance. The second part of this book will cover the various components of the JRockit Mission Control Suite, which is an ideal toolbox for performance analysis.

The JRockit code pipeline

Given that the frontend of the JIT compiler is finished with the bytecode, having turned it into some other form that is easier to process, what happens next? Typically, the code goes through several levels of transformations and optimizations, each level becoming increasingly platform-dependent. The final level of code is native code for a particular platform. The native code is emitted into a code buffer and executed whenever the function it represents is called.

Naturally, it makes sense to keep the JIT compiler portable as far as possible. So, most optimizations are usually done when the intermediate code format is still platform-independent. This makes it easier to port the JIT compiler to different architectures. However, low-level, platform-specific optimizations must naturally be implemented as well to achieve industrial strength performance.

This section describes how the JIT compiler gets from bytecode to native code and the stages involved. We concentrate on the JRockit JIT compiler, but in general terms the process of generating native code is similar between JVMs.

Why JRockit has no bytecode interpreter

JRockit uses the code generation strategy total JIT compilation.

When the JRockit project started in 1998, the JVM architects realized early on that pure server-side Java was a niche so far unexploited, and JRockit was originally designed to be only a server-side JVM. Most server-side applications, it was argued, stay running for a long time and can afford to take some time reaching a steady state. Thus, for a server-side-only JVM, it was decided that code generation time was a smaller problem than efficient execution. This saved us the trouble of implementing both a JIT compiler and a bytecode interpreter as well as handling the state transitions between them.

It was quickly noted that compiling every method contributed to additional startup time. This was initially not considered to be a major issue. Server-side applications, once they are up and running, stay running for a long time.

Later, as JRockit became a major mainstream JVM, known for its performance, the need to diversify the code pipeline into client and server parts was recognized. No interpreter was added, however. Rather the JIT was modified to differentiate even further between cold and hot code, enabling faster "sloppy" code generation the first time a method was encountered. This greatly improved startup time to a satisfying degree, but of course, getting to pure interpreter speeds with a compile-only approach is still very hard.

Another aspect that makes life easier with an interpreter is **debuggability**. Bytecode contains meta information about things like variable names and line numbers. These are needed by the debugger. In order to support debuggability, the JRockit JIT had to propagate this kind of information all the way from per-bytecode basis to per-native instruction basis. Once that bookkeeping problem was solved, there was little reason to add an interpreter. This has the added benefit that, to our knowledge, JRockit is the only virtual machine that lets the user debug optimized code.

The main problems with the compile-only strategy in JRockit are the code bloat (solved by garbage collecting code buffers with methods no longer in use) and compilation time for large methods (solved by having a sloppy mode for the JIT).

The compile-only strategy is sometimes less scalable than it should be. For example, sometimes, JRockit will use a lot of time generating a relatively large method, the typical example being a JSP. Once finished, however, the response time for accessing that JSP will be better than that of an interpreted version.

If you run into problems with code generation time using JRockit, these can often be worked around. More on this will be covered in the *Controlling code generation in JRockit* section at the end of this chapter.

Bootstrapping

The "brain" of the JRockit JVM is the runtime system itself. It keeps track of what goes on in the world that comprises the virtual execution environment. The runtime system is aware of which Java classes and methods make up the "world" and requests that the code generator compiles them at appropriate times with appropriate levels of code quality.

To simplify things a bit, the first thing the runtime wants to do when the JVM is started, is to look up and jump to the `main` method of a Java program. This is done through a standard JNI call from the native JVM, just like any other native application would use JNI to call Java code.

Searching for `main` triggers a complex chain of actions and dependencies. A lot of other Java methods required for bootstrapping and fundamental JVM behavior need to be generated in order to resolve the `main` function. When finally `main` is ready and compiled to native code, the JVM can execute its first native-to-Java stub and pass control from the JVM to the Java program.

To study the bootstrap behavior of JRockit, try running a simple Java program with the command-line switch `-Xverbose:codegen`. It may seem shocking that running a simple "Hello World" program involves JIT compiling around 1,000 methods. This, however, takes very little time. On a modern Intel Core2 machine, the total code generation time is less than 250 milliseconds.

Runtime code generation

Total JIT compilation needs to be a lazy process. If any method or class referenced from another method would be fully generated depth first at referral time, there would be significant code generation overhead. Also, just because a class is referenced from the code doesn't mean that every method of the class has to be compiled right away or even that any of its methods will ever be executed. Control flow through the Java program might take a different path. This problem obviously doesn't exist in a mixed mode solution, in which everything starts out as interpreted bytecode with no need to compile ahead of execution.

Trampolines

JRockit solves this problem by generating stub code for newly referred but not yet generated methods. These stubs are called **trampolines**, and basically consist of a few lines of native code pretending to be the final version of the method. When the method is first called, and control jumps to the trampoline, all it does is execute a call that tells JRockit that the real method needs to be generated. The code generator fulfils the request and returns the starting address of the real method, to which the trampoline then dispatches control. To the user it looks like the Java method was called directly, when in fact it was generated just at the first time it was actually called.

```
0x1000: method A                     0x3000: method C
  call method  B @ 0x2000              call method B @ 0x2000

0x2000: method B (trampoline)        0x4000: The "real" method B
  call JVM.Generate(B) -> start        . . .
  write trap @ 0x2000
  goto start @ 0x4000
```

Consider the previous example. method A, whose generated code resides at address 0x1000 is executing a call to method B, that it believes is placed at address 0x2000. This is the first call to method B ever. Consequently, all that is at address 0x2000 is a trampoline. The first thing the trampoline does is to issue a native call to the JVM, telling it to generate the real method B. Execution then halts until this code generation request has been fulfilled, and a starting address for method B is returned, let's say 0x4000. The trampoline then dispatches control to method B by jumping to that address.

Note that there may be several calls to method B in the code already, also pointing to the trampoline address 0x2000. Consider, for example, the call in method C that hasn't been executed yet. These calls need to be updated as well, without method B being regenerated. JRockit solves this by writing an illegal instruction at address 0x2000, when the trampoline has run. This way, the system will trap if the trampoline is called more than once. The JVM has a special exception handler that catches the trap, and patches the call to the trampoline so that it points to the real method instead. In this case it means overwriting the call to 0x2000 in method C with a call to 0x4000. This process is called **back patching**.

Back patching is used for all kinds of code replacement in the virtual machine, not just for method generation. If, for example, a hot method has been regenerated to a more efficient version, the cold version of the code is fitted with a trap at the start and back patching takes place in a similar manner, gradually redirecting calls from the old method to the new one.

Again, note that this is a lazy approach. We don't have time to go over the entire compiled code base and look for potential jumps to code that has changed since the caller was generated.

If there are no more references to an older version of a method, its native code buffer can be scheduled for garbage collection by the run time system so as to unclutter the memory. This is necessary in a world that uses a total JIT strategy because the amount of code produced can be quite large.

Code generation requests

In JRockit, **code generation requests** are passed to the code generator from the runtime when a method needs to be compiled. The requests can be either synchronous or asynchronous.

Synchronous code generation requests do one of the following:

- Quickly generate a method for the JIT, with a specified level of efficiency
- Generate an optimized method, with a specified level of efficiency

An asynchronous request is:

- Act upon an invalidated assumption, for example, force regeneration of a method or patch the native code of a method

Internally, JRockit keeps synchronous code generation requests in a **code generation queue** and an **optimization queue**, depending on request type. The queues are consumed by one or more code generation and/or optimization threads, depending on system configuration.

The code generation queue contains generation requests for methods that are needed for program execution to proceed. These requests, except for special cases during bootstrapping, are essentially generated by trampolines. The call "generate me" that each trampoline contains, inserts a request in the code generation queue, and blocks until the method generation is complete. The return value of the call is the address in memory where the new method starts, to which the trampoline finally jumps.

Optimization requests

Optimization requests are added to the optimization queue whenever a method is found to be hot, that is when the runtime system has realized that we are spending enough time executing the Java code of that method so that optimization is warranted.

The optimization queue understandably runs at a lower priority than the code generation queue as its work is not necessary for code execution, but just for code performance. Also, an optimization request usually takes orders of magnitude longer than a standard code generation request to execute, trading compile time for efficient code.

On-stack replacement

Once an optimized version of a method is generated, the existing version of the code for that method needs to be replaced. As previously described, the method entry point of the existing cold version of the method is overwritten with a trap instruction. Calls to the old method will be back patched to point to the new, optimized piece of code.

If the Java program spends a very large amount of time in a method, it will be flagged as hot and queued for replacement. However, consider the case where the method contains a loop that executes for a very long time. This method may well be hotspotted and regenerated, but the old method still keeps executing even if the method entry to the old method is fitted with a trap. Obviously, the performance enhancement that the optimized method contributes will enter the runtime much later, or never if the loop is infinite.

Some optimizers swap out code on the existing execution stack by replacing the code of a method with a new version in the middle of its execution. This is referred to as **on-stack replacement** and requires extensive bookkeeping. Though this is possible in a completely JIT-compiled world, it is easier to implement where there is an interpreter to fall back to.

JRockit doesn't do on-stack replacement, as the complexity required to do so is deemed too great. Even though the code for a more optimal version of the method may have been generated, JRockit will continue executing the old version of the method if it is currently running.

Our research has shown that in the real world, this matters little for achieving performance. The only places we have encountered performance penalties because of not doing on-stack replacement is in badly written micro benchmarks, such as when the `main` function contains all the computations in a very long loop. Moving the bulk of the benchmark into a separate function and calling this repeatedly from `main` will resolve this problem. We will thoroughly discuss the most important aspects of benchmarking in Chapter 5.

Bookkeeping

The code generator in the JVM has to perform a number of necessary bookkeeping tasks for the runtime system.

Object information for GC

For various reasons, a garbage collector needs to keep track of which registers and stack frame locations contain Java objects at any given point in the program. This information is generated by the JIT compiler and is stored in a database in the runtime system. The JIT compiler is the component responsible for creating this data because type information is available "for free" while generating code. The compiler has to deal with types anyway. In JRockit, the object meta info is called **livemaps**, and a detailed explanation of how the code generation system works with the garbage collector is given in *Chapter 3, Adaptive Memory Management*.

Source code and variable information

Another bookkeeping issue in the compiled world is the challenge of preserving source code level information all the way down to machine language. The JVM must always be able to trace program points back from an arbitrary native instruction to a particular line of Java source code. We need to support proper stack traces for debugging purposes, even stack traces containing optimized code. This gets even more complicated as the optimizer may have transformed a method heavily from its original form. A method may even contain parts of other methods due to **inlining**. If an exception occurs anywhere in our highly optimized native code, the stack trace must still be able to show the line number where this happened.

This is not a difficult problem to solve—bookkeeping just involves some kind of database, as it is large and complex. JRockit successfully preserves mappings between most native instructions and the actual line of Java source code that created them. This, obviously, is much more work in a compiled world than in an interpreted one. In the Java bytecode format, local variable information and line number information are mapped to individual bytecodes, but JRockit has to make sure that the mapping survives all the way down to native code. Each bytecode instruction eventually turns into zero or more native code instructions that may or may not execute in sequence.

Assumptions made about the generated code

Finally, as we have already discussed, remembering what assumptions or "gambles" have been made while generating methods is vital in Java. As soon as one of the assumptions is violated, we need to send asynchronous code regeneration requests for whatever methods are affected. Thus, an assumption database is another part of the JRockit runtime that communicates with the code generator.

A walkthrough of method generation in JRockit

Let us now take a look at what happens on the road from bytecode to native code in the JRockit JIT compiler. This section describes how a small method is transformed to native code by the JRockit JIT. Large parts of this process are similar in other JIT compilers (as well as in other static compilers), and some parts are not. The end result, native code, is the same.

Let us, consider the following Java method as an example:

```
public static int md5_F(int x, int y, int z) {
  return (x & y) | ((~x) & z);
}
```

This is part of the well known **MD5 hash function** and performs bit operations on three pieces of input.

The JRockit IR format

The first stage of the JRockit code pipeline turns the bytecode into an **Intermediate Representation** (**IR**). As it is conceivable that other languages may be compiled by the same frontend, and also for convenience, optimizers tend to work with a common internal intermediate format.

JRockit works with an intermediate format that differs from bytecode, looking more like classic text book compiler formats. This is the common approach that most compilers use, but of course the format of IR that a compiler uses always varies slightly depending on implementation and the language being compiled.

Aside from the previously mentioned portability issue, JRockit also doesn't work with bytecode internally because of the issues with unstructured control flow and the execution stack model, which differs from any modern hardware register model.

Because we lack the information to completely reconstruct the ASTs, a method in JRockit is represented as a directed graph, a **control flow graph,** whose nodes are **basic blocks**. The definition of a basic block is that if one instruction in the basic block is executed, all other instructions in it will be executed as well. Since there are no branches in our example, the md5_F function will turn into exactly one basic block.

Data flow

A basic block contains zero to many operations, which in turn have operands. Operands can be other operations (forming expression trees), variables (virtual registers or atomic operands), constants, addresses, and so on, depending on how close to the actual hardware representation the IR is.

Control flow

Basic blocks can have multiple entries and multiple exits. The edges in the graph represent control flow. Any control flow construct, such as a simple fallthrough to the next basic block, a `goto`, a conditional jump, a `switch`, or an exception, produces one or more edges in the graph.

When control enters a method, there is a designated start basic block for the execution. A basic block with no exits ends the method execution. Typically such a block ends with a `return` or `throw` clause.

A word about exceptions

A small complication is the presence of exceptions, which, if consistent to this model, should form conditional jumps from every bytecode operation that may fault to an appropriate catch block, where one is available.

This would quickly turn into a combinatorial explosion of edges in the flow graph (and consequently of basic blocks), severely handicapping any $O(|V||E|)$ (nodes x edges) graph traversal algorithm that needs to work on the code. Therefore, exceptions are treated specially on a per-basic block basis instead.

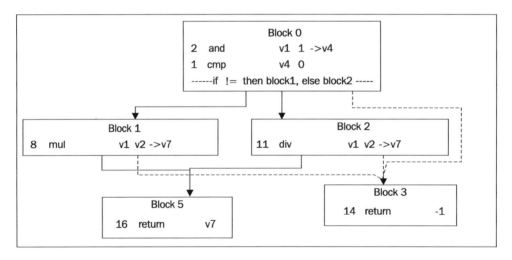

This figure shows the basic block graph of a slightly larger example. Method entry is at **Block 0** that has three exits—two normal ones, as it contains a conditional branch, and an exception edge. This means that **Block 0** is a `try` block, whose `catch` starts at **Block 3**. The same `try` block spans **Block 1** and **Block 2** as well. The method can exit either by triggering the exception and ending up in **Block 3** or by falling through to **Block 5**. Both these blocks end with `return` instructions. Even though the only instruction that can trigger an exception is the `div` in **Block 2** (on division by zero), the `try` block spans several nodes because this is what the bytecode (and possibly the source code) looked like. Optimizers may choose to deal with this later.

JIT compilation

This following figure illustrates the different stages of the JRockit code pipeline:

Generating HIR

The first module in the code generator, BC2HIR, is the frontend against the bytecode and its purpose is to quickly translate bytecodes into IR. **HIR** in this case stands for **High-level Intermediate Representation**. For the md5_F method, where no control flow in the form of conditional or unconditional jumps is present, we get just one basic block.

The following code snippet shows the md5_F method in bytecode form:

```
public static int md5_F(int, int, int);
     Code:         Stack contents:                    Emitted code:
  0:  iload_0      v0
  1:  iload_1      v1
  2:  iand         (v0&v1)
  3:  iload_0      (v0&v1), v0
  4:  iconst_m1    (v0&v1), v0, -1
  5:  ixor         (v0&v1), (v0^-1)
  6:  iload_2      (v0&v1), (v0^-1), v2
  7:  iand         (v0&v1), ((v0^-1) & v2)
  8:  ior          ((v0&v1) | ((v0^-1) & v2))
  9:  ireturn                                         return ((v0&v1) |
                                                      ((v0^-1) & v2));
```

The JIT works by computing a control flow graph for the IR by examining where the jumps in the bytecode are, and then filling its basic blocks with code. Code is constructed by emulating the contents of the evaluation stack at any given location in the program. Emulating a bytecode operation results in changes to the evaluation stack and/or code being generated. The example has been annotated with the contents of the emulated evaluation stack and the resulting generated code after each bytecode has been processed

 Bit negation (~) is implemented by `javac` as an xor with `-1` (`0xffffffff`), as bytecode lacks a specific `not` operator.

As we can see, by representing the contents of a variable on the evaluation stack with a variable handle, we can reconstruct the expressions from the original source code. For example, the `iload_0` instruction, which means "push the contents of variable 0" turns into the expression "variable 0" on the emulated stack. In the example, the emulator gradually forms a more and more complex expression on the stack, and when it is time to pop it and return it, the expression in its entirety can be used to form code.

This is the output, the High-level IR, or HIR:

```
params: v1 v2 v3
   block0: [first] [id=0]
    10 @9:49    (i32)    return {or {and v1 v2} {and {xor v1 -1} v3}}
```

 In JRockit IR, the annotation @ before each statement identifies its program point in the code all the way down to assembler level. The first number following the @ is the bytecode offset of the expression and the last is the source code line number information. This is part of the complex meta info framework in JRockit that maps individual native instructions back to their Java program points.

The variable indexes were assigned by JRockit, and differ from those in the bytecode. Notice that operations may contain other operations as their operands, similar to the original Java code. These nested expressions are actually a useful byproduct of turning the bytecode stack back into expressions. This way we get a High-level Representation instead of typical "flat" compiler code with temporary variable assignments, where operations may not contain other operations. The HIR lends itself well to some optimizations that are harder to do on another format; for example, discovering if a sub-expression (in the form of a subtree) is present twice in an expression. Then the sub-expression can be folded into a temporary variable, saving it from being evaluated twice.

Emulating the bytecode stack to form HIR is not without problems though. Since at compile time, we only know what expression is on the stack, and not its value, we run into various problems. One example would be in situations where the stack is used as memory. Take for example the construct `result = x ? a : b`. The bytecode compiles into something like this:

```
/* bytecode for: "return x ? a : b" */
static int test(boolean x, int a, int b);
   0:   iload_0    //push x
   1:   ifeq    8  //if x == false then goto 8
   4:   iload_1    //push a
```

```
5:   goto   9
8:   iload_2     //push b
9:   ireturn     //return pop
```

When the emulator gets to the `ireturn` instruction, the value popped can be either
a (local variable 1) or b (local variable 2). Since we can't express "either a or b" as a
variable, we need to replace the loads at offsets 4 and 8 with writes to one and the
same temporary variable, and place that on the stack instead.

The BC2HIR module that turns bytecodes into a control flow graph with expressions
is not computationally complex. However, it contains several other little special
cases, similar to the earlier one, which are beyond the scope of this book. Most of
them have to do with the lack of structure in byte code and with the evaluation stack
metaphor. Another example would be the need to associate `monitorenter` bytecodes
with their corresponding `monitorexit`(s), the need for which is explained in great
detail in Chapter 4.

MIR

MIR or Middle-level Intermediate Representation, is the transform domain where
most code optimizations take place. This is because most optimizations work best
with **three address code** or rather instructions that only contain atomic operands,
not other instructions. Transforming HIR to MIR is simply an in-order traversal
of the expression trees mentioned earlier and the creation of temporary variables.
As no hardware deals with expression trees, it is natural that code turns into
progressively simpler operations on the path through the code pipeline.

Our `md5_F` example would look something like the following code to the JIT
compiler, when the expression trees have been flattened. Note that no operation
contains other operations anymore. Each operation writes its result to a temporary
variable, which is in turn used by later operations.

```
params: v1 v2 v3
block0: [first] [id=0]
    2 @2:49*      (i32)   and      v1 v2 -> v4
    5 @5:49*      (i32)   xor      v1 -1 -> v5
    7 @7:49*      (i32)   and      v5 v3 -> v5
    8 @8:49*      (i32)   or       v4 v5 -> v4
   10 @9:49*      (i32)   return   v4
```

If the JIT compiler is executing a code generation request from the optimizer, most
optimizations on the way down to native code are carried out on MIR. This will be
discussed later in the chapter.

LIR

After MIR, it is time to turn platform dependent as we are approaching native code. **LIR**, or Low-level IR, looks different depending on hardware architecture.

Consider the Intel x86, where the biggest customer base for JRockit exists. The x86 has legacy operations dating back to the early 1980s. The RISC-like format of the previous MIR operations is inappropriate. For example, a logical and operation on the x86 requires the same first source and destination operand. That is why we need to introduce a number of new temporaries in order to turn the code into something that fits the x86 model better.

If we were compiling for SPARC, whose native format looks more like the JRockit IR, fewer transformations would have been needed.

Following is the LIR for the md5_F method on a 32-bit x86 platform:

```
params: v1 v2 v3
block0: [first] [id=0]
    2 @2:49*        (i32)   x86_and     v2 v1 -> v2
   11 @2:49         (i32)   x86_mov     v2 -> v4
    5 @5:49*        (i32)   x86_xor     v1 -1 -> v1
   12 @5:49         (i32)   x86_mov     v1 -> v5
    7 @7:49*        (i32)   x86_and     v5 v3 -> v5
    8 @8:49*        (i32)   x86_or      v4 v5 -> v4
   14 @9:49         (i32)   x86_mov     v4 -> eax
   13 @9:49*        (i32)   x86_ret     eax
```

A couple of platform-independent mov instructions have been inserted to get the correct x86 semantics. Note that the and, xor, and or operations now have the same first operand as destination, the way x86 requires. Another interesting thing is that we already see hard-coded machine registers here. The JRockit calling convention demands that integers be returned in the register eax, so the register allocator that is the next step of the code pipeline doesn't really have a choice for a register for the return value.

Register allocation

There can be any number of virtual registers (variables) in the code, but the physical platform only has a small number of them. Therefore, the JIT compiler needs to do **register allocation**, transforming the virtual variable mappings into machine registers. If at any given point in the program, we need to use more variables than there are physical registers in the machine at the same time, the local stack frame has to be used for temporary storage. This is called **spilling**, and the register allocator implements spills by inserting move instructions that shuffle registers back and forth from the stack. Naturally spill moves incur overhead, so their placement is highly significant in optimized code.

Register allocation is a very fast process if done sloppily, such as in the first JIT stage, but computationally intensive if a good job is needed, especially when there are many variables in use (or live) at the same time. However, because of the small number of variables, we get an optimal result with little effort in our example method. Several of the temporary mov instructions have been **coalesced** and removed.

Our md5_F method needs no spills, as x86 has seven available registers (15 on the 64-bit platforms), and we use only three.

```
params: ecx eax edx
block0: [first]  [id=0]
    2 @2:49*          (i32)  x86_and        eax ecx -> eax
    5 @5:49*          (i32)  x86_xor        ecx -1 -> ecx
    7 @7:49*          (i32)  x86_and        ecx edx -> ecx
    8 @8:49*          (i32)  x86_or         eax ecx -> eax
   13 @9:49*          (void) x86_ret        eax
```

Every instruction in our register allocated LIR has a native instruction equivalent on the platform that we are generating code for.

Just to put spill code in to perspective, following is a slightly longer example. The main method of the Spill program does eight field loads to eight variables that are then used at the same time (for multiplying them together).

```
public class Spill {
   static int aField, bField, cField, dField;
   static int eField, fField, gField, hField;
   static int answer;

   public static void main(String args[]) {
      int a = aField;
      int b = bField;
      int c = cField;
      int d = dField;
      int e = eField;
      int f = fField;
      int g = gField;
      int h = hField;
      answer = a*b*c*d*e*f*g*h;
   }
}
```

We will examine the native code for this method on a 32-bit x86 platform. As 32-bit x86 has only seven available registers, one of the intermediate values has to be spilled to the stack. The resulting register allocated LIR code is shown in the following code snippet:

 Assembly or LIR instructions that dereference memory typically annotate their pointers as a value or variable within square brackets. For example, [esp+8] dereferences the memory eight bytes above the stack pointer (esp) on x86 architectures.

```
block0: [first] [id=0]
  68           (i32)  x86_push ebx                //store callee save reg
  69           (i32)  x86_push ebp                //store callee save reg
  70           (i32)  x86_sub   esp 4 -> esp  //alloc stack for 1 spill
  43 @0:7*     (i32)  x86_mov  [0xf56bd7f8] -> esi  //*aField->esi (a)
  44 @4:8*     (i32)  x86_mov  [0xf56bd7fc] -> edx  //*bField->edx (b)
  67 @4:8      (i32)  x86_mov  edx -> [esp+0x0]     //spill b to stack
  45 @8:9*     (i32)  x86_mov  [0xf56bd800] -> edi  //*cField->edi (c)
  46 @12:10*   (i32)  x86_mov  [0xf56bd804] -> ecx  //*dField->ecx (d)
  47 @17:11*   (i32)  x86_mov  [0xf56bd808] -> edx  //*eField->edx (e)
  48 @22:12*   (i32)  x86_mov  [0xf56bd80c] -> eax  //*fField->eax (f)
  49 @27:13*   (i32)  x86_mov  [0xf56bd810] -> ebx  //*gField->ebx (g)
  50 @32:14*   (i32)  x86_mov  [0xf56bd814] -> ebp  //*hField->ebp (h)
  26 @39:16    (i32)  x86_imul esi [esp+0x0] -> esi //a *= b
  28 @41:16    (i32)  x86_imul esi edi -> esi       //a *= c
  30 @44:16    (i32)  x86_imul esi ecx -> esi       //a *= d
  32 @47:16    (i32)  x86_imul esi edx -> esi       //a *= e
  34 @50:16    (i32)  x86_imul esi eax -> esi       //a *= f
  36 @53:16    (i32)  x86_imul esi ebx -> esi       //a *= g
  38 @56:16    (i32)  x86_imul esi ebp -> esi       //a *= h
  65 @57:16*   (i32)  x86_mov  esi -> [0xf56bd818]  //*answer = a
  71 @60:18*   (i32)  x86_add   esp, 4 -> esp       //free stack slot
  72 @60:18    (i32)  x86_pop  -> ebp       //restore used callee save
  73 @60:18    (i32)  x86_pop  -> ebx       //restore used callee save
  66 @60:18    (void) x86_ret                       //return
```

We can also note that the register allocator has added an epilogue and prologue to the method in which stack manipulation takes place. This is because it has figured out that one stack position will be required for the spilled variable and that it also needs to use two **callee-save** registers for storage. A register being callee-save means that a called method has to preserve the contents of the register for the caller. If the method needs to overwrite callee-save registers, they have to be stored on the local stack frame and restored just before the method returns. By JRockit convention on x86, callee-save registers for Java code are ebx and ebp. Any calling convention typically includes a few callee-save registers since if every register was potentially destroyed over a call, the end result would be even more spill code.

Native code emission

After register allocation, every operation in the IR maps one-to-one to a native operation in x86 machine language and we can send the IR to the code emitter. The last thing that the JIT compiler does to the register allocated LIR is to add mov instructions for parameter marshalling (in this case moving values from in-parameters as defined by the calling convention to positions that the register allocator has picked). Even though the register allocator thought it appropriate to put the first parameter in ecx, compilers work internally with a predefined calling convention. JRockit passes the first parameter in eax instead, requiring a shuffle mov. In the example, the JRockit calling convention passes parameters x in eax, y in edx, and z in esi respectively.

 Assembly code displayed in figures generated by code dumps from JRockit use Intel style syntax on the x86, with the destination as the first operand, for example "and ebx, eax" means "ebx = ebx & eax".

Following is the resulting native code in a code buffer:

```
[method is md5_F(III)I [02DB2FF0 - 02DB3002]]

    02DB2FF0:   mov     ecx,eax
    02DB2FF2:   mov     eax,edx
    02DB2FF4:   and     eax,ecx
    02DB2FF6:   xor     ecx,0xffffffff
    02DB2FF9:   and     ecx,esi
    02DB2FFC:   or      eax,ecx
    02DB2FFF:   ret
```

Generating optimized code

Regenerating an optimized version of a method found to be hot is not too dissimilar to normal JIT compilation. The optimizing JIT compiler basically piggybacks on the original code pipeline, using it as a "spine" for the code generation process, but at each stage, an optimization module is plugged into the JIT.

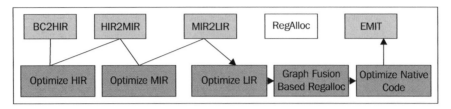

A general overview

Different optimizations are suitable for different levels of IR. For example, **HIR** lends itself well to value numbering in expression trees, substituting two equivalent subtrees of an expression with one subtree and a temporary variable assignment.

MIR readily transforms into **Single Static Assignment (SSA)** form, a transform domain that makes sure that any variable has only one definition. SSA transformation is part of virtually every commercial compiler today and makes implementing many code optimizations much easier. Another added benefit is that code optimizations in SSA form can be potentially more powerful.

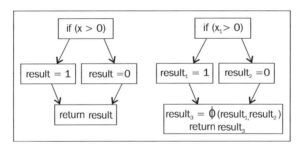

The previous flow graph shows what happens before and after transformation to SSA form. The `result` variable that is returned by the program is assigned either `1` or `0` depending on the value of `x` and the branch destination. Since SSA form allows only one assignment of each variable, the `result` variable has been split into three different variables. At the `return` statement, `result` can either be $result_1$ or $result_2$. To express this "either" semantic, a special **join operator**, denoted by the Greek letter phi (Φ), is used. Trivially, no hardware platform can express this ambiguity, so the code has to be transformed back to normal form before emission. The reverse transform basically replaces each join operator with preceding assignments, one per flow path, to the destination of the `join` instruction.

Many classic code optimizations such as **constant propagation** and **copy propagation** have their own faster SSA form equivalents. This mostly has to do with the fact that given any use of a variable, it is unambiguous where in the code that variable is defined. There is plenty of literature on the subject and a thorough discussion on all the benefits of SSA form is beyond the scope of this book.

LIR is platform-dependent and initially not register allocated, so transformations that form more efficient native operation sequences can be performed here. An example would be replacing dumb copy loops with specialized Intel SSE4 instructions for faster array copies on the x86.

When generating optimized code, register allocation tends to be very important. Any compiler textbook will tell you that optimal register allocation basically is the same problem as **graph coloring**. This is because if two variables are in use at the same time, they obviously cannot share the same register. Variables in use at the same time can be represented as connected nodes in a graph. The problem of register allocation can then be reduced to assigning colors to the nodes in the graph, so that no connected nodes have the same color. The amount of colors available is the same as the number of registers on the platform. Sadly enough, in computational complexity terms, graph coloring is NP-hard. This means that no efficient (polynomial time) algorithm exists that can solve the problem. However, graph coloring can be approximated in quadratic time. Most compilers contain some variant of the graph coloring algorithm for register allocation.

The JRockit optimizer contains a very advanced register allocator that is based on a technique called **graph fusion**, that extends the standard graph coloring approximation algorithm to work on subregions in the IR. Graph fusion has the attractive property that the edges in the flow graph, processed early, generate fewer spills than the edges processed later. Therefore, if we can pick hot subregions before cold ones, the resulting code will be more optimal. Additional penalty comes from the need to insert **shuffle code** when fusing regions in order to form a complete method. Shuffle code consists of sequences of move instructions to copy the contents of one local register allocation into another one.

Finally, just before code emission, various **peephole optimizations** can be applied to the native code, replacing one to several register allocated instructions in sequence with more optimal ones.

Clearing a register is usually done by XORing the register with itself. Replacing instructions such as `mov eax, 0` with `xor eax, eax`, which is potentially faster, is an example of a peephole optimization that works on exactly one instruction. Another example would be turning a multiplication with the power of two followed by an `add` instruction into a simple `lea` instruction on x86, optimized to do both.

How does the optimizer work?

A complete walkthrough of the JRockit code pipeline with the algorithms and optimizations within would be the subject for an entire book of its own. This section merely tries to highlight some of the things that a JVM can do with code, given adequate runtime feedback.

Generating optimized code for a method in JRockit generally takes 10 to 100 times as long as JITing it with no demands for execution speed. Therefore, it is important to only optimize frequently executed methods.

Grossly oversimplifying things, the bulk of the optimizer modules plugged into the code pipeline work like this:

```
do {
  1) get rid of calls, exposing more control flow
     through aggressive inlining.
  2) apply optimizations on enlarged code mass, try to shrink it.
} while ("enough time left" && "code not growing too fast");
```

Java is an object-oriented language and contains a lot of getters, setters, and other small "nuisance" calls. The compiler has to presume that calls do very complex things and have side effects unless it knows what's inside them. So, for simplification, small methods are frequently **inlined**, replacing the call with the code of the called function. JRockit tries to aggressively inline everything that seems remotely interesting on hot execution paths, with reasonable prioritization of candidates using sample and profiling information.

In a statically compiled environment, too aggressive inlining would be total overkill, and too large methods would cause instruction cache penalties and slow down execution. In a runtime, however, we can hope to have good enough sample information to make more realistic guesses about what needs to be inlined.

After bringing in whatever good inlining candidates we can find into the method, the JIT applies optimizations to the, now usually quite large, code mass, trying to shrink it. For example, this is done by folding constants, eliminating expressions based on escape analysis, and applying plenty of other simplifying transforms. **Dead code** that is proved never to be executed is removed. Multiple loads and stores that access the same memory location can, under certain conditions, be eliminated, and so on.

Surprisingly enough, the size of the total code mass after inlining and then optimizing the inlined code is often less than the original code mass of a method before anything was inlined.

The runtime system can perform relatively large simplifications, given relatively little input. Consider the following program that implements the representation of a circle by its radius and allows for area computation:

```
public class Circle {

  private double radius;

  public Circle(int radius) {
    this.radius = radius;
  }

  public double getArea() {
    return 3.1415 * radius * radius;
  }

  public static double getAreaFromRadius(int radius) {
    Circle c = new Circle(radius);
    return c.getArea();
  }

  static int areas[]  = new int[0x10000];
  static int radii[]  = new int[0x10000];
  static java.util.Random r = new java.util.Random();
  static int MAX_ITERATIONS = 1000;

  public static void gen() {
    for (int i = 0; i < areas.length; i++) {
      areas[i] = (int)getAreaFromRadius(radii[i]);
    }
  }

  public static void main(String args[]) {
    for (int i = 0; i < radii.length; i++) {
      radii[i] = r.nextInt();
    }
    for (int i = 0; i < MAX_ITERATIONS; i++) {
      gen(); //avoid on stack replacement problems
    }
  }
}
```

Running the previous program with JRockit with the command-line
flag -Xverbose:opt,gc, to make JRockit dump all garbage collection
and code optimization events, produces the following output:

```
hastur:material marcus$ java -Xverbose:opt,gc Circle
[INFO ][memory ] [YC#1] 0.584-0.587: YC 33280KB->8962KB (65536KB),
   0.003 s, sum of pauses 2.546 ms, longest pause 2.546 ms
[INFO ][memory ] [YC#2] 0.665-0.666: YC 33536KB->9026KB (65536KB),
   0.001 s, sum of pauses 0.533 ms, longest pause 0.533 ms
[INFO ][memory ] [YC#3] 0.743-0.743: YC 33600KB->9026KB (65536KB),
   0.001 s, sum of pauses 0.462 ms, longest pause 0.462 ms
[INFO ][memory ] [YC#4] 0.821-0.821: YC 33600KB->9026KB (65536KB),
   0.001 s, sum of pauses 0.462 ms, longest pause 0.462 ms
[INFO ][memory ] [YC#5] 0.898-0.899: YC 33600KB->9026KB (65536KB),
   0.001 s, sum of pauses 0.463 ms, longest pause 0.463 ms
[INFO ][memory ] [YC#6] 0.975-0.976: YC 33600KB->9026KB (65536KB),
   0.001 s, sum of pauses 0.448 ms, longest pause 0.448 ms
[INFO ][memory ] [YC#7] 1.055-1.055: YC 33600KB->9026KB (65536KB),
   0.001 s, sum of pauses 0.461 ms, longest pause 0.461 ms
[INFO ][memory ] [YC#8] 1.132-1.133: YC 33600KB->9026KB (65536KB),
   0.001 s, sum of pauses 0.448 ms, longest pause 0.448 ms
[INFO ][memory ] [YC#9] 1.210-1.210: YC 33600KB->9026KB (65536KB),
   0.001 s, sum of pauses 0.480 ms, longest pause 0.480 ms
[INFO ][opt     ][00020] #1 (Opt)
   jrockit/vm/Allocator.allocObjectOrArray(IIIZ)Ljava/lang/Object;
[INFO ][opt     ][00020] #1 1.575-1.581 0x9e04c000-0x9e04c1ad 5
   .72 ms 192KB 49274 bc/s (5.72 ms 49274 bc/s)
[INFO ][memory ] [YC#10] 1.607-1.608: YC 33600KB->9090KB
   (65536KB), 0.001 s, sum of pauses 0.650 ms, longest pause 0.650 ms
[INFO ][memory ] [YC#11] 1.671-1.672: YC 33664KB->9090KB (65536KB),
   0.001 s, sum of pauses 0.453 ms, longest pause 0.453 ms.
[INFO ][opt     ][00020] #2 (Opt)
   jrockit/vm/Allocator.allocObject(I)Ljava/lang/Object;
[INFO ][opt     ][00020] #2 1.685-1.689 0x9e04c1c0-0x9e04c30d 3
   .88 ms 192KB 83078 bc/s (9.60 ms 62923 bc/s)
[INFO ][memory ] [YC#12] 1.733-1.734: YC 33664KB->9090KB
   (65536KB), 0.001 s, sum of pauses 0.459 ms, longest pause 0.459 ms.
[INFO ][opt     ][00020] #3 (Opt) Circle.gen()V
[INFO ][opt     ][00020] #3 1.741-1.743 0x9e04c320-0x9e04c3f2 2
   .43 ms 128KB 44937 bc/s (12.02 ms 59295 bc/s)
[INFO ][opt     ][00020] #4 (Opt) Circle.main([Ljava/lang/String;)V
[INFO ][opt     ][00020] #4 1.818-1.829 0x9e04c400-0x9e04c7af 11
   .04 ms 384KB 27364 bc/s (23.06 ms 44013 bc/s)
hastur:material marcus$
```

No more output is produced until the program is finished.

The various log formats for the code generator will be discussed in more detail at the end of this chapter. Log formats for the memory manager are covered in Chapter 3.

It can be noticed here, except for optimization being performed on the four hottest methods in the code (where two are JRockit internal), that the garbage collections stop after the optimizations have completed. This is because the optimizer was able to prove that the `Circle` objects created in the `getAreaFromRadius` method aren't escaping from the scope of the method. They are only used for an area calculation. Once the call to `c.getArea` is inlined, it becomes clear that the entire lifecycle of the `Circle` objects is spent in the `getAreaFromRadius` method. A `Circle` object just contains a radius field, a single `double`, and is thus easily represented just as that `double` if we know it has a limited lifespan. An allocation that caused significant garbage collection overhead was removed by intelligent optimization.

Naturally, this is a fairly trivial example, and the optimization issue is easy for the programmer to avoid by not instantiating a `Circle` every time the area method is called in the first place. However, if properly implemented, adaptive optimizations scale well to large object-oriented applications.

The runtime is always better than the programmer at detecting certain patterns. It is often surprising what optimization opportunities the virtual machine discovers, that a human programmer hasn't seen. It is equally surprising how rarely a "gamble", such as assuming that a particular method never will be overridden, is invalidated. This shows some of the true strength of the adaptive runtime.

Unoptimized Java carries plenty of overhead. The `javac` compiler needs to do workarounds to implement some language features in bytecode. For example, string concatenation with the + operator is just syntactic sugar for the creation of `StringBuilder` objects and calls to their `append` functions. An optimizing compiler should, however, have very few problems transforming things like this into more optimal constructs. For example, we can use the fact that the implementation of `java.lang.StringBuilder` is known, and tell the optimizer that its methods have no harmful side effects, even though they haven't been generated yet.

Similar issues exist with boxed types. Boxed types turn into hidden objects (for example instances of `java.lang.Integer`) on the bytecode level. Several traditional compiler optimizations, such as escape analysis, can often easily strip down a boxed type to its primitive value. This removes the hidden object allocation that `javac` put in the bytecode to implement the boxed type.

Controlling code generation in JRockit

JRockit is designed to work well out of the box, and it is generally discouraged to play around too much with its command-line options. Changing the behavior of code generation and optimization is no exception. This section exists mostly for informational purposes and the user should be aware of possible unwanted side effects that can arise from changing the behavior of the code generators.

> This section applies mainly to the versions of JRockit from R28 and later. For earlier versions of JRockit, please consult the JRockit documentation for equivalent ways of doing the same thing. Note that all R28 functionality does not have equivalents in earlier versions of JRockit.

Command-line flags and directive files

In the rare case that the code generator causes problems in JRockit, or an application behaves strangely or erroneously, or it just takes too long time to optimize a particular method, the JRockit code generator behavior can be altered and controlled. Naturally, if you know what you are doing, code generation can be controlled for other purposes as well.

Command-line flags

JRockit has several command-lines flags that control code generation behavior in a coarse grained way. For the purpose of this text, we will only mention a few.

Logging

The `-Xverbose:codegen` (and `-Xverbose:opt`) options make JRockit output two lines of information per JIT compiled (or optimized) method to `stderr`.

Consider the output for a simple `HelloWorld` program. Every code generation event produces two lines in the log, one when it starts and one when it finishes.

```
hastur:material marcus$ java -Xverbose:codegen HelloWorld
[INFO ][codegen][00004] #1 (Normal) jrockit/vm/RNI.transitToJava(I)V
[INFO ][codegen][00004] #1 0.027-0.027 0x9e5c0000-0x9e5c0023 0
  .14 ms (0.00 ms)
[INFO ][codegen][00004] #2 (Normal)
  jrockit/vm/RNI.transitToJavaFromDbgEvent(I)V
[INFO ][codegen][00004] #2 0.027-0.027 0x9e5c0040-0x9e5c0063 0
  .03 ms (0.00 ms)
[INFO ][codegen][00004] #3 (Normal) jrockit/vm/RNI.debuggerEvent()V
```

```
[INFO ][codegen][00004] #3 0.027-0.027 0x9e5c0080-0x9e5c0131 0
  .40 ms 64KB 0 bc/s (0.40 ms 0 bc/s)
[INFO ][codegen][00004] #4 (Normal)
  jrockit/vm/ExceptionHandler.enterExceptionHandler()
    Ljava/lang/Throwable;
[INFO ][codegen][00004] #4 0.027-0.028 0x9e5c0140-0x9e5c01ff 0
  .34 ms 64KB 0 bc/s (0.74 ms 0 bc/s)
[INFO ][codegen][00004] #5 (Normal)
  jrockit/vm/ExceptionHandler.gotoHandler()V
[INFO ][codegen][00004] #5 0.028-0.028 0x9e5c0200-0x9e5c025c 0
  .02 ms (0.74 ms)
...
[INFO ][codegen][00044] #1149 (Normal) java/lang/Shutdown.runHooks()V
[INFO ][codegen][00044] #1149 0.347-0.348 0x9e3b4040-0x9e3b4106 0
  .26 ms 128KB 219584 bc/s (270.77 ms 215775 bc/s)


hastur:material marcus$
```

The first log line of a code generation request (event start) contains the following information from left to right:

- **Info tag and log module identifier** (code generator).

- **The thread ID of the thread generating the code**: Depending on the system configuration, there can be more than one code generator thread and more than one code optimizer thread.

- **The index of the generated method**: The first method to be generated starts at index 1. As we notice, at the beginning of the output, code generation is single threaded, and the order between the start and end of a code generation event is maintained, forming consecutive entries. This doesn't have to be the case if multiple code generation and optimization threads are working.

- **The code generation strategy:** The code generation strategy tells you how this particular method will be generated. As it is too early to have received runtime feedback information, all methods are generated using a normal code generator strategy, or even a quick one that is even sloppier. The quick strategy is applied for methods that are known to be of exceedingly little importance for the runtime performance. This can be, for example, static initializers that will run only once and thus make no sense to even register allocate properly.

- **The generated method**: This is uniquely identified by class name, method name, and descriptor.

The second line of a code generation request (event end) contains the following information from left to right:

- **Info tag and log module identifier** (code generator).
- **The thread ID of the thread generating the code**.
- **The index of the generated method**.
- **Start and end time for the code generation event**: This is measured in seconds from the start of the JVM.
- **The address range**: This is where the resulting native code is placed in memory.
- **Code generation time**: The number of milliseconds it took for the code generator to turn this particular method into machine language (starting from bytecode).
- **Maximum amount of thread local memory used**: This is the maximum amount of memory that the code generator thread needed to allocate in order to generate the method.
- **Average number of bytecodes per second**: The number of bytecodes processed per second for this method. 0 should be interpreted as infinity — the precision was not good enough
- **Total code generation time**: The total number of milliseconds this thread has spent in code generation since JVM startup and average bytecodes compiled per second for the thread so far.

Turning off optimizations

The command-line flag `-XnoOpt`, or `-XX:DisableOptsAfter=<time>` turns off all optimization in the compiler, optionally after a specified number of seconds after the start of the JVM. The flag `-XnoOpt` makes programs compile faster, but run slower, and can be used if there is a suspected problem with the JRockit optimizer or if compile time turns out to be a very big issue, for example in application response time.

Changing the number of code generation threads

Depending on the machine configuration, it might make sense to change the number of code generation and optimization threads that the JVM should use. Code generation and code optimization is a process that can, with the exception of emitting code into native code buffers and some aspects of class loading, be parallelized. The number of JIT compiler threads can be changed with the `-XX:JITThreads=<n>` option. The number of optimizing threads can be changed with the `-XX:OptThreads=<n>` option. Note that optimizations typically are quite memory and CPU intensive, even if the machine has plenty of cores.

Directive files

A more versatile method for code generation control is provided by **directive files**. Here, wild card patterns for interesting methods can be specified, for which the code generator should customize its behavior. The amount of available customizations is very large, and this section serves merely to introduce the concept of directive files, not serve as a reference of any kind.

> Warning! Directive files are a completely unsupported way of controlling JRockit code generation. The directives in the files are undocumented externally and are subject to change without notice. Oracle will not give support to JRockit configurations that use directive files.

A directive file is passed to JRockit by the flag `-XX:OptFile=<filename>`. It can also be added to or removed from the runtime state using JRCMD or through the JRockit Java API, both of which will be covered later in this book. In order to be able to use directive files, the command-line switch `-XX:+UnlockDiagnosticVMOptions` needs to be passed on the command line as well. Diagnostic VM options are subject to change without notice between releases and should be used at your own risk.

A directive file is a tuple of directives in a format compatible with the **JavaScript Object Notation (JSON)** format. An example would be:

```
{
  //pattern to match against class+method+signature
  match: "java.dingo.Dango.*",
  enable: jit
}
```

This is a very simple file that forbids the optimization of any method whose descriptor matches `java.dingo.Dango.*`. This is because the `enable` directive only contains the word `jit`, not the word `hotspot`, which would allow the matched methods to be selected for optimization through sampling.

If, on the other hand, we want to force optimization of the matched methods on their first code generation, we'd use something like this:

```
{
  match: "java.dingo.Dango.*",
  //types of "reasons" for codegen we allow
  enable: jit,
  jit: {
    preset : opt
  }
}
```

This means that we only allow the JIT strategy for the method, but when it is compiled we should use the preset optimization strategy on it. JRockit contains a number of preset strategies that are also directives, and `opt` means "immediately generate this method with full optimization".

> Applying full optimization to a method the first time it is generated by the system doesn't necessarily produce the same code or performance as it would have done if that method was detected to be hot and queued for normal optimization by the runtime. If a method is optimized too early, the risk is that we don't know enough about the program yet to do a good enough job. The fact is that the method might even have been queued for optimization, since the runtime has learned new things about the running program, but not optimized yet. Forcing the immediate optimization of many methods is not only expensive in clock cycles, but it is also not guaranteed to perform as well as it would by just letting things run their natural course.

The code generation strategy can be overridden in a more fine-grained way as well, for example, by turning off individual optimizations that are normally run, or by forbidding the inlining of a particular method.

The following is an example of a directive file with multiple directives:

```
//Using more than one directive, should use an array '['.
[
  //directive 1
  {
    match: "java.dingo.Dango.*",
    enable: [ jit, hotspot ], //allow both jit and optimization
    hotspot: {
       fusion_regalloc : false; //forbid graph fusion for opt
    },
    jit_inline : false, //forbid jit inlining
  },
```

```
    //directive 2
    {
      match: [ "java.lang.*", "com.sun.*" ],
      enable: jit ,
      jit: {
        //copy the opt preset, i.e. force optimization
        //for jit, but disable inlining
        preset : opt,
        opt_inline : false,
        },
    },

    //directive 3
    {
      match: "com.oracle.*",
      //force optimizer to always inline java.util methods
      //force optimizer to NEVER inline com.sun.methods
      inline: [ "+java.util.*", "-com.sun.*" ],
    }
  ]
```

 Practically, any part of compilation to native code for each kind of code generation strategy in JRockit, down to individual optimizations, can be controlled through a directive file. All aspects of directive files and names of directives are generally not documented. While directive files are a great instrument for helping you track down problems in a dialogue with JRockit support, playing around too much with them on your own is generally discouraged.

When using a directive file, it is a good idea to run with the -Xverbose:opt command-line flag enabled, in order to make sure that the file is actually read and understood by the JVM.

Summary

This chapter discussed code generation in a runtime environment. The topic was introduced as a general problem, comparing adaptive compilation to static compilation. We also explained special situations that apply to code generation in a Java Virtual Machine.

We have discussed some aspects of the Java bytecode format, its pros and cons, and the challenges of making Java code run fast, using different techniques from interpretation to total JIT compilation.

Furthermore, we have discussed the challenges of an adaptive runtime, where new code can enter the system at any time, and how to overcome them by "educated guesses", or "gambling". This means that JVM takes the optimistic approach when optimizing that made assumptions rarely change. We also mentioned the equation compilation speed versus execution speed, depending on method "hotness".

Finally, the chapter introduced the code pipeline in the JRockit Virtual Machine and its state of the art optimizations, using a comprehensive example with snapshots of a method generation cycle, all the way to native code. At the end of the chapter, some ways of modifying JRockit code generation behavior through command-line flags and directive files were explained.

The next chapter covers another fundamental aspect of adaptive runtimes; the memory management system, and techniques for efficient garbage collection, both as an overview, for garbage collected languages in general and specifically for Java with the JRockit JVM.

3
Adaptive Memory Management

This chapter is an introduction to automatic and adaptive memory management in the Java runtime. It provides a background on techniques for garbage collection and looks at the history of automatic memory management. It also discusses the advantages and disadvantages of automatic memory management compared to static solutions.

You will learn the following from this chapter:

- The concepts of automatic and adaptive memory management and understanding the problems and possibilities associated with these

- How a garbage collector works, including algorithms for garbage collection and implementation details

- How a garbage collector must be implemented in order to perform well and be scalable

- About the latency versus throughput equation

- The problems of object allocation in a runtime and algorithms for doing efficient object allocation

- The most important Java APIs for memory management, for example, the `java.lang.ref` package

- How the JRockit Real Time product and deterministic garbage collection works

- How to write Java code that plays well with the garbage collector, and common pitfalls and false optimizations

- How to use the most fundamental command-line flags associated with the memory subsystem

The concept of automatic memory management

Automatic memory management is defined as any garbage collection technique that automatically gets rid of stale references, making a `free` operator unnecessary. This is quite an old idea—implementations have been with us for almost as long as the history of modern computer science, probably starting out as reference counting methods in early Lisp machines. After that, other heap management strategies were developed. Most are refinements of tracing techniques, which involve traversing live object graphs on the heap in order to determine what can be garbage collected.

 We will use the term **heap** throughout this chapter to mean all the non-thread local memory available for objects in a garbage collected environment.

Adaptive memory management

As we have already seen in the previous chapter, basing JVM behavior on runtime feedback is a good idea. JRockit was the first JVM to recognize that adaptive optimizations based on runtime feedback could be applied to all subsystems in the runtime and not just to code generation. One of these subsystems is memory management.

We will use the term **adaptive memory management** to describe a memory management system whose behavior is based heavily on runtime feedback. Adaptive memory management is a special case of **automatic memory management**. Automatic memory management should be taken to mean just that some kind of garbage collection technique is employed. Garbage collection means, of course, that the user does not have to explicitly remove objects that are no longer in use. The system will automatically detect and free those resources.

Adaptive memory management must correctly utilize runtime feedback for optimal performance. This can mean changing GC strategies, automatic heap resizing, getting rid of memory fragmentation at the right intervals, or mainly recognizing when it is most appropriate to "stop the world". **Stopping the world** means halting the executing Java program, which is a necessary evil for parts of a garbage collection cycle.

Advantages of automatic memory management

The first and foremost advantage of automatic memory management is its contribution to the speed of the software development cycle. Any support organization knows that, with the possible exception of erroneous multi-threaded behavior, some of the most common causes for problems in software are memory allocation bugs, buffer overruns, and memory leaks. All of these are fairly hard to debug. It may not be a trivial matter to spot a one-byte-off allocation that leads to a crash much later in the program lifetime, when, for example, a totally different object is freed.

Both memory allocation bugs and buffer overruns are impossible in Java due to the intrinsic properties of the Java language. Memory allocation bugs can't occur because automatic memory management exists and buffer overruns can't occur because the runtime does not allow them. For example, whenever the program tries to write outside an array, an `ArrayIndexOutOfBoundsException` is thrown.

While memory leaks are still possible in a garbage collected world, modern JVMs provide ways of detecting them. There are also constructs in the Java language that can help the developer work around them. In the case of JRockit, the JRockit Mission Control suite contains a tool that can, with very low overhead, detect memory leaks in a running application. This is possible, as the garbage collector in the JVM already collects a lot of useful information that can be used for multiple purposes. The **Memory Leak Detector tool** is covered in detail in Chapter 10 of this book. It is a prime example of a value add, stemming from automatic memory management.

 It is the authors opinion that built-in automatic memory management and the shorter development cycles it enabled, was one of the main factors behind today's widespread Java adoption. Complex server applications crash less often with automatic memory management.

An additional advantage is that an adaptive memory manager may pick the appropriate garbage collection strategy for an application based on its current behavior, appropriately changing the number of garbage collecting threads or fine tuning other aspects of garbage collection strategies whenever needed. This might be compared to the adaptive behavior of the code generator, as explained in the previous chapter. The code generator can use runtime feedback to, for example, optimize only hot parts of methods and leave cold parts alone until they become hot at some later stage.

Disadvantages of automatic memory management

It is often argued that automatic memory management can slow down execution for certain applications to such an extent that it becomes impractical. This is because automatic memory management can introduce a high degree of non-determinism to a program that requires short response times. To avoid this, extensive workarounds may be needed to get enough application performance.

In truth, giving up control of memory management to the runtime may result in slowdowns, but this is rarely the case anymore, at least for well written applications.

The main bottleneck for a garbage collector tends to be the amount of live data on the heap, not the actual heap size. Any garbage collection algorithm will break down given too large an amount of live data. This could indeed be less of a problem in a non-garbage collecting system, but humans are fallible and there is no guarantee that manual memory management would fare any better with a large live data set.

Finally, there may still be memory leaks in a garbage collected environment. If the program erroneously holds on to references that should have been garbage collected, these will be treated as **live**. A common example is a broken cache implementation, for example in the form of a `java.util.HashMap` that doesn't throw away all old objects as it should. The system has no way of knowing that a forgotten object, still referenced by a key/value pair in a `HashMap` that is still in use, should be reclaimed.

Fundamental heap management

Before addressing actual algorithms for garbage collection, we need to talk about allocation and deallocation of objects. We will also need to know which specific objects on the heap to garbage collect, and we need to briefly discuss how they get there and how they are removed.

Allocating and releasing objects

Allocation on a per-object basis normally, in the common case, never takes place directly on the heap. Rather, it is performed in thread local buffers or similar constructs that are promoted to the heap from time to time. However, in the end, allocation is still about finding appropriate space on the heap for the newly allocated objects or collections of objects.

In order to put allocated objects on the heap, the memory management system must keep track of which sections of the heap are free (that is, those which contain no live objects). Free heap space is usually managed by maintaining a **free list**—a linked list of the free memory chunks on the heap, prioritized in some order that makes sense.

A best fit or first fit can then be performed on the free list in order to find a heap address where enough free space is available for the new object. There are many different algorithms for this, with different advantages.

Fragmentation and compaction

It is not enough to just keep track of free space in a useful manner. **Fragmentation** is also an issue for the memory manager. When dead objects are garbage collected all over the heap, we end up with a lot of **holes** from where objects have been removed.

Fragmentation is a serious scalability issue for garbage collection, as we can have a very large amount of free space on the heap that, even though it is free, is virtually unusable. This is because there is not enough contiguous space for the allocation of new objects—no hole is big enough. Typically, this will lead to the runtime system triggering more and more GCs in order to attempt clean up of the mess, but still isn't able to reclaim enough contiguous space for new objects. Untreated fragmentation is a classic performance death spiral.

The following figure shows a heap occupied by several objects:

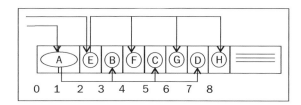

The heap section shown is completely occupied by live objects. The object **A** is two heap units in size and the other objects are just one heap unit in size. The application has two objects reachable from a program point where garbage collection takes place, **A** that references the object graph **ABCD** and **E** that references the object graph **EFGH**, where ABCD and EFGH are mutually independent.

If **E** is assigned `null` and thus removed from the scope of the program, E and its children can be garbage collected. The resulting heap after garbage collection will look like in the following figure:

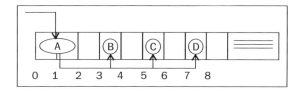

There is now free space on the heap, but even though there is a total amount of four free heap units, there is no place on the heap with more than one free unit in sequence. If the memory manager now attempts to find space for a new object that is, say, two heap units in size, an OutOfMemoryError will be thrown, even though there are four free units on the heap. This illustrates why fragmentation is problematic.

It follows that a memory management system needs some logic for moving objects around on the heap, in order to create larger contiguous free regions. This process is called **compaction,** and involves a separate GC stage where the heap is defragmented by moving live objects so that they are next to one another on the heap.

The following figure shows the heap from our example after compaction has taken place:

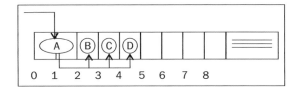

Now, we have four consecutive free heap units, and so we are able to allocate larger objects than before with the same amount of free space.

Compaction is difficult to do without stopping the world, but we will discuss some ways of making it more efficient later in this chapter (and to some extent in Chapter 5 and 13).

By looking at the object reference graph and by gambling that objects referencing each other are likely to be accessed in sequence, the compaction algorithm may move these objects so that they are next to one another on the heap. This is beneficial for the cache, and hopefully, the object lifetimes are similar so that larger free heap holes are created upon reclamation.

Intrinsic properties of different garbage collection algorithms also prevent some degree of fragmentation (generational GCs) or allow for automatic compaction (stop and copy). These are discussed later in this chapter.

Garbage collection algorithms

All techniques for automatic memory management boil down to keeping track of which objects are being used by the running program, in other words, which objects are referenced by other objects that are also in use. Objects that are no longer in use may be garbage collected. We will use the terms **live** and **in use** interchangeably.

It is hard to exactly place garbage collection techniques in different categories. With the risk of drawing fire from the academic community, we will use the term "tracing garbage collection" for everything except reference counting. **Tracing garbage collection** means building a graph of live objects at a collection event and discarding unreachable ones. The only other kind of technique that we will cover is reference counting.

Reference counting

Reference counting is a memory management technique where the runtime keeps track of how many live objects point to a particular object at a given time.

When the reference count for an object decreases to zero, the object has no referrers left, and trivially, the object is available for garbage collection. This approach was first used in Lisp implementations and is fairly efficient, except for the obvious flaw that cyclic constructs can never be garbage collected. If two objects refer to each other but have no outside referrers, their reference counts are obviously non-zero but they are still unreachable by the GC, consequently turning into a memory leak.

The main advantage of reference counting, aside from its obvious simplicity, is that any unreferenced object may be reclaimed immediately when its reference count drops to zero.

However, keeping the reference counts up to date can be expensive, especially in a parallel environment where synchronization is required. There are no commercial Java implementations today where reference counting is a main garbage collection technique in the JVM, but it might well be used by subsystems and for simple protocols in the application layer.

Tracing techniques

The concept of a tracing garbage collector is very simple. Start by marking all objects currently seen by the running program as live. Then recursively mark all objects reachable from those objects live as well.

Naturally, the variations to this theme are endless.

From now on, we will use the term **root set** to mean the initial input set for this kind of search algorithm, that is the set of live objects from which the trace will start. Typically, the root set includes all Java objects on local frames in whatever methods the program is executing when it is halted for GC. This includes everything we can obtain from the user stack and registers in the thread contexts of the halted program. The root set also contains global data, such as static fields. Or even simpler—the root set contains all objects that are available without having to trace any references.

We will discuss how to identify the root sets in more detail later in this chapter.

Mark and sweep

The mark and sweep algorithm is the basis of all the garbage collectors in all commercial JVMs today. Mark and sweep can be done with or without copying or moving objects (see the section on *Generational garbage collection* and the section on *Compaction* for details). However, the real challenge is turning it into an efficient and highly scalable algorithm for memory management. The following pseudocode describes a naive mark and sweep algorithm:

```
Mark:
   Add each object in the root set to a queue
     For each object X in the queue
        Mark X reachable
        Add all objects referenced from X to the queue
Sweep:
   For each object X on the heap
      If the X not marked, garbage collect it
```

As can be inferred from the previous algorithm and the explanation of tracing techniques, the computational complexity of mark and sweep is both a function of the amount of live data on the heap (for mark) and the actual heap size (for sweep).

The following figure shows a heap before the mark phase:

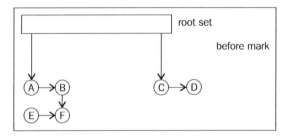

First, the live object graph needs to be traversed for marking. Then the entire heap needs to be traversed to identify unmarked objects. This is not necessarily optimal and there are several ways that have been addressed in research over the years to make faster and more parallelizable variants.

In the following figure, the mark phase is done. All objects that are reachable from the root set have been marked. Only E is not reachable from the root set.

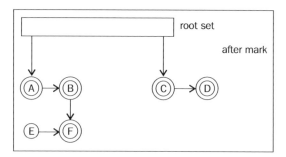

The simplest version of mark and sweep assumes that the object graph doesn't change during the mark phase. This means that all code execution that may modify the object graph through, for example, field reassignments, must be halted when the mark takes place. This is never good enough for modern applications with large data sets.

The following figure shows the heap after the sweep phase has taken place and E has been garbage collected:

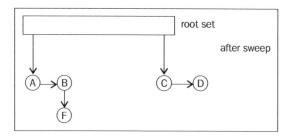

In naive mark and sweep implementations, a **mark bit** is typically associated with each reachable object. The mark bit keeps track of if the object has been marked or not. Objects are typically allocated so that they are aligned on even addresses in memory. Thus, the lowest bit in an object pointer is always zero. This is one example of a good place to keep the mark bit.

A variant of mark and sweep that parallelizes better is **tri-coloring mark and sweep**. Basically, instead of using just one binary mark bit per object, a **color**, or ternary value is used. The color associated with each object in the object graph is conventionally referred to as **white**, **grey**, or **black**. White objects are considered dead and should be garbage collected. Black objects are guaranteed to have no references to white objects. Initially, there are no black objects—the marking algorithm needs to find them. No black object is ever allowed to reference a white object. Grey objects are live, but with the status of their children unknown. Initially, the root set is colored grey to make the algorithm explore the entire reachable object graph. All other objects start out as white.

The tri-color algorithm is fairly simple:

```
Mark:
    All objects are White by default.
    Color all objects in the root set Grey.
    While there exist Grey objects
      For all Grey Objects, X
        For all White objects (sucessors) Y, that X references
          Color Y Grey.
        If all edges from X lead to another Grey object,
          Color X black.
Sweep:
  Garbage collect all White objects
```

The main idea here is that as long as the invariant that no black nodes ever point to white nodes is maintained, the garbage collector can continue marking even while changes to the object graph take place. These changes may be caused by, for example, allocations and field assignments in the executing program. Typically, the marking is "outsourced" so that many parts of the memory manager help maintain the coloring while the program is running. For example, objects may be marked immediately upon allocation.

There are several variants to parallelizing mark and sweep beyond the scope of this chapter. This section merely serves as an example of how mark and sweep can be improved for incremental and parallel garbage collection.

Stop and copy

Stop and copy can be seen as a special case of tracing GC, and is intelligent in its way, but is impractical for large heap sizes in real applications.

Stop and copy garbage collection requires partitioning the heap into two regions of equal size. Only one region is in use at a time, which is quite wasteful and ensures that only a maximum of half the available heap memory can be utilized for live data. In its simplest form, stop and copy garbage collection goes through all live objects in one of the heap regions, starting at the root set, following the root set pointers to other objects and so on. The marked live objects are moved to the other heap region. After garbage collection, the heap regions are switched so that the other half of the heap becomes the active region before the next collection cycle.

This approach is advantageous as fragmentation can't become an issue. Surviving objects are laid out first-fit in the new heap section on each garbage collection. As objects are laid out in their referencing order as the object graph is explored, stop and copy can significantly decrease cache overhead for the running program by keeping objects and the objects they reference close on the heap.

The obvious disadvantage of this approach is of course that all live data must be copied each time a garbage collection is performed, introducing a serious overhead in GC time as a function of the amount of live data, not to mention the very serious cache performance issues for the GC itself. More importantly, only using half of the heap at a time is an unforgivable waste of memory.

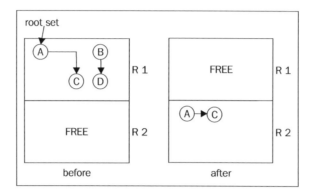

This figure illustrates a stop and copy cycle. The heap is divided into two regions. The root set contains only the object **A** at the start of garbage collection. **A** references **C** and no other objects. The mark phase of the GC cycle determines that **A** and **C** are the only live objects, and they are moved to the new region, **R2**. **B** and **D** are garbage collected. **A** and **C** were not adjacent in memory in **R1**, but will be automatically adjacent in **R2** as objects are laid out first-come-first-serve from tracing the object graph.

Stopping the world

Stopping the world, that is halting all executing Java threads for garbage collection, is the main Achilles' heel of automatic memory management. Even though an algorithm such as mark and sweep may run mostly in parallel, it is still a complicated problem that references may change during actual garbage collections. If the Java program is allowed to run, executing arbitrary field assignments and move instructions at the same time as the garbage collector tries to clean up the heap, mutual bookkeeping between the program and the garbage collector is needed. Ultimately this means synchronization, and synchronization, even in a smart algorithm, means stopping the world. Stopping the world for short periods of time is necessary for all languages where garbage collection and heap management is involved. This is one of the main sources of latencies and non-determinism in a runtime.

Garbage collection may move objects around on the heap, for example by compaction. If a register in a thread context of a running program contains a pointer to an object and that object is moved to another location in memory, it is easy to realize that the program will break if it is just allowed to continue running without the GC updating the register contents in the thread context. This is done by synchronously modifying the thread context of the executing thread. The same applies to any object reference that points out an object on the heap whose address has changed as an effect of the garbage collection.

The easy way out would be to stop the world for a long period of time and just brute force garbage collect as much as possible with as many threads as possible. Before resuming the threads, all registers are updated. Normally, however, this isn't possible because low latencies are usually the main requirement for a modern server-side application. It doesn't do to halt execution for hundreds of milliseconds at a time. Thus, for low latency environments, which seek to minimize application response time, the garbage collector needs to do as much work as it can while the Java program is still running, and still handle these possible pointer reassignments. This is the difficult part. However, there is no getting around stopping the world completely at some point, unless the application has very special behavior. The real challenge is keeping these pauses as short as possible.

Conservative versus exact collectors

As we have discussed earlier, the virtual machine needs to provide some information to the memory system so that it can identify which positions on a local stack frame contain objects. This is needed to build the root set of objects that will form the first nodes of the live object graph. Every thread that is executing Java code handles objects, and if the thread is stopped, we need to know where in its context they are.

It is easy to identify objects in fields of other objects, as all object layouts are known to the garbage collector. If all instances of object X contain a field of type Y, the pointer to the field contents of Y for all X instances is always at the same offset from the start of an X instance. An object is little more than a C `struct` to the JVM. However, the GC doesn't automatically know where objects are on a stack frame.

Finding the method in which a particular thread has stopped is simple. We can just use a lookup table or search tree to find out in which Java method an instruction pointer belongs. Objects occur in the scope of this method, either present from the beginning of its execution as in-parameters, or as the result of field loads or function calls in the method. Move instructions may also copy objects from one register to another. Given an arbitrary point in the code of the method, the point where the execution has been halted, there is no way to backtrack the context where the thread is stopped to the context in which these objects were created. We have no way of knowing which code was just executed to get us to this particular address. However, the GC must, given a stack frame, know where objects are stored to form a correct root set.

Trivially, one might tell the compiler to only use certain registers and positions on the local stack frame for objects and certain other registers and positions for non-objects, such as integers. For example on x86, one might force the code generator to place objects only in the registers `esi` and `edi` and integers only in all other registers. One might spill objects only to stack positions whose offsets are even multiples of the pointer size (`[esp+0*4]`, `[esp+2*4]` and so on) and integers only to stack positions that are odd multiples (`[esp+1*4]`, `[esp+3*4]` and so on). This makes it simple for the GC, as our "objects only" locations can only contain a valid object or `null`. Other locations need not be processed by the GC at all, as they never contain objects. However, limiting the number of registers for generic use by the compiler requires the register allocator to produce more spills. This is completely impractical for performance reasons, especially on architectures like x86, where the amount of available general purpose registers is limited.

One way to get around this is to use a **conservative garbage collector**, treating every location that looks like an object pointer as an object pointer. Trivially, values like `17` and `4711` can be disregarded and are known to be integers, but values that look like addresses must be examined and checked against the heap. This produces overhead, and is necessary if we want to add automatic memory management to some languages, such as C, which is weakly typed. Conservative garbage collectors also have problems with unintentional object retention to varying degrees and with moving objects in memory.

In Java, however, we can get by with an **exact garbage collector** that knows precisely where object pointers are and where they are not. We only need a way to get this information to the garbage collector. Typically, this is done by generating meta info along with code for a Java method.

Livemaps

In JRockit, a piece of meta info that consists of a collection of registers and stack positions containing objects at a given program point is called a **livemap**. An additional bit of info per object pointer tells us whether it is an **internal pointer** or the actual start of an object. Internal pointers refer to some piece of information inside an object, thus pointing to the heap, but not to an object header. Internal pointers need to be tracked as they must be updated along with their **base object** if it is moved in memory, but they cannot be treated as base objects themselves.

A typical example of the use of internal pointers is when iterating through an array. In Java no internal pointers to objects may exist, but compiled code may well run faster if a sequence like:

```
for (int i = 0; i < array.length; i++) {
   sum += array[i];
}
```

were to be compiled to native code equivalent to:

```
for (int ptr = array.getData();
   ptr < sizeof(int) * array.length;
   ptr += sizeof(int)) {
      sum += *ptr;
}
```

In this case, the GC has to know that `ptr` is an internal pointer to the array so that it can be updated as well if `array` is moved to another position in memory. The code potentially runs faster since the pointer to the array element data need not be computed at every iteration in the loop.

So, it is clear that object pointers and internal object pointers need to be stored in meta info, livemaps, for the garbage collector. To illustrate how this information looks to the memory system, the following is a small example of compiled Java code in JRockit annotated with livemap info. The code example is a simple method that computes the sum of the elements of an array.

```
public static Integer sum(Integer array[]) {
   Integer sum = 0;
   for (int i = 0; i < array.length; i++) {
      sum += array[i];
   }
   return sum;
}
```

Letting JRockit generate the method on a 64-bit x86 platform produces the following assembly code:

```
[SumArray.sum([Ljava/lang/Integer;)Ljava/lang/Integer;
7a8c90: push    rbx                    7a8cc7: jle     0x7a8cf7
7a8c91: push    rbp                       *----- [rsib, rbxb]
7a8c92: sub     rsp,8                  7a8cc9: mov     [rsp+0],rbx
7a8c96: mov     rbx,rsi                7a8ccd: mov     ebx,r9d
   *----- [rsib, rbxb]                    *----- [rsib, [rsp+0]b]
7a8c99: test    eax,[0x7fffe000]       7a8cd0: mov     r9d,[rsi+8]
   *--B-- [rsib, rbxb]                    *--B-- [[rsp+0]b]
7a8ca0: mov     ebp,[rsi+8]            7a8cd4: test    eax,[0x7fffe000]
7a8ca3: test    ebp,ebp                7a8cdb: mov     r11,[rsp+0]
7a8ca5: jg      7a8cb1                    *----- [r11b, [rsp+0]b]
   *----- [nothing live]               7a8cdf: mov ecx,[r11+4*rbx+16]
7a8ca7: xor     rax,rax                   *--B-- [rcxb, [rsp+0]b]
   *----- [nothing live]               7a8ce4: add     r9d,[rcx+8]
7a8caa: call Integer.valueOf(I)        7a8ce8: mov     eax,r9d
   *C---- [rsib]                          *----- [[rsp+0]b]
7a8caf: jmp     0x7a8cf7               7a8ceb: call Integer.valueOf(I)
   *--B-- [rsib, rbxb]                    *C-B-- [rsib, [rsp+0]b]
7a8cb1: mov     r9d,[rsi+16]           7a8cf0: add     ebx,1
   *----- [r9b, rbxb]                  7a8cf3: cmp     ebx,ebp
7a8cb5: mov     eax,[r9+8]             7a8cf5: jl      7a8cd0
   *----- [rbxb]                          *--B-- [rsib]
7a8cb9: call Integer.valueOf(I)        7a8cf7: pop     rcx
   *C---- [rsib, rbxb]                 7a8cf8: pop     rbp
7a8cbe: mov     r9d,1                  7a8cf9: pop     rbx
7a8cc4: cmp     rbp,1                  7a8cfa: ret
```

Though it is not important to understand what the code generator has done here in detail, the main idea is that several program points in the assembly code are annotated with liveness information. In this case, the optimization level is not sufficiently high to generate the inner pointer pattern described earlier. Also, the calls to `Integer.valueOf` have not been inlined.

The livemap information under annotated operations tells the garbage collector which registers and stack positions contain objects at the given program point. Notice, for example, that the calls to `Integer.valueOf`, by calling convention always return a new integer object in `rsi` (the b after `rsi` means "base pointer" as opposed to "internal pointer").

The livemaps also tell us that `rsi` and `rbx` contain objects after the frame entry at the beginning of the method. This follows from the `mov rbx, rsi` at address `7a8c96`, which is a register allocator artifact that shuffles the in-parameter from register `rsi` to register `rbx`.

 As `rbx`, in the JRockit calling convention is **callee save** (not destroyed over calls), the compiler chooses, for efficiency reasons, to keep the object alive in a register over the calls to `Integer.valueOf`. This way, the register allocator avoids doing a spill.

So, where can the garbage collector stop the world? Intuitively, it is too expensive to tag every single native instruction, each being a potential thread suspension point, with liveness information. As can be seen from the previous example, this is neither the case.

In JRockit, only certain instructions are tagged with livemaps, for example loop headers or headers of basic blocks with multiple entries, where it isn't possible to know which way control flow took to get there. Another example of instructions annotated with livemaps are `call` instructions. This is because liveness information must, for execution speed, be available immediately when computing a stack trace.

Recall from Chapter 2 that JRockit performs tasks like back patching calls. This means that the JVM must be equipped with a mechanism to understand and decompile native code. Originally, this mechanism was extended to make it possible to also emulate all native instructions from an address, given an operating system thread context as a starting point. If a livemap wasn't available at a certain instruction pointer in the context of a stopped thread, JRockit simply emulated the code, instruction by instruction, from that position until a livemap was reached. This is called **rollforwarding**.

 Rollforwarding was abandoned with JRockit R28. JRockit now uses a more traditional safepoint-based approach.

The advantages to this approach were that threads could be stopped anywhere. This was implemented using the signaling mechanisms of the underlying operating system. No extra instructions in the generated code were required.

The disadvantages were that emulation still took time and that large emulation frameworks needed to be in place, one for each supported hardware architecture. This was extremely difficult to test, as the set of inputs was virtually infinite, and emulation itself was very error prone. In addition, porting to a new hardware architecture became very expensive, requiring the implementation of a new complete emulation framework for that particular piece of silicon. Bugs in the emulators were usually subtle and generated intermittent and hard-to-find problems.

Throughout the years, there were also several problems with the signaling approach to stopping threads. It turns out that certain operating systems, especially Linux, seem to be poorly tested when it comes to applications that use a lot of signals. There were also issues with third-party native libraries that did not respect signal conventions, causing signal collisions. The external dependency on signals proved too error-prone to be completely reliable.

Newer versions of JRockit use a more traditional **safepoint** approach instead. Throughout the code, **safepoint instructions** that dereference a certain **guard page** in memory are inserted. At these instruction pointers, a complete livemap is always guaranteed to be in place. Whenever a Java thread is to be stopped, the runtime protects the guard page from access. This makes the safepoint instruction trigger a fault when executed. Variants of this technique are, as far as we know, employed in all commercial JVMs today. Loop headers are a typical example of program points where it makes sense to place safepoint instructions. We cannot allow a situation where the program will continue executing without ever trying to dereference a guard page. Thus, constructs like potentially infinite loops cannot be left without safepoint instructions.

The disadvantage here is that explicit code for dereferencing the guard page has to be inserted in the generated code, contributing to some execution overhead. But the advantages easily pay for this small inconvenience.

By now we have covered a lot of material on garbage collection, but only the basic concepts and algorithms. We've also discussed the surprisingly difficult problem of generating root sets for our garbage collectors. We will now attempt to cross the bridge to the "real world" and move on to discuss how garbage collection can be optimized and made more scalable.

Generational garbage collection

In object-oriented languages, a very important observation is that most objects are temporary or short-lived.

For temporary objects, escape analysis at compile time might be able to stop them from being allocated on the heap altogether, but in an imperfect world this is not always possible. Especially in a language like Java.

However, performance improvements for handling short-lived objects on the heap can be had if the heap is split into two or more parts called **generations**. New objects are allocated in the "young" generations of the heap, that typically are orders of magnitude smaller than the "old" generation, the main part of the heap. Garbage collection is then split into **young** and **old collections**, a young collection merely sweeping the young spaces of the heap, removing dead objects and **promoting** surviving objects by moving them to an older generation.

Collecting a smaller young space is orders of magnitude faster than collecting the larger old space. Even though young collections need to happen far more frequently, this is more efficient because many objects die young and never need to be promoted. Ideally, total throughput is increased and some potential fragmentation is removed.

JRockit refers to the young generations as **nurseries**.

Multi generation nurseries

While generational GCs typically default to using just one nursery, sometimes it can be a good idea to keep several small nursery partitions in the heap and gradually age young objects, moving them from the "younger" nurseries to the "older" ones before finally promoting them to the "old" part of heap. This stands in contrast with the normal case that usually involves just one nursery and one old space.

Multi generation nurseries may be more useful in situations where heavy object allocation takes place.

We assume that the most freshly allocated objects will live for a very short period of time. If they live just a bit longer, typically if they survive a first nursery collection, the standard behavior of a single generation nursery collector, would cause these objects to be promoted to the old space. There, they will contribute more to fragmentation when they are garbage collected. So it might make sense to have several young generations on the heap, with different age spans for young objects in different nurseries, to try to keep the heap holes away from the old space where they do the most damage.

Of course the benefits of a multi-generational nursery must be balanced against the overhead of copying objects multiple times.

Write barriers

In generational GC, objects may reference other objects located in different generations of the heap. For example, objects in the old space may point to objects in the young spaces and vice versa. If we had to handle updates to all references from the old space to the young space on GC by traversing the entire old space, no performance would be gained from the generational approach. As the whole point of generational garbage collection is only to have to go over a small heap segment, further assistance from the code generator is required.

In generational GC, most JVMs use a mechanism called **write barriers** to keep track of which parts of the heap need to be traversed. Every time an object **A** starts to reference another object **B**, by means of **B** being placed in one of **A**'s fields or arrays, write barriers are needed. Write barriers consist of a small amount of helper code that needs to be executed after each field or array store in the executing Java code.

The traditional approach to implementing write barriers is to divide the heap into a number of small consecutive sections (typically about 512 bytes each) that are called **cards**. The address space of the heap is thus mapped to a more coarse grained **card table**. Whenever the Java program writes to a field in an object, the card on the heap where the object resides is "dirtied" by having the write barrier code set a **dirty bit**.

Now, the traversion time problem for references from the old generation to the nursery is shortened. When doing a nursery collection, the GC only has to check the portions of the old space represented by dirty cards.

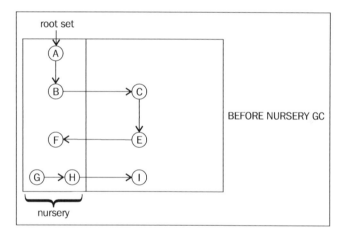

Consider the previous figure. The runtime is about to do a nursery collection. If the root set contains object **A** only, at the start of the collection, we would easily detect **A** and **B** as live by pointer tracing **A** to **B**. The pointer trace from **B** to **C** would be ignored, as **C** is in the old space. However, for the GC to work, we must add **E** in the old space to the root set, as it references an object in the nursery. With write barriers, we don't have to go over the entire old space to find **E**, but we just have to check the areas of the old space that correspond to dirty cards. In this example, the card for **E** was dirtied by the write barrier code after a previous assignment of **F** to a field in **E**. Thus, we can add **F** to the set of objects to be traced by the nursery GC.

A and **B** are root reachable and will be promoted to the old space after the nursery collection. **G** and **H** are not, and will be garbage collected. **E** and **F** were root reachable, and thus **F** will be promoted. While **I** is dead, it is part of the old space and won't be handled until the next old collection. The following figure shows the heap after the completed nursery collection and promotion. The objects in the old space are untouched, as this was a nursery collection.

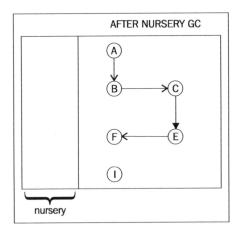

Throughput versus low latency

Recollect from Chapter 2 that the main factor that the JVM wants to minimize is the total runtime. In code generation, the total runtime is defined by the time to compile the code plus the time to execute the code. As we saw, we can only minimize one factor at the cost of another.

In memory management, the equation is simpler. All time spent in GC is of course detrimental to runtime. Minimizing the time spent in GC might seem the proper and only solution to lower the total runtime.

However, recollect that garbage collection requires stopping the world, halting all program execution, at some stage. Performing GC and executing Java code concurrently requires a lot more bookkeeping and thus, the total time spent in GC will be longer. If we only care about throughput, stopping the world isn't an issue —just halt everything and use all CPUs to garbage collect, one part of the heap per CPU. However, to most applications, latency is the main problem, and latency is caused by not spending every available cycle executing Java code.

Thus, the tradeoff in memory management is between maximizing throughput and maintaining low latencies. In an imperfect world, we can't expect to have both.

Optimizing for throughput

In some cases, latencies do not matter at all in an application, for example, in offline jobs that do large amounts of object crunching. A batch job running overnight may not be as vulnerable to response times as a client/server application.

If pause times up to several seconds are permissible, throughput can be maximized to a degree that is not possible if low latency is critical.

There are many variants of high throughput GC. The simplest approach is to stop the world and then garbage collect the heap with as many threads as possible, at least as many as the number of cores on the platform, each handling a separate part of the heap. Naturally, some synchronization between GC threads is still required for references that point to other heap parts. JRockit refers to this as **parallel garbage collection**.

We can still achieve levels of throughput not attainable in a low latency environment with other, less intrusive variants of this parallel approach. One example would be by using **generations** in the heap.

Optimizing for low latency

Optimizing for low latencies is basically a matter of avoiding stopping the world, and therefore also Java execution, by any means necessary. But naturally, if the garbage collector gets too little total CPU time and it can't keep up with the allocation frequency, the heap will fill up and an OutOfMemoryError will be thrown by the JVM. We need a GC that performs large parts of its work when the program is running.

JRockit refers to this kind of GC as **concurrent garbage collection**, using a term from one of the first scientific papers describing this technique, by Boehm and others. Later, the term **mostly concurrent** was introduced for improved versions of this algorithm.

There is a slight degree of confusion in the terminology here. The **parallel**, throughput oriented GC, described in the previous section, does not run at the same time as the Java program executes. It is known as "parallel" because it uses as many threads as possible in parallel to garbage collect the heap. Garbage collection that runs at the same time as the Java program executes, as described in this section, is known as **concurrent** GC.

The concurrent garbage collector is also parallel, in the traditional meaning of the word, because it uses several worker threads. However, the terms concurrent and parallel used in the manner of this book are not just specific to JRockit. This is often the standard way of referring to these respective GC techniques in academic research and other commercial implementations.

Many stages of a mark and sweep garbage collection algorithm can be made to run concurrently with the executing Java program. Marking is the most critical of the stages, as it usually takes up around 90 percent of the total garbage collection time. Fortunately, marking is very parallelizable and large parts of a mark phase can also be run concurrently with executing Java code. Sweeping and compaction, however, tend to be more troublesome, even though it is fairly simple to compact parts of the heap while others are swept, thus achieving better throughput.

The main idea behind mostly concurrent garbage collection is to spend as much time running garbage collection as possible, while the Java program still executes. Throughout the GC cycle, several shorter stop the world phases are used, where some merely seek to synchronize the GC with the object graph, as the running Java program continuously makes changes to it. This is trivially not an issue if no Java execution is allowed to take place during GC. As far as we know, all commercial JVMs use variants of the mostly concurrent approach for low latency garbage collection.

The section on *Near-real-time garbage collection*, later in this chapter, goes into further details on how to achieve both performance and low latencies. And specifically, how JRockit does it.

Garbage collection in JRockit

The backbone of the GC algorithm used in JRockit is based on the tri-coloring mark and sweep algorithm described earlier in this chapter. However, several optimizations and improvements have been made to make it more parallel, both to enable it to run at the same time as the Java program is executing and to use an optimal number of threads. For nursery collections, heavily modified variants of stop and copy are used.

Garbage collection in JRockit can work with or without generations, depending on what we are optimizing for. Garbage collection strategies and adaptive implementation thereof is covered later in this chapter.

The JRockit garbage collector can chose to tag any object on the heap as **pinned** for a shorter or longer period of time. This makes concurrent garbage collection algorithms more flexible. It can also enable I/O performance in that things like buffers can be kept in the same place on the heap for an entire I/O operation. This makes memory-intensive operations significantly faster. Pinned objects are a relatively simple concept in a GC, but for some reason, JRockit seems to be one of the few commercial JVMs that implements it.

Old collections

The mark and sweep algorithm that is the fundament of all JRockit garbage collectors, parallel or concurrent, uses two colors and not three, for its objects, but still allows for efficient parallelization in the manner described in the section on *Mark and sweep* earlier in this chapter. Objects belong to one of two sets. One set is used to mark live objects. JRockit calls this set the **grey bits**, even though it is actually the semantic equivalent of a mix of grey and black objects in traditional tri-coloring. The distinction between grey and black objects is instead handled by putting grey objects in **thread local queues** for each garbage collecting thread. This approach has two advantages. First of all it allows parallel threads to work on thread local data instead of competing for a synchronized common set. Furthermore, it is possible to efficiently use **prefetching** on the contents of the queues as their elements are accessed both in FIFO order and close in time to one another. The general advantages of prefetching in memory management will be discussed later in this chapter.

For concurrent collectors in JRockit, an additional set called the **live bits** is used. It keeps track of all live objects in the system, including the newly created ones. This makes it possible for JRockit to quickly find objects that have been created during a concurrent mark phase, that is one running at the same time as the Java application.

JRockit uses a **card table** not only for generational GCs, but also to avoid searching the entire live object graph when a concurrent mark phase cleans up. This is because JRockit needs to find any new objects that may have been created by the running program during that mark phase. Recollect that write barriers in the running code continuously update the card table. The card table also has one card per region in the live object graph. As described, a card can be dirty or clean and all cards where objects have been newly created or have had their object references modified are marked as dirty. At the end of a concurrent mark phase, JRockit only needs to look at the dirty cards and scan the objects in the corresponding heap regions that have their live bit set. This guarantees that all objects, freshly allocated and old ones, are found even after a concurrent mark phase.

Nursery collections

For nursery collections, JRockit uses a variant of stop and copy. All threads are halted, and all objects in the nursery are copied or promoted to the old space.

The copying is done hierarchically in breadth first manner, which increases cache locality (objects that reference each other should be stored close to each other in memory for maximum cache efficiency). The breadth-first copy algorithm is parallelizable in a way that automatically contributes to good load balancing.

Only live objects are copied to the old space. Instead of having to scan the entire heap to find out what objects in the nursery are live, the young collection uses the live bits and the card table that were mentioned in the previous section. As we start out with an empty nursery and because all objects that have their references updated get the corresponding card in the card table marked as dirty by write barrier code, all live objects in the nursery can be found by merely scanning objects that have their live bit set in a region corresponding to a dirty card.

Nursery collections in JRockit are always parallel but never concurrent. However, for efficiency reasons, young collections may occur at any time during a concurrent old collection. This complicates matters, especially because both the young collection and the old collection depend heavily on the same data structures.

However, it turns out that these data structures, the bit sets and the card table, can be shared as long as an old collection is guaranteed to see all cards that have become dirty during a concurrent phase. This is achieved by having an extra card table that records all dirty cards from the original card table. JRockit calls this union of all card table changes the **modified union set**. The nursery collection is free to process and clear dirty cards as long as the modified union set is kept intact for the old collection. So the young and old collector can operate at the same time without getting in the way of each other.

JRockit also uses a concept called **keep area**. The keep area is a region in the nursery where objects are not copied to old space during a young collection. By making sure that the youngest objects are allocated in the keep area, JRockit can ensure that newly created objects have an extra chance to become garbage collected before they are considered long lived, and copied to old space. This is the rough, simpler, equivalent to a multi-generational approach.

Permanent generations

One thing that sets JRockit apart from the HotSpot VM is the lack of a **permanent generation** on the heap. In HotSpot, a heap part of predefined size, the permanent generation, is used to store metadata about, for example, class objects. Once the data is in the permanent generation, the default behavior is that it remains there forever (this might vary between garbage collection policies). This means that if a large amount of classloading takes place, the permanent generation will fill up and `OutOfMemoryErrors` will be thrown. We have seen customer cases, where the problem with a permanent generation gets so bad that the JVM and the Java application have to be restarted regularly.

JRockit is different in that it stores metadata off the heap in native memory instead. Code buffers for generated methods along with metadata pointed to by `ClassLoaders` that are no longer used are also constantly garbage collected. The problem of running out of memory for metadata in JRockit is not that different from the same problem in HotSpot, except for the fact that it is native memory instead of heap memory. There are, however, two significant differences. Firstly, in JRockit, cleaning up stale metadata is always enabled by default and secondly, there is no fixed size limit for the space used to store metadata. One of the larger problems with HotSpot is probably that intuitively, it is very hard to pick a size for the permanent generation. Is 128 MB enough? No? What about 256 MB? It is really very difficult to know for any given application. JRockit, being completely dynamic in its metadata allocation, need not consider size limits. It will, out of the maximum amount of native memory, allocate as much space as it needs for its metadata at any given time.

Compaction

In JRockit, compaction is always single-threaded and non-concurrent. However, for parallel collectors, compaction runs at the same time as the sweep phase. As compaction is always done with a single thread, it is important that it is fast and that the time spent doing compaction can be controlled. JRockit limits compaction time by only compacting a part of the heap in each garbage collection. Most of the time, heuristics are used for choosing where on the heap to compact, and how much. The heuristics are also used to decide between different types of compactions—**internal compaction** just within one heap partition or **external compaction** (also referred to as **evacuation**) between different areas on the heap.

In order to make it more efficient to update all references to an object when it is moved, JRockit lets the mark phase keep track of all references that point to objects inside a heap region that is to be compacted. This information can also be used to determine if it is possible to do any compaction at all or if certain popular objects should be excluded from compaction as too many other objects reference them.

Speeding it up and making it scale

This section addresses what a modern runtime can do to speed up memory management, going from impractical and "academic" algorithms to real world performance.

Thread local allocation

One technique, used in JRockit, that significantly speeds up object allocation is the concept of **thread local allocation**. It is normally much cheaper to allocate an object locally in a buffer in the running Java thread than going through the synchronized process of placing it directly on the heap. A naive garbage collector doing direct heap allocations would need a global heap lock for each allocation. This would quickly be the site for a nightmarish amount of contention. On the other hand, if each Java thread keeps a thread local object buffer, most object allocations may be implemented simply as the addition of a pointer, one assembly instruction on most hardware platforms. We refer to these thread local buffers as **Thread Local Areas (TLA)**. The TLAs naturally have to processed by the garbage collector as well.

For cache and performance reasons, each TLA is typically between 16 and 128 kilobytes, but this can be modified from the command line. Whenever a thread local buffer is full, everything in it is promoted to the heap. We can think of a thread local buffer as a small thread local nursery.

Whenever a `new` operator in Java is compiled and the JIT set to a sufficiently high level of optimization, the allocation code turns into a construct that can be illustrated by the following pseudocode:

```
Object allocateNewObject(Class objectClass) {
  Thread current = getCurrentThread();
  int objectSize = alignedSize(objectClass);
  if (current.nextTLAOffset + objectSize > TLA_SIZE) {
      current.promoteTLAToHeap(); //slow and synchronized
      current.nextTLAOffset = 0;
  }
  Object ptr = current.TLAStart + current.nextTLAOffset;
  current.nextTLAOffset += objectSize;

  return ptr;
}
```

The pseudocode just seen presents a somewhat simplified view of the world, in order to illustrate the point. Objects that are larger than a certain threshold value or that are too big to fit in any available TLA are still allocated directly on the heap. As of JRockit R28, a measurement used to better optimize TLA usage, called the **TLA waste limit**, has been introduced. This is discussed to a greater extent in Chapter 5.

In certain architectures where registers are plentiful, further performance gains can be achieved by always keeping the `nextTLAOffset`, and possibly the pointer to the TLA itself, in registers for the thread that is currently executing Java code. On x86 with its limited register set, however, this is a luxury we can't afford.

Larger heaps

As the complexity of a well written GC is mostly a function of the size of the live data set, and not the heap size, it is not too costly to support larger heaps for the same amount of live data. This has the added benefit of it being harder to run into fragmentation issues and of course, implicitly, the possibility to store more live data.

32-Bits and the 4-GB Barrier

On a 32-bit system, a maximum 4 GB of memory can be addressed. This is the theoretical maximum size of any heap, but of course there are other things that need to be kept in memory as well, such as the operating system. Some operating systems, for example Windows, are very picky about how they lay out kernel and libraries in memory. On Windows, the kernel often lies almost in the middle of the address space, making it difficult to fully utilize all available memory as one contiguous Java heap. Most JVMs only support heaps that consist of contiguous chunks of memory, so this can be a problem.

To our knowledge, JRockit is the only JVM that supports non-contiguous heaps and is able to utilize the memory both above and below the operating system kernel and any other external libraries for its heap space.

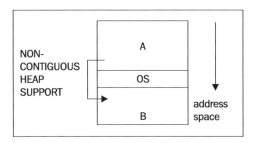

In the previous figure, the OS resides roughly in the middle of the address space, effectively limiting the maximum virtual address space for a process. The memory areas **A** and **B** come before and after the operating system respectively. **A** is slightly larger than **B**, so **A** corresponds to the largest heap that we can use without support for non-contiguous heaps. A non-contiguous heap implementation would allow us to use the combined memory in **A** and **B** for our heap at the price of a small bit of extra bookkeeping overhead. This is implemented by basically pretending that the OS area is a large pinned object in the middle of the address space.

While 32-bit architectures tend to grow less and less common with the 64-bit revolution, there are still scenarios where they are used a lot. Currently, virtualized environments seem to be such a place, and so it still makes sense to maximize performance for 32-bit platforms, with the limited address space that entails.

The 64-bit world

On a 64-bit system, even when running a 32-bit JVM, the larger available virtual address space can be tweaked so that we don't need to work around occupied areas of the address space.

Most modern architectures are 64-bit, and the theoretical amount of data that fits into a 64-bit address range, 16 exabytes, is staggeringly huge. Currently, it is not affordable to populate that large an address space with physical memory.

There are both benefits and disadvantages to using a 64-bit architecture for automatic memory management, unlike with code generation, which tends to see only benefits (such as more registers, wider registers, and lager data bandwidth).

Pointers on a 64-bit machine are 8 bytes wide instead of 4 bytes. This consumes more bandwidth and CPU cache space. Simplifying a bit, dereferencing a 32-bit pointer is faster than dereferencing a 64-bit one, so a 64-bit 4.1 GB heap, although only slightly larger than a 32-bit 4 GB one, may actually be a lot slower to use.

Compressed references

A fair compromise is the **compressed reference** optimization that JRockit was the first JVM to implement. If a JVM running on a 64-bit system uses less than 4 GB of heap space, it obviously makes no sense to represent objects as 64-bit pointers. 32 bits are enough, and consequently all object access will be a lot quicker.

Native pointers outside the heap that are still part of the runtime environment must be system wide, 64 bits, on a 64-bit system. The typical example is handles that represent JNI references to Java objects. Transitions to and from native code through JNI may occur in any Java program. For the sake of native code and to some extent the GC, which needs to operate on native pointers internally, we need ways to go from the transform domain of compressed references to that of ordinary system wide pointers. We refer to these transforms as **reference compression** and **reference decompression**.

Following is the pseudocode for compression and decompression of a 4 GB heap on a 64-bit platform. The virtual address of the heap base can be placed anywhere in memory.

```
CompRef compress(Ref ref) {
   return (uint32_t)ref; //truncate reference to 32-bits
}


Ref decompress(CompRef ref) {
   return globalHeapBase | ref;
}
```

When compressed references are 32-bit, it suffices to use a logical or with the actual (64-bit) heap base to decompress them into system-wide pointers. This operation has the added benefit that it can be applied an arbitrary number of times without further changing the pointer. However, depending on the number of bits in a compressed reference, this representation isn't always possible and strict state machines must therefore be maintained so we know when a reference is compressed and when it isn't, for example in stubs to and from native code or when the code refers to actual 64-bit handles to objects.

Note that 4-GB heaps aren't the only application of compressed references. For example, consider a 64-GB heap, where instead of using all 64 bits to represent an object, we can use 4 + 32 bits, where four of the bits are used to point out which of sixteen possible 4-GB heap sections an object resides in. Note that this requires four free bits in the object, which in turn requires that allocated objects are aligned on 16-byte boundaries. This may waste some heap space, but can still be a win performance-wise.

```
CompRef compress(Ref ref) {
   return (uint32_t)(ref >> log₂(objectAlignment));
}

Ref decompress(CompRef ref) {
   return globalHeapBase | (ref << log₂(objectAlignment));
}
```

The method can be made even simpler, if we keep the 16-byte object alignment and make sure that the virtual address space starts at address 0 and ends at address "64 GB". Then a reference may be decompressed by just shifting it four bits left, and compressed by shifting it four bits right, not needing to involve a global heap base. This is how JRockit does it, thereby maintaining 32-bit wide compressed references for the general case. JRockit, for convenience, still wants address 0 to be used for `null` pointers, so the lowest 4 GB of the virtual space is not used for anything else, effectively reducing the 64 GB of heap to 60 GB, but this is of little importance for performance. If the difference between a 64-GB heap and a 60-GB heap matters to you, you are in trouble anyway.

This method is generic as it works for all heap sizes larger than or equal to 4 GB. The generic approach, however, has a new drawback. The attractive property that decompression can be applied an infinite number of times, to both uncompressed and compressed references, disappears.

Naturally, 64 GB isn't a theoretical limit but just an example. It was mentioned because compressed references on 64-GB heaps have proven beneficial compared to full 64-bit pointers in some benchmarks and applications. What really matters, is how many bits can be spared and the performance benefit of this approach. In some cases, it might just be easier to use full length 64-bit pointers.

JRockit R28 supports compressed references in different configurations that can support theoretical heap sizes up to 64 GB. Parts of the compressed references framework is adaptive.

Some variant of compressed references is always enabled by default in JRockit if the maximum heap size is either unspecified or set to a value less than or equal to 64 GB. The required object alignment (and therefore implementation) varies depending on maximum heap size. Compressed references can be explicitly disabled from the command line.

In JRockit, what we are mostly trying to maximize with the compressed reference approach is the available heap space and the amount of objects that fit in the L1 cache. To avoid a number of problematic special cases, references on a local stack frame in a method are never compressed. Basically, code inserted after every field load decompresses a reference and code inserted before every field store re-compresses it. The overhead from doing this is negligible.

Cache friendliness

It is also important for the garbage collector to care about other aspects of the underlying system architecture. The most important issue to consider is cache friendliness. Repeated cache misses can cause significant performance degradation.

CPUs contain both instruction and data caches (along with several specialized caches for other purposes). In this section we are addressing data cache issues. A cache consists of several cache-lines of data, which is the smallest accessible cache unit. When data is retrieved from memory, it is placed into the caches so that it can be quickly accessed again in the near future. Accessing data in a cache is orders of magnitude faster than retrieving it from memory.

A CPU cache is usually hierarchical and multi level (for example, with three levels). The first level of cache is the fastest, smallest, and closest to the CPU. On modern architectures, each core tends to have its own L1 cache, while higher level caches may or may not be shared between cores. An L1 cache is usually on the order of kilobytes and an L2 cache on the order of megabytes. Accessing an L2 cache is more expensive than an L1 cache, but still much cheaper than having to go to memory, which will be the case if the highest level cache in the hierarchy misses.

Intelligent prefetching of data into a cache before it is to be accessed can both reduce the number of cache misses if it is the correct data, or destroy cache performance if cache contents are replaced by irrelevant data. An adaptive runtime seems like an ideal environment to find out what data is likely to be relevant.

In code generation, this can be remedied by using runtime feedback to determine which object accesses in Java code cause cache misses and compensate by generating code that does intelligent **prefetching**. In the memory system, we need to care about things like object placement on the heap, alignment, and allocation strategies.

Prefetching

Using software prefetching to load data that is soon to be accessed, thus getting it into the cache during cycles of other activity, can be very beneficial. This is because when the data is accessed "for real", the cache won't miss.

Explicit prefetching done by the program is known as **software prefetching**. It should be noted that modern hardware architectures also have advanced **hardware prefetching** built in that can do an excellent automatic prefetching job if any memory access pattern is regular and predictable enough.

One example of when intelligent prefetching improves garbage collection speed in JRockit stems from the fact that the thread local areas for allocation are divided into many small chunks. When a chunk is first to be used, the next chunk is heuristically prefetched. This means that the following allocations will already have the next chunk of the TLA in the cache.

Done correctly, there are significant performance improvements in using prefetching to improve cache hits.

The downside is of course that every time an item is loaded into the cache, other cached data is destroyed. Prefetching too often may decrease cache functionality. Also, a prefetch retrieves an entire cache line, which takes time, so unless the prefetch operation can be **pipelined**, or hidden in parallel with other actions before its data is to be used, it has no or even negative effects.

Data placement

If we know certain data accesses to be sequential or close in time, it makes a lot of sense for the GC to try to place the objects involved on the same cache line—spatial locality follows temporal locality. An example is that a `java.lang.String` and the `char` array which it contains are almost always accessed in sequence. The more runtime feedback the memory system has, the better guesses it can make which data should belong together.

There are of course good static guesses as well, that usually pay off, such as trying to best-fit an object on the heap next to other objects that it may reference and an array next to its elements.

NUMA

Modern **Non-Uniform Memory Access (NUMA)** architectures provide even more challenges for a garbage collector. Typically, in a NUMA architecture, the address space is divided between processors. This is in order to avoid the bus (and possibly cache) latency bottleneck when several CPUs try to access the same memory. Each CPU owns a part of the address space and memory on a CPU-specific bus. A CPU that wants to access its own memory handles this very quickly, while the further away that the memory is that it wants to access, the longer it takes (depending on the configuration). The traditional approach is **Uniform Memory Access (UMA)**, where all CPUs uniformly access memory and where access time to a particular memory location is independent of which CPU requests it.

Two of the modern NUMA architectures that are used in several server-side environments are the AMD Opteron and the newer Intel Nehalem architecture.

The following figure illustrates a NUMA node configuration:

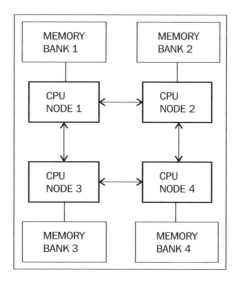

Here, any CPU, or NUMA node, has to perform at most two communication hops with the other NUMA nodes in the system to get at arbitrary memory. The ideal (and the fastest) memory access consists of zero hops (the node's own memory). There is not necessarily be a one-to-one mapping between CPUs and NUMA nodes. For example, one NUMA node may contain several CPUs who share local memory.

So, to perform well on a NUMA architecture, the garbage collector threads should be structured in a beneficial way. If a CPU is executing a mark thread in the GC it should be the one working on the parts of the heap memory that belong to the CPU itself. This way NUMA performance is maximized. As referenced objects may, in worst case, appear anywhere on the heap, on NUMA the GC usually needs an additional object moving heuristic. This is to make sure that objects referenced near other objects in time appear near them in memory as well, evacuating them from suboptimal NUMA nodes. If this works correctly, there are substantial performance gains to be had. The main problem is keeping objects from being moved back and forth, "ping ponging", between memory sections that are the responsibilities of different NUMA nodes. Theoretically, an adaptive runtime could be very good at this.

This is another example of an optimization that can work well in an adaptive runtime, but perhaps not so much in a static environment. Command-line flags that modify memory allocation behavior in the JVM and change NUMA node affinity for the JVM process will be discussed in greater detail in Chapter 5.

> NUMA is a challenging architecture to implement good memory management for. However, research on JRockit shows that it is still possible to get pretty good performance without specific NUMA optimizations as long as prefetching and cache behavior is intelligent enough in the JVM.

Large pages

At the base of all memory allocations lies the operating system and its page table. An OS divides the physical memory into pages, a page typically being the smallest possible memory allocation unit. Traditionally, a page is somewhere in the order of 4 KB. A process in an OS only sees a virtual address space, not a physical one. In order for a CPU to map a virtual page to the actual physical page in memory, a cache called the **Translation Lookaside Buffer (TLB)** is used to speed things up. If pages are too small, TLB misses are consequently more common.

This problem can be remedied if pages were several orders of magnitude larger; megabytes instead of kilobytes. All modern operating systems tend to support **large pages** in some form.

Obviously, in an OS where many processes allocate memory in separate address spaces and where pages are much larger than a couple of KB, fragmentation becomes a bigger problem because more page space is wasted. An allocation that requires slightly more memory than the size of a page suddenly carries a lot of dead weight. This doesn't matter to a runtime that does its own memory management in one process and owns a large part of the memory, but even if it were a problem it could be remedied by providing abstraction for many different page sizes on an underlying large page.

> A performance increase of at least 10 percent can usually be gained for a memory intensive application if it runs on large pages instead of normal ones. JRockit has support for this and can use large pages if enabled on the underlying operating system.

Typically, on most operating systems, enabling large page support is a privileged operation that requires administrator access, which makes it slightly harder to just "plug and play".

Adaptability

As we have discussed to a great extent in the chapter on code generation, adaptability is the key to success in a runtime for a mobile language such as Java. Traditionally, only code was adaptively reoptimized and was subject to hotspot analysis. However, the JRockit designers recognized from the start that all aspects of the runtime system should be made adaptive if possible.

So, JRockit may heuristically change garbage collection behavior at runtime, based on feedback from the memory system and adjust parameters such as heap size, number of generations in the heap, and even the overall strategy used to garbage collect.

Here is an example output generated by running JRockit with the -Xverbose:gc flag:

```
marcusl@nyarlathotep:$ java -Xmx1024M -Xms1024M -Xverbose:gc
  -cp dist/bmbm.jar com.oracle.jrpg.bmbm.minisjas.server.Server
[memory] Running with 32 bit heap and compressed references.
[memory] GC mode: Garbage collection optimized for throughput,
  initial strategy: Generational Parallel Mark & Sweep.
[memory] Heap size: 1048576KB, maximal heap size: 1048576KB,
  nursery size: 524288KB.
[memory] <s>-<end>: GC <before>KB-><after>KB (<heap>KB), <pause>ms.
[memory] <s/start> - start time of collection (seconds since jvm start).
[memory] <end>     - end time of collection (seconds since jvm start).
[memory] <before>  - memory used by objects before collection (KB).
[memory] <after>   - memory used by objects after collection (KB).
[memory] <heap>    - size of heap after collection (KB).
[memory] <pause>   - total sum of pauses
  during collection (milliseconds).
[memory]                run with -Xverbose:gcpause to see
  individual pauses.
[memory] [YC#1] 28.298-28.431: YC 831035KB->449198KB
  (1048576KB), 132.7 ms
[memory] [OC#1] 32.142-32.182: OC 978105KB->83709KB
  (1048576KB), 40.9 ms
```

```
[memory] [OC#2] Changing GC strategy to Parallel Mark & Sweep

[memory] [OC#2] 39.103-39.177: OC 1044486KB->146959KB
  (1048576KB), 73.0 ms

[memory] [OC#3] Changing GC strategy to Generational
  Parallel Mark & Sweep

[memory] [OC#3] 45.433-45.495: OC 1048576KB->146996KB
  (1048576KB), 61.8 ms

[memory] [YC#2] 50.547-50.671: YC 968200KB->644988KB
  (1048576KB), 124.4 ms

[memory] [OC#4] 51.504-51.524: OC 785815KB->21012KB
  (1048576KB), 20.2 ms

[memory] [YC#3] 56.230-56.338: YC 741361KB->413781KB
  (1048576KB), 108.2 ms

...

[memory] [YC#8] 87.853-87.972: YC 867172KB->505900KB
  (1048576KB), 119.4 ms

[memory] [OC#9] 90.206-90.234: OC 875693KB->67591KB
  (1048576KB), 27.4 ms

[memory] [YC#9] 95.532-95.665: YC 954972KB->591713KB
  (1048576KB), 133.2 ms

[memory] [OC#10] 96.740-96.757: OC 746168KB->29846KB
  (1048576KB), 17.8 ms

[memory] [YC#10] 101.498-101.617: YC 823790KB->466860KB
  (1048576KB), 118.8 ms

[memory] [OC#11] 104.832-104.866: OC 1000505KB->94669KB
  (1048576KB), 34.5 ms

[memory] [OC#12] Changing GC strategy to Parallel Mark & Sweep

[memory] [OC#12] 110.680-110.742: OC 1027768KB->151658KB
  (1048576KB), 61.9 ms

[memory] [OC#13] Changing GC strategy to Generational
  Parallel Mark & Sweep

[memory] [OC#13] 116.236-116.296: OC 1048576KB->163430KB
  (1048576KB), 59.1 ms.

[memory] [YC#11] 121.084-121.205: YC 944063KB->623389KB
  (1048576KB), 120.1 ms
```

JRockit versions from R28 tend not to change garbage collection strategies at runtime. Default values will be picked depending on configuration. This, along with better garbage collectors, was found to provide a larger degree of determinism for customers.

The previous output is from the R27 line of JRockit releases. For R28, non-standard GC strategies should be explicitly specified on the command line. R28 defaults to a generational parallel mark and sweep (optimized for throughput). The R28 memory management system still adaptively modifies many aspects of the garbage collection behavior, but to a lesser extent than R27.

All garbage collections in the previous example take place using a parallel mark and sweep algorithm, optimized for throughput. However, the JVM heuristically decides whether nurseries should be used or not depending on feedback from the runtime system. In the beginning, these changes are fairly frequent, but after a warm-up period and maintained steady-state behavior, the idea is that the JVM should settle upon an optimal algorithm. If, after a while, the steady-state behavior changes from one kind to another, the JVM may once again change strategies to a more optimal one.

Near-real-time garbage collection

Real-time systems tend to fit badly in a garbage collecting world. No matter how well a garbage collector performs, we still have a non-deterministic runtime overhead. Even if the latencies introduced by the GC are few and stopping the world completely is a rare event, a certain degree of non-determinism cannot be avoided.

So what do we mean by real-time? The terminology suffers from a certain degree of misuse. To avoid some of the confusion associated with real-time, we will divide the concept into **hard real-time** and **soft real-time**.

Hard and soft real-time

Hard real-time should be understood as the more traditional real-time system—perhaps a synthesizer or a pacemaker, a system where 100 percent determinism is an absolute requirement. There are few runtimes with automatic memory management that can work for this kind of environment, at least not without extensive modifications to the application and some kind of program language constructs for controlling the garbage collection.

A typical example is the Java real-time effort as specified in **Java Specification Request (JSR) 1**, which specifies an API (`javax.realtime`) for interacting with the runtime and for controlling the occurrence of garbage collection at certain program points. When using Java to develop a new application, this might be a feasible way to go ahead, but porting an existing Java production system to use a new API with new semantics is often very challenging or downright impossible. Even if it is technically feasible, modifying the key aspects of an existing system is very costly. Hence, the concept soft real-time.

We use the term **soft real-time** to mean a runtime system where it is possible to specify a quality of service level for latencies, and control pause times so that, even though they are non-deterministic, no single pause will last longer than a certain amount of time. This is the technique that is implemented in the product JRockit Real Time.

JRockit Real Time

It turns out that guaranteeing a quality of service level in the form of a maximum pause time setting is sufficient for most complex systems that require a certain degree of determinism. It is enough for the system to guarantee that latencies stay below the given bound. If this works as it should, the immediate benefit is of course that more deterministic and lower latencies can be gained without modifying an existing application.

The main selling point of JRockit Real Time is that getting deterministic latencies requires no modifications to the application—it just plugs in. The only thing that needs to be specified from the user side is the pause time target in milliseconds. Current JRockit releases have no problems maintaining single millisecond pause time targets on modern CPU architectures.

No world is perfect, however, and as we have discussed in the section about concurrent GC, the price of low latencies has to be paid for with longer total garbage collection time. Recollect that it is more difficult to garbage collect efficiently when the application is running, and if we have to interrupt GC more often, it might be even more problematic. In practice, this has turned out not to be a problem. It is more important to most customers who want JRockit Real Time that the degree of predictability and latency is deterministic, than that the total garbage collection time goes down. Most customers feel that response times is their main problem and that a sudden increase in pause time while large garbage collections take place is more harmful than if the total time spent in GC increases.

The following graph illustrates response times over time for a running application. The application in question is a benchmark for WebLogic SIP Server, a product for the telecom industry. JRockit Real Time is not enabled. As can be seen, the deviation in response times is large.

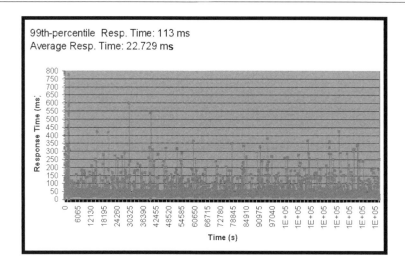

99th-percentile Resp. Time: 113 ms
Average Resp. Time: 22.729 ms

Does the soft real-time approach work?

The soft real-time approach in JRockit Real Time has turned out to be a major winner. But how can a non-deterministic system like a garbage collector provide the degree of determinism required to never have longer than single millisecond pause times? The complete answer is that it can't, but the boundary cases are rare enough so that it doesn't matter.

Of course there is no silver bullet, and there are indeed scenarios when a pause time target cannot be guaranteed. It turns out, however, that practically all standard applications, with live data sets up to about 30 to 50 percent of the heap size, can be successfully handled by JRockit Real Time with pause times shorter than, or equal to, the supported service level. This fits the majority of all Java applications that customers run. The live data set bound of 30 to 50 percent is constantly being improved by tuning and gets better with each new JRockit Real Time release. The minimum supported pause time is also continuously made lower.

In the event that JRockit Real Time isn't a perfect first fit for an application, several other things can be done to tune the behavior of the garbage collector. When looking for the cause of latencies in a Java program, there are frequently non GC-related user issues involved. For example, it is common that a lock in the Java code is so contended that it is actually contributing more to program latencies than the GC itself. JRockit Mission Control contains a set of diagnostic tools that can fairly easily point out problems like this from a runtime recording.

We often hear success stories from the field, such as when a trading system started making tens of thousands of dollars more per day because of lower latencies and consequently faster response times. The system could complete a significant number of more trades per day on the same hardware. No other action than switching VMs to JRockit Real Time was required.

The following graph shows the same benchmark run as before, with JRockit Real Time enabled and a maximum latency service level set to 10 milliseconds using the -XpauseTarget flag. Note that after the initial warm-up spikes, there is virtually no unpredictability left in the latencies.

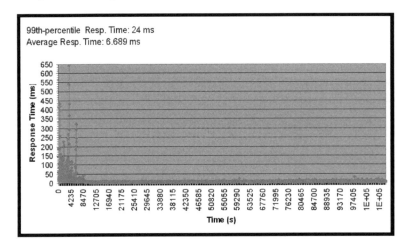

One might easily theorize that the spikes in the beginning of the run are caused by the VM aggressively trying to reach a steady state, for example through large amounts of code optimization. This can be true, and indeed this kind of pattern can show up. For this particular benchmark run, however, the initial latencies were actually caused by a bug in the Java application, unrelated to GC or adaptive optimization. The problem was subsequently fixed.

We also note that JRockit Real Time has no trouble fulfilling the 10 millisecond guarantee it was given. All of this comes at the affordable price of a slightly longer total time spent in garbage collection.

How does it work?

So how can JRockit deliver this kind of garbage collection performance? There are three key issues at work here:

- Efficient parallelization
- Splitting garbage collection work into **work packets**, transactions that may be rollbacked or aborted if they fail to complete in time
- Efficient heuristics

Efficient parallelization isn't a novel concept. There are several concurrent garbage collectors in existing literature, and there are few conceptual changes or technological leaps in how JRockit Real Time handles concurrency. Performance is, as always, in the details—synchronize efficiently, avoid locks if possible, make sure existing locks aren't saturated, and schedule the worker threads in an efficient manner.

The key to low latency is still to let the Java program run as much as possible, and keep heap usage and fragmentation at a decent level. We can think of JRockit Real Time as a greedy strategy for keeping Java programs running. The basic strategy is postponing stopping the world for as long as possible, hoping that whatever problem that caused us to want to stop the world in the first place will resolve itself, or that the time required to stop the world will go down once it is inevitable. Hopefully, there are fewer objects to compact or sweep when we finally pause.

All garbage collector work in JRockit Real Time is split up into work packets. If we start to execute a work packet, for example a compaction job for part of the heap, with the Java program halted, and it takes too long, we can throw away whatever work it has done so far and restart the application. Sometimes the partial work can be kept, but the entire transaction doesn't have time to complete. The time to completion while the world is stopped is governed by the quality of service level for latencies that the user has specified. If a very low latency bound has been specified we might have to throw away more of a partially completed transaction in order to keep the Java program running than with a higher one.

The mark phase is, as has already been covered, simple to modify, so that it runs concurrently with the Java program. However, both the sweep phase and compaction need to stop the world at times. Luckily, mark time tends to make up around 90 percent of the total garbage collection time. If the phases that need stopping the world take too long, we just have to make sure we can terminate what they are doing and restart the concurrent phase, hoping that the problem goes away in the meantime. The work package abstraction makes it easier to implement this functionality.

There are, of course, several heuristics involved. Slight modifications to the runtime system helps JRockit Real Time make more informed decisions. One example is a somewhat more complex write barrier that keeps track of the number of cards dirtied on a per-thread basis. The code takes a little bit more time to execute than that of a traditional generational GC write barrier, but provides more adequate profiling data to the GC. If one thread is much more active at dirtying cards than others, it probably needs special attention. JRockit also uses the sum of all executed write barriers in a thread as a heuristic trigger.

The Java memory API

This section covers some of the unique constructs of the Java language, related to memory management.

Dreaming of `delete` or `free` operators for Java or trying to explicitly control the garbage collection behavior in a JVM by, for example, hanging on to objects longer than their natural lifespans is a sure way of shooting yourself in the foot. There are, however, some mechanisms in the Java language that make it possible to help the GC by giving it "hints". Some of the available mechanisms are good and some are bad. Some should be used with caution to avoid unwanted side effects.

Finalizers

In Java, since Java 1.0, every object contains a method called `finalize` that may be freely overridden by any implementer. The contract is that the `finalize` method is called just before the object in question is about to be garbage collected. This might seem like a good idea, making it possible to do cleanups before the object goes away, such as closing any open file handles that the object may hold on to.

However, since a `finalize` method can contain arbitrary code, there are several potentially bad scenarios to consider as well, for example, the case that a finalizer **resurrects** the object, or clones a new object from the dying one, in effect preventing an object from being garbage collected. In addition, placing code that releases limited resources, such as file handles, in a finalizer may cause resource starvation. This is because there is never a predictable point in time where finalizers are guaranteed to be run. System resources should always be released explicitly in a situation where the programmer has control.

Furthermore, finalizers can also be called at any time in any thread, no matter which locks the thread is holding. This is extremely bad and can lead to all kinds of unintended deadlock situations and violations of mutual exclusion semantics.

It is not just the authors' opinion, but that of the Java community in general, that finalizers are a bad design choice and that their use should be avoided at any cost.

References

When programming Java, one might think that there is only one kind of object reference. An object is either live or unreachable, eventually leading to it being garbage collected and removed from the system. There are, however, several kinds of references in Java, which may be thought of as *references with varying degrees of liveness*. We refer to the normal references or standard object references, as **strong references**.

The package `java.lang.ref` contains several classes that wrap Java objects and thereby provide a classification for the object's reference type. The different reference classes all extend `java.lang.ref.Reference`. All `Reference` objects in Java have a `get` method that will return the actual object being referenced or `null` if that particular object isn't reachable, i.e. if the object has been garbage collected.

Java also provides the class `java.lang.ref.ReferenceQueue`, where objects that change reachability or scope are enqueued, for example when the object a `Reference` points to gets garbage collected. A `Reference` object can be bound to a `java.lang.ref.ReferenceQueue` at instantiation. By polling an instance of the `ReferenceQueue`, a small amount of insight into what the memory management system is doing can be gained programmatically.

There are four main types of references in Java—**strong, weak, soft and phantom** references.

Weak references

A **weak reference** that points to an object isn't strong enough to force that object to remain in memory. The `java.lang.ref.WeakReference` class is in effect a wrapper around a strong reference, tagging it as weak.

```
WeakReference weak = new WeakReference(object);
```

In the example, to get the actual object the reference points to, use `weak.get()`. As `object` may be garbage collected at any time, this call returns `null` when `object` is no longer in memory.

A typical application for weak references is the `java.util.WeakHashMap` class, which gets rid of an entry if its key is no longer referenced. This is ideal for caches. Using weak references in the memory leak prone `HashMap` cache example, introduced in the first section of this chapter, would prevent leaks caused by forgotten objects left in the hash table. It would also have the added benefit of not requiring that hash table contents are cleared out in order for it to ever be garbage collected. Weak references can provide an intrinsic protection against memory leaks.

Soft references

A **soft reference** is a weak reference that the garbage collector is more reluctant to throw away. Typically, the garbage collector tries to keep them around as long as possible, but they are the first to go if memory is running low.

How much stronger a soft reference should be, than a weak reference, is left to the JVM implementation. In theory, a soft reference may behave exactly like a weak reference and not violate the Java semantics.

Phantom references

Phantom references are the preferred way of implementing finalization. They are designed to supersede the use of finalizers that, as we have seen, are deeply flawed. Phantom references wrap ordinary objects similar to weak and soft references, but their `get` method always returns `null`.

Phantom references are accessed through the `java.lang.ref.ReferenceQueue` class mentioned earlier, by polling an instance to which the phantom references one is interested in are bound. Polling the reference queue at regular intervals (or doing a blocking `remove`) reveals if a new phantom reference is available for garbage collection. If this is the case, as the `get` method of phantom references always returns `null`, there is no possible way to get hold of a handle to the object in question and resurrect it. This avoids the problems with finalizers and provides all the benefits of a similar mechanism.

Here is a code example that prints the number of finalized `TestObject`s in the system using finalizers:

```
/**
 * Prints the number of finalized objects
 */
public class Finalize {
  static class TestObject {
    static int nObjectsFinalized = 0;

    protected void finalize() throws Throwable {
      System.err.println(++nObjectsFinalized);
    }
```

```
    }
  public static void main(String[] args) {
    for (;;) {
      TestObject o = new TestObject();
      doStuff(o);
      o = null;    //clear any remaining refs to "o"
      System.gc(); //try to force gc
    }
  }
}
```

The equivalent approach with PhantomReferences in a ReferenceQueue might look something like this:

```
/**
 * Prints the number of finalized objects using PhantomReferences
 */
import java.lang.ref.*;

public class Finalize {
  static class TestObject {
    static int nObjectsFinalized = 0;
  }

  static ReferenceQueue<TestObject> q =
    new ReferenceQueue<TestObject>();

  public static void main(String[] args) {
    Thread finalizerThread = new Thread() {
      public void run() {
        for (;;) {
          try {
            //block until PhantomReference is available
            Reference ref = q.remove();
            System.err.println(++TestObject.nObjectsFinalized);
          } catch (InterruptedException e) {
          }
        }
      }
    };
    finalizerThread.start();

    for (;;) {
      TestObject o = new TestObject();
      PhantomReference<TestObject> pr =
        new PhantomReference<TestObject>(o, q);
      doStuff(o);
      o = null; //clear any remaining refs to "o"
      System.gc(); //try to force GC
    }
  }
}
```

Differences in JVM behavior

The most important thing to remember is that all of the above language constructs merely provide *hints* to the GC. The Java language, by design, gives no exact control over the memory system. It is a bad practice to assume, for example, that just because soft references are alive in a cache for a certain amount of time in one VM vendor's implementation, the same will be true for another vendor's implementation too.

Another example, which recurs quite frequently among customers, is misuse of the `System.gc` method. The `System.gc` method is only defined as a hint to the runtime that "now will be a good time to garbage collect". In some VMs this hint is taken almost all the time, leading to extensive GCs and the possible freeing of massive amounts of memory. In other VMs it is ignored most of the time.

In the authors' old line of work as performance consultants, we have time and time again seen this function abused. More than once, the simple removal of a couple of calls to `System.gc` has led to immense speedups for quite a few customer applications. This is the story behind the JRockit `-XX:AllowSystemGC=false` flag that basically just tells JRockit to ignore all `System.gc` calls.

Pitfalls and false optimizations

As with code generation, it is fairly common to see false optimizations in Java applications, implemented with the belief that they will assist the garbage collector. Again, premature optimization is the root of all evil. At the Java level there is really very little to be known about how the GC will treat the program. The general sin is believing that the garbage collector will always behave in a certain way and try to manipulate it.

We have already discussed the case of `System.gc` that is not required to do anything at all, or might do a full-heap-GC stopping the world every time, or anything in between.

Another false optimization is different types of **object pooling**. Keeping a pool of objects alive and reusing them, instead of allocating new objects, is often believed to increase garbage collection performance. But not only does this add complexity to the Java application, it is also easy to get wrong. Using the `java.lang.ref.Reference` classes for caching or simply making sure to set object references to `null` as soon as they aren't needed anymore is usually sufficient enough for any modern garbage collector. Keeping objects alive longer than their natural lifespan can backfire. Generational GC usually takes care of temporary objects quickly, but if they are artificially kept alive and reused, they will eventually clog up the old space instead.

Java is not C++

Frequently, people express the belief that there should be a static way to control all aspects of Java garbage collection, complete with `free` or `delete` operators as well as the ability to turn off and on garbage collection at arbitrary intervals. Another example is wishing for ways to get at and modify objects as native pointers directly in the JVM. Both these strategies would be extremely dangerous if introduced in Java, and successful usage would, in the authors' opinion, be very hard or impossible.

There are several advantages of automatic memory management, and some disadvantages, chief of which is non-determinism. JRockit Real Time has tried to provide good enough ways around this without the need for modifying an application or interfacing with the GC.

 We still recall with horror the "Java should have a `free` operator" discussion that swamped the entire HotSpot session at JavaOne 1999. The guy who started it raised his hand and opened up with the now classic line "Many of my friends are C++ programmers..."

In truth, a well-written Java program that uses all the allowed tricks in the book correctly, such as the correct `java.lang.ref.Reference` classes, and takes heed of the dynamic nature of Java, should run fine on a modern JVM. If a program has real-time needs that require further manipulation, maybe it shouldn't have been written in Java to begin with, but rather in a static language where the programmer's control over the memory system is more absolute.

Automatic memory management, while being a helpful tool that shortens development cycles and reduces program complexity, isn't a golden hammer that can be applied to all programmatic problems.

Controlling JRockit memory management

This section covers the most fundamental command-line switches that control garbage collection in JRockit. For more advanced manipulation of the memory system, for example tuning compaction, please refer to *Chapter 5, Benchmarking and Tuning*.

Basic switches

Following are the most fundamental command-line switches for interacting with the JRockit memory system.

Outputting GC data

Running JRockit with `-Xverbose:gc` will, similar to `-Xverbose:codegen`, output plenty of verbose information on what the JVM memory management system is doing. This information includes garbage collections, where they take place (nurseries or old space), changes of GC strategy, and the time a particular garbage collection takes.

`-Xverbose:gc` (or `-Xverbose:memory`) is, except for JRockit Mission Control, the main information provider when it comes to studying garbage collector behavior for an application.

Here is an example of the output generated by `-Xverbose:gc`:

```
hastur:material marcus$ java -Xverbose:gc GarbageDemo
[INFO ][memory ] GC mode: Garbage collection optimized for
  throughput, strategy: Generational Parallel Mark & Sweep.
[INFO ][memory ] Heap size: 65536KB, maximal heap size:
  382140KB, nursery size: 32768KB.
[INFO ][memory ] [YC#1] 1.028-1.077: YC 33232KB->16133KB
  (65536KB), 0.049 s, sum of pauses 48.474 ms, longest pause 48.474 ms.
[INFO ][memory ] [YC#2] 1.195-1.272: YC 41091KB->34565KB
  (65536KB), 0.077 s, sum of pauses 76.850 ms, longest pause 76.850 ms.
[INFO ][memory ] [YC#3] 1.857-1.902: YC 59587KB->65536KB
  (65536KB), 0.045 s, sum of pauses 45.122 ms, longest pause 45.122 ms.
[INFO ][memory ] [OC#1] 1.902-1.912: OC 65536KB->15561KB
  (78644KB), 0.010 s, sum of pauses 9.078 ms, longest pause 9.078 ms.
[INFO ][memory ] [YC#4] 2.073-2.117: YC 48711KB->39530KB
  (78644KB), 0.044 s, sum of pauses 44.435 ms, longest pause 44.435 ms.
```

Typically, the log shows things such as garbage collection strategy changes and heap size adjustments, as well as when a garbage collection take place and for how long.

OC or YC means **Old Collection** or **Young Collection** (nursery), followed by the sequence number of the particular collection. Sequence numbers start at 1.

After the OC and YC identifier comes the time span in seconds, since the start of the JVM, that was spent in this particular GC.

Then JRockit reports how much live data the particular heap region that was collected contained before and after the GC, the total size of the region, and the time that particular garbage collection took. We can see that the GC chooses to gradually grow the heap in this particular example.

Finally, the sum of pauses, that is for how long the world was stopped during the last garbage collection, is reported along with the longest individual pause. In the previous example, we can infer that as these values are the same, we are dealing with complete stop-the-world-collections, i.e. parallel GC. They each consist of one large pause.

For advanced users, as has been covered, each garbage collection consists of several phases, and if you want more granularity on them, a flag called -Xverbose:gcpause will provide it. It should be noted, however, that JRockit Mission Control with its graphic illustration of garbage collection behavior probably provides more insight into application behavior.

Set initial and maximum heap size

The -Xms and -Xmx flags are standard and variants are available in all JVMs. They specify initial and maximum heap size to be allocated to the JVM. If no arguments are given, the heap will grow and shrink heuristically during runtime. Consider the following example:

```
java -Xms1024M -Xmx2048M <application>
```

The code shown in the previous example will force the initial heap size to 1 GB and prevent it from ever growing above 2 GB. If enough heap to accommodate the demands isn't available, an OutOfMemoryError will be thrown.

Controlling what to optimize for

Unless you really know what you are doing, the -XgcPrio flag is the preferred way to tell JRockit what garbage collection strategies to run. Instead of fixing a GC strategy, JRockit will heuristically determine what is best for the application, depending on what the user thinks is important and change strategies at runtime when appropriate.

- -XgcPrio:throughput: This optimizes for throughput, not caring about pause times

- -XgcPrio:pausetime: This optimizes for low latency

- -XgcPrio:deterministic: This activates the JRockit Real Time functionality, striving for extremely short pauses at the cost of some additional runtime overhead

The maximum pause time target for the GC (not applicable for `-XgcPrio:throughput`) can be set with the flag `-XpauseTarget`. Depending on the amount of live data on the heap and system configuration, JRockit may or may not be able to keep up. Experimenting with different pause time targets for a particular application is encouraged.

Following is command-line example for enabling deterministic GC (JRockit Real Time) with an upper pause time target of five milliseconds:

```
java -XgcPrio:deterministic -XpauseTarget:5ms <application>
```

Specifying a garbage collection strategy

For even further control over GC behavior, a more fine grained garbage collection strategy can be set from the command line using the `-Xgc` flag. This fixes a garbage collection strategy for the JVM and prevents it from being changed at runtime. The strategy can be made more fine grained than with one of the three `-XgcPrio` choices. Again, we use the terms concurrent and parallel to describe if we are optimizing for low latencies or throughput. The possible options are `-Xgc:singlecon` (single generational concurrent), `-Xgc:gencon` (generational concurrent), `-Xgc:singlepar` (single generational parallel) and `-Xgc:genpar` (generational parallel). "Generational", as opposed to "single generational", means that a nursery is used.

Compressed references

As already mentioned, given a maximum heap size smaller than 64 GB, JRockit will use some form of compressed references by default. But the usage of compressed references can also be explicitly controlled with the `-XXcompressedRefs` flag. The flag takes two arguments—whether compressed references should be enabled at all and in that case the maximum size of the heap that they should support.

The following command-line example disables compressed references, and forces JRockit to use native size pointers for all objects:

```
java -XXcompressedRefs:enable=false <application>
```

This following command-line example enables compressed references that can support up to 64-GB heaps:

```
java -XXcompressedRefs:enable=true,size=64GB <application>
```

Advanced switches

It should be noted that playing around too much with JVM switches doesn't necessarily lead to increased performance and might interfere with more optimal runtime behavior.

If memory performance is believed to be an application bottleneck, it is recommended to use the JRockit Mission Control suite for instrumentation. Chapters in the second part of this book will explain how to do a runtime recording with JRockit and how to analyze it. Collecting as much information as possible about an application before starting to modify non-standard parameters is strongly recommended.

Almost any aspect of the garbage collector can be tuned from the command line —everything from the size of the thread local buffers used for allocation to the strategies used for heap compaction.

Some less fundamental switches that control memory management are covered in Chapter 5. Please study the JRockit documentation for a more in-depth description of all memory management options.

Summary

This chapter covered automatic memory management in detail, concentrating on adaptive memory management, where feedback from the runtime system is continuously used to optimize GC performance.

We explained the mark and sweep as well as the stop and copy strategies for garbage collection and discussed how more advanced variants of these can work in a modern runtime, especially JRockit. We discussed how to implement fast scalable GC on all levels from software to hardware.

Every GC needs to stop the world at some point, for example when sweeping or compacting. Stopping the world introduces latencies. The main lesson is that we can optimize either for throughput or for low latencies, one at the cost of the other.

We introduced the product JRockit Real Time, that provides a degree of determinism and pause time targets for the JVM. JRockit Real Time can massively improve response times and decrease their deviation for most applications without the need to modify the applications.

Some of the constructs available in the Java language that can help control garbage collection and memory management were introduced, followed by a section on false optimizations. It is dangerous to believe that complete deterministic control can be exerted over as non-deterministic a system as a garbage collector.

Finally, the most common command-line options used to control memory management in JRockit were explained.

Now code generation and memory management in an adaptive runtime environment have been introduced. In the next chapter, we will cover the final fundamental building block that makes up a Java runtime—threads and synchronization.

4

Threads and Synchronization

This chapter covers threads and synchronization in Java and in the Java Virtual Machine. **Threads** are the de facto mechanism for running several parallel tasks in a process. **Locks** are the de facto mechanism for constraining access to a critical section of code to one thread at a time. These are the building blocks we need in order to implement parallelism in software.

You will learn the following from this chapter:

- How fundamental parallel concepts such as threads and synchronization work in Java and how the Java APIs can be used for synchronization. This includes concepts like `wait`, `notify`, and the often misunderstood `volatile` keyword. We will also briefly look at the `java.util.concurrent` package.

- The concept of the Java Memory Model, and why it is required. Understanding the memory model is the key to writing working multithreaded Java programs.

- How the JVM can efficiently implement threads and synchronization and a discussion about a few different models.

- How the JVM can optimize threads and synchronization using different types of locks, locking policies, and code optimizations, all based on adaptive runtime feedback.

- How to avoid common pitfalls and false optimizations in parallel Java programming—learning to stay clear of things like deprecated `java.lang.Thread` methods and double checked locking.

- How to work with JRockit to modify thread and synchronization behavior as well as an introduction on how to do lock profiling.

Fundamental concepts

Java was, from its inception, a language designed for parallelism. It has intrinsic mechanisms like the `java.lang.Thread` class as an abstraction for threads, a `synchronized` keyword and `wait` and `notify` methods in every object. This made it fairly unique at the time of its release, at least outside academia. The most common approach for commercially proven languages so far was to use platform-dependent OS library calls for thread management. Naturally, Java needed a platform-independent way to do the same, and what can be better than integrating the mechanisms for parallelism and synchronization into the language itself?

Java is a nice language to work with, when it comes to synchronization. Not only does it have explicit constructs that can be used for threads, locks, and semaphores but it was also designed so that every object in a Java program can conveniently be used as the limiting resource, or monitor object, constraining access to code in a critical section. As of Java 1.5, the JDK also contains a package full of useful parallel data structures, `java.util.concurrent`.

 The term **monitor** is used to represent a handle to a synchronized resource—only one thread can hold the monitor at a time, thus being allowed exclusive access to the resource.

The advantages of this are obvious—Java synchronization involves no third-party library calls and the semantics for locking are well-defined. It is easy to use locks and threads when programming Java.

A disadvantage may be that it is too easy. It is simple to add synchronization anywhere and everywhere "just to be sure", resulting in possible performance loss.

There are, of course, also questions of implementation overhead. As every object is allowed to be a monitor, every object also needs to carry synchronization information (for example whether the object is used in a lock right now, how that lock is implemented, and so on). Typically, to enable quick access, this information is stored in a **lock word** that exists in the header of every object. For more than the simplest form of automatic memory management, similar performance concerns also exist. Therefore, fundamental GC info, such as what GC state an object is in, must also be available for quick access. Recollect, for example, the discussion about mark bits from the section on tracing garbage collection in Chapter 3. Thus, both locking and GC need certain kinds of information to be quickly available on a per-object basis. Consequently, JRockit also uses a few bits in the lock word to store garbage collection state information. However, we will still refer to this word as the "lock word" for convenience throughout this text.

Naturally, too compact a meta info representation in every object header introduces extra execution overhead for decoding and encoding the information. A too large representation introduces extra memory overhead in every object instead. Thus, some care has to be taken when choosing a representation for the lock and GC bits for the object.

Another thing that needs to go into every object header is a pointer to its type information. JRockit calls this the **class block**.

The following figure shows the layout of a Java object in JRockit. All words in the header are 32-bit wide on all platforms to save memory and provide faster dereferencing. The class block is a 32-bit pointer to an external structure, with type information for the object and virtual dispatch tables.

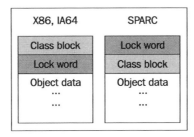

In JRockit, and as far as we know in most JVMs, a complete object header is represented by two 32-bit words. JRockit stores type information at the 0th offset of an object pointer and the lock word four bytes into the object. On SPARC, the layout is reversed because there it is cheaper to execute atomic instructions that manipulate pointers with no offset. As the class block, unlike the lock word, is not subject to any atomic operations, it can be placed later in the header on SPARC.

 We define an **atomic instruction** as a native instruction that can only be either fully executed or not executed at all. When it is fully executed, its results are guaranteed to be visible to all potential accessors.

Atomic operations are required for reads and writes to the **lock word,** as they have to be exclusive—they are the most fundamental building block of the synchronization state machine in the JVM.

 Various academic research has shown that there is relatively little to be gained by compressing an object header further, for example into a single 32-bit word. The extra processing overhead does not make it worthwhile, even though it saves some more memory per object.

Hard to debug

True for most platforms and programming languages is that a single concurrency problem may manifest itself in many different ways such as **deadlocks**, **livelocks**, or plain crashes. The common denominator is usually non-determinism. This is a classic challenge. As concurrency problems tend to depend on timing, attaching a debugger to the running program before it breaks might not necessarily reproduce the issue. Timing changes with the added debugger overhead.

> A **deadlock** occurs when two threads are sleeping, both waiting for the other to finish using a resource that each of them needs. Obviously, they never wake up. A **livelock** is similar, but involves active processing from the threads. One can liken it to the case when two people meet in a narrow corridor and step out of each other's way, but happen to do it in the same direction so that they end up blocking each other again.

Because of these kinds of issues, debugging parallel systems is generally difficult. The greatest help comes from visualization aids and debuggers that can untangle thread and lock dependencies.

JRockit, like all major JVMs, supports dumping stack traces from all threads in a running Java application to the console, along with lock holder information. This is enough to resolve simple deadlock problems, where it is possible to determine which mutually dependent threads are stuck waiting for a single resource. Examples will be given later in this chapter.

The JRockit Mission Control suite can also be used to visualize lock information in a more convenient way.

Difficult to optimize

It is also very common that performance issues arise from using synchronization. Every lock is a bottleneck, as it introduces a critical section that can only be accessed by one thread at a time. The more threads trying to get at a critical section, the more contention will arise as threads have to wait their turn. If a lock is badly placed or covers too wide a section in the interest of easier debugging (or just because of general laziness) performance penalties will almost certainly occur.

Sadly enough, it seems to be quite a common case in commercial software that a single lock or a just a few locks cause the majority of the latency in a program. We have seen this more than once when debugging third-party applications. The programmer is normally not aware of this. Luckily, if the problematic locks are few and can be identified, the latency problem is simple to fix. Again, the JRockit Mission Control suite can be used to easily establish which locks are most contended in a running program.

A lock is said to be **contended** when many threads spend significant time competing to acquire it

Latency analysis

The JRockit Mission Control suite comes with a unique component for latency analysis that, given a JRockit flight recording of a Java program, visualizes latency data for the program. Latency analysis can be the programmer's best friend when optimizing concurrent programs with plenty of synchronization. Instead of taking the traditional profiler's approach of displaying where the program spends its active runtime, the latency analyzer provides information on where it *does not*. Any nanosecond where a thread isn't executing Java code is mapped and laid out in a thread graph. This way, it can be determined if the idle time is spent waiting for I/O or the network, or, which is potentially more serious, in Java locks, i.e. code waiting to enter `synchronized` blocks or methods.

Latency analysis with JRockit Mission Control is covered in greater detail in the next section of this book, where the JRockit Mission Control suite is introduced, specifically in *Chapter 8, The Runtime Analyzer* and *Chapter 9, The Flight Recorder*.

The following screenshot shows the latency analysis tab in the JRockit Runtime Analyzer. The data comes from a recording of a running server application and the recording is now about to be examined offline. One colored bar per thread in the program represents where the program spent its time during the recording. The time axis goes from left to right. A different color is used for each latency generating activity. In the following screenshot, all thread bars are mostly the same color. In this case red, meaning "blocked in Java". This is bad, as it means almost all program time was spent waiting for a Java lock, for example in a synchronized block. To be precise, all colors except green mean "not executing Java". This might entail native threads waiting for I/O or network traffic or any other source of latency.

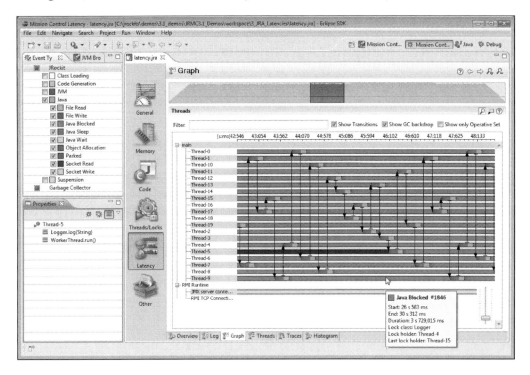

Recollect our intuitive latency argument on memory management from Chapter 3—if the JVM spends clock cycles garbage collecting, these cannot be used to execute Java code. Similarly, if the clock cycles are spent waiting for file I/O or Java locks, latency arises. This is the same kind of latency—time spent outside Java execution. It affects response times and is the root of most performance problems.

 JRockit Flight Recorder can help locate sources of latency in your Java programs. In the example above, it turns out that virtually all latency comes from a single badly placed Java lock in a logging module.

Java API

This section covers the built-in synchronization mechanisms in Java. These are convenient to have as intrinsic mechanisms in the language. There are, however, potential dangers of misusing or overusing Java synchronization mechanisms.

The synchronized keyword

In Java, the keyword `synchronized` is used to define a critical section. Both code blocks inside a method and entire methods can be synchronized. The following code example illustrates a synchronized method:

```java
public synchronized void setGadget(Gadget g) {
  this.gadget = g;
}
```

As the method is synchronized, only one thread at a time can write to the `gadget` field in a given object.

In a synchronized method, the monitor object is implicit. Static synchronized methods use the class object of the method's class as monitor object, while synchronized instance methods use `this`. So, the previous code would be equivalent to:

```java
public void setGadget(Gadget g) {
  synchronized(this) {
    this.gadget = g;
  }
}
```

The java.lang.Thread class

The built-in thread abstraction in Java is represented by the class `java.lang.Thread`. This class is a somewhat more generic thread representation than that of corresponding OS implementations. It contains, among other things, fundamental methods for starting threads and for inserting the thread payload code. This is symmetrical with typical OS thread implementations where payload is passed as a function pointer to the main thread function by the creator of the thread. Java uses an object-oriented approach instead, but the semantics are the same. Any class implementing the `java.lang.Runnable` interface can become a thread. The run method inherited from the interface must be implemented and filled with payload code. `java.lang.Thread` can also be subclassed directly.

There is also a simple priority mechanism in the `java.lang.Thread` class that may or may not be efficiently mapped to the underlying OS variant. The `setPriority` method can be used to change the priority level of a thread, hinting to the JVM that it's more important (real-time) or less important. Normally, for most JVMs, little is gained by setting thread priorities explicitly from Java. The JRockit JVM may even ignore Java thread priorities when the runtime "knows better".

Threads can be made to `yield` the rest of their scheduled time slice to other threads, go to `sleep` or `join` (that is, wait for this thread to die).

Threads can be arranged in `java.lang.ThreadGroups`, a *NIX process like abstraction, which can also contain other thread groups. Thread operations may be applied to all threads in a thread group.

A thread may hold thread local object data, represented by the `java.lang.ThreadLocal` class. Each thread will own a copy of any `ThreadLocal` it contains. This is a very useful mechanism that has been around since Java 1.2. Even though it is a somewhat clumsy retrofit for a language without the concept of stack local object allocation, it can be a performance life saver. Given that the programmer knows what he is doing, explicitly declaring data thread local in Java may lead to significant speed ups.

The `java.lang.Thread` class has suffered some changes and deprecations to its API during its lifetime. Originally, it came with methods for stopping, suspending, and resuming threads. These turned out to be inherently unsafe. They still occur from time to time in Java programs, and we will discuss why they are dangerous in the section *Pitfalls and false optimizations*, later in this chapter.

The java.util.concurrent package

The `java.util.concurrent` package, introduced in JDK 1.5, contains several classes that implement data structures useful for concurrent programming. One example is the `BlockingQueue` that halts execution and waits for space to become available in the queue before storing elements and for elements to be inserted before retrieving them. This is the classic synchronized producer/consumer pattern.

The `java.util.concurrent` package helps the programmer spend less effort on re-implementing the most fundamental building blocks of synchronization mechanisms. Effort has also been made to ensure that the concurrent classes are optimized for scalability and performance.

Possibly, even more useful is the child package `java.util.concurrent.atomic` that contains lightweight thread safe mechanisms for modifying fields. For example, representations of integers (`java.util.concurrent.atomic.AtomicInteger`) and longs (`java.util.concurrent.atomic.AtomicLong`) that can be atomically incremented and decremented and have native-style atomic compares applied to them. Using the atomic package, when applicable, can be a good way of avoiding explicit heavyweight synchronization in the Java program.

Finally, the concurrent package includes the sub package `java.util.concurrent.locks` that contains implementations of data structures with common locking semantics. This includes reader/writer locks, another useful pattern that the programmer no longer has to implement from scratch.

 A **reader/writer lock** is a lock that allows unsynchronized reads from the data it protects, but enforces exclusiveness for writes to the data.

Semaphores

A semaphore is a synchronization mechanism that can come in handy when one thread tries to acquire a resource and fails because the resource is already being held by another thread. In case of failure, the thread that wanted the resource may want to go to sleep until explicitly woken up when the resource has been released. This is what semaphores are for. Semaphores are a common locking mechanism with abstraction and library calls present in every operating system, modern as well as antique. They are also enabled by an integral feature of the Java language.

In Java, each object contains methods named `wait`, `notify`, and `notifyAll` that may be used to implement semaphores. They are all inherited from the `java.lang.Object` class. The methods are meant to be used in the context of a monitor object, for example in a `synchronized` block. If there is no monitor available in the context they are called from, an `IllegalMonitorStateException` will be thrown at runtime.

Calling `wait` suspends the executing thread. It will be woken up as soon as a notification is received. When `notify` is called, one of the threads waiting for the synchronized resource will be arbitrarily selected and woken up by the thread scheduler in the JVM. The executing thread will go to sleep and block. When `notifyAll` is called, all threads waiting for the lock will be woken up. Only one of them will succeed in acquiring the lock and the rest will go to sleep again. The `notifyAll` method is safer than `notify`, as everyone will get a chance to acquire the lock, and deadlock situations are easier to avoid. The downside to `notifyAll` is that it carries a greater overhead than `notify`. So, if you know what you are doing, `notifyAll` should probably be avoided.

The `wait` method also comes with an optional timeout argument, which, when exceeded, always results in the suspended thread being woken up again.

To exemplify how semaphores work in Java, we can study the following code. The code is a component that can be used in a classic producer/consumer example, a **message port**, with the instance `this` used as an implicit monitor object in its synchronized methods.

```java
public class Mailbox {
  private String  message;
  private boolean messagePending;

  /**
   * Places a message in the mailbox
   */
  public synchronized void putMessage(String message) {
    while (messagePending) { //wait for consumers to consume
      try {
        wait(); //blocks until notified
      } catch (InterruptedException e) {
      }
    }

    this.message = message;     //store message in mailbox
    messagePending = true;      //raise flag on mailbox
    notifyAll();                //wake up any random consumer
  }

  /**
   * Retrieves a message from the mailbox
   */
  public synchronized String getMessage() {
    while (!messagePending) { //wait for producer to produce
      try {
        wait(); //blocks until notified
      } catch (InterruptedException e) {
      }
    }

    messagePending = false; //lower flag on mailbox
    notifyAll();                //wake up any random producer

    return message;
  }
}
```

Multiple producer and consumer threads can easily use a `Mailbox` object for synchronized message passing between them. Any consumer wanting to retrieve a message from an empty `Mailbox` by calling `getMessage` will block until a producer has used `putMessage` to place a message in the `Mailbox`. Symmetrically, if the `Mailbox` is already full, any producer will block in `putMessage` until a consumer has emptied the `Mailbox`.

We have deliberately simplified things here. Semaphores can be either binary or counting. **Binary semaphores** are similar to the `Mailbox` example described above—there is an explicit "true or false" control over a single resource. **Counting semaphores** can instead limit access to a given number of accessors. This is exemplified by the class `java.util. concurrent.Sempahore`, which is another excellent tool that can be used for synchronization.

The volatile keyword

In a multi-threaded environment, it is not guaranteed that a write to a field or a memory location will be seen simultaneously by all executing threads. We will get into some more details of this in the section on *The Java Memory Model*, later in this chapter. However, if program execution relies on all threads needing to see the same value of a field at any given time, Java provides the **volatile** keyword.

Declaring a field `volatile` will ensure that any writes to the field go directly to memory. The data cannot linger in caches and cannot be written later, which is what may cause different threads to simultaneously see different values of the same field. The underlying virtual machine typically implements this by having the JIT insert memory barrier code after stores to the field, which naturally is bad for program performance.

While people usually have trouble with the concept that different threads can end up with different values for a field load, they tend not to suffer from the phenomenon. Usually, the memory model of the underlying machine is strong enough or the structure of the program itself isn't too prone to causing problems with non-volatile fields. However, bringing an optimizing JIT compiler into the picture might wreak some additional havoc on the unsuspecting programmer. Hopefully, the following example explains why it is important to think about memory semantics in all kinds of Java programs, even (especially) in those where problems do not readily manifest themselves:

```java
public class MyThread extends Thread {
  private volatile boolean finished;

  public void run() {
    while (!finished) {
      //
    }
  }

  public void signalDone() {
    this.finished = true;
  }
}
```

If `finished` isn't declared `volatile` here, the JIT compiler may theoretically choose, as an optimization, to load its value from memory only once, before the `while` loop is run, thus breaking the thread ending criterion. In that case, as `finished` starts out as `false`, the `while` loop condition will be forever `true` and the thread will never exit, even though `signalDone` is called later on. The Java Language Specification basically allows the compiler to create its own thread local copies of non-volatile fields if it sees fit to do so.

For further insight about volatile fields, consider the following code:

```java
public class Test {
  volatile int a = 1;
  volatile int b = 1;

  void add() {
    a++;
    b++;
  }

  void print() {
    System.out.println(a + " " + b);
  }
}
```

Here, the `volatile` keyword implicitly guarantees that b never appears greater than a to any thread, even if the `add` and `print` functions are frequently called in a multithreaded environment. An even tougher restriction would be to declare the `add` method `synchronized`, in which case a and b would always have the same value when `print` is called (as they both start at 1). If none of the fields are declared `volatile` and the method is not synchronized, it is important to remember that Java guarantees no relationship between a and b!

`volatile` fields should be used with caution, as their implementation in the JIT usually involves expensive barrier instructions that may ruin CPU caches and slow down program execution.

Naturally, synchronized mechanisms incur runtime overhead to a greater degree than unsynchronized ones. Instead of readily using volatile and synchronized declarations, with their potential slowdowns, the programmer should sometimes consider other ways of propagating information if it doesn't change the semantics of the memory model.

Implementing threads and synchronization in Java

Once again, it's time to look inside the JVM. This section covers some of the issues implementing threads and synchronization in a Java runtime. The aim is to provide enough insight and technical background so that the reader will be better equipped to handle parallel constructs and understand how to use synchronization without too much performance loss.

The Java Memory Model

On modern CPU architectures, data caches exist, which is a necessary mechanism for speeding up data access for loads and stores and for reducing contention on the processor bus. As with any cache mechanism, invalidation issues are a problem, especially on multiprocessor systems where we often get the situation that two processors want to access the same memory at the same time.

A memory model defines the circumstances under which different CPUs will and won't see the same data. Memory models can be strong (x86 is fairly strong), where multiple CPUs almost automatically see the same, newly stored, data after one of them does a write to memory. In strong memory models, multiple writes to memory locations as good as always occur in the same order as they were placed in the code. Memory models can also be weak (such as IA-64), where there is virtually no guarantee (unless the CPU writing the data executes a special barrier instruction) when field accesses and, more generally, all Java induced memory accesses should be visible to all.

Subtle differences handling read-after-write, write-after-read and write-after-write dependencies of the same data exist on different hardware platforms. Java, being a hardware agnostic language, needs to define strict semantics for how these dependencies should be interpreted for threads in the JVM. This is a complication not present in a static language like C++ that compiles to hardware specific code and lacks a memory model per se. Although there is a `volatile` keyword in C++ as well as in Java, parts of the C++ program behavior are still impossible to decouple from that of the hardware architecture for which it is compiled. Parts of the "de facto" memory model in a C++ program also reside outside the language itself—in thread libraries and in the semantics of operating system calls. On architectures with weak memory models such as Intel IA-64, the programmer may even have to explicitly put calls to memory barrier functions in the C++ program. Anyway, once compiled, the behavior of the native code generated from the C++ will remain the same within the chosen architecture.

But how can the programmer make sure that the same behavior applies to a compiled Java program, no matter if it is running on x86, Itanium, PowerPC, or SPARC? There are no explicit memory barriers in Java, and probably shouldn't be either, because of its platform independence.

Early problems and ambiguities

The need for a unified memory model for Java that guarantees identical behavior across different hardware architectures was acknowledged from the start. Java 1.0 through 1.4 implemented the memory model as specified in the original Java Language Specification. However, the first Java Memory Model contained several surprising issues that were counter-intuitive and even made standard compiler optimizations invalid.

The original memory model allowed volatile and non-volatile writes to be reordered interchangeably. Consider the following code:

```
volatile int x;
int y;
volatile boolean finished;

/* Code executed by Thread 1 */
x = 17;
y = 4711;
finished = true;
/* Thread 1 goes to sleep here */

/* Code executed by Thread 2 */
if (finished) {
  System.err.println(x):
  System.err.println(y);
}
```

In the old memory model, the previous code was guaranteed to print out `17`, but not necessarily `4711`, once Thread 2 was woken up. This had to do with the semantics for `volatile`. They were clearly defined, but not in relation to non-volatile reads or writes. To a person used to working closer to hardware than a Java programmer, this might not be too surprising, but often Java programmers intuitively expected that constructs like the assignment to `finished` shown earlier would act as a barrier, and commit all earlier field stores to memory, including the non-volatile ones. The new memory model has enforced stricter barrier behavior for `volatile`, also with respect to non-volatile fields.

Recollect from our "infinite loop" example in the introduction to `volatile` earlier in this chapter, that the JIT compiler may optimize code by creating thread local copies of any non-volatile field.

Consider the following code:

```
int operation(Item a, Item b) {
    return (a.value + b.value) * a.value;
}
```

The compiler might choose to optimize the previous method to the assembly equivalent of:

```
int operation(Item a, Item b) {
    int tmp = a.value;
    return (tmp + b.value) * tmp;
}
```

Notice how two field loads turned into one. Depending on CPU architecture, this will lead to a smaller or larger performance increase if the method is hot. However, it is almost certainly a good idea for the JIT compiler to try to eliminate loads wherever possible, as memory access is always orders of magnitude more expensive than register access. The equivalent optimization is performed by compilers in virtually all statically compiled languages, and not being able to perform it in Java would lead to severe performance loss in comparison.

Originally, through some oversights in the original Java Memory Model, this kind of optimization wasn't guaranteed to be allowed (if it couldn't be proven that a and b were the same object). Luckily, the new Java Memory Model allows this kind of optimization as long as the `value` field isn't declared `volatile`. The new memory model allows any thread to keep local copies of non-volatile field values, as was also illustrated with the potentially infinite loop on the field `finished` earlier in this chapter.

Immutability

One of the most surprising problems in the original Java Memory Model was that objects that were declared `final` were sometimes not in fact `final` (immutable) at all. `final` objects were defined to require no synchronization, intuitively through their immutability, but there were problems. These manifested themselves to the ordinary user in unexpected ways. A final instance field in a Java object is assigned its one and only value in a constructor, but as all uninitialized fields, it also has an implicit default value (`0` or maybe `null`) before the constructor is run. Without explicit synchronization, the old memory model could allow a different thread to temporarily see this default value of the field before the assignment in the constructor had been committed to memory.

This issue typically led to problems with `String` instances. A `String` instance contains a `char` array with its text, a start offset in the array for where the text begins and a length. All these fields are `final` and immutable, just like `String`s themselves are guaranteed to be in the Java language. So, two `String` objects can save memory by reusing the same immutable `char` array. For example, the `String` "cat" may point out the same `char` array as the `String` "housecat", but with a start offset of 5 instead of 0. However, the old memory model would allow the `String` object for "cat" to be visible with its uninitialized (zeroed) start offsets for a very short period of time, before its constructor was run, basically allowing other threads to think it was spelling out "housecat" very briefly until it became "cat". This clearly violates the immutability of a `java.lang.String`.

The new memory model has fixed this problem, and final fields without synchronization are indeed immutable. Note that there can still be problems if an object with final fields is badly constructed, so that the `this` reference is allowed to escape the constructor before it has finished executing.

JSR-133

Redesigning the memory model in Java was done through the Java community process, in **Java Specification Request (JSR)** 133. It was ready as of Sun's reference implementation of Java 1.5, which was released in 2004. The JSR document itself, and the updated Java Language Specification, are fairly complex, full of precise and formal language. Getting into the details of JSR-133 is beyond the scope of this book. The reader is, however, encouraged to examine the documents, to become a better Java programmer.

There are also several great resources on the Internet about the Java Memory Model that are easier to read. One example is the excellent *JSR-133 FAQ* by *Jeremy Manson and Brian Goetz*. Another is *Fixing the Java memory Model by Brian Goetz*. Both are referenced in the bibliography of this book.

For this text, it suffices to say that JSR-133 cleaned up the problem with reordering fields across volatiles, the semantics of final fields, immutability, and other visibility issues that plagued Java 1.0 through 1.4. Volatiles were made stricter, and consequently, using `volatile` has become slightly more expensive.

JSR-133 and the new Java Memory Model was a huge step in making sure that intrinsic synchronized semantics were simpler and more intuitive. The intuitive approach to using `volatile` declarations in Java became the approach that also provided correct synchronization. Of course, a Java programmer may still stumble upon counterintuitive effects of memory semantics in the new memory model, especially if doing something stupid. But the worst unpredictable issues are gone. Maintaining proper synchronization discipline and understanding locks and volatiles will keep the number of synchronization bugs (or races) down to a minimum.

Implementing synchronization

Now that we have covered specification and semantics, we'll see how synchronization is actually implemented, both in Java bytecode and inside the JVM.

Primitives

On the lowest level, i.e. in every CPU architecture, are atomic instructions which are used to implement synchronization. These may or may not have to be modified in some way. For example on x86, a special **lock prefix** is used to make instructions maintain atomicity in multiprocessor environments.

Usually, standard instructions such as increments and decrements can be made atomic on most architectures.

A **compare and exchange** instruction is also commonly available, for atomically and conditionally loading and/or storing data in memory. Compare and exchange examines the contents of a memory location and an input value, and if they are equal, a second input value is written to the memory location. The compare and exchange may write the old memory contents to a destination operand or set a conditional flag if the exchange succeeded. This way, it can be used to branch on. Compare and exchange can, as we shall see later, be used as a fundamental building block for implementing locks.

Another example is **memory fence** instructions that ensure that reads or writes from memory can be seen by all CPUs after execution of the fence. Fences can be used, for example, to implement Java volatiles by having the compiler insert a fence after each store to a `volatile` field.

Atomic instructions introduce overhead, as they enforce memory ordering, potentially destroy CPU caches, and disallow parallel execution. So, even though they are a necessary ingredient for synchronization, the runtime should use them with care.

A simple optimization in the JVM is to use atomic instructions as **intrinsic calls** for various JDK functions. For example, certain calls to `java.util.concurrent.atomic` methods can be implemented directly as a few inline assembly instructions if the virtual machine is programmed to recognize them. Consider the following code:

```java
import java.util.concurrent.atomic.*;

public class AtomicAdder {
  AtomicInteger counter = new AtomicInteger(17);

  public int add() {
    return counter.incrementAndGet();
  }
}

public class AtomicAdder {
  int counter = 17;

  public int add() {
    synchronized(this) {
      return ++counter;
    }
  }
}
```

Given the first case, the virtual machine knows what is intended and uses an atomic add instruction in the generated code instead of even contemplating generating whatever code is inside `AtomicInteger.incrementAndGet`. We can do this because `java.util.concurrent.AtomicInteger` is a system class that is part of the JDK. Its semantics are well defined. In the case without atomics, it is possible, but a little bit harder, to deduce that the synchronization contains a simple atomic add.

Trivially, using synchronization to gain exclusive access to a resource is expensive, as a program that might have been running faster in parallel doesn't anymore. But beside from the obvious issue that the code in a critical section can be run only by one thread at a time, the actual synchronization itself might also add overhead to execution.

On the micro-architecture level, what happens when a locking atomic instruction executes varies widely between hardware platforms. Typically, it stalls the dispatch of the CPU pipeline until all pending instructions have finished executing and their memory writes have been finalized. The CPU also typically blocks other CPUs from the particular cache line with the memory location in the instruction. They continue to be blocked until the instruction has completed. A fence instruction on modern x86 hardware may take a large amount of CPU cycles to complete if it interrupts sufficiently complex multi-CPU execution. From this it can be concluded that not only are too many critical sections in a program bad for performance, but the lock implementation of the platform also matters — especially if locks are frequently taken and released, even for small critical sections.

Locks

While any lock may be implemented as a simple OS call to whatever appropriate synchronization mechanism the native platform provides, including one that puts threads to sleep and handles wait queues of monitor objects competing for the lock, one quickly realizes that this one-size-fits-all approach is suboptimal.

What if a lock is never contended and is acquired only a small number of times? Or what if a lock is severely contended and many threads compete for the resource that the particular lock protects? It is once more time to bring the power of the adaptive runtime into play. Before we discuss how the runtime can pick optimal lock implementations for a particular situation, we need to introduce the two fundamental types of lock implementations — **thin locks** and **fat locks**.

Thin locks are usually used for fast uncontended locks that are held for a short time only. Fat locks are used for anything more complex. The runtime should be able to turn one kind of lock into the other, depending on the current level of contention.

Thin locks

The simplest implementation of a thin lock is the **spinlock**. A spinlock spends its time in a `while` loop, waiting for its monitor object to be released — that is, burning CPU cycles. Typically, a spinlock is implemented with an atomic compare and exchange instruction to provide the basic exclusivity, and a conditional jump back to the compare and exchange if the test failed to acquire the lock.

Following is the pseudocode for a very simple spinlock implementation:

```
public class PseudoSpinlock {
   private static final int LOCK_FREE = 0;
   private static final int LOCK_TAKEN = 1;

   //memory position for lock, either free or taken
   static int lock;

   /**
    * try to atomically replace lock contents with
    * LOCK_TAKEN.
    *
    * cmpxchg returns the old value of [lock].
    * If lock already was taken, this is a no-op.
    *
    * As long as we fail to set the taken bit,
    * we spin
    */
   public void lock() {
      //burn cycles, or do a yield
      while (cmpxchg(LOCK_TAKEN, [lock]) == LOCK_TAKEN);
   }

   /**
    * atomically replace lock contents with "free".
    */
   public void unlock() {
      int old = cmpxchg(LOCK_FREE, [lock]);
      //guard against recursive locks, i.e. the same lock
      //being taken twice
      assert(old == LOCK_TAKEN);
   }
}
```

Due to the simplicity and low overhead of entering a spinlock, but because of the relatively high overhead maintaining it, spinlocks are only optimal if used in an implementation where locks are taken for very short periods of time. Spinlocks do not handle contention well. If the lock gets too contended, significant runtime will be wasted executing the loop that tries to acquire the lock. The cmpxchg itself is also dangerous when frequently executed, in that it may ruin caches and prevent any thread from running at maximum capacity.

Spinlocks are referred to as "thin" if they are simple to implement and take up few resources in a contention free environment. Less intrusive varieties can be implemented with slightly more complex logic (for example adding a yield or CPU pause to the spin loop), but the basic idea is the same.

As the implementation is nothing but a `while` loop with an atomic check, spinlocks cannot be used to support every aspect of Java synchronization. One example is the `wait`/`notify` mechanism that has to communicate with the thread system and the scheduler in order to put threads to sleep and wake them up when so required.

Fat locks

Fat locks are normally an order of magnitude slower than thin locks to release or acquire. They require a more complex representation than the thin lock and also have to provide better performance in a contended environment. Fat lock implementations may, for example, fall back to an OS level locking mechanism and thread controls.

Threads waiting for a fat lock are suspended. A **lock queue** for each fat lock is typically maintained, where the threads waiting for the lock are kept. The threads are usually woken up in FIFO order. The lock queue may be rearranged by the runtime as the scheduler sees fit or based on thread priorities. For objects used in `wait` / `notify` constructs, the JVM may also keep a **wait queue** for each monitor resource where the threads that are to be notified upon its release are queued.

A word on fairness

In scheduling, the term **fairness** is often used to describe a scheduling policy where each thread gets an equally sized time quantum to execute. If a thread has used its quantum, another thread gets an opportunity to run.

If fairness is not an issue—such as when we don't need a certain level of even **thread spread** over CPUs and threads perform the same kind of work—it is, in general, faster to allow whatever thread that gets a chance to run to keep running. Simply put, if we are just concerned about maximizing Java execution cycles, it can be a good idea to let a thread that just released a lock reacquire it again. This avoids expensive context switching and doesn't ruin the caches. Surprisingly enough, unfair behavior like this from the scheduler can, in several cases, improve runtime performance.

When it comes to thin locks, there is actually no fairness involved by design. All locking threads race with each other when attempting to acquire a lock.

With fat locks, in principle, the same thing applies. The lock queue is ordered, but threads will still have to race for the lock if several threads at once are awoken from the queue.

The lock word in JRockit

Recollect the 2 x 32-bit word header of any object in JRockit. One word is the class block that contains a pointer to type information for the object. The other word is the lock and GC word. Of the 32 bits in the lock and GC word, JRockit uses 8 bits for GC information and 24 bits for lock information.

The lock word and object header layout described in this section reflects the current state of the implementation in JRockit R28 and is subject to change without notice between releases. The bit-level details are only introduced to further help explaining lock states and their implementation.

In JRockit, every lock is assumed to be a thin lock when first taken. The lock bits of a thin locked object contain information about the thread that is holding the lock, along with various extra information bits used for optimization. For example for keeping track of the number of lock transfers between threads to determine if a lock is mostly thread local, and thus mostly unnecessary.

A fat lock requires a JVM internal monitor to be allocated for lock and semaphore queue management. Therefore, most of the space in the lock word for fat locks is taken up by an index (handle) to the monitor structure.

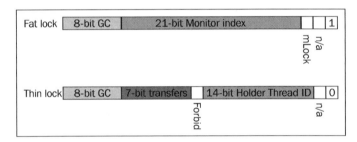

The JRockit lock bits are one example of an implementation of helper data structures for thin and fat locks, but of course both object header layout and contents vary between different vendors' JVM implementations. The various state diagrams that follow, go into some more detail on how thin locks and fat locks are converted to each other in JRockit and how lock words are affected by the state transitions.

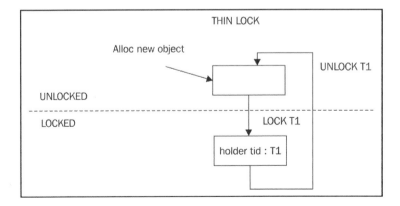

The previous figure shows the relatively simple transitions between a locked and unlocked state if only thin locks are involved. An unlocked object is locked when thread **T1** executes a successful lock on the object. The lock word in the object header now contains the thread ID of the lock taker and the object is flagged as thin locked. As soon as **T1** executes an unlock, the object reverts back to unlocked state and the lock holder bits are zeroed out in the object header.

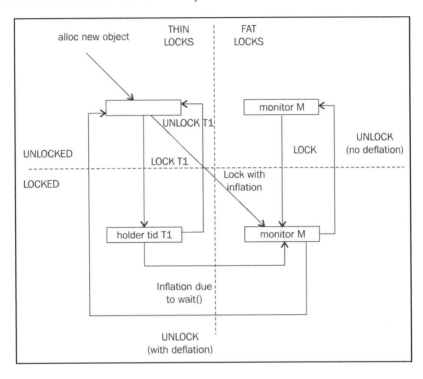

If we add fat locks to the picture, things get a little bit more complex. Recollect that a thin lock can be inflated into a fat lock if it is determined that it is too contended or if a call to wait is applied to it, such as a call to wait. The object can go directly to fat locked if thread **T1** attempts to acquire it and it is known to be contended. There is also a path from the thin locked version of the lock to the fat locked version in the event of a wait call. As a fat lock keeps its allocated JVM internal monitor, along with the handle to it, in the lock word, unlocking a fat lock without finding the need to deflate it will retain the monitor ID in the lock word, reusing the monitor structure.

The section on *Pitfalls and false optimizations* later in this chapter will further discuss how the runtime adaptively turns thin locks and fat locks into one another using contention based heuristics.

The Java bytecode implementation

Java bytecode defines two opcodes for controlling synchronization—monitorenter and monitorexit. They both pop a monitor object from the execution stack as their only operand. The opcodes monitorenter and monitorexit are generated by javac when there are synchronized regions with explicit monitor objects in the code. Consider the following short Java method that synchronizes on an implicit monitor object, in this case this, as it is an instance method:

```java
public synchronized int multiply(int something) {
    return something * this.somethingElse;
}
```

The bytecode consists of the seemingly simple sequence shown as follows:

```
public synchronized int multiply(int);
  Code:
    0:   iload_1
    1:   aload_0
    2:   getfield     #2; //Field somethingElse:I
    5:   imul
    6:   ireturn
```

Here, the runtime or JIT compiler has to check that the method is synchronized by examining an access flag set for this particular method in the .class file. Recollect that a synchronized method has no explicit monitor, but in instance methods this is used and in static methods a unique object representing the class of the object is used. So, the earlier source code is trivially equivalent to:

```java
public int multiply(int something) {
    synchronized(this) {
        return something * this.somethingElse;
    }
}
```

But, the previous code compiles to this rather more complex sequence:

```
public int multiply(int);
  Code:
    0:   aload_0
    1:   dup
    2:   astore_2
    3:   monitorenter
```

```
4:   iload_1

5:   aload_0

6:   getfield    #2; //Field somethingElse:I

9:   imul

10:  aload_2

11:  monitorexit

12:  ireturn

13:  astore_3

14:  aload_2

15:  monitorexit

16:  aload_3

17:  athrow
   Exception table:
     from   to   target type
       4    12     13    any
      13    16     13    any
```

What `javac` has done here, except for generating `monitorenter` and `monitorexit` instructions for `this`, is that it has added a generic catch-all try block for the entire code of the `synchronized` block, bytecode 4 to bytecode 9 in the previous example. Upon any unhandled exception, control will go to bytecode 13, the catch block, which will release the lock before re-throwing whatever exception was caught.

Compiler intervention in this fashion is the standard way of solving the issue of unlocking a locked object when an exception occurs. Also notice that if there are exceptions in the catch block from bytecode 13 to bytecode 16, it will use itself as the catch-all, creating a cyclic construct that isn't possible to express in Java source code. We explained the problems with this in Chapter 2.

Naturally, we could treat this as unstructured control flow, but as the recursive catch is a common pattern, and as we don't want it to complicate control flow analysis, it is treated specially by the JRockit compiler. Otherwise it would be considered obfuscated code, and a number of optimizations would be forbidden from being done.

JRockit internally translates all methods with an implicit monitor object into methods with an explicit one, similar to what is shown in the second part of example, in order to avoid the special case with the synchronized flag.

Lock pairing

Other than the previous bytecode issue there is a more serious one — monitorenter and monitorexit are not **paired**. It is simple to generate weird bytecode where, for example, a monitorexit is executed on an unlocked object. This would lead to an IllegalMonitorStateException at runtime. However, bytecode where a lock is taken in one method and then released in another is also possible (and perfectly legal at runtime). The same applies to various many-to-many mappings of monitorenter and monitorexit for the same lock. Neither of these constructs have Java source code equivalents. The problem of the power of expression comes back to bite us.

For performance reasons, in a JIT compiler, it is very important to be able to identify the matching lock for a particular unlock operation. The type of the lock determines the unlock code that has to be executed. As we shall soon see, given even more kinds of locks than just thin and fat ones, this becomes increasingly important. Sadly, we cannot assume that locks are nicely paired, because of the non-symmetrical semantics of the bytecode. Unpaired locks don't occur in ordinary bytecode and in ordinary programs, but as it is possible, JRockit needs to be able to handle unpaired synchronization constructs as well.

The JRockit code generator does control flow analysis upon method generation and tries to match every monitorenter to its corresponding monitorexit instruction(s). For structured bytecode that was compiled from Java source, this is almost always possible (if we treat the anomalous catch produced by synchronized blocks as a special case). The match is done when turning the stack-based metaphor into a register-based one, piggybacking on the BC2HIR pass of the code generator, which, as explained in Chapter 2, has to do control flow analysis anyway.

JRockit uses a mechanism called **lock tokens** to determine which monitorenter and monitorexit instructions belong together. Each monitorenter is translated into an instruction with a lock token destination. Its matching monitorexit is translated into an instruction with that particular lock token as a source operand.

Following is a pseudocode example of the transformation of a Java synchronized region to JRockit matched (or paired) locks:

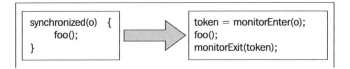

```
synchronized(o)  {
     foo();
}
```

```
token = monitorEnter(o);
foo();
monitorExit(token);
```

In the rare case that a `monitorenter` can't be mapped to a particular `monitorexit`, JRockit tags these instructions with a special "unmatched" flag. While, this is still supported by the runtime, and needs to be for full bytecode compliance, we shall soon see that handling unmatched locks is orders of magnitude more expensive than handling tokenized locks.

From a practical perspective, unmatched locks never occur in standard compiled bytecode, but may show up in obfuscated code or as the result of various bytecode profilers. Running JRockit with verbose code generator output (`-Xverbose:codegen`) will display information about unmatched locks if they are detected. In JRockit versions from R28, there is also special JRockit Flight Recorder event for unmatched locks that can be used for performance profiling. If unmatched locks show up in your Java program, all performance bets are off. You probably need to get rid of them.

A special case, where lock pairing can never be done is in native code. Calls from native code, accessed through JNI, to `monitorenter` and `monitorexit` equivalents will always be treated as unmatched locks, as once the program is executing native code, we have no control over the stack. However, JNI marshalling overhead, i.e. executing the stub code to get from Java code to native code, is orders of magnitude slower than taking locks anyway. So, the key to lock performance may lie elsewhere if we enter and exit native code frequently.

So what is a lock token? JRockit implements a lock token as a reference to a monitor object, the operand to `monitorenter`, with a couple of bits added at the end. As we have seen in Chapter 3, objects are typically aligned on even addresses, in practice on 8 byte boundaries (or more for compressed references with larger heaps). So, we always have the lowest bits of any object pointer available for storing arbitrary information. Whenever any of the three lowest bits in an object pointer are non-zero, JRockit takes this to mean that the object is used as a monitor, locked with a lock token. The seven different possible non-zero bit configurations can be used to communicate different information about the lock, for instance if it is thin, taken recursively by the same thread, fat, or unmatched. Lock tokens can only exist in local stack frames, never on the heap. Since JRockit doesn't use compressed references in local frames, we are guaranteed to be able to claim the alignment bits of any object for token information.

Recollect from the previous chapter that all live registers at any given time are explicitly determined by the compiler and stored as livemaps, metadata accessible to the code generator. The same thing applies to lock tokens.

Trivially, because of the implicit lock pairing in structured Java code, one lock cannot be released before another one, taken inside that lock. It is easy to look at an object in a livemap and determine whether it is a lock token or not, but in order to be able to unlock tokens in the correct order upon, for example, an exception being thrown, nesting information is required as well. If many locks are taken when an exception occurs, the runtime needs to know the order in which they were locked. Consequently, the livemap system also provides the nesting order of lock tokens.

For unmatched unlocks, an expensive stack walk is required in order to discover the matching lock operation and update the lock state in its lock token reference. The JVM needs to look for it on all previous frames on the stack. This requires stopping the world and is several orders of magnitude slower than with perfect lock pairing that can be immediately handled by modifying a lock token on the local stack frame. Luckily, unmatched locks are rare. No code that is compiled with `javac` is likely to contain unmatched locks.

Implementing threads

This section briefly covers some different types of thread implementations. It is fairly brief, as unmodified OS threads are the preferred way of implementing threads in a JVM these days.

Green threads

Green threads usually refers to implementing threads with some kind of multiplexing algorithm, using one OS thread to represent several or all Java threads in the JVM. This requires that the runtime handle the thread scheduling for the Java threads inside the OS thread. The advantages to using green threads is that the overhead is a lot smaller than for OS threads when it comes to things like context switches and starting a new thread. Many early JVMs tended to favor some kind of green thread approach.

However, aside from the added complexity of having to implement lifecycle and scheduling code for the green threads, there is also the intrinsic problem of Java native code. If a green thread goes into native code that then blocks on the OS level, the entire OS thread containing all the green threads will be suspended. This most likely causes a deadlock issue by preventing any other Java thread contained in the same OS thread from running. So, a mechanism for detecting this is needed. Early versions of JRockit used green threads and solved the OS-level suspension problem with a mechanism called **renegade threads**, basically branching off a native thread from the main OS thread whenever a native operation was to be performed. If this happened frequently, the green thread model incrementally turned into a model where Java threads were one-to-one mapped to OS threads.

N x M threads

A variety of the green thread approach is to use several OS threads that in turn represent several green threads—sort of a hybrid solution. This is referred to as an **n x m thread model**. This can somewhat alleviate the green thread problem of blocking in native code.

In the early days of server-side Java, certain kinds of applications lent themselves well to this model—applications where thread scalability and low thread start overhead was everything. Several of the first paying JRockit customers had setups with the need for a very large number of concurrent threads and for low thread creation overhead, the prime example being chat servers. JRockit 1.0 used the n x m model and was able to provide massive performance increases in these very specialized domains.

As time went by and Java applications grew more complex, the added complexity of multiplexing virtual threads on OS threads, the common reliance on native code, and the refinement of other techniques such as more efficient synchronization, made the n x m approach obsolete.

To our knowledge, no modern server-side JVM still uses a thread implementation based on green threads. Because of their intrinsic simplicity and the issues mentioned earlier, OS threads are the preferred way of representing Java threads.

OS threads

Naturally, the most obvious implementation of a `java.lang.Thread` is to use an underlying operating system thread, for example a POSIX thread on *NIX, one-to-one-mapped against each `java.lang.Thread` object. This has the advantage that most of the semantics are similar and little extra work needs to be done. Thread scheduling can also be outsourced to the operating system.

This is the most common approach and as far as we know, it is used in all modern JVM implementations. Other approaches often aren't worth the complexity anymore, at least not for standard server-side applications. In, for example, embedded environments, it may still make sense to use other approaches, but then, on the other hand, implementation space is constrained.

Thread pooling

If we can rely on threads being OS threads, optimization techniques with slightly bad reputations, such as **thread pooling**, also make a certain amount of sense. The creation and starting of OS threads introduces a significantly larger overhead than if the VM uses some kind of green thread model. Under special circumstances, in a `java.lang.Thread` implementation based on OS threads, it might make sense to reuse existing thread objects in a Java program, to try to reduce this overhead. This is typically done by keeping finished threads in a thread pool and reusing them for new tasks instead of allocating new threads. The authors of this book generally frown upon trying to outsmart the JVM, but this is a case where it might sometimes pay off. However, serious profiling should be done before trying thread pooling to determine if it is really necessary.

Also, if the underlying thread implementation is not using pure OS threads, thread pooling may be disruptive and counterproductive. In a green thread model, starting a thread is extremely cheap. While to our knowledge no other JVM thread implementation than OS threads exists today, Java is still supposed to be a platform-independent language. So, proceed with caution.

Optimizing threads and synchronization

This section discusses how threads and synchronization can be optimized in an adaptive runtime environment.

Lock inflation and lock deflation

As was mentioned when the different types of locks were introduced, one of the most important optimizations in an adaptive runtime is the ability to convert thin locks to fat locks and vice versa, depending on load and contention. Both the code generator and the lock implementation will attempt to solve this problem as efficiently as possible.

In an adaptive environment, the runtime has the benefit of free lock profiling information (at least a small amount of free lock profiling information, as, we shall see, doing complete in-depth lock profiling incurs some runtime overhead). Whenever a lock is taken or released, information can be logged about who is trying to get the lock and how many times it has been contended. So, if a single thread has failed to acquire a thin lock in too many subsequent attempts, it makes good sense for the virtual machine to convert it to a fat lock. The fat lock is better suited for handling contention, in that waiting threads sleep instead of spin and therefore use less CPU cycles. We refer to the practice of converting a thin lock to a fat lock as **lock inflation**.

JRockit, by default, also uses a small spinlock to implement a fat lock while it has been recently inflated and held only for a very short time. This might seem counterintuitive, but is generally beneficial. This behavior can be turned off from the command line (with the flag -XX:UseFatSpin=false), if deemed too slow—for example, in an environment with highly contended locks with long waiting periods. The spinlock that is part of the fat lock can also be made adaptive and based on runtime feedback. This is turned off by default, but can be enabled with the command-line flag -XX:UseAdaptiveFatSpin=true.

In the same manner, when many subsequent unlocks of a fat lock have been done without any other thread being queued on its lock or wait queue, it makes sense to turn the fat lock into a thin lock again. We refer to this as **lock deflation**.

JRockit uses heuristics to perform both inflation and deflation, thus adapting to the changed behavior of a given program where, for example, locks that were contended in the beginning of program execution stop being contended. Then these locks are candidates for deflation.

The heuristics that trigger transitions between thin and fat locks can be overridden and modified from the command line if needed, but this is generally not recommended. The next chapter will briefly discuss how to do this.

Recursive locking

It is permissible, though unnecessary, for the same thread to lock the same object several times, also known as recursive locking. Code that does so occurs, for example, where inlining has taken place or in a recursive synchronized method. Then the code generator may remove the inner locks completely, if no unsafe code exists within the critical section, (such as volatile accesses or escaping calls between the inner and outer locks).

This can be combined with optimizing for the recursive lock case. JRockit uses a special lock token bit configuration to identify recursive locks. As long as a lock has been taken at least twice by one thread without first being released, it is tagged as recursive. So, forced unlock operations upon exceptions can still be correctly implemented, resetting the recursion count to the correct state, with no extra synchronization overhead.

Lock fusion

The JRockit optimizing JIT compiler also uses a code optimization called **lock fusion** (sometimes also referred to as **lock coarsening** in literature). When inlining plenty of code, especially synchronized methods, the observation can be made that frequent sequential locks and unlocks with the same monitor object are common.

Consider code that, after inlining, looks like:

```
synchronized(x) {
  //Do something...
}

//Short snippet of code...
x = y;

synchronized(y) {
  //Do something else...
}
```

Classic alias analysis by the compiler trivially gives us that x and y are the same object. If the short piece of code between the synchronized blocks carries little execution overhead, less than the overhead of releasing and reacquiring the lock, it is beneficial to let the code generator fuse the lock regions into one.

```
synchronized(x) {
  //Do something...
  //Short snippet of code...
  x = y;
  //Do something else...
}
```

Additional requirements are of course that there are no escaping or volatile operations in the code between the synchronized blocks, or the Java Memory Model semantics for equivalence would be violated. There are of course a few other code optimization issues that have to be handled that are beyond the scope of this chapter. An example would be that any exception handlers for the regions that are to be fused need to be compatible.

Naturally, it might not be beneficial just to fuse every block of code we see, but we can avoid some overhead if the blocks to fuse are picked cleverly. And if enough sampling information is available for the short snippet of code, we can make clever adaptive guesses to whether a lock fusion would be beneficial or not.

To summarize, this code optimization all boils down to not releasing a lock unnecessarily. The thread system itself can, by making its state machine a little bit more complicated, implement a similar optimization, independent of the code generator, known as **lazy unlocking**.

Lazy unlocking

So what does the previous observation really mean, if it can be showed that there are many instances of thread local unlocks and re-locks that simply slow down execution? Perhaps this is the case almost all the time? Perhaps the runtime should start assuming that each individual unlock operation is actually not needed?

This gamble will succeed each time the lock is reacquired by the same thread, almost immediately after release. It will fail as soon as another thread tries to acquire the seemingly unlocked object, which semantics must allow it to do. Then the original thread will need to have the lock forcefully unlocked in order to make it seem as if "nothing has happened". We refer to this practice as **lazy unlocking** (also referred to as **biased locking** in some literature).

Even in the case that there is no contention on a lock, the actual process of acquiring and releasing the lock is expensive compared to doing nothing at all. Atomic instructions incur overhead to all Java execution in their vicinity.

In Java, sometimes it is reasonable to assume that most locks are thread local. Third-party code often uses synchronization unnecessarily for a local application, as the authors of third-party libraries cannot be sure if the code is to run in a parallel environment or not. They need to be safe unless it is explicitly specified that thread safety is not supported. There are plentiful examples of this in the JDK alone, for example the `java.util.Vector` class. If the programmer needs vector abstraction for a thread local application, he might pick `java.util.Vector` for convenience, not thinking about its inherent synchronization, when `java.util.ArrayList` virtually performs the same job but is unsynchronized.

It seems sensible that if we assume most locks are thread local and never shared, we would gain performance in such cases, taking a lazy unlocking approach. As always, we have a trade off—if another thread needs to acquire a lazy unlocked object, more overhead is introduced than in a non-lazy model, as the seemingly free object must be located and released.

It seems reasonable to assume that, as an overall approach, always gambling that an unlock won't be needed, isn't such a safe bet. We need to optimize for several different runtime behaviors.

Implementation

The semantics of a lazy unlocking implementation are fairly simple.

For the lock operation, `monitorenter`:

- If the object is unlocked, the thread that locks the object will reserve the lock, tagging the object as lazily locked.

- If the object is already tagged as lazily locked:

  ○ If the lock is wanted by the same thread, do nothing (in principle a recursive lock).

  ○ If the lock is wanted by another thread, we need to stop the thread holding the lock, detect the "real" locking state of the object, i.e. is it locked or unlocked. This is done with an expensive stack walk. If the object is locked, it is converted to a thin lock, otherwise it is forcefully unlocked so that it can be acquired by the new thread.

For the unlock operation, `monitorexit`:

- Do nothing for a lazily locked object and leave the object in a locked state, that is, perform lazy unlocking.

In order to revoke a reservation for a thread that wants the lock, the thread that did the reservation needs to be stopped. This is extremely expensive. The actual state of the lock to be released is determined by inspecting the thread stack for lock tokens. This is similar to the approach of handling unmatched locks described earlier. Lazy unlocking uses a lock token of its own, whose bit configuration means "this object is lazily locked".

If we never had to revert a lazy locked object, that is if all our locks are in fact thread local, all would be well and we would see immense performance gains. In the real world, however, we cannot afford to take the very steep penalty of releasing lazy locked objects time and time again, if our guess proves to be wrong. So, we have to keep track of the number of times a lazy lock is transferred between threads—the number of penalties incurred. This information is stored in the lock word of the monitor object in the so called **transfer bits**.

If the number of transfers between threads is too large, a particular object or its entire type (class) and all its instances can be forbidden from further lazy locking and will just be locked and unlocked normally using standard thin and fat lock mechanisms.

Object banning

When a transfer limit is hit, the **forbid bit** in a JRockit object lock word is set. This bit indicates that a specific object instance is unsuitable for lazy unlocking. If the forbid bit is set in an object header, this particular object cannot be used for lazy unlocking ever again.

Also, if a lock is contended, regardless of other settings, lazy unlocking is immediately banned for its monitor object.

Further locking on a banned object will behave as ordinary thin and fat locks.

Class banning

Just banning certain instances from being used in lazy unlocking may not be enough. Several objects of the same type often use locks similarly. Thus an entire class can be tagged so that none of its instances can be subject to lazy unlocking. If too many instances of a class are banned or too many transfers take place for instances of a class, the entire class is banned.

A dynamic twist to class bans and object bans can be introduced by letting the bans "age"—the runtime system gets a new chance to retry lazy unlocking with a certain object if a significant amount of time has been spent since the last ban. If we end up with the same ban in effect again, the aging can be set to be restarted, but run more slowly, or the ban can be made permanent.

The following figure tries to better illustrate the complexities of states involved in lazy unlocking:

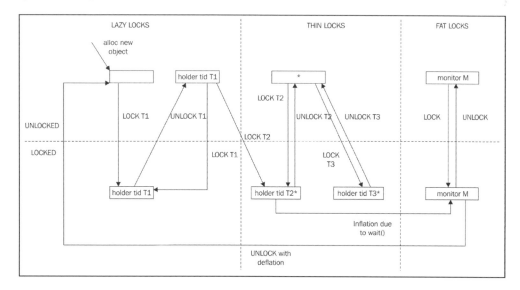

Now, we have three lock domains, as opposed to two (thin and fat) shown in the state graphs earlier in this chapter. The new domain "lazy" is added, which is where locking of hitherto unseen objects starts—we hope our "gamble" that locks are mostly thread local pays off.

Just as before, starting at the unlocked, previously untouched object, a `monitorenter` by thread **T1** will transition it to lazy locked state (just as with the thin locked state before). However, if **T1** performs a `monitorexit` on the object, it will pretend to be unlocked, but really remain in a locked state, with the thread ID for **T1** still flagging ownership in the lock bits. Subsequent locks by **T1** will then be no-ops.

If another thread, **T2** now tries to lock the object, we need to respect that, take the penalty for our erroneous guess that the lock was taken mostly by **T1**, flush out **T1** from the thread ID bits and replace them with **T2**. If this happens often enough, the object may be subject to banning from lazy unlocking and then we must transfer the object to a normal thin locked state. Pretending that this was the case with the first `monitorenter` **T2** did on our object, this moves the state diagram to the familiar thin locked domain. Objects that are banned from lazy unlocking in the figure are denoted by (*). If thread **T3** tries to lock a banned (but unlocked) object, we notice that we remain in the thin locked section of the picture. No lazy unlocking is allowed.

In similar fashion as before, thin locks are inflated to fat locks if they get contended or their objects are used with `wait` / `notify`, which requires wait queues. This is true for objects in the lazy domain as well.

Results

Most commercial JVM implementations maintain some kind of mechanism for lazy unlocking. Somewhat cynically, this may have its origin in the popular SPECjbb2005 benchmark, which has many thread local locks and where small optimization efforts towards hanging on to locks result in huge performance gains.

 SPEC and the benchmark name SPECjbb2005 are trademarks of the **Standard Performance Evaluation Corporation**.

However, there are also several real-world applications, for example, application servers where it turns out that lazy unlocking can deliver performance. This is just because the sheer complexity and many abstraction layers has made it hard for developers to see if synchronization across threads needs be used at all.

Some versions of JRockit, such as the x86 implementation running JDK 1.6.0, come with lazy unlocking and banning heuristics enabled out of the box. This can be turned off from the command line if needed. To find out if a particular shipment of JRockit uses lazy unlocking as a default option, please consult the section on locks in the JRockit documentation.

Pitfalls and false optimizations

As in previous chapters, we will finish up with a discussion of obvious caveats. This section discusses things to be aware of when working with threads and synchronization in Java.

Thread.stop, Thread.resume and Thread. suspend

The single most dangerous part of the Java thread API, are the methods in the `java. lang.Thread` class called `stop`, `resume`, and `suspend`. They were included in Java 1.0, but immediately found unsafe and deprecated. This however, was a bit too late, and, even today, they are widely used both in legacy code and new applications, despite the deprecation warnings. We are sad to report that we've come across them in commercial code that was developed as late as 2008.

The `stop` method (meant to halt the execution of a thread) is unsafe. This is because stopping the execution of a thread that is modifying global data would possibly leave the global data in an inconsistent, broken state. A thread that receives a stop signal will unlock all of the locks that it was holding, thus making the data under modification by these locks briefly visible to the rest of the world, which violates the Java sandbox model.

Stopping threads should instead be handled by `wait` / `notify` or (volatile) variables, properly synchronized when this needs to be the case.

What about suspension? Suspending a thread is inherently deadlock prone. That is, if a thread is holding a lock and then is suspended, no other thread can access the resource protected by the lock until the suspended thread is resumed. If the thread responsible for the `resume` call, waking up the suspended thread, tries to acquire that lock, a deadlock will occur. Thus, `Thread.resume` and `Thread.suspend` are deemed too dangerous to leave to the user and were deprecated as well.

Consequently, never use `Thread.stop`, `Thread.resume` or `Thread.suspend` in any program and be aware of their issues when working with legacy code.

Double checked locking

Lack of understanding of the underlying memory model and CPU architecture, can cause trouble in the highest levels of platform-independent Java as well. Consider the following thread safe code that returns a singleton object, instantiated once only upon demand:

```
public class GadgetHolder {

  private Gadget theGadget;

  public synchronized Gadget getGadget() {
    if (this.theGadget == null) {
      this.theGadget = new Gadget();
    }
    return this.theGadget;
  }
}
```

The previous example works fine for multiple threads, as the method is synchronized, using the GadgetHolder instance itself as the monitor. However, when the Gadget constructor has run once, further synchronization might seem unnecessary and expensive. Therefore, one might be tempted to optimize the method as:

```
public Gadget getGadget() {
  if (this.theGadget == null) {
    synchronized(this) {
      if (this.theGadget == null) {
        this.theGadget = new Gadget();
      }
    }
  }
  return this.theGadget;
}
```

The previous optimization might seem like a clever trick. If the object exists, which will be the usual case, we can return it immediately without synchronization. The singleton instantiation is still synchronized, including the original null check, retaining thread safety.

The problem here is that we have created a common anti-pattern known as **double checked locking**. Now, one thread can start initializing the Gadget field upon completing the inner null check in the synchronization. This thread might start allocating and writing the object to the Gadget field, which may well be a non-atomic process, containing several writes to memory without guaranteed ordering. If this happens in the middle of a context switch, another thread can come in, see the partially written object in the field and thus fail the first null check. Then the partially allocated object may be returned. The same thing can happen not just with objects, but with other field types as well. For example, `longs` on a 32-bit platform often need to be initialized by two 32-bit writes to memory. A 32-bit `int`, on the other hand (just one memory write on initialization) would slip past the trap.

The problem may, though only in the new version of the Java Memory Model, be gotten around by declaring the `theGadget` field `volatile`, but this incurs overhead anyway. Possibly less overhead than the original synchronization, but still overhead. For clarity, and because underlying memory model implementations may not be correct, double checked locking should be avoided! There are several good web pages explaining why double checked locking should be considered an anti-pattern in several languages, not just Java.

> The danger with problems like this is that on strong memory models they rarely break down. Intel IA-64 deployment is a typical real-world scenario where Java applications that previously have been running flawlessly start malfunctioning. Intel IA-64 has a notoriously weak memory model. It is all too easy to suspect a bug in the JVM instead of in the Java program if it runs fine on x86 but breaks on IA-64.

For static singletons, initialization can be performed with **initialize on demand**, providing the same semantics and avoiding double checked locking.

```
public class GadgetMaker {
   public static Gadget theGadget = new Gadget();
}
```

Java guarantees that the class initialization is atomic, and as the `GadgetMaker` class has no other contents, `theGadget` will always be atomically assigned when the class is first referenced. This works both in the old and the new memory model.

In conclusion, there are plenty of caveats when programming parallel Java, but most of them can be avoided by understanding the Java Memory Model. Furthermore, even if you don't care about the underlying hardware, not understanding the Java Memory Model can still be a sure way of shooting yourself in the foot.

JRockit flags

This section covers the most important command-line flags that can be used to control and instrument JRockit lock behavior.

While plenty of information can be gleaned from log files using some of these flags, synchronization is a complex business and the preferred and best way to visualize multithreaded behavior is through the JRockit Mission Control suite.

Examining locks and lazy unlocking

This section explains the most important flags for studying and manipulating lock behavior.

Lock details from -Xverbose:locks

This flag makes JRockit report information related to synchronization in the running program. Most of the information that the -Xverbose:locks flag produces has to do with the lazy unlocking optimization. This is a good way to see, for example, which types and objects are temporarily or permanently banned for lazy unlocking, or if lazy unlocking performs as efficiently as it should, without having to revert its assumptions all the time.

Following is a sample output from -Xverbose:locks. We can see that lazy unlocking is determined inappropriate for a couple of classes, whose instances are competed for by different threads. These classes are banned from further lazy unlocking.

```
hastur:SPECjbb2005 marcus$ java -Xverbose:locks -cp jbb.jar:check.
  jar spec.jbb.JBBmain -propfile SPECjbb.props >/dev/null

[INFO ][locks  ] Lazy unlocking enabled
[INFO ][locks  ] No of CPUs: 8
[INFO ][locks  ] Banning spec/jbb/Customer for lazy unlocking.
  (forbidden 6 times, limit is 5)
[INFO ][locks  ] Banning spec/jbb/Address for lazy unlocking.
  (forbidden 6 times, limit is 5)
[INFO ][locks  ] Banning java/lang/Object for lazy unlocking.
  (forbidden 5 times, limit is 5)
[INFO ][locks  ] Banning spec/jbb/TimerData for lazy unlocking.
  (forbidden 6 times, limit is 5)
[INFO ][locks  ] Banning spec/jbb/District for lazy unlocking.
  (forbidden 6 times, limit is 5)
```

Controlling lazy unlocking with –XX:UseLazyUnlocking

Depending on the platform and JRockit version, lazy unlocking may or may not be enabled out of the box. Please refer to the JRockit Documentation to find out what applies to a particular platform or study the output from `-Xverbose:locks`. Given that adaptive reversion strategies form part of the lazy unlocking algorithm, it is more often the case than not, that when enabled, lazy unlocking will contribute to increased performance.

The default lazy unlocking behavior can be overridden with the flag:

> `-XX:UseLazyUnlocking=false` or `-XX:UseLazyUnlocking=true`.

Finally, `-Xverbose:codegen` will, as mentioned earlier in the chapter, output warnings for any method where the compiler failed to create matched locks and unlocks.

Using SIGQUIT or Ctrl-Break for Stack Traces

Issuing a SIGQUIT signal to a JRockit process, typically by executing `kill -QUIT <PID>` or `kill -3 <PID>` in *NIX environments or by pressing *Ctrl-Break* in a console window on Windows, will dump complete stack traces (where available) for all the threads in the JVM, both native and Java threads. The locks taken by the threads are also displayed, along with their types. This is a "poor man's way" of quickly detecting deadlocks, by finding out if a thread is waiting for a resource held by another suspended thread.

Following is an example thread dump including lock holders, what type of lock they are holding and where on the execution stacks the locks were taken:

```
===== FULL THREAD DUMP ================
Tue Jun 02 14:36:39 2009
BEA JRockit(R) R27.6.3-40_o-112056-1.6.0_11-20090318-2104-windows-ia32

"Main Thread" id=1 idx=0x4 tid=4220 prio=5 alive,
  in native, sleeping, native_waiting
    at java/lang/Thread.sleep(J)V(Native Method)
    at spec/jbb/JBButil.SecondsToSleep(J)V(Unknown Source)
    at spec/jbb/Company.displayResultTotals(Z)V(Unknown Source)
    at spec/jbb/JBBmain.DoARun(Lspec/jbb/Company;SII)V(Unknown Source)
    at spec/jbb/JBBmain.runWarehouse(IIF)Z(Unknown Source)
    at spec/jbb/JBBmain.doIt()V(Unknown Source)
    at spec/jbb/JBBmain.main([Ljava/lang/String;)V(Unknown Source)
    at jrockit/vm/RNI.c2java(IIIII)V(Native Method)
    -- end of trace
```

```
"(Signal Handler)" id=2 idx=0x8 tid=1236 prio=5 alive, in native, daemon
"(GC Main Thread)" id=3 idx=0xc tid=5956 prio=5 alive,
    in native, native_waiting, daemon
"(GC Worker Thread 1)" id=? idx=0x10 tid=5884 prio=5 alive,
    in native, daemon
"(GC Worker Thread 2)" id=? idx=0x14 tid=3440 prio=5 alive,
    in native, daemon
"(GC Worker Thread 3)" id=? idx=0x18 tid=4744 prio=5 alive,
    in native, daemon
"(GC Worker Thread 4)" id=? idx=0x1c tid=5304 prio=5 alive,
    in native, daemon
"(GC Worker Thread 5)" id=? idx=0x20 tid=5024 prio=5 alive,
    in native, daemon
"(GC Worker Thread 6)" id=? idx=0x24 tid=3632 prio=5 alive,
    in native, daemon
"(GC Worker Thread 7)" id=? idx=0x28 tid=1924 prio=5 alive,
    in native, daemon
"(GC Worker Thread 8)" id=? idx=0x2c tid=5144 prio=5 alive,
    in native, daemon
"(Code Generation Thread 1)" id=4 idx=0x30 tid=3956 prio=5 alive,
    in native, native_waiting, daemon
"(Code Optimization Thread 1)" id=5 idx=0x34 tid=4268 prio=5 alive,
    in native, native_waiting, daemon
"(VM Periodic Task)" id=6 idx=0x38 tid=6068 prio=10 alive,
    in native, native_blocked, daemon
"(Attach Listener)" id=7 idx=0x3c tid=6076 prio=5 alive,
    in native, daemon
...
"Thread-7" id=18 idx=0x64 tid=4428 prio=5 alive
    at spec/jbb/infra/Util/TransactionLogBuffer.privText
        (Ljava/lang/String;IIIS)V(UnknownSource)[optimized]
    at spec/jbb/infra/Util/TransactionLogBuffer.putText
        (Ljava/lang/String;IIIS)V(Unknown Source)[inlined]
    at spec/jbb/infra/Util/TransactionLogBuffer.putDollars
        (Ljava/math/BigDecimal;III)V(Unknown Source)[optimized]
    at spec/jbb/NewOrderTransaction.processTransactionLog()
        V(Unknown Source)[optimized]
    ^-- Holding lock: spec/jbb/NewOrderTransaction@0x0D674030[biased lock]
    at spec/jbb/TransactionManager.runTxn(Lspec/jbb/Transaction;JJD)
        J(Unknown Source)[inlined]
    at spec/jbb/TransactionManager.goManual(ILspec/jbb/TimerData;)
        J(Unknown Source)[optimized]
```

```
at spec/jbb/TransactionManager.go()V(Unknown Source)[optimized]
at spec/jbb/JBBmain.run()V(Unknown Source)[optimized]
at java/lang/Thread.run(Thread.java:619)[optimized]
at jrockit/vm/RNI.c2java(IIIII)V(Native Method)
-- end of trace


"Thread-8" id=19 idx=0x68 tid=5784 prio=5 alive,
  in native, native_blocked
  at jrockit/vm/Locks.checkLazyLocked(Ljava/lang/Object;)
    I(Native Method)
  at jrockit/vm/Locks.monitorEnterSecondStage(Locks.java:1225)
  at spec/jbb/Stock.getQuantity()I(Unknown Source)[inlined]
  at spec/jbb/Orderline.process(Lspec/jbb/Item;Lspec/jbb/Stock;)
    V(Unknown Source)[optimized]
  at spec/jbb/Orderline.validateAndProcess(Lspec/jbb/Warehouse;)
    Z(Unknown Source)[inlined]
  at spec/jbb/Order.processLines(Lspec/jbb/Warehouse;SZ)
    Z(Unknown Source)[inlined]
  at spec/jbb/NewOrderTransaction.process()Z(Unknown Source)[optimized]
  ^-- Holding lock: spec/jbb/Orderline@0x09575D00[biased lock]
  ^-- Holding lock: spec/jbb/Order@0x05DDB4E8[biased lock]
  at spec/jbb/TransactionManager.runTxn(Lspec/jbb/Transaction;JJD)
    J(Unknown Source)[inlined]
  at spec/jbb/TransactionManager.goManual(ILspec/jbb/TimerData;)
    J(Unknown Source)[optimized]
  at spec/jbb/TransactionManager.go()V(Unknown Source)[optimized]
  at spec/jbb/JBBmain.run()V(Unknown Source)[optimized]
  at java/lang/Thread.run(Thread.java:619)[optimized]
  at jrockit/vm/RNI.c2java(IIIII)V(Native Method)
  -- end of trace


"Thread-9" id=20 idx=0x6c tid=3296 prio=5 alive,
  in native, native_blocked
  at jrockit/vm/Locks.checkLazyLocked(Ljava/lang/Object;)
    I(Native Method)
  at jrockit/vm/Locks.monitorEnterSecondStage(Locks.java:1225)
  at spec/jbb/Stock.getQuantity()I(Unknown Source)[inlined]
  at spec/jbb/Orderline.process(Lspec/jbb/Item;Lspec/jbb/Stock;)
    V(Unknown Source)[optimized]
```

```
    at spec/jbb/Orderline.validateAndProcess(Lspec/jbb/Warehouse;)
      Z(Unknown Source)[inlined]

    at spec/jbb/Order.processLines(Lspec/jbb/Warehouse;SZ)
      Z(Unknown Source)[inlined]

    at spec/jbb/NewOrderTransaction.process()Z(Unknown Source)[optimized]

    ^-- Holding lock: spec/jbb/Orderline@0x09736E10[biased lock]

    ^-- Holding lock: spec/jbb/Order@0x09736958[biased lock]

    at spec/jbb/TransactionManager.runTxn(Lspec/jbb/Transaction;JJD)
      J(Unknown Source)[inlined]

    at spec/jbb/TransactionManager.goManual(ILspec/jbb/TimerData;)
    J(Unknown Source)[optimized]

    at spec/jbb/TransactionManager.go()V(Unknown Source)[optimized]

    at spec/jbb/JBBmain.run()V(Unknown Source)[optimized]

    at java/lang/Thread.run(Thread.java:619)[optimized]


===== END OF THREAD DUMP ===============
```

Lock profiling

JRockit can produce extensive profiling information about each lock in a running program at the cost of some overhead. Typically, running with lock profiling adds about three percent or possibly more to the total runtime, depending heavily on the application.

For more information about analyzing lock profiling info, please see the chapters on JRockit Mission Control.

Enabling lock profiling with -XX:UseLockProfiling

For more extensive information about where a Java application spends its time, the flag -XX:UseLockProfiling=true can be used. This will instrument all locks and unlocks in the Java program and store information under which condition it was taken and the number of times it has been in use. Lock profiling can be augmented with information on native locks inside the JVM, such as code buffer locks or locks taken by the garbage collector. In order to get this information as well, use the flag -XX:UseNativeLockProfiling=true.

JRockit Mission Control can be used to analyze any JRockit Flight Recording with lock profiling information. Any lock in the Java program (or JVM) can be studied in detail, revealing, for example, how many times it was thin, fat, contended, lazily reserved, recursive, and so on.

Following is a screenshot of the lock profiling tab in JRockit Mission Control:

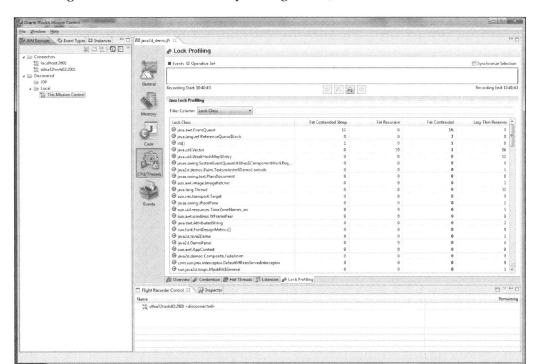

For further information about generating and using lock profiling information, please consult the JRockit Documentation.

JRCMD

The lock profile can also be controlled through the JRCMD command-line instrumentation tool that is part of the JRockit JDK. Whenever JRockit is run with the lock profiling flag enabled, JRCMD will respond to the commands `lockprofile_reset` and `lockprofile_print` that will respectively clear all lock performance counters and dump them to the console.

A detailed explanation on how to use JRCMD and its diagnostic commands is given in *Chapter 11, JRCMD*.

Setting thread stack size using -Xss

The `-Xss` flag specifies how much stack each thread should be allocated. Thread stacks are the memory areas allocated for each Java thread for their internal use. This is where the thread stores its execution state. It normally makes little sense to increase this size, unless there is plenty of recursion or a large amount of stack local information. For example, `-Xss:256k` will set the thread stack size to 256 KB.

The default stack size varies between platforms. Please refer to the official JRockit Documentation to find the default stack size for a particular platform.

`StackOverflowError`(s) in a Java program might be resolved by using larger thread stacks, unless they are the product of infinite recursion.

Controlling lock heuristics

Finally, there are several flags for controlling heuristics for the JRockit locks. One example would be the ability to disable the spinlock part of a fat lock (`-XX:UseFatSpin=false`) that is otherwise enabled by default. Another would be `-XX:UseAdaptiveFatSpin=true` that enables adaptive runtime feedback to adjust the behavior of the spinlock part of a fat lock. It is disabled by default.

There are also several default values for lazy unlocking heuristics, lock inflation, and lock deflation heuristics that can be modified. This is generally not needed. To satisfy the curious readers, some more advanced JRockit lock tweaks are described in *Chapter 5, Benchmarking and Tuning*. The JRockit documentation also contains information on all applicable command-line flags.

Summary

It is hard to code and debug in a parallel environment. Java can give us some help here, with its built-in mechanisms for synchronization and the data structures in the JDK. As synchronization is integrated into the Java language, using it comes naturally. Every object in Java may be a monitor object and used for synchronization. The downside is that if it is too easy to use synchronization, it might be used unnecessarily.

This chapter also covered the Java Memory Model that is meant to unify the parallel behavior of multithreaded Java across all hardware architectures, as well as the problems therein.

We covered the implementation of synchronization and threads in a virtual machine and went over the most common ways of implementing adaptive locks, using thin locks and fat locks. In an adaptive runtime, locks can be inflated or deflated, based on runtime feedback, turning one into another depending on contention level.

Some basic optimizations were explained; most notably the lazy unlocking framework and the shortcuts the code generator can provide, by running lock fusion.

At the end of the chapter, some common caveats were reviewed, the most important ones being the usage of the deprecated methods `Thread.stop`, `Thread.suspend` and `Thread.resume` and the anti-pattern known as double checked locking. The biggest trap of all when writing complex multithreaded Java applications is to not understand the Java Memory Model.

Finally, common JRockit command-line flags for instrumenting and examining threads and synchronization, as well as modifying the behavior of the JVM were introduced.

The next chapter will talk about the necessity of benchmarking an application, both in order to guard against regressions and to provide information that can be used for performance improvements. Benchmarking and instrumentation can only be done well if you are equipped with a good understanding of JVM internals and of how Java works. Hopefully, enough fundamentals for this, on code generation, memory management, and threads and synchronization has been provided by the chapters so far.

5
Benchmarking and Tuning

This chapter introduces benchmarking as a fundamental method to measure the performance of a Java application. It also covers the JVM side of performance, discussing how the virtual machine can be made to execute Java faster.

Benchmarking can, and should, be used to regression test an application during development, to ensure that new code modifications do not impact performance. Time and time again during our careers, we have seen unexpected performance regressions crop up from seemingly innocent changes. Continuous, preferably automated, benchmarking is the best way to prevent this from happening. Each software project should have a performance goal and benchmarking is the way to make sure that this goal is achieved.

Once we have discussed the hows and whys of good benchmarks, we will go on to discuss how to draw conclusions from what is measured and when there is a need to change the application or to just reconfigure the JVM by tuning parameters and setup. Tuning will be discussed in general terms, but concrete examples will be JRockit specific.

You will learn the following from this chapter:

- The relevance of benchmarking an application for finding bottlenecks, in order to avoid regressions and in order to make sure that performance goals for your software are achieved.

- How to create a benchmark appropriate for a particular problem set. This includes deciding what to measure and making sure that the benchmark actually does that. This also includes correctly extracting core application functionality into a smaller benchmark.

- How some of the various industry-standard benchmarks for Java work.

- How to use benchmark results to tune an application and the JVM for increased runtime performance.

- How to recognize bottlenecks in a Java program and how to avoid them. This includes standard pitfalls, common mistakes, and false optimizations.

Throughout this chapter, we will, among other things, discuss the SPEC benchmarks. SPEC (www.spec.org) is a non-profit organization that establishes, maintains, and endorses standardized benchmarks to evaluate performance for the newest generation of computing systems. Product and service names mentioned within this chapter are SPEC's intellectual property and are protected by trademarks and service marks.

Reasons for benchmarking

Benchmarking is always needed in a complex environment. There are several reasons for benchmarking, for example making sure that an application is actually usable in the real world or to detect and avoid performance regressions when new code is checked in. Benchmarking can also help optimize a complex application by breaking it down into more manageable problem domains (specialized benchmarks) that are easier to optimize. Finally, benchmarking should not be underestimated as a tool for marketing purposes.

Performance goals

Benchmarking is relevant in software development on all levels, from OEM or Java Virtual Machine vendors to developers of standalone Java applications. It is too often the case in software development that while the functionality goals of an application are well specified, no performance goals are defined at all. Without performance goals and benchmarks in place to track the progress of those goals, the end result may be stable but completely unusable. During our careers we have seen this many times, including during the development of business critical systems. If a critical performance issue is discovered too late in the development cycle, the entire application may need to be scrapped.

Performance benchmarking needs to be a fundamental part of any software development process—set a performance goal, create benchmarks for it, examine the benchmarking results, tune the application, and repeat until done.

Typically, in order to avoid these kinds of embarrassments, performance must be a fundamental requirement of a system throughout the entire software development process, and it needs to be verified with regular benchmarking. The importance of application performance should never be underestimated. Inadequate performance should be treated as any other bug.

Performance regression testing

An application that is developed without a good Quality Assurance (QA) infrastructure in place from day one is likely to be prone to bugs and instabilities. More specifically, an application without good functional unit tests that run whenever new code is checked in, is likely to break, no matter how well the new code has been reviewed. This is conventional wisdom in software engineering.

The first and foremost purpose of regression testing is to **maintain stability**. Whenever a new bug is discovered along with its fix, it is a good practice to check-in a **regression test** in the form of a **reproducer**, possibly based on code left over from debugging the problem. The ideal reproducer is a program with a few lines of code in a main function that breaks whatever was wrong with the system, but reproducers can also be more complex. It is almost always worth it to spend time turning a more complex reproducer into a regression test. Keeping the regression test running upon new source code check-ins will prevent the particular problem from recurring, potentially saving future hours of debugging an issue that has been fixed at least once already. Naturally, all functionality tests don't easily break down into simple regression tests or self-contained reproducers. Extensive runs of large, hard-to-setup applications are still often needed to validate stability.

The other side of regression testing is to **maintain performance**. For some reason this has not been as large a part of the conventional wisdom in software engineering as functionality testing, but it is equally important. New code might as easily introduce performance regressions as functional problems. The former is harder to spot, as performance degradations normally don't cause a program to actually break down and crash. Thus, including **performance tests** as part of the QA infrastructure makes a lot of sense. Discovering too late that application performance has gone down requires plenty of detective work to figure out exactly where the regression happened. Possibly this involves going over a large number of recent source code check-ins, recompiling the application at different changes and rerunning the affected application until the guilty check-in is spotted. Thus, integrating simple performance regression tests into the source code check-in criteria to guard against regressions makes as much sense as with unit tests or regression tests for functionality.

A good QA infrastructure should contain benchmarking for the purpose of detecting slowdowns as well as traditional functionality tests for the purpose of detecting bugs. A performance regression should be treated as no less serious than any other traditional bug.

Performance regression testing is also good for detecting unexplained performance boosts. While this might seem like a good thing, sometimes this indicates that a bug has been introduced, for example important code may no longer be executed. In general, all unexpected performance changes should be investigated and performance regression tests should trigger warnings both if performance unexpectedly goes up as well as if it goes down.

A cardinal rule when regression testing performance is to have as many points of measurements as possible, in order to quickly detect regressions. One per source control modification or check-in is ideal, if the infrastructure and test resources allow for it.

Let us, for a moment, disregard large and complex tests in the QA infrastructure and concentrate on simple programs that can serve as unit tests. While a unit test for functionality usually takes the form of a small program that either works or doesn't, a unit test for performance is a **micro benchmark.** A micro benchmark should be fairly simple to set up, it should run only for a short time, and it can be used to quickly determine if a performance requirement is reached. We will extensively discuss techniques for implementing micro benchmarks as well as more complex benchmarks later in this chapter.

Easier problem domains to optimize

Another reason for keeping a collection of relevant benchmarks around is that performance is a difficult thing to quantify—are we talking about high throughput or low latency? Surely we can't have both at the same time, or can we? If so, how can we ensure that our application is good enough in both these problem domains?

While running an application with a large set of inputs and workloads is a good idea for the general QA perspective, it might provide too complex a picture to illustrate where the application performs well and where it requires improvements.

A lot of trouble can be avoided if a program can be broken down into sub-programs that can be treated as individual benchmarks and if it can be made sure that all of them perform well. Not only is it easier to understand the different aspects of the performance of the program, it is also easier to work on improving these aspects on a simpler problem domain that only measures one thing at a time. Furthermore, it is also simpler to verify that code optimizations actually result in performance improvements. It should be common sense for an engineer that the fewer factors that are affected at once, the easier it is to measure and draw conclusions from the results.

Also, if a simple and self-contained benchmark correctly reflects the behavior of a larger application, performance improvements to the benchmarks will most likely be applicable to the larger application as well. In that case, working with the benchmark code instead of with the complete application may significantly speed up the development process.

Commercial success

Finally, a large number of industry-standard benchmarks for various applications and environments exist on the Internet. These are useful for verifying and measuring performance in a specific problem domain, for example, XML processing, decoding mp3s, or processing database transactions.

Industry benchmarks also provide standards with which to measure the performance of an application against competing products. Later in this chapter, we will introduce a few common industrial benchmarks, targeting both the JVM itself as well as Java applications on various levels in the stack.

 Marketing based on standard benchmark scores is naturally a rather OEM centric (or JVM centric) practice. It can also be important when developing a competing product in a market segment with many vendors. It is not as relevant for more unique third-party software.

Being the world leader on a recognized benchmark makes for good press release material and excellent marketing.

What to think of when creating a benchmark

Creating a benchmark, large as well as small, for an application without knowing much about the application behavior is a fairly futile exercise. In order to understand which benchmarks may be relevant for performance testing an application, the application needs to be well profiled.

There are several tools available for examining Java applications that either work by creating a special version of the application by inserting instrumentation code in the bytecode or through online analysis of an unmodified program. The JRockit Mission Control suite is an example of the latter. The next part of this book extensively explains how to use the JRockit Mission Control suite for profiling purposes.

Profiling an application will reveal things such as in which methods most of the run time is spent, common patterns in garbage collection, and which locks are often contended versus those that do not matter for overall performance.

Naturally, profiling or instrumenting an application does not necessarily require advanced tools. In some cases, it can be as simple as using `System.out.println` to occasionally output statistics to the console and examine them.

Once enough data about an application has been collected, suitable subsets of the application can hopefully be isolated for benchmarking. However, before creating a benchmark, we need to determine if it is relevant, and whether the benchmark and the application are subject to the same kind of performance issues or not.

When normalizing a benchmark against an application, **warm-up time** is an important factor to consider. If an application requires warm-up time to reach a steady state, as most server-side applications do, the benchmark might require this as well. Can the application be turned into a small self-contained benchmark with lower startup time, for the sake of simplicity? Is it still a case of comparing apples with apples if the benchmarking time is shrunk to five minutes from an application runtime of an hour, including warm-up, or does this kind of scaledown not work? Has the benchmark turned into an application with a completely different kind of behavior?

> An example of a complex application that needs to be broken down into benchmark domains is an application server, which typically is a collection of a vast number of subcomponents with varying functions.

The ideal benchmark is a small self-contained program that emulates a relevant part of an application. If this isn't easy to implement, maybe individual subsystems of the application can still be broken out as "black boxes" that can be fed with limited subsets of the input data. Then the subsystems may still form a simpler basis for measurements than the entire application, which might be hard to set up and require multiple input sources.

Measuring outside the system

For anything but very small benchmarks and small pieces of proof of concept code, it is usually a good idea to measure "outside the system". By that, we mean running the benchmark with some kind of external **driver**. The driver is an application independent of the actual benchmark code on which the performance evaluation is to take place.

Working with a driver usually means that the driver injects a workload into the benchmark, for example over the network. The entire response time, including network traffic, for the benchmark to run its payload code and respond is then measured.

Using a driver has the benefit that response times can be accurately measured without mixing up the measurements with the data generation or load generation. The driver can also be moved to another machine, and can be run under lower total load, to make sure that neither data generation nor load generation is a bottleneck in the benchmark.

The need for externalizing certain measurements can perhaps be more simply illustrated by a smaller example. Consider the following benchmark that measures how fast an implementation of the **MD5** message digest algorithm runs on random data:

```
import java.util.Random;
import java.security.*;

public class Md5ThruPut {
  static MessageDigest algorithm;
  static Random r = new Random();
  static int ops;

  public static void main(String args[]) throws Exception {
    algorithm = MessageDigest.getInstance("MD5");
    algorithm.reset();
    long t0 = System.currentTimeMillis();
    test(100000);
    long t1 = System.currentTimeMillis();
    System.out.println((long)ops / (t1 - t0) + " ops/ms");
  }

  public static void test(int size) {
    for (int i = 0; i < size; i++) {
      byte b[] = new byte[1024];
      r.nextBytes(b);
      digest(b);
    }
  }
}
```

```
    public static void digest(byte [] data) {
      algorithm.update(data);
      algorithm.digest();
      ops++;
    }
  }
```

If our goal was to only measure the performance of the MD5 algorithm, the previous benchmark is less than optimal, as the generation of the random input data is part of the time of an operation being measured. So, the total runtime will not only reflect the performance of the MD5 algorithm, but it will also reflect the performance of the random number generator. This was probably not intended. A better version of the MD5 benchmark would look like the following program:

```
import java.util.Random;
import java.security.*;

public class Md5ThruPutBetter {
  static MessageDigest algorithm;
  static Random r = new Random();
  static int ops;
  static byte[][] input;

  public static void main(String args[]) throws Exception {
    algorithm = MessageDigest.getInstance("MD5");
    algorithm.reset();
    generateInput(100000);
    long t0 = System.currentTimeMillis();
    test();
    long t1 = System.currentTimeMillis();
    System.out.println((long)ops / (t1 - t0) + " ops/ms");
  }

  public static void generateInput(int size) {
    input = new byte[size];
    for (int i = 0; i < size; i++) {
      input[i] = new byte[1024];
      r.nextBytes(input[i]);
    }
  }

  public static void test() {
    for (int i = 0; i < input.length; i++) {
      digest(input[i]);
    }
  }
```

```
public static void digest(byte [] data) {
    algorithm.update(data);
    algorithm.digest();
    ops++;
  }
}
```

Measuring several times

It is also of the utmost importance to collect a large amount of statistics before drawing any conclusions from a benchmark. The simplest way to do this is to repeat the measurements many times—do multiple benchmark runs. This way, a better grasp of the standard deviations in benchmark results can be obtained. Relevant benchmark scores can only be recorded if the size of deviation for the score in your benchmarking setup is known.

If possible, multiple runs should also be spread over multiple equivalent machines. That way, configuration errors can be discovered and removed from the data. For example, a forgotten load generator may be running on one of the benchmarking machines, contributing to lower scores. If all runs take place on that machine, erroneous measurements will be recorded.

Micro benchmarks

Micro benchmarks are benchmarks that contain a very small amount of code and only measure a small piece of functionality, for example, how quickly the JVM multiplies instances of `java.math.BigInteger` or how quickly it does AES encryption. Micro benchmarks are simple to write and often require just a single or a few function calls that contain the algorithmic payload.

Micro benchmarks are convenient, as they are simple to write and simple to run. They may prove invaluable in understanding a particular bottleneck in a very large application. They form an excellent backbone both for regression testing against performance loss and for optimizing the execution of known problems in the code, as discussed in the first section of this chapter.

We strongly encourage any application developer to keep a number of micro benchmarks around for regression testing, the same way as we encourage creating and keeping unit tests around when fixing bugs. In both cases, this is to verify that a resolved issue doesn't ever happen again and causes a regression.

If any large application could be reduced to a number of micro benchmarks, or at least "mini benchmarks", life would be easier. Sadly, for modern complex applications this is rarely the case. However, almost always, a fair (but for industrial purposes, incomplete) amount of micro benchmarks can be created from the understanding gained by profiling an application and figuring out what it does. The following code is a function from a real world micro benchmark that is used as a performance regression test for the JRockit JVM:

```java
public Result testArrayClear(Loop loop, boolean validate) {
  long count = 0;

  OpsPerMillis t = new OpsPerMillis("testArrayClear");
  t.start();
  loop.start();

  while (!loop.done()) {
    int[] intArray = new int[ARRAYSIZE];
    System.arraycopy(this.sourceIntArray, 0, intArray, 0, ARRAYSIZE);

    //Introduce side effects:
    //This call prevents dead code elimination
    //from removing the entire allocation.
    escape(intArray);
    count++;
  }
  t.end();
  return new OpsPerMillis(count, t.elapsed());
}
```

Java requires that objects are cleared on allocation, so that all their fields are initiated to their default values. The code optimizer in JRockit should be able to detect that the newly allocated array `intArray` is immediately and completely overwritten by data, and so, as it is non-volatile, need not be cleared. If, for some reason, this code optimization starts to fail, this benchmark will take longer to complete, and the QA infrastructure will trigger a warning while examining the result database.

Micro benchmarks can (and should) also be created from scratch for problems that are known to be performance-critical in an application. For example for an XML parser, it makes sense to create a small benchmark that operates on a set of auto-generated XML files of different sizes. For a math package that wants to use `java.math.BigDecimal`, it makes sense to write a couple of small self-contained applications that operate on `BigDecimal` instances.

Creating micro benchmarks that aren't valid or that don't produce useful results for the problem set is not just a waste of time and effort, but it is also potentially harmful if the benchmark is believed to accurately measure all important aspects of a problem. For example, testing an implementation of `java.util.HashMap` by just creating a `HashMap` and filling it up with data might not be good enough. How long does rehashing take? Extracting elements? What about collisions in `HashMaps` of different sizes?

Similarly, testing a `java.math.BigDecimal` implementation by just performing a large number of additions is almost certainly not good enough. What if there is a fatal performance flaw in the division algorithm?

 When creating a micro benchmark, the main rule is always to understand what you are measuring. Verify that the benchmark is valid and that the result is useful.

While the previous two examples might seem somewhat artificial, they are still examples of the kind of thinking that can lead you astray when creating benchmarks. A somewhat more relevant example might be the case of benchmarking an important synchronized operation in a class library. If the lock in the synchronized operation is contended in an application, this obviously won't show up in a single threaded micro benchmark. It may seem trivial that reducing the load from many to fewer threads fundamentally changes the lock behavior, but this is one of the main reasons that benchmarks fail to represent the real workload. Make sure that any lock in a benchmark is actually stressed by many threads, if this is the case in the real application.

Finally, it might make sense to try to eliminate parts of the runtime that aren't relevant to the problem from the benchmark. If you want to measure pure code performance for some algorithm, it probably makes little sense to create large numbers of objects and stress the garbage collector at the same time. Or at least, pick a good garbage collection strategy that won't interfere too much with the execution of the algorithm (large heap, no nursery, and optimized for throughput).

Micro benchmarks and on-stack replacement

Another common benchmarking mistake is to assume that any JVM will perform **on-stack replacement**, i.e. that any method can be optimized and replaced in the middle of its execution. As was also mentioned in Chapter 2 on adaptive code generation, all VMs do not perform on-stack replacement. Thus, if the entire payload of the benchmark exists in a loop in the `main` function, code replacement may never have a chance to take place, even though all relevant methods are flagged as hot and reoptimized into more optimal versions.

The following benchmark executes some kind of complex operation in each iteration of a loop in `main`. A JVM that, like JRockit, doesn't use on-stack replacement may well select `main` for optimization and make the operation in the loop execute a lot faster. However, since `main` never returns during the execution of the benchmark, the new code is never run. Moving the main benchmark operation into a separate method, and calling that method each iteration in the loop would solve the problem.

```
public class BadMicro {
  public static void main(String args[]) {
    long t0 = System.currentTimeMillis();
    for (int i = 0; i < 1000000; i++) {
      // complex benchmarking operation
    }
    long t1 = System.currentTimeMillis();
    System.out.println("Time: " + (t1 - t0) + " ms");
  }
}
```

Micro benchmarks and startup time

Recall, from the chapter on code generation, that JVM startup time is dependent on the time it takes to load initial classes and generate bootstrap code. If the intention is to measure only the runtime of the benchmark payload, startup time needs to be subtracted from the overall runtime. The problem can also be solved by having the benchmark perform enough operations so that startup time won't be a factor.

It is important to realize that if a micro benchmark does its work quickly and then exits, the JVM startup time contributes significantly to the overall benchmark runtime. A micro benchmark that measures the time it takes to multiply 100 floating point numbers will be all startup time and nothing else, but if it multiplies trillions of floating point numbers instead, startup time won't matter.

This point is somewhat more relevant for JVMs, such as JRockit, that lack interpreters and consequently start up slightly slower than JVMs that use bytecode interpretation for cold or previously unseen code.

So, it is important to start timing the micro benchmark only when the main workload function is called, and not from the start of `main`. Similarly, using an external library for timing that measures the time a Java program takes from start to finish will also implicitly factor in startup time.

 There may of course be cases where startup time is a very relevant thing to measure, even in a micro benchmark.

The runtime of the benchmark in the following example will almost certainly only be startup time, since the required time to get the VM up and running significantly exceeds the time required to add 1,000 random numbers.

```
import java.util.Random;

public class AnotherBadMicro {

    static Random r = new Random();
    static int sum;

    public static void main(String args[]) {
        long t0 = System.currentTimeMillis();
        int s = 0;
        for (int i = 0; i < 1000; i++) {
            s += r.nextInt();
        }
        sum = s;
        long t1 = System.currentTimeMillis();
        System.out.println("Time: " + (t1 - t0) + " ms");
    }
}
```

Give the benchmark a chance to warm-up

Different VMs use different optimization heuristics that trigger at different times. So, it might be possible to improve the quality of measurements and decrease deviation by doing a small amount of "dry runs" or **warm-up rounds** before starting the actual measurements. The warm-up gives the VM a chance to retrieve runtime feedback from the executing code and perform optimizations in relevant places, before measurements start. This ensures that the measurements are done in a steady optimized state.

Many industry standard benchmarks, such as the SPECjvm2008 suite mentioned later in this chapter, come with warm-up rounds built into the benchmark.

Deciding what to measure

Deciding what a benchmark should measure depends on the kind of application for which it should assist performance tuning.

Throughput

An application that is optimized for throughput has relatively simple needs. The only thing that matters is performing as many operations as possible in a given time interval. Used as a regression test, a throughput benchmark verifies that the application still can do x operations in y seconds on the baselined hardware. Once this criterion is fulfilled, the benchmark can be used to verify that it is maintained.

Again, as we have learned from the chapter on memory management, throughput alone is not usually a real life problem (except in, for example, batch jobs or offline processing). However, as can be easily understood, writing a benchmark that measures throughput is very simple. Its functionality can usually be extracted from a larger application without the need for elaborate software engineering tricks.

Throughput with response time and latency

Throughput benchmarks can be improved to more accurately reflect real life use cases. Typically, throughput can be measured with a fixed response time demand. The previously mentioned and easily extractable throughput benchmark can usually, with relatively small effort, be modified to accommodate this.

If a fixed response time is added as a constraint to a throughput benchmark, the benchmark will also factor in latencies into its problem set. The benchmark can then be used to verify that an application keeps it service level agreements, such as preset response times, under different amounts of load.

 The internal JRockit JVM benchmark suite used by JRockit QA contains many throughput benchmarks with response time requirements. These benchmarks are used to verify that the deterministic garbage collector fulfils its service level agreements for various kinds of workloads.

Low latency is typically more important to customers than high throughput, at least for client/server type systems. Writing relevant benchmarks for low latency is somewhat more challenging.

Normally, simple web applications can get through with response times on the order of a second or so. In the financial industry, however, applications that require pause time targets of less than 10 milliseconds, all the way down to single digits, are becoming increasingly common. A similar case can be made for the telecom industry that usually requests pause times of no more than 50 milliseconds. Both the customer and the JVM vendor need to do latency benchmarking in order to understand how to meet these challenges. For this, relevant benchmarks are required.

Scalability

Benchmarking for scalability is all about measuring resource utilization. Good scalability means that service levels can be maintained while the workload is increasing. If an application does not scale well, it isn't fully utilizing the hardware. Consequently, throughput will suffer. In an ideal world, linearly increasing load on the application should at most linearly degrade service levels and performance.

The following figure illustrates a nice example of near linear scalability on a per-core basis. It shows the performance in ops per second for an older version of the JRockit JVM running the well-known SPECjbb2005 benchmark. SPECjbb2005 is a multithreaded benchmark that gradually increases load on a transaction processing framework.

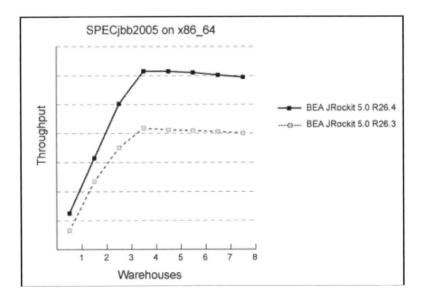

A SPECjbb run starts out using fewer load generating worker threads than cores in the physical machine (one thread per virtual warehouse in the benchmark). Gradually, throughout the run, threads are added, enabling more throughput (sort of an incremental warm-up). From the previous graph, we can see that adding more threads (warehouses) makes the throughput score scale linearly until the number of threads equals the number of cores, that is when saturation is reached. Adding even more warehouses maintains the same service level until the very end. This means that we have adequate scalability. SPECjbb will be covered in greater detail later in this chapter.

A result like this is good. It means that the application is indeed scalable on the JVM. Somewhat simplified, if data sets grow larger, all that is required to ensure that the application can keep up is throwing more hardware at it. Maintaining scalability is a complex equation that involves the algorithms in the application as well as the ability of the JVM and OS to keep up with increased load in the form of network traffic, CPU cycles, and number of threads executing in parallel.

While scalability is a most desirable property, as a target goal, it is usually enough to maximize performance up to the most powerful hardware specification (number of cores, and so on) that the application will realistically be deployed on. Optimizing for good scalability on some theoretical mega-machine with thousands of cores may be wasted effort. Focusing too much on total scalability may also run the risk of decreasing performance on smaller configurations. It is actually quite simple to construct a naive but perfectly scalable system that has horrible overall performance.

Power consumption

Power consumption is a somewhat neglected benchmarking area that is becoming increasingly more important. Power consumption matters, not only in embedded systems, but also on the server side if the server cluster is large enough. Minimizing power consumption is becoming increasingly important due to cooling costs and infrastructure issues. Power consumption is directly related to datacenter space requirements. **Virtualization** is an increasingly popular way to get more out of existing hardware, but it also makes sense to benchmark power consumption on the general application level.

Optimizing an application for low power consumption may, for example, involve minimizing used CPU cycles by utilizing locks with OS thread suspension instead of spin locks. It may also be the other way around—doing less frequent expensive transitions between OS and application can be the key to low power usage instead.

One might also take a more proactive approach by making sure during development that performance criteria can be fulfilled on lower CPU frequencies or with the application bound only to a subset of the CPUs in a machine.

Other issues

Naturally, these are just a few of the possible areas where application performance might need to be benchmarked. If performance for an application is important in a completely different area, another kind of benchmark will be more appropriate. Sometimes, just quantifying what "performance" should mean is surprisingly difficult.

Industry-standard benchmarks

The industry and the academic community continuously strive to provide generic benchmarks that emulate many common programmatic problems for Java. This is, of course, is of interest to JVM vendors and hardware vendors (to make sure that the JVM itself performs well and also for marketing purposes). However, the standardized benchmarks often provide some insights on tuning the JVM for a specific problem. It is recommended to have a look at some of the things that the industry tries to benchmark in order to understand how Java can be applied to different problem domains.

Naturally, standard benchmarks for anything and everything exists. Many software stacks are subject to performance measurement standardization, with organizations releasing benchmarks for everything from application servers down to network libraries. Finding and using industry-standard benchmarks is a relevant exercise for the modern Java developer.

This section is written from a somewhat JVM centric perspective. We are JVM developers and it has been in our interest to make sure that the JVM performs as well as possible on many configurations. So, we have chosen to highlight many standard benchmarks that JVM vendors tend to use. However, a lot of the effort we have spent optimizing the JVM has had very real impact on all kinds of Java applications. This is exactly the point that this chapter has tried to make so far — optimizing for good benchmarks that accurately represent real-world applications leads to real-world application performance.

Some of the benchmarks we mention, such as SPECjAppServer also work well as generic benchmarks for larger software stacks.

The SPEC benchmarks

The **Standard Performance Evaluation Corporation (SPEC)** is a non-profit organization that strives to maintain and develop a set of benchmarks that can be used to measure performance in several runtime environments on modern architectures. This section will quickly introduce the most well known SPEC benchmarks that are relevant to Java.

None of the SPEC benchmarks mentioned in this section are available for free, with the sole exception of SPECjvm2008.

The SPECjvm suite

SPECjvm—its first incarnation released in 1998 as SPECjvm98 (now retired)—was designed to measure the performance of a JVM/Java Runtime Environment. The original SPECjvm98 benchmark contained almost only single-threaded, CPU-bound benchmarks, which indeed said something about the quality of the code optimizations in a JVM, but little else. Object working sets were quickly, after a few years, deemed too small for modern JVMs. SPECjvm98 contained simple problem sets such as compression, mp3 decoding, and measuring the performance of the `javac` compiler.

The current version of SPECjvm, SPECjvm2008, is a modification of the original SPECjvm98 suite, including several new benchmarks, updated (larger) workloads, and it also factors in multi-core aspects. Furthermore, it tests out of the box settings for the JVM such as startup time and lock performance.

Several real-life applications have recently been added to SPECjvm, such as the Java database Derby, XML processors, and cryptography frameworks. Larger emphasis than before has been placed on warm-up rounds and on measuring performance from a steady state.

The venerable scientific computing benchmark SciMark has also been integrated into SPECjvm2008. The original standalone version of SciMark suffered from the on-stack replacement problem in that the `main` function contained the main work loop for each individual benchmark, which compromised, for example, the JRockit JVM and made it hard to compare its results with those of other virtual machines. This has been fixed in the SPECjvm2008 implementation.

The SPECjAppServer / SPECjEnterprise2010 suite

SPECjAppServer is a rather complex benchmark, and a rather good one, though hard to set up. It started its life called ECPerf and has gone through several generations—SPECjAppServer2001, SPECjAppServer2002, and SPECjAppServer2004. The latest version of this benchmark has changed names to SPECjEnterprise2010, but the basic benchmark setup is the same.

The idea behind this benchmark is to exercise as much of the underlying infrastructure, hardware, and software, as possible, while running a typical J2EE application. The J2EE application emulates a number of car dealerships interacting with a manufacturer. The dealers use simulated web browsers to talk to the manufacturer, and stock and transactions are updated and kept in a database. The manufacturing process is implemented using RMI. SPECjEnterprise2010 has further modernized the benchmark by introducing web services and more Java EE 5.0 functionality.

The SPECjAppServer suite is not just a JVM benchmark but it can also be used to measure performance in everything from server hardware and network switches to a particular brand of an application server. The publication guidelines specify that the complete stack of software and hardware needs to be provided along with the score. SPECjAppServer / SPECjEnterprise2010 is an excellent benchmark in that any part of a complete system setup can be measured against a reference implementation. This makes it relevant for everyone from hardware vendors to application server developers. The benchmark attempts to measure performance of the middle tier of the J2EE application, rather than the database or the data generator (driver).

The benchmark is quite complicated to set up and hard to tune. However, theoretically, once set up, it can run self-contained on a single machine, but is rather resource heavy, and this will not produce any interesting results.

A typical setup requires a **System Under Test (SUT)**, consisting of network infrastructure, application servers, and a database server, all residing on different machines. A driver, external to the test system, injects load into the setup. This is an example of the technique for measuring outside the system that was explained earlier in this chapter. In SPECjEnterprise2010, one of the more fundamental changes, compared to earlier versions, is that database load has been significantly reduced so that other parts of the setup (the actual application on the application server) becomes more relevant for performance.

In a complete setup, the performance of everything, from which network switch to which RAID solution the disk uses, matters. For a JVM, SPECjAppServer is quite a good benchmark. It covers a large Java code base and the execution profile is spread out over many long stack traces with no particular "extra hot" methods. This places strict demands on the JIT to do correct inlining. It can no longer look for just a few bottleneck methods and optimize them.

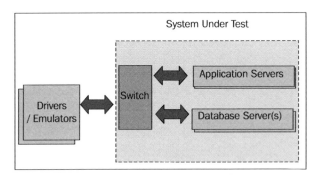

As of SPECjAppServer2004, in order to successfully run the benchmark, a transaction rate (TxRate) is used for work packet injection. This is increased as long as the benchmark can keep up with the load, and as soon as the benchmark fails, the maximum TxRate for the benchmark system can thus be determined. This is used to compute the score.

The realism is much better in newer generations of the benchmark. Application servers use more up-to-date standards and workloads have been increased to fit modern architectures. Support for multiple application servers and multiple driver machines has also been added. Measurements have also been changed to more accurately reflect performance.

The SPECjbb suite

SPECjbb is probably one of the most widespread Java benchmarks in use today. It is interesting because it has been used frequently in academic research, and has been a point of competition between the big three JVM providers, Oracle, IBM, and Sun Microsystems. The big three, in cooperation with hardware vendors, have taken turns publishing press releases announcing new world records.

SPECjbb has existed in two generations, SPECjbb2000 (retired), and lately SPECjbb2005, that is still in use. SPECjbb, similar to SPECjAppServer, emulates a transaction processing system in several tiers, but is run on one machine in a self-contained application.

SPECjbb has done the Java world some good in that a lot of optimizations that JVMs perform, especially code optimizations, have been driven by this benchmark, producing beneficial spin-off effects. There are also many examples of real-life applications that the quest for SPECjbb scores has contributed performance to—for example, more efficient garbage collection and locks.

> Here are some examples of functionality and optimizations in the JRockit JVM that are a direct result of trying to achieve high scores on SPECjbb. There are many more. All of these optimizations have produced measurable performance increases for real-world applications, outside the benchmark:
>
> - Lazy unlocking (biased locking)
> - Better heuristics for object prefetching
> - Support for large pages for code and heap
> - Support for non-contiguous heaps
> - Improvements to array handling such as `System.arraycopy` implementations, clear-on-alloc optimizations, and assignments to arrays
> - Advanced escape analysis that runs only on parts of methods

A downside of SPECjbb is that it is, in fact, quite hardware-dependent. SPECjbb is very much memory bound, and just switching architectures to one with a larger L2 cache will dramatically increase performance.

Another downside to SPECjbb is that it is possible to get away with only caring about throughput performance. The best scores can be achieved if all execution is occasionally stopped and then, massive amounts of parallel garbage collection is allowed to take place for as long as it takes to clean the heap.

SPECjbb2005 has also been used as the basis for the SPECpower_ssj2008 benchmark that utilizes the same transaction code, but with an externalized driver. It is used to quantify transactions per Watt at different levels of load, to provide a basis for measuring power consumption.

Here's another benchmarking anecdote. Sometimes an optimization designed for a benchmark is only that and has no real world applications. An example from JRockit is calls to `System.currentTimeMillis`. This is a Java method that goes to native and finds out what the system time is, expressed in milliseconds since January 1, 1970. Because this typically involves a system call or a privileged operation, very frequent calls to `System.currentTimeMillis` could be a bottleneck on several platforms.

Irritatingly enough, it turned out that calls to `System.currentTimeMillis` made up several percent of the total runtime of SPECjbb2000. On some platforms, such as Windows and Solaris, quick workarounds to obtain system time were available, but not on Linux. On Linux, JRockit got around the bottleneck by using its own signal-based OS timers instead. The Linux JVM uses a dedicated thread to catch an OS-generated signal every 10 milliseconds. Each time the signal is caught, a local time counter is increased. This makes timer granularity a little worse than with the system timer. However, as long as the timer is safe (that is, it cannot go backwards) this maintains Java semantics and SPECjbb runs much faster.

Today on JRockit versions for Linux, native-safe timers are disabled. If you, for some weird reason, have problems with the performance of `System.currentTimeMillis` in your application, they can still be enabled with the hidden flag `-XX:UseSafeTimer=true`. We have never heard of anyone who needs this.

SipStone

SipStone (`www.sipstone.org`) provides a suite of benchmarks that are interesting for the telecom industry, making it possible to benchmark implementations of the **Session Initiation Protocol (SIP)**.

Real life scenarios for testing telecom applications are provided. One of the benchmarks used is Proxy200, where the SIP application is provided by the benchmark user. Typically, the benchmark user is a SIP server provider. This benchmark is interesting as it provides a standardized proxy for testing SIP performance.

The DaCapo benchmarks

The DaCapo (`www.dacapobench.org`) suite is a free benchmark suite created by the DaCapo group, an academic consortium that does JVM and runtime research. The idea behind the initiative is to create a benchmark with more GC-intensive loads and more modern Java applications.

The benchmark suite includes, for example, a parser generator, a bytecode optimizer, a Java based Python interpreter, and some of the non-GUI unit tests for the Eclipse IDE. It is fairly simple to run and makes for an interesting collection of benchmarks that stresses some typical applications of Java.

Real world applications

Of course, one should not underestimate the usefulness of keeping a library of real world applications around for benchmarking, if they can exercise relevant areas of your code. For example, for developers of a Java web server, including a couple of free Java web servers in the benchmarking matrix is probably a good idea to make sure that competitive advantage is maintained over them.

The authors of this book, and their JVM development teams use, with kind permission, a collection of customer applications that have caused performance issues with JRockit over the years. This enables us to better understand performance and make sure that no regressions appear. These applications have been turned into benchmarks that are executed in known environments in nightly or weekly performance runs. Smaller benchmarks are run more often.

Having "thrashatons" for a development team every now and then is a fun and useful activity. Have the developers spend a few days deploying their product on every kind of relevant (and not so relevant) compatible application platform downloaded from the web. This helps weed out bugs and performance problems. While, naturally, finding thrashaton fodder for a JVM or a compiler is easy (the input is any Java program), there is still plenty of source out there for testing more specialized platforms. Also look for load generators, network tests, and other platform-agnostic products that can stress an application until unknown issues pop up.

Our recommendation is always to keep a large "zoo" of applications around, for platform testing. If your platform is a J2EE application, deploy it on several application servers. If it is a mathematical package, run it with several JVMs and different `java.lang.math` implementations, and so on. Storage is cheap—so never throw anything away. Test, benchmark, improve, and repeat!

The dangers of benchmarking

It is sometimes all too easy to focus too much on the results of a particular benchmark and let this "tunnel vision" take over all performance work.

It is very important that a wide selection of standard industry benchmarks exists, as they will be used by anyone from hardware vendors to undergraduate researchers, for ultimately increasing performance for various runtimes and applications. Conclusions drawn, given a benchmark setup, can have wide-ranging implications.

One danger is, of course, if a mainstream benchmark gets too well adopted. Classic examples here are the SPECjvm benchmark suite and later the SPECjbb benchmark.

To put it bluntly, if a graduate student can run a benchmark from his workstation with a simple command line, the problems it addresses will get much love and research. If not, they won't. SPECjbb has a simple command line, SPECjAppServer doesn't. SPECjAppServer, in itself, is an excellent benchmark that pretty much stresses any desired portion of a Java platform stack and can be used to test everything from application servers to network cards in a realistic environment. SPECjAppServer requires quite a lot of hardware and has an extensive hard-to-configure setup. Consequently, few relevant publications have been released using SPECjAppServer in the academic world, but plenty of SPECjbb results are still published, even though it may not be that relevant for all aspects of modern performance research.

Tuning

Once a working benchmark is in place in your test infrastructure, be it a version of an application that can be run in a controlled environment or a subset of the algorithmic problem that an application tries to solve, regression testing can be performed. This ensures that no performance is lost during future code alterations.

Another purpose of the benchmark is to provide a small self-contained sandbox that can be used to tune the runtime environment in order to provide optimal performance for that particular application and to make sure that performance goals set for the software project are reached.

Whereas, in some cases, it may be obvious from benchmarking that parts of an application need to be rewritten using more efficient algorithms, sometimes it may just be enough to provide a more optimal runtime environment by tuning the JVM parameters.

Out of the box behavior

The previous three chapters on code generation, memory management, and threads and synchronization have all, quite strongly, made the case for adaptive runtime environments. All the feedback that a runtime collects can be put to powerful use by the JVM for optimization.

Indeed, in Utopia, an adaptive runtime would never need tuning at all, as the runtime feedback alone would determine how the application should behave for any given scenario at any given time. Sadly enough, a human always knows more about some aspects of application runtime and lifecycles than a machine can deduce. The machine may beat the human at things such as picking the hottest methods to optimize first, and at inflating and deflating locks depending on the current contention level. However, if the human knows, for example, that the heap never needs to be resized, as it is large enough for the application, or that heap compaction should never take place because fragmentation won't ever become much of an issue, the JVM may need to be told that from the start for optimal performance. On the other hand, the human may think he knows more than the machine and misguidedly change the runtime configuration for the worse. Playing around with a JVM configuration with too little information is always dangerous and strongly discouraged.

In-depth data about application behavior can (and should) be collected by running thorough profiling analyses on the application. JRockit provides an excellent selection of tools for non-intrusive profiling of Java programs that can be used to do low cost live recordings of an application. The recordings can then be analyzed offline.

Before attempting to tune the performance of an application, it is important to know where the bottlenecks are. That way no unnecessary effort is spent on adding complex optimizations in places where it doesn't really matter. Again, this is a lesson learned from our previous discussions on adaptive runtimes. For example, if network overhead is the main performance bottleneck (as revealed by latency analysis in a JRockit Flight Recorder), it might be too early to turn the ten lines of code that comprise a very readable search algorithm into one hundred lines of "more optimal" code. Low hanging fruit should always be handled first, to avoid introducing unnecessary complexity to the application.

In some cases, when the analysis is finished, no actual modification of the application needs to be done. The analysis might reveal that the problem is such that some runtime option can be added to handle it, helping our imperfect non-out of the box world a bit. However, before we introduce command-line flags that can modify anything and everything, we want to stress that good out of the box behavior is a research area that always gets plenty of attention, both by Oracle and by other JVM vendors. For JRockit, dramatic improvements have taken place for each new release. It makes sense to optimize out of the box behavior to make it easier for the customer to achieve the performance he needs and to off-load support, who instead should be concentrating on actual bugs.

A final word of warning—modifying JVM behavior through command-line switches may produce unexpected results and functionality lock-ins and should always be done with plenty of caution. A combination of switches that work well for performance in a particular version of a JVM may very well be harmful instead in a new version of the same JVM. Typically, JRockit flags that start with –XX can never be relied on to be unchanged between releases.

What to tune for

Recollect from Chapter 3 that no matter what tasks the underlying JVM performs, tuning is universal. We can, for example, tune for throughput, low pause times, or real-time performance, the latter being a stronger variant of low pause times.

While the general aspects of this have already been covered in previous chapters, we will proceed to go over a selection of important JVM parameters that may be beneficial to use for reconfiguration. This section covers JRockit parameters only, as the innermost workings of other JVMs are beyond the scope of this book. However, while parameters vary between different JVMs, some of the techniques presented below, such as modifying heap size, are relevant on all runtimes.

Before attempting to use any of the switches, the JRockit Documentation, particularly the *JRockit Diagnostics Guide*, should be consulted to ensure that their full implications are understood. Much insight can also be gained by using the JRockit Mission Control suite to do recordings before and after a parameter change, to understand how the overall runtime behavior was affected.

In the interest of keeping this section fairly short, extensive examples of using the mentioned flags will not be included. Extensive examples, along with default values for different configurations, are available in the JRockit Documentation and the *JRockit Diagnostics Guide*.

Flags and options presented here are specific to the R28 versions of the JRockit JVM. Earlier versions may have different flags for doing the same thing, or lack the functionality altogether. Please consult the JRockit Documentation to find out what is supported for a particular JRockit version.

Tuning memory management

This section covers command-line parameters specific to the memory management system and garbage collector.

Heap sizes

Recollect from Chapter 3 that the most fundamental way to tune the memory system is to specify initial heap size using the `-Xms` flag and maximum heap size using the `-Xmx` flag.

While tuning for real time, it is usually helpful to set both values to a fixed maximum size that the system has enough resources to allocate. Thus, unnecessary heap resizing, a somewhat costly process, will be prevented from occurring during run time.

Example: `java -Xms1024M -Xmx1024M <application>` (set both the initial and maximum heap size to 1 GB)

The GC algorithm

Furthermore, pick a GC algorithm that makes sense for the current application. For real-time performance targets, do not forget to specify a service level agreement, using the `-XpauseTarget` option.

For batch processing and throughput optimization, `-XgcPrio:throughput` is the way to go.

Example: `java -XgcPrio:pausetime -XpauseTarget:250ms` (set up GC optimizing for low pause times with a pause time target of maximum 250 milliseconds)

Compaction

It is inevitable that a heap gets fragmented over time. Traditionally, the "stone age" approach to handling fragmentation for a long running program has been to restart the server during a nightly service interval. This contributes to latencies, generates downtime, and costs CPU cycles. However, experience has shown that by using partial compaction, which is the default in JRockit, the problem is handled very well. The JRockit compaction heuristics are mostly self-tuning.

One of the worst GC bottlenecks is compaction. Since compaction is not a fully concurrent operation, if anything is known about fragmentation and object sizes (for example from JRockit Flight Recorder data), it might be beneficial to tune compaction as well. In JRockit, this can be done through the `-XXcompaction` flag and its arguments.

The compaction algorithm in JRockit divides the heap into a number of equally large parts. Each of these is subject to separate compaction that occasionally may stop the world. The default is to use 4,096 heap parts, but it might be beneficial to increase this number if compaction is too disruptive or decrease it if compaction fails to keep up with fragmentation. Typically, for strategies other than throughput, GC compaction areas are dynamically sized depending on how busy they are. Setting the number of heap parts is done by passing the subcommand `heapParts` to `-XXcompaction`.

Compaction in JRockit is divided into **internal** and **external compaction** (the latter also referred to as **evacuation**). Internal compaction never moves objects outside a heap part, but completely compacts that heap part by moving objects to its beginning. External compaction works on several heap parts and strives to move objects to the start of the heap as is needed to keep overall fragmentation down. Consequently, external compaction is less concurrent and requires stopping the world for longer periods of time.

Compaction takes place inside a sliding window that gradually moves over the entire heap. Currently, JRockit interleaves the use of internal and external compaction between GCs. If one GC does internal compaction, the next does external compaction, and so on.

The maximum percentages of the heap to compact for internal and external compaction per GC compaction event can be set with the `internalPercentage` flag for internal compaction and `externalPercentage` flag for external compaction.

If the object allocation strategies in the program are well known and latencies need to be decreased, the flag `-XXcompaction:enable=false` will turn off all compaction in the JRockit garbage collector. Before enabling this option, JRockit Mission Control should be used to establish that fragmentation is not an issue. Turning off compaction will dramatically reduce the need for memory management to halt Java execution. However, death by fragmentation is a likely outcome for large and long running applications that run with compaction switched off. This will manifest itself as `OutOfMemoryError`s.

If, on the other hand, latencies aren't an issue and optimizing for throughput is the only concern, `-XXcompaction:full` will force full heap compaction at every GC, keeping fragmentation at a minimum but at the cost of large pause times. Enabling full compaction may be a dangerous experiment. Performing full compaction for every GC can, in some cases, be so slow and cause such long pauses that throughput is reduced to unusable levels anyway.

 Full compaction is also sometimes referred to as **exceptional compaction** in the JRockit Mission Control suite.

In GCs that optimize for short pausetimes, compaction can be aborted if the world has been stopped for too long. The default in throughput GC is not to allow this, in the interest of battling fragmentation. Abortable compactions can be forced by using the `-XXcompaction:abortable` flag.

There are several additional ways to tune compaction that are beyond the scope of this chapter. Please refer to the *JRockit Diagnostics Guide* for in-depth guidance. Finally, note that playing around with compaction parameters when tuning for real-time, might result in larger performance deviations and in less deterministic pause times. Some of the ways to tune compaction are:

Example: `java –XXcompaction:enable=false <application>` (turn off all compaction)

Example: `java –XXcompaction:full <application>` (compact as much as possible, optimizing for throughput)

Example: `java –XXcompaction:internalPercentage=1.5, externalPercentage=2,heapParts=512 <application>` (use 512 heap parts. Use up to two percent of the heap per external compaction and up to 1.5 percent of the heap per internal compaction)

Example: `java –XgcPrio:throughput –XXcompaction:abortable=true` (use throughput oriented GC, but soften the latency blow somewhat by allowing abortable compaction)

Tweaking System.gc

The flag `–XX:AllowSystemGC` may be used to turn calls to `System.gc` into no-ops. For example `java –XX:AllowSystemGC=false <application>` is used to turn any `System.gc` call into a no-op. This can be a quick fix for applications that frequently call `System.gc` in ways detrimental to their performance. The default is to allow `System.gc`, which may or may not do full heap garbage collections when invoked. Please see *Chapter 3, Adaptive Memory Management*, and the section *Common bottlenecks and how to avoid them* at the end of this chapter for more information.

For high throughput setups, on the other hand, `System.gc` can be made to force the JVM to do a full heap garbage collection each time it is called. This is done with the `–XX:FullSystemGC` flag. This flag should be used with caution

Example: `java –XX:FullSystemGC=true <application>` (force any `System.gc` to perform a full heap garbage collection)

Nursery size

Recall from Chapter 3 that nurseries are the young generations of short-lived objects on the heap. Nurseries are normally adaptively resized by the JVM. Specifying the size of the nursery in the heap, by using the `-Xns` (nursery size) parameter, may be an option if the application uses generational GC and produces large amounts of temporary objects. In that case the size of the nursery should be increased. When tuning for high throughput, it is most likely a good idea to skip generational GCs altogether and run with `-XgcPrio:throughput`.

Example: `java -Xns:10M <application>` (set the nursery size to 10 MB of heap)

GC strategies

If, for some reason, the adaptive garbage collection strategy changes are too frequent and incur an overhead, strategy changes can be disabled altogether by using the command-line option `-XXdisableGCHeuristics`. Compaction and nursery size heuristics aren't affected.

 This flag works for JRockit versions prior to R28 only. As of JRockit R28, GC heuristic changes are disabled altogether or are far less intrusive, so this flag has been deprecated.

Thread local area size and large objects

Recollect that each thread allocates objects in a thread local area that is promoted to the heap when full. The size of the TLA can be controlled by the flag `-XXtlaSize`. The JVM may allocate larger objects directly on the heap, if they don't fit into a TLA or would lead to too much waste of space within the TLA. This is to prevent the thread local areas from filling up too quickly and incurring extra overhead.

Large objects can be a problem for an application, and, sometimes, if something is known about common object sizes in the running application, it helps to play around with various TLA settings.

Example: `java -XXtlaSize:min=2k,preferred=8k <application>` (allocate a preferred size of 8 KB for the TLAs, but down to 2 KB is also acceptable)

In JRockit versions earlier than R28, large objects were allocated immediately on the heap and never in a TLA. A flag called -XXlargeObjectLimit was provided to tell JRockit the minimum number of bytes an object should be of in order to be treated as "large". The default was 2 KB. JRockit post R28 uses a **waste limit** for TLA space instead. This constrains the amount of TLA space that can be thrown away for each TLA when large objects are allocated and is a more flexible solution.

The R28 allocation algorithm now works like this—JRockit tries to allocate every object regardless of its size in the current TLA. If it doesn't fit and the waste limit is less than the space left in the TLA, the object goes directly on the heap. Otherwise, JRockit will "waste" the rest of this TLA and try to allocate the object in a new TLA or directly on the heap, depending on the size of the object.

Example: `java –XXlargeObjectLimit:16k <application>` (raise the large object limit to 16 KB, only pre R28)

Example: `java –XXtlaSize:min=16k,preferred=256k,wasteLimit=8k <application>` (TLAs should be 256 KB, but down to 16 KB is acceptable. Never waste more than 8 KB of a TLA—rather allocate too large objects directly on the heap)

Tuning for large objects will be covered in further detail in the "*Common Bottlenecks*" section of this chapter. It suffices to say that there is a natural trade-off between heap fragmentation and the overhead of frequently allocating new TLAs—constantly promoting objects to the heap from TLAs with lots of space left in them is wasteful and defeats the lock-free purpose of TLA allocation.

Number of GC threads

JRockit, out of the box, tends to assume that it has the computer all to itself, and strives to increase the number of parallel GC threads to a limit bounded by the OS and the physical hardware. Typically, JRockit uses as many GC threads as there are cores in the machine. If this is inappropriate for some reason, for example if other applications need CPU time on the machine as well, the number of GC threads can be explicitly set with the -XXgcThreads option.

Using too few GC threads introduces the risk that the garbage collector cannot keep up with the growing set of dead objects. In extreme cases, this will lead to OutOfMemoryErrors being thrown. However, it is more likely that in order to save itself, the GC repeatedly needs to do emergency full heap garbage collections. This leads to stalls and unacceptable latencies.

Example: `java –XXgcThreads:4 <application>` (use four GC threads)

NUMA and CPU affinity

Most modern operating systems have some notion of changing or setting processor affinity for a process, making it possible to lock that process to one or more particular CPUs. In NUMA environments, this might be most important, as better locality can be achieved by binding the JVM process to a small number of NUMA nodes. The trade-off is of course less dynamism and not being able to use some of the memory efficiently. The application behavior must be very well understood before trying to modify the process affinity.

The flag `-XX:BindToCPUs` can be used to force JRockit to only use certain CPUs in the machine.

Example: `java -XX:BindToCPUs=0,2 <application>` (used to set JRockit CPU affinity to CPU 0 and 2 only)

For NUMA, a separate affinity flags exists for NUMA nodes (`-XX:BindToNumaNodes`) as well as a flag that can control the NUMA memory allocation policy. This enables the user to specify if JRockit should interleave allocated pages evenly across all NUMA nodes or bind them in the local node where the memory allocation takes place. A "preferred local" policy can also be selected, that is JRockit should try to use the local node, but interleaved allocation is also fine.

Example: `java -XX:NumaMemoryPolicy=strictlocal <application>` (force local NUMA allocation. Other values are `preferredlocal` and `interleave`)

Tuning code generation

This section covers parameters specific to the code generator.

Call profiling

By using the flag `-XX:UseCallProfiling`, the JRockit code generator can be told to add additional instrumentation to code while it is JITed, in order to collect data for more intelligent decisions about inlining once a method is found to be a candidate for optimization.

Normally, the execution overhead in JIT code is deemed too large to efficiently allow arbitrary instrumentation code. However, if the application will run for a long time, most methods where runtime is spent are likely to be optimized and won't have any instrumentation code left in them. The resulting optimized methods will potentially run faster if the optimizer has extra call profiling information to base inlining decisions on.

This flag is disabled by default, but may be enabled by default for future versions of JRockit. It is especially beneficial for an application with long call chains.

Example: `java -XX:UseCallProfiling=true <application>` (enable call profiling as an additional way of collecting hotness information)

Changing the number of optimization threads

Code optimization in JRockit is a fairly aggressive operation that uses plenty of CPU time and memory. However, it might not make sense to spend too many CPU cycles doing it. Recall from Chapter 2 that the number of code generation threads and the number of optimization threads in the JRockit JIT compiler can be controlled.

If there are CPU cycles to spare and the application is to be deployed on a large multi-core platform, steady state might be achieved faster by enabling a larger number of code optimization threads.

The number of code optimization threads can be set with the `-XX:OptThreads` option.

The default is one optimization thread only. Benchmarking should be made to establish if more optimization threads are more efficient. Eventually, the application will reach a steady state anyway. The number of JIT compiler threads can be modified in similar fashion.

Example: `java -XX:JITThreads=2 <application>` (use two JIT compiler threads instead of one, which is the default)

Example: `java -XX:OptThreads=2 <application>` (use two optimization threads instead of one, which is the default)

Turning off code optimizations

Sometimes, code optimization, being a fairly CPU-intensive operation, may incur unacceptable overhead, either in the form of too long warm-up periods or by introducing latency spikes. All code optimizations can be switched off with the `-XnoOpt` flag. This will lead to a much more predictable JVM behavior. However, severe performance penalties for the executing code should be expected. Optimizations can also be turned off after a specific amount of time (in seconds), by using the `-XX:DisableOptsAfter` switch.

Example: `java -XnoOpt <application>` (disable all code optimizations)

Example: `java -XX:DisableOptsAfter=600 <application>` (disable all code optimization after 10 minutes of runtime)

Tuning locks and threads

When it comes to lock tuning, it is often a good idea to leave well enough alone and not modify the default behavior. It is rare that the user can add anything by modifying lock heuristics. It is more often the case that performance gains can come from modifying the application. However, for the sake of completeness, this section presents some switches that control lock behavior in JRockit.

Lazy unlocking

Recall from Chapter 4 that lazy unlocking is beneficial in an environment where a particular lock is frequently taken and released by the same thread. If we know that the same thread will soon reacquire the lock, it makes little sense to release it for just a short period of time.

Lazy unlocking is enabled by default in JRockit (except when running with deterministic GC on versions earlier than Java 1.6). It can be explicitly turned on and off with the flag `-XX:UseLazyUnlocking`.

Example: `java -XX:UseLazyUnlocking=false <application>` (explicitly turn off lazy unlocking)

Class banning, i.e. the heuristic that stops a certain class from being used for lazy unlocking after too many erroneous guesses, can be switched off with the flag `-XX:UseLazyUnlockingClassBan=false`.

Enforcing thread priorities

The `java.lang.Thread` class supports different priorities for thread execution, but they are rarely implemented by the VM by default. This is because the potential for trouble tends to be greater than the gain. Messing around with thread scheduling policies at the Java level might lead to unforeseen problems.

JRockit supports forcing the VM to respect thread priorities set through the `setPriority` method of `java.lang.Thread`. The default is to ignore thread priorities, but they can be enabled with the `-XX:UseThreadPriorities` flag.

Example: `java -XX:UseThreadPriorities=true <application>` (enable thread priority changes)

Thresholds for inflation and deflation

Finally, advanced users may find it useful to tune the heuristic thresholds for lock deflation and lock inflation, i.e. the criteria with which a lock is turned from thin to fat or vice versa.

Example: `java -XX:ThinLockConvertToFatThreshold=100 <application>` (no more than 100 iterations are allowed to run in the thin lock spin loop before a lock is inflated)

The JRockit spin loop isn't pure CPU wastage, as it does some kind of micropause or yield each iteration. Naturally, specifying a limit for the number of iterations in the spinlock loop modifies timing in completely incomparable ways between architectures and CPUs.

Example: `java -XX:UseFatLockDeflation=false <application>` (never deflate a fat lock. The default is `true`)

Example: `java -XX:FatLockDeflationThreshold=10 <application>` (deflate a fat lock to thin again after 10 uncontended entries)

Recall from the last chapter that a spinlock is part of the JRockit fat lock implementation. It is used as a "second chance" when a lock is inflated, but only for a short period of time before entering the real fat lock. This behavior can be modified as well.

Example: `java -XX:UseFatSpin=false <application>` (never use a spinlock as part of a fat lock)

Example: `java -XX:UseAdaptiveFatSpin=false <application>` (never try to adaptively change the spinlock part of a fat lock based on runtime feedback)

There are several other advanced flags for controlling lock heuristics. For more information, please refer to the *JRockit Diagnostics Guide*. In general, be careful when messing around with lock settings—it can produce strange and unexpected results.

Generic tuning

Finally, we present some switches and aspects that have to do with tuning and don't fit into a particular category or span several.

Compressed references

Recall from the chapter on memory management that compressed references are enabled by default on 64-bit platforms for most heap sizes. So, they shouldn't need to be configured manually. JRockit will, by default, enable different flavors of compressed references depending on maximum heap size for all heap sizes up to 64 GB. This can be explicitly overridden. Consult the documentation to decide whether this is appropriate or not.

Example: `java -XXcompressedRefs:enable=false <application>` (never use compressed references)

Example: `java –XXcompressedRefs:enable=true,size=64GB <application>`
(enable compressed references supporting heaps up to 64 GB)

Large pages

Large pages can be used for both code buffers and for the heap. This can be controlled by using the `–XX:UseLargePagesForCode` and `–XX:UseLargePagesForHeap` options. The default is to not use large pages for anything.

If appropriate support for large pages is enabled and available in the underlying OS, having the JVM use large pages reduces TLB misses to a large extent. On memory intensive applications, it is not unusual to achieve a performance gain of 10-15 percent.

We definitely recommend trying out large pages for any large long running application to see if there is a performance gain. If the underlying operating system doesn't support large pages, JRockit will print a warning and fall back to normal behavior.

Example: `java –XX:UseLargePagesForCode=true <application>` (use large pages for code buffers)

Example: `java –XX:UseLargePagesForHeap=true <application>` (use large pages for the heap)

Common bottlenecks and how to avoid them

As in most of our chapters so far, we will finish by reviewing a few common mistakes and false optimizations. In the benchmarking world, this is all about understanding the bottlenecks and the anti patterns that frequently show up in application code and how they can be avoided.

Care should be taken that any instrumentation is not too intrusive. If, for example, the chosen instrumentation tool inserts extra bytecode operations all over the application code, the overall timing of the program can change completely. This may make the resulting profile useless for drawing any kinds of conclusions about the original program behavior. While small bytecode instrumenters may be handy for things like implementing counters for specific kinds of events, they rarely produce a true execution profile. Bytecode instrumenters also make it necessary to recompile and restart the application. The JRockit Mission Control suite, on the other hand, can plug in at runtime and profiles the application with virtually no extra overhead.

A benchmark or instrumentation result can provide great insights into why an application contains performance bottlenecks. Over the years, the authors of this book have examined many applications to determine why they aren't running as fast as they should. Some findings keep recurring, and the following section provides information on several common areas that cause performance problems and what practices should be avoided or used with caution when programming Java.

The –XXaggressive flag

From one time to another we discover customers using the undocumented and experimental –XXaggressive flag for JRockit. This flag is a wrapper for other flags that tell JRockit to perform at high speed and try to reach a stable state as soon as possible. The cost of this is more resource use at startup. The parameters that this option modifies are subject to change from release to release. Because of its experimental nature, the frivolous use of –XXaggressive is discouraged. However, it can be useful to try as one of many different setups when doing profiling. Use this flag at your own risk.

Too many finalizers

Finalizers are, as we have already discussed in Chapter 3, unsafe in that they can resurrect objects and interfere with the GC. They usually incur processing overhead in the JVM as well.

Objects waiting for finalization have to be kept track of separately by the garbage collector. There is also call overhead when the `finalize` method is invoked (not to mention the execution time of the `finalize` method itself, if it does something fairly complex). Finalizers should simply be avoided.

Too many reference objects

As with finalizers, the garbage collector has to treat soft, weak, and phantom references specially. Although all of these can provide great aid in, for example, simplifying a cache implementation, too many live `Reference` objects will make the garbage collector run slower. A `Reference` object is usually a magnitude more expensive than a normal object (strong reference) to bookkeep.

To get information on `Reference` object processing along with garbage collections, JRockit can be started with the flag `-Xverbose:refobj`. Following is an example of its output:

```
hastur:material marcus$ java -Xverbose:refobj GarbageCollectionTest
  [INFO ][refobj ] [YC#1] SoftRef: Reach:   25 Act: 0 PrevAct: 0 Null: 0
  [INFO ][refobj ] [YC#1] WeakRef: Reach: 103 Act: 0 PrevAct: 0 Null: 0
  [INFO ][refobj ] [YC#1] Phantom: Reach:    0 Act: 0 PrevAct: 0 Null: 0
  [INFO ][refobj ] [YC#1] ClearPh: Reach:    0 Act: 0 PrevAct: 0 Null: 0
  [INFO ][refobj ] [YC#1] Finaliz: Reach:   12 Act: 3 PrevAct: 0 Null: 0
  [INFO ][refobj ] [YC#1] WeakHnd: Reach: 217 Act: 0 PrevAct: 0 Null: 0
  [INFO ][refobj ] [YC#1] SoftRef: @Mark: 25
    @Preclean: 0 @FinalMark:   0
  [INFO ][refobj ] [YC#1] WeakRef: @Mark: 94
    @Preclean: 0 @FinalMark:   9
  [INFO ][refobj ] [YC#1] Phantom: @Mark:  0
    @Preclean: 0 @FinalMark:   0
  [INFO ][refobj ] [YC#1] ClearPh: @Mark:  0
    @Preclean: 0 @FinalMark:   0
  [INFO ][refobj ] [YC#1] Finaliz: @Mark:  0
    @Preclean: 0 @FinalMark:  15
  [INFO ][refobj ] [YC#1] WeakHnd: @Mark:  0
    @Preclean: 0 @FinalMark: 217
  [INFO ][refobj ] [YC#1] SoftRef: SoftAliveOnly: 24 SoftAliveAndReach:1
  [INFO ][refobj ] [YC#1] NOTE: This count only
    applies to a part of the heap.
```

The program in the previous example seems to have only a small number of `Reference` objects and the GC has no trouble keeping up. Beware of applications where each GC needs to handle hundreds of thousands of soft references.

Object pooling

As was discussed in the chapter on memory management, **object pooling**, the practice of keeping a collection of objects alive for reuse in order to reduce allocation overhead, is usually a bad idea.

Apart from interfering with GC workloads and heuristics, pooling objects will also cause objects to live longer, and thus eventually force their promotion to the old generation on the heap. This introduces extra overhead and contributes to fragmentation. Recall from Chapter 3 that large amounts of live data is a GC bottleneck and the GC is optimized to handle many objects with short life spans. Object pooling contributes both to more live data and to longer object life spans.

Also, allocating fresh objects instead of keeping old objects alive, will most likely be more beneficial to cache locality.

No rule without exception, however. In very specific applications, allocation time is actually a program bottleneck, especially the clearing part of allocations. As Java guarantees that every new object is initialized with `null`, freshly allocated objects have to be cleared. Performance in an environment with many large objects, for example large arrays, may therefore occasionally benefit from object pooling. JRockit tries to remove unnecessary object clearings if it can prove that they are not needed.

In general, though, it is probably a good idea to just keep things simple.

Bad algorithms and data structures

It should be fairly obvious that a hash table is a better data structure for fast element lookups than a linked list. It should also be clear that a QuickSort algorithm of runtime complexity $O(n\ log\ n)$ is better than a naively implemented BubbleSort of $O(n^2)$. We assume that the reader is fairly proficient in picking the correct algorithms and data structures in order to minimize algorithm complexity.

Classic textbook issues

However, when working with a poorly written third-party application, bad data structures can still be a problem. By benchmarking and by working backwards from where the program spends its time, serious runtime improvements can sometimes be made.

```
public List<Node> breadthFirstSearchSlow(Node root) {
  List<Node> order = new LinkedList<Node>();
  List<Node> queue = new LinkedList<Node>();

  queue.add(root);

  while (!queue.isEmpty()) {
    Node node = queue.remove(0);
    order.add(node);
    for (Node succ : node.getSuccessors()) {
      if (!order.contains(succ) && !queue.contains(succ)) {
        queue.add(succ);
      }
    }
  }

  return order;
}
```

The previous code is a standard breadth first search algorithm for (possibly cyclic) graphs. Given a root node, the algorithm uses a queue to traverse its successors in breadth first order. In order to avoid duplicates and potentially infinite loops, a check to see if a node has been already processed is done before adding it to the queue.

The method `contains`, used for finding an element in a linked list, is implemented in the JDK as a linear scan of the entire list. This means that in the worst case, our search algorithm is quadratic to the number of nodes, which will be very slow for large data sets.

```
public List<Node> breadthFirstSearchFast(Node root) {
   List<Node> order   = new LinkedList<Node>();
   List<Node> queue   = new LinkedList<Node>();
   Set<Node>  visited = new HashSet<Node>();

   queue.add(root);
   visited.add(root);

   while (!queue.isEmpty()) {
     Node node = queue.remove(0);
     order.add(node);

     for (Node succ : node.getSuccessors()) {
       if (!visited.contains(succ)) {
         queue.add(succ);
         visited.add(succ);
       }
     }
   }

   return order;
}
```

The previous code corrects the problem by adding a `HashSet` type data structure to keep track of visited nodes. Constant time lookups replace the linear traversal when checking if a node already has been visited. The potential difference for large data sets is enormous.

Unwanted intrinsic properties

There are however other, more subtle problems caused by picking the wrong data structure. Consider a queue implementation in the form of a linked list. This is seemingly a good general purpose data structure that can be used as a queue without any modifications. It provides the ability of inserting elements last in the list and removing elements from the list head. These are both constant time operations and no other functionality is required. So, what can go wrong? First of all, even if your program never iterates over the entire linked list, the garbage collector still has to.

If the queue contains large amounts of data, many objects are kept alive as long as they are referenced from the linked list. As the linked list elements consist of object references that both point out the next list element and wrap a payload of data, the queue elements may exist anywhere on the heap. Thus, accessing objects in a linked list may actually lead to bad cache locality and long pause times. Bad cache locality can ensue because payloads or element wrappers aren't guaranteed to be stored next to each other in memory. This will cause long pause times as, if the object pointers are spread over a very large heap area, a garbage collector would repeatedly miss the cache while doing pointer chasing during its mark phase.

So, seemingly innocent data structures with low complexities for the operations involved can turn out to introduce intrinsic problems in systems with automatic memory management.

Misuse of System.gc

There is no guarantee from the Java language specification that calling `System.gc` will do anything at all. But if it does, it probably does more than you want or doesn't do the same thing every time you call it. To reiterate, don't confuse the garbage collector by trying to tell it what to do. To be safe, don't call `System.gc`.

Too many threads

While it is a good thing to be able to break up a problem into many computational threads with little inter-thread communication, context switches always incur overhead anyway. We have been over the different thread implementations, from green threads to OS threads in Chapter 4. However, true for all thread implementation is that some kind of context switch, during which no useful program execution can be performed, takes place while shifting execution from one thread to another. The number of context switches grows proportionally to the number of fairly scheduled threads, and there may also be hidden overhead here.

 A worst-case example from real life is the Intel IA-64 processor, with its massive amount of registers, where a native thread context is on the order of several KB. Every memory copy performed in order to initiate a new thread context after a context switch contributes to the overhead. This makes many threads executing in parallel particularly expensive as their contexts are large.

One contended lock is the global bottleneck

Contended locks are bottlenecks, as their presence means that several threads want to access the same resource or execute the same piece of code at the same time. It is not uncommon that one lock is the main source of all contention in a program. A typical example is an application using some third-party library for logging that acquires a global lock each time log file information is to be written. When many, mutually independent, threads are trying to log output at the same time, the log lock might be the one bottleneck that brings an otherwise well written application to its knees.

Unnecessary exceptions

Handling exceptions takes time and interrupts normal program flow. Using exceptions for the common case in a program as means of communicating results or implementing control flow is definitely bad practice.

It is useful to try to create some kind of exception profile of the program to find out what exceptions are thrown and from where. Unnecessary hardware exceptions such as null pointers and divisions by zero should be removed wherever possible. Hardware exceptions are the most expensive type of exception, as they are triggered by an interrupt at the native level, whereas throwing a Java exception explicitly from code keeps most of the (though still expensive) work of handling the exception inside the JVM.

> We have seen cases with customer applications throwing tens of thousands of unnecessary `NullPointerExceptions` every second, as part of normal control flow. Once this behavior was rectified, performance gains of an order of magnitude were achieved.

The simplest way to discover which exceptions, both caught and uncaught, are thrown by JRockit, is to use the flag `-Xverbose:exceptions`. An example of its output is shown as follows:

```
hastur:~ marcus$ java -Xverbose:exceptions Jvm98Wrapper _200_check
  [INFO ][excepti][00004] java/io/FileNotFoundException:
    /localhome/jrockits/R28.0.0_R28.0.0-454_1.6.0/jre/classes
  [INFO ][excepti][00004] java/lang/ArrayIndexOutOfBoundsException: 6
  [INFO ][excepti][00004] java/lang/ArithmeticException: / by zero
  [INFO ][excepti][00004] java/lang/ArithmeticException: fisk
  [INFO ][excepti][00004] java/lang/ArrayIndexOutOfBoundsException: 11
  [INFO ][excepti][00004] java/lang/RuntimeException: fisk
```

Each line in the log corresponds to a thrown exception. To get stack traces along with the exceptions, use `-Xverbose:exceptions=debug`. The JRockit Mission Control suite also contains frameworks for profiling exceptions and for introspecting them in a more user friendly way. The following is an example output that shows exceptions along with their stack traces, as they are thrown by the JVM:

```
hastur:~ marcus$ java -Xverbose:exceptions=debug Jvm98Wrapper _200_check
  [DEBUG][excepti][00004] java/lang/ArrayIndexOutOfBoundsException: 6
    at spec/jbb/validity/PepTest.testArray()Ljava/lang/String;
      (Unknown Source)
    at spec/jbb/validity/PepTest.instanceMain()V(Unknown Source)
    at spec/jbb/validity/Check.doCheck()Z(Unknown Source)
    at spec/jbb/JBBmain.main([Ljava/lang/String;)V(Unknown Source)
    at jrockit/vm/RNI.c2java(JJJJJ)V(Native Method)
    --- End of stack trace
  [DEBUG][excepti][00004] java/lang/ArithmeticException: / by zero
    at jrockit/vm/Reflect.fillInStackTrace0(Ljava/lang/Throwable;)
      V(Native Method)
    at java/lang/Throwable.fillInStackTrace()Ljava/lang/Throwable;
      (Native Method)
    at java/lang/Throwable.<init>(Throwable.java:196)
    at java/lang/Exception.<init>(Exception.java:41)
    at java/lang/RuntimeException.<init>(RuntimeException.java:43)
    at java/lang/ArithmeticException.<init>(ArithmeticException.java:36)
    at jrockit/vm/RNI.c2java(JJJJJ)V(Native Method)
    at jrockit/vm/ExceptionHandler.throwPendingType()V(Native Method)
    at spec/jbb/validity/PepTest.testDiv()Ljava/lang/String;
      (Unknown Source)
    at spec/jbb/validity/PepTest.instanceMain()V(Unknown Source)
    at spec/jbb/validity/Check.doCheck()Z(Unknown Source)
    at spec/jbb/JBBmain.main([Ljava/lang/String;)V(Unknown Source)
    at jrockit/vm/RNI.c2java(JJJJJ)V(Native Method)
    --- End of stack trace
  [DEBUG][excepti][00004] java/lang/ArithmeticException: fisk
    at spec/jbb/validity/PepTest.testExc1()Ljava/lang/String;
      (Unknown Source)
    at spec/jbb/validity/PepTest.instanceMain()V(Unknown Source)
    at spec/jbb/validity/Check.doCheck()Z(Unknown Source)
    at spec/jbb/JBBmain.main([Ljava/lang/String;)V(Unknown Source)
```

```
      at jrockit/vm/RNI.c2java(JJJJJ)V(Native Method)
   --- End of stack trace
[DEBUG][excepti][00004] java/lang/ArrayIndexOutOfBoundsException: 11
   at spec/jbb/validity/PepTest.testExc1()Ljava/lang/String;
      (Unknown Source)
   at spec/jbb/validity/PepTest.instanceMain()V(Unknown Source)
   at spec/jbb/validity/Check.doCheck()Z(Unknown Source)
   at spec/jbb/JBBmain.main([Ljava/lang/String;)V(Unknown Source)
   at jrockit/vm/RNI.c2java(JJJJJ)V(Native Method)
   --- End of stack trace
[DEBUG][excepti][00004] java/lang/RuntimeException: fisk
   at spec/jbb/validity/PepTest.testExc2()Ljava/lang/String;
      (Unknown Source)
   at spec/jbb/validity/PepTest.instanceMain()V(Unknown Source)
   at spec/jbb/validity/Check.doCheck()Z(Unknown Source)
   at spec/jbb/JBBmain.main([Ljava/lang/String;)V(Unknown Source)
   at jrockit/vm/RNI.c2java(JJJJJ)V(Native Method)
   --- End of stack trace
```

Any JRockit Flight Recording contains an exception profile of the running program that can be examined using JRockit Mission Control.

Large objects

Large objects sometimes have to be allocated directly on the heap and not in thread local areas. The rationale is that they would mostly contribute to overhead in a small TLA and cause frequent evacuations. In JRockit versions prior to R28, an explicit large object size could be given and objects that were larger were never allocated in a TLA. Post R28, the waste limit for a TLA is instead the modifiable property, allowing large objects to be allocated in a TLA if they fit well enough.

Large objects on the heap are bad in that they contribute to fragmentation more quickly. This is because they might not readily fit in most spaces provided by the **free list**, where smaller "normal" objects have been previously garbage collected.

Allocation time increases dramatically on a fragmented heap, and juggling many large objects extensively contributes to fragmentation. As large objects may be allocated directly on the heap and not in the TLA, large object allocation in JRockit also contributes to overhead because it may require taking a global heap lock on allocation.

The worst case scenario is that an overuse of large objects leads to full heap compaction being done too frequently, which is very disruptive and requires stopping the world for large amounts of time.

As it is hard to pick a "one size fits all" value as an explicit large object limit, for any given application, the large object limit in JRockit (or the TLA waste limit in R28) can be changed. This is useful if analysis shows that there are, for example, a large number of fixed size objects slightly larger than the default, or if many direct-to-heap allocations take place as the TLAs want to be too tightly packed. In that case, it might be beneficial to increase the large object limit or TLA waste limit, depending on JRockit version.

The bad corner cases, the large object death spirals, occur when objects frequently are on the orders of several megabytes. The real world examples are typically database query results or very large arrays. Avoid them at all costs. Do whatever it takes to keep them off the heap, even implement a native layer for them, but do not let your Java Virtual Machine juggle a large number of humongous objects.

Native memory versus heap memory

To the JVM, all memory that exists is system memory, available from the underlying operating system. Some of this system memory is used by the JVM to allocate the Java heap. The amount of memory used for the heap can be controlled by the `-Xms` (initial heap size) and `-Xmx` (maximum heap size) flags.

The JVM will throw `OutOfMemoryError` both from inside the JVM, when there is not enough memory available to complete some internal operation, and from Java, when a program tries to allocate more objects than will fit on the current heap.

A JVM is a native application that also consumes system memory for its own purposes, for example, to allocate data structures used for code optimization. Internal JVM memory management is, to a large extent, kept off the Java heap and allocated natively in the operating system, through system calls like `malloc`. We refer to non-heap system memory allocated by the JVM as **native memory**.

While heap memory can be reclaimed when the JVM garbage collects objects in running program, native memory can't. If all native memory management was handled by the JVM alone, and the JVM was economic enough in its native memory usage, all would be well. However, there are complications.

In certain scenarios, we can run out of native memory. One example is when several parallel threads perform code optimizations in the JVM. Code optimization typically is one of the JVM operations that consumes the largest amounts of native memory, though only when the optimizing JIT is running and only on a per-method basis. There are also mechanisms that allow the Java program, and not just the JVM, to allocate native memory, for example through JNI calls. If a JNI call executes a native `malloc` to reserve a large amount of memory, this memory will be unavailable to the JVM until it is freed.

Mechanisms for tracking native memory usage are available in JRockit, and can be accessed through the JRockit Mission Control suite or JRCMD. Histograms that show the native memory usage of individual JVM modules are also available.

If the heap is too large, it may well be the case that not enough native memory is left for JVM internal usage—bookkeeping, code optimizations, and so on. In that case, the JVM may have no other choice than to throw an `OutOfMemoryError` from native code. For JRockit, increasing the amount of available native memory is done implicitly by lowering the maximum Java heap size using `-Xmx`.

Wait/notify and fat locks

Recall from the last chapter that `wait` and `notify` always inflates thin locks to fat locks in JRockit. Locks that are frequently taken and released, but are only held for a short time might do better as thin locks. So, immediately using `wait` or `notify` on a new object will create a new monitor and consequently a fat lock that might lead to performance overhead.

Wrong heap size

Another common problem that causes performance issues is using the wrong heap size for the JVM. Too small heaps trigger frequent and time consuming garbage collections. Too large heaps lead to longer mean GC times and may cause the JVM to run out of native memory. It makes sense to do profiling runs to figure out the memory requirements of your application and try to find an optimal maximum heap size. JRockit Mission Control will almost always provide good data on the memory requirements for a particular application.

Too much live data

As we have discussed in the chapter on garbage collection, the main contributor to runtime complexity in memory management is not the heap size per se, but rather the amount of live data on the heap. Large amounts of live data almost certainly create garbage collection overhead. Again, profiling can help figure out if there are any large object clusters kept in memory even though there shouldn't be.

The Memleak tool, which is part of the JRockit Mission Control suit is ideal for this kind of analysis.

Java is not a silver bullet

Finally, Java is a powerful and versatile language that contributes to short application development time because of its friendly semantics and built-in memory management. However, Java is not a silver bullet. The last caveat this chapter will warn of is trying to use Java to solve a problem that in fact is totally inappropriate for Java.

- Is the application a telecom application with virtually tens of thousands of concurrent threads that need near-real-time support?

- Does the application contain a database layer that frequently returns 20 MB query results of binary data in the form of byte arrays?

- Is the application completely dependent on the underlying OS scheduler for performance and determinism, with bad overhead problems if the scheduling semantics change even slightly?

- Is the application a device driver?

- Has the development team implemented a C/Fortran/COBOL-to-Java automatic translator, so that those 100,000 lines of legacy code can "easily" be deployed on a modern Java runtime?

- Is the program highly concurrent or embarrassingly parallel, that is, it tries to use a divide and conquer strategy that branches off tens of thousands of threads that run computations for a short period of time before fusing the partial results?

In these cases, and there are probably plenty of others, it might be considered doubtful if using Java is the correct approach. Java is highly attractive in that the JVM provides an abstract layer on top of the operating system and in that Java programs can be compiled once, and run everywhere. But, stretching it a bit, so can ANSI C. Just ship the source code and make sure it is portable. Choose your tool with care. Java is a lovely multi-purpose hammer, but not every problem is a nail!

Summary

This chapter has covered benchmarking and tuning. We have motivated the need for benchmarking, mostly since having a benchmark framework in place prevents performance regressions, but also because well understood and easy-to-setup sub-problems are simpler to work with than complex applications. We also stressed the importance of having performance goals for commercial software development, another area where benchmarking is of a great help. It can also be useful to maintain a set of third-party applications as part of a benchmark suite.

We have discussed micro benchmarks to some extent and explained why they are useful and when they are not. We also talked about the importance of knowing what you are measuring.

Profiling always needs to be done to understand where the bottlenecks are in an application and to make sure that external benchmarks really address these bottlenecks. Profiling can be done with several levels of complexity, and with several levels of intrusiveness. For JRockit, low cost profiling is easily facilitated by the JRockit Mission Control suite.

We went on to present some industrial standard benchmarks, most famously the SPEC suite, and discussed where they can do some good for everyone from hardware vendors to application developers.

Once an application is well understood, it is time to decide if tuning JVM parameters alone can improve performance or if rewriting certain parts of the program is required. Using JRockit as an example JVM, we covered the parameters that can be used to tune application behavior in the memory system, in the code generator, and elsewhere.

Finally, we presented a section on common bottlenecks or anti-patterns that are frequently seen in Java applications and taught the reader how to avoid them.

This concludes the first part of this book. The next part of the book will go over the versatile and powerful tools in JRockit Mission Control in great detail. Hopefully this chapter contained enough philosophy on benchmarking and tuning to provide an excellent primer for understanding how to apply the necessary tools to solve your performance problems.

6
JRockit Mission Control

JRockit, as a Java runtime, is required to constantly monitor the running Java application. As has been explained in previous chapters, JRockit must, among other things, be able to find out in which methods the Java application is spending the most time executing code. JRockit is also responsible for keeping track of the memory usage and memory allocation behavior of the application—it would be fairly upsetting if JRockit forgot a few objects, or if memory was not reclaimed when objects were no longer referenced.

The wealth of data that JRockit already collects is, of course, a very good source of information when profiling your Java program or when doing diagnostics.

In this, the second part of the book, the JRockit tools suite is presented. The following chapters introduce four of the tools that are included in the JRockit distribution—the JRockit Mission Control Console, the JRockit Runtime Analyzer (which was superseded by the JRockit Flight Recorder in R28), the JRockit Memory Leak Detector, and JRCMD.

The first three tools are included in the JRockit Mission Control tools suite. The last one, JRCMD, is a command-line tool that ships as part of the JRockit JDK. A common denominator for the tools is their ability to interact with an already running JVM. There is no need to pre-configure the JVM or the application to be able to later attach the tools. Also, the tools add virtually no overhead, making them suitable for use in live production environments.

In this chapter you will learn:

- How to start JRockit Mission Control, both as a standalone application and inside the Eclipse IDE
- How to configure JRockit JVM instances so that they can be managed by JRockit Mission Control from remote locations

- How to make JRockit Mission Control automatically discover remotely running JRockit instances

- How to configure the management agent that is part of the JRockit JVM

- How to use JRockit Mission Control and the JRockit Management Agent in a secure environment

- How to troubleshoot connections between JRockit Mission Control and JRockit

- Various ways to get more debug information from JRockit Mission Control

- About the **Experimental Update Site for JRockit Mission Control** and how to extend JRockit Mission Control with plug-ins from the Experimental Update Site

While not necessary for the bigger picture, parts of this chapter assume various degrees of familiarity with Eclipse IDE. For more information about Eclipse, see the Eclipse homepage at `http://www.eclipse.org`.

Background

JRockit Mission Control started out as a set of internal tools used by the JRockit team to monitor and tune the JRockit JVM in order to make it a better Java runtime. The early analysis tools were initially not available to end customers. However, after we used the tools to resolve a couple of high profile customer issues, the word started to spread. We realized that customers found the tools useful when tuning and profiling their Java applications, and consequently the tools were made more user friendly, packaged together, and released as the Java tools suite known as JRockit Mission Control.

Today, the JRockit Mission Control tools suite is a set of tools for monitoring, managing and profiling Java applications running on JRockit. It also includes a powerful tool for tracking down memory leaks. The JRockit Mission Control tools can, with very little overhead, retrieve a profile that is a fair approximation of the actual runtime behavior of an application. Most other profilers cause significant slowdowns which, in turn, can alter the behavior of the running application. As mentioned in *Chapter 5, Benchmarking and Tuning,* if a lot of overhead is incurred from the actual profiler, it is fair to say that what is being observed is no longer a true representation of the application behavior. It is rather the behavior of the application, plus that of the profiler itself, that is being profiled.

Behavior change in an application due to profiling is sometimes referred to as the **observer effect** — when the act of observation alters what is being observed. The term **Heisenberg effect** is also sometimes used. The Heisenberg Uncertainty Principle is related to, and often conflated with, the observer effect.

In a BEA internal study, before the Oracle acquisition, the BEA performance team was benchmarking different profilers. They were looking for a low overhead tool to profile a J2EE benchmark on WebLogic Server. Several different profilers were examined, and the overhead as a function of change in response time was calculated. For this particular benchmark, the overhead for Mission Control was 0.5 percent. The second best tool, a leading Java profiler, incurred 93.8 percent (!) overhead on that very same benchmark.

Sampling-based profiling versus exact profiling

Naturally, different tools have different strengths and weaknesses. The data captured by JRockit Mission Control aims to provide a statistically accurate representation of what is going on in the JRockit JVM. It will not always be exact, but it will usually provide the information required to solve important problems. We call this **sampling-based profiling**. Sampling-based profiling lends itself well to when a statistical approach can be used to periodically record a state. The most common variants in JRockit Mission Control are time-based sampling and sampling based on a subset of state changes. The JVM, being a large state machine, can cheaply provide a large amount of samples and events. The data can be readily exposed by the JVM to a consumer, for example Mission Control. Sampling-based profiling has the additional benefit that it is much easier to estimate the profiling overhead.

For example, the best way to find out where an application is spending the most execution time is to use the JRockit Flight Recorder tool to look at the **hot methods list**. The list provides a statistically representative view of what methods JRockit spent the most time executing, using information from the code profiling thread in the JRockit code generator. It will, however, not provide information about every single method call or exactly how much wall clock time was spent executing the method.

There are some **exact profiling** alternatives in JRockit Mission Control, as well, that can provide such metrics. These, however, may incur a much larger overhead if enabled. It is, for instance, possible (but please don't try this at home) to connect the JRockit Management Console to a running application and enable exact timing and invocation counters for each and every method in the system. Doing exact profiling always incurs extra runtime overhead. Enabling exact profiling for every method in the system will require the JVM to both generate and execute a large amount of extra profiling code. This will not only adversely affect performance, but it is also quite difficult to determine the exact performance implications. Some of the JRockit code is written in Java. Instrumenting all allocation and locking code would almost certainly bring the application to its knees. If the aim is to determine what parts of the application would benefit most from improvements and optimization, the sampling-based approach is superior.

One might think that the cost of overhead for exact profiling is paid for in better measurements. For example, given exact data, the timing values for all the methods in the system can then be measured, and the one with the highest invocation count multiplied by execution time would be the natural one to target for optimization first, wouldn't it?

It might, but in a sufficiently complex system the data will be misleading and distorted. The overhead of the methods on the critical paths in the system will quite likely increase drastically and the overall system performance will degrade. Furthermore, applying the exact method profiler to every single method in the system would most likely severely change the behavior of the application, rendering the measurements inaccurate.

Using the JRockit Mission Control Management Console to retrieve exact method timings and invocation counts is one of the rare cases where the overhead of running the JRockit tools suite is very difficult to estimate. The time it takes to calculate the profiling data can be considered to be constant. Invocation counting code is mainly placed at method entries and method exits. So, the distortion caused by the profiling is proportional to how often the method is invoked and inversely proportional to the time the method takes to execute. If the method is frequently called, the overhead will add up. If the method already takes a long time to execute, the overhead may be less noticeable. In multi-threaded scenarios, the non-determinism of exact profiling with the Management Console is even greater.

A different animal to different people

JRockit Mission Control is used in very different ways by different people. Outside Oracle, it is most commonly used as a very capable profiling tool.

Some people use JRockit Mission Control to track down application problems. This is the main use case for Oracle Support. The authors also find it enlightening to turn JRockit Mission Control on itself during the development phase to find both performance issues and bugs.

There are also the ultra nerds, the authors included, who use the JRockit Mission Control tools suite to squeeze out that extra percentage of performance from JRockit by doing benchmarking and by tuning the JVM for a very specific application.

Here are a few typical JRockit Mission Control use cases:

- **Finding hotspots**: Where should we start optimizing an application? Is the application even computationally bound or is it experiencing latency related issues? Which method is being executed the most and would thus be the most important to improve for better performance?

- **Tracking latencies**: Finding out why application throughput is worse than expected or why response times are too long. In applications with latency-related throughput problems, the CPU is typically not saturated. Over-reliance on synchronization may cause thread stalls. Why are all the worker threads blocking most of the time? Why is the system starting to time out on requests while utilizing only 20 percent of the CPU?

- **Memory profiling**: Useful when trying to find out what is causing all those garbage collections. Where is the pressure on the memory system created? What part of the program is causing all those garbage collections? How much time is spent doing garbage collections? What phase of a garbage collection is making them take so long? How badly fragmented is the heap?

- **Exception profiling**: Throwing and handling a lot of unnecessary exceptions can be taxing on a system. How many exceptions are being thrown? Where do they originate? Tracking down and eliminating the sources of unnecessary exceptions often leads to significant increases in runtime performance.

- **Heap analysis**: Finding out what type of data is on the heap in various phases of a running program can provide insight on how to choose, for example, garbage collector strategies or compaction strategies. It can also identify and help get rid of situations where too many `Reference` objects are used.

"George, why does your ticker quote cache contain a `HashMap` holding on to 96 percent of the heap? It is still growing by the way, and I expect the server will throw an `OutOfMemoryError` in two hours at this rate. We need to restart our server twice a week. Otherwise we will get an `OutOfMemoryError`. But that's okay. Everyone does that..."

- **Tuning the memory system**: The out of the box behavior for the memory system is usually good enough, but some extra performance can usually be gained by tuning it a little. For some corner case applications, tuning may even be necessary to get the required performance. In those cases, JRockit Mission Control can quickly reveal why the garbage collector fails to keep up.

Mission Control overview

The different tools currently available in JRockit Mission Control 4.0 are:

- **The JRockit Management Console**: Usually referred to as just the console, this tool is used for monitoring the JVM and the application running in the JVM. The Management Console supports customizable graphs, **trigger rules** (so that actions can be taken on user-defined conditions), and more.

- **JRockit Flight Recorder**: Normally referred to as the Flight Recorder or JFR. A low overhead, always on, recorder that creates a profile of what JRockit has been up to lately. The recording can be dumped from the JRockit Mission Control GUI and the contents analyzed offline. JRockit Flight Recorder is the main profiling tool in the suite and supersedes the old (prior to R27.x/3.x) **JRockit Runtime Analyzer (JRA)**.

- **The JRockit Memory Leak Detector**: Memleak for short. A powerful, online, heap analyzer that visualizes memory usage trends, relationships between instances of different classes on the heap, and more. Memleak can quickly detect quite slow memory leaks that only become problematic over time. It accomplishes this by doing trend analysis on the live set for each type in the system.

Mission Control consists of two major parts—a set of APIs, agents and protocols built into the JRockit JVM and the JRockit Mission Control client. The different tools rely on different sets of APIs, but they all initiate communication with the JRockit JVM using JMX.

A full discussion on JMX is beyond the scope of this book, but we'll briefly discuss the basic concepts. The JMX standard is a three-layered architecture. It consists of:

- **The Instrumentation Level**: This is where applications running in the JVM expose resources for manageability through **Managed Beans (MBeans)**. An MBean is a type of Java Bean that is defined by its attributes, its operations, and the notifications it can emit.

- **The Agent Level**: The **agent** is the component managing the MBeans. The most important agent-level component is the **MBean server**, which is a container where MBeans are registered and managed.

- **The Remote Management Level**: This level provides protocol adapters that enable communication with the MBean server from outside the JVM process.

The following figure shows how the different architectural levels of JMX apply in a typical JRockit deployment:

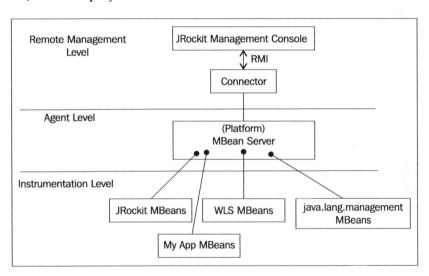

Mission Control server-side components

From a high-level Mission Control perspective, the monitored JRockit JVM consists of:

- A set of server-side APIs:
  - ○ **JMXMAPI**: JRockit JVM-specific extensions to the MBeans available in the platform MBean server. MBeans and the platform MBean server will be discussed in the next chapter.
  - ○ **JRockit internal local Java APIs**: For example the **JRockit Management API (JMAPI)**.
  - ○ **Server-side native APIs**: APIs that are built into JRockit and not implemented in Java. For example, the native API used by Memleak.

- Agents exposing the previously mentioned APIs and miscellaneous services:
  - ○ **The default JMX agent**
  - ○ **The Memleak server**: A native server that exposes the native Memleak API over the proprietary **Memleak Protocol (MLP)**
  - ○ **The JRockit Discovery Protocol (JDP) server**: An optional service that broadcasts the locations of JVM instances on the network

Mission Control client-side components

As of JRockit Mission Control 2.0, the JRMC client is based on Eclipse RCP (Rich Client Platform) Technology. This provides a series of architectural advantages, such as an OSGi-based component model and being able to run JRockit Mission Control both as a standalone application and inside the Eclipse IDE.

 Mission Control 2.0 was internally codenamed Energy, as $E=mc^2$. Yes, we're nerds!

The Rich Client Platform is the base platform for the Eclipse IDE. It contains, among other things, the Standard Widget Toolkit (SWT), JFace, the Eclipse OSGi implementation (Equinox), and an integrated mechanism to deliver and update RCP applications. OSGi is a standardized dynamic module system for Java, backed by numerous large corporations. RCP provides an excellent base platform for writing and delivering highly modular applications with a look and feel that is native to the host operating system.

For more information on RCP, please see `http://www.eclipse.org/home/categories/rcp.php`.

For more information on OSGi, please see `http://www.osgi.org/`.

The client-side of JRockit Mission Control is highly modular—new tools can easily be plugged in, and the tools themselves can be extended.

From a high-level Mission Control perspective, the Mission Control Client consists of:

- **RCP**: The Eclipse **Rich Client Platform**
- **Client-side APIs**:
    - **RJMX**: Extended JMX services, such as an MBean attribute subscription framework, triggers, proxies for the old proprietary, and obsolete RMP protocol (used in 1.4 versions of JRockit)
    - **Memleak API**: For communicating with the Memleak server
    - **Flight Recorder Model**: For parsing JRockit Flight Recorder recordings
    - **JDP Client API**: For detecting JRockit instances running on the network
- **JRockit Mission Control core**: Contains the core framework for the JRockit Mission Control client and defines the core extension points
- **The JVM Browser**: Keeps track of the detected and/or user-defined connections to JVMs
- **The Tools**: The various tools that can be launched from the JVM browser—the Management Console, the Flight Recorder, and Memleak

The following figure shows a simplified breakdown of the plug-ins in the 4.0.0 version of JRockit Mission Control:

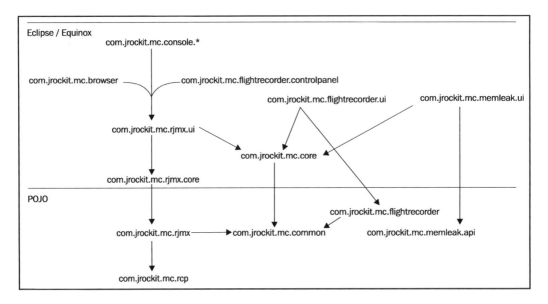

The rest of this chapter will focus on how to get JRockit Mission Control up and running and how to troubleshoot JRockit Mission Control. The different tools in JRockit Mission Control will be explained in detail in the chapters that follow.

Terminology

In order to efficiently communicate about the JRockit Mission Control client, a common terminology is needed. The terms discussed here apply when running Mission Control standalone as well as inside Eclipse.

 The reader familiar with Eclipse may note that we use the same terminology as with Eclipse and the Eclipse Workbench.

In an Eclipse RCP application, the main window is called the **workbench**. Inside the workbench there are two types of windows — **views** and **editors**. The editors occupy the center of the workbench — the **editor area**. The views are normally located around the editor area.

As shown in the following screenshot, the JVM Browser is the view to the left:

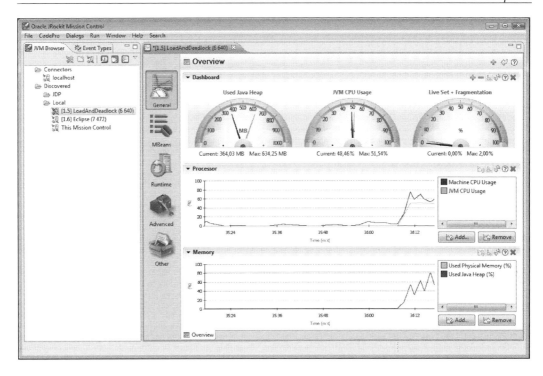

Views are normally used to show a specialized presentation of the contents of the selected editor, to manipulate the contents of an editor, or to launch new editors. Several views can be docked on each other by dragging a view on top of another view into the same **view folder**.

A certain configuration of which views to show, along with how they should be located, is called a **perspective**. In the screenshot, the Mission Control perspective is used, that shows the **JVM Browser** view and the **Event Types** view co-located in the same view folder to the left. Should you ever lose a view or mistakenly rearrange the views in a way you are not satisfied with, the perspective can easily be reset from the workbench menu (**Window | Reset Perspective**).

The editor currently opened in the editor area in the screenshot above is a JRockit Mission Control Console. It is being used to monitor a locally running application where the main class is called LoadAndDeadlock.

In Eclipse parlance, the JRockit tools are built as **editors**—any tool that is started will open up in the editor area. Several editors can be open at the same time. They will show as multiple tabs in the editor area. Several editors can also be viewed side-by-side by dragging an editor by the tab and docking it at any side of another editor. Views, such as the JVM Browser, cannot be docked into the editor area. They can, however, be docked to any side of the editor area.

To the left in the Management Console (in the editor area) is the **tab group toolbar** that selects tabs that are currently visible in the tab container at the bottom of the editor. A tab group toolbar is available in other JRockit Mission Control tools as well. In JRockit Mission Control 3.1, the **General** tab group, which is automatically selected when a Management Console is started, contains only a single tab—the **Overview** tab.

Running the standalone version of Mission Control

JRockit Mission Control exists both as a standalone executable and as a plug-in for the Eclipse IDE. The version of JRockit Mission Control included in the JRockit JDK is the standalone version.

Starting Mission Control in standalone mode is simple. Just run the executable named jrmc (or jrmc.exe on Windows) in the bin directory of the JRockit distribution.

Do not attempt to start JRockit Mission Control in standalone mode through any mechanism other than running the jrmc executable. Sometimes we run into homegrown customer setups where Mission Control is started by running the jar files in the Mission Control directory with some elaborate class path configuration. This is generally a very bad idea and is strongly discouraged. The jrmc launcher ensures, among other things, that the correct version of JRockit is being used to launch JRockit Mission Control, and that the class path is correctly configured.

For example:

JROCKIT_HOME/bin/jrmc

On Windows systems, JRockit Mission Control, when installed, will also be available in the start menu.

Once JRockit Mission Control has been started, an empty workspace (JRockit Mission Control 3.x), or a welcome screen (JRockit Mission Control 4.0) is displayed. If everything is correctly set up, JRockit Mission Control will automatically discover JVMs running on the local system. Even if there are no other Java applications running, the JRockit JVM used to execute the JRockit Mission Control client will be discovered and displayed as **This Mission Control** in the **JVM Browser**.

From the JVM Browser, the different JRockit Mission Control tools can be launched against a selected JVM.

Most of the tools require the JVM to be a JRockit JVM, as they are relying on JRockit specific APIs. The Management Console is currently the only exception among the tools, as it can be connected to any JMX compliant JVM. Some functionality will however be unavailable if connected to anything but a JRockit JVM.

Finding and monitoring locally running JVMs is simple and convenient—no additional setup is required. However, having the Mission Control client running on the same machine as the monitored JVM is usually a bad idea, especially in an enterprise configuration. The resources required by the client will be taken from whatever mission critical application executing on the JVM that is to be profiled. Of course, in a testing or development environment, this may be acceptable. Also, changes made to the settings, for instance the addition of an attribute to a graph in the JRockit Management Console, are stored on a per-connection basis. They are, however, not stored at all for local connections.

To add a user-defined connection, simply click on the **Connectors** folder and click on the **Create Connection** button.

The Connection Wizard, as shown in the previous screenshot, will open. Here, the details of the connection can be specified. It is usually enough to enter the **Host** and **Port**, but the following is worth noting:

- If connecting to a JDK 1.4 version of JRockit, select the **JDK 1.4** radio button.

- Selecting the **Custom JMX service URL** radio button will allow full control over the JMX Service URL. The JMX Service URL is a URL that specifies how to connect to a JMX agent. Specifying a custom URL is useful if a protocol other than JMX over RMI is required by the agent.

  The protocol used by the default agent is **JMX over RMI (JMXRMI)**. Other possible protocols include JMXMP (as described in the Java SE documentation) and IIOP. There are also proprietary protocols, such as WebLogic Server's t3. If using a custom agent and a custom protocol, see the agent documentation for more information.

- Passwords can be stored by checking the **Store password in settings file (encrypted)** check box. If storing passwords is enabled, a **master password** will be used each time the password is encrypted or decrypted. If no master password is set, one will be asked for. The master password can be reset by clicking on the **Reset Master Password** button in the JRockit Mission Control preferences.

- The **Test connection** button is very useful for validating that a connection is correctly configured before leaving the wizard.

Running JRockit Mission Control inside Eclipse

There are some advantages to running JRockit Mission Control inside the Eclipse IDE, there are however no fundamental differences in functionality. One advantage, if the source code for the application being monitored is in the Eclipse workspace, is that it is possible to jump directly to the corresponding source whenever a class, method, or stack frame is shown in the JRockit Mission Control client.

If you are unfamiliar with Eclipse, or if you do not plan to use it for Java development, you can safely skip this section, as it assumes some familiarity with the Eclipse IDE.

In order to start JRockit Mission Control inside Eclipse, the JRockit Mission Control plug-ins from the JRockit Mission Control update site must first be installed. The latest version of the update site will be available from the JRockit Mission Control home page on **Oracle Technology Network**. At the time of writing, the JRockit Mission Control homepage is located at `http://www.oracle.com/technology/products/jrockit/missioncontrol/index.html`.

As that's a handful to remember, it can also be reached at `http://www.tinyurl.com/missioncontrol`.

Installation instructions can be found at the update site and will not be discussed in detail here. To fully take advantage of all of the features in the JRockit Mission Control plug-ins, Eclipse should be run on a JRockit JVM. Most of the functionality is available, even if Mission Control is running in an Eclipse instance executing on another JVM, but features such as local JVM discovery and some JRockit specific functionality in the Management Console will not work.

There are additional benefits of running Eclipse on JRockit. JRockit Real Time, discussed in *Chapter 3, Adaptive Memory Management* can be used to make any interactive application more responsive.

In the Eclipse home folder, there is a configuration file, `eclipse.ini`, that can be altered to change the command-line flags of the JVM running Eclipse. Here is an example `eclipse.ini` file that the authors use:

```
-showsplash
org.eclipse.platform
-framework
plugins\org.eclipse.osgi_3.4.3.R34x_v20081215-1030.jar
-vm
d:\jrockits\R27.6.3_R27.6.3-16_1.5.0\bin
-vmargs
-Xms512m
-Xmx512m
-XgcPrio:deterministic
-XpauseTarget:20
```

The previous example is for Eclipse 3.4 and JRockit R27, but it is very similar in Eclipse 3.5 and JRockit R28. To make it work with R28, simply specify the path to the R28 JVM after the -vm argument, and keep everything after the -vmargs.

 There are differences in command-line flags between R27 and R28, and the JRockit Documentation should be consulted for more elaborate JVM configurations.

To start JRockit Mission Control once it is installed in Eclipse, **the Mission Control perspective** must be opened. There are two Mission Control perspectives available in 3.x—the **Mission Control** main perspective and the **Mission Control Latency** perspective. The latter is used to study JRA recordings containing latency data. In the 4.0 version of JRockit Mission Control, there is only one perspective optimized to work with all the tools.

As shown in the following screenshot, the Mission Control perspectives can be found in the **Window | Open Perspective | Other...** menu:

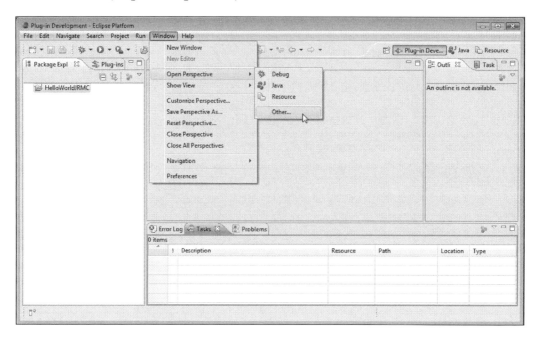

Once the Mission Control perspective has been opened, things will look pretty much the same as when using the standalone version of JRockit Mission Control. As mentioned, one benefit of running JRockit Mission Control from within Eclipse is the ability to open up the corresponding application source code from most places where JRockit Mission Control shows a class or method, as shown in the following screenshot:

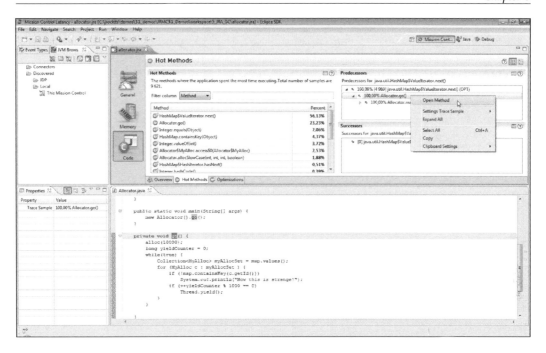

Starting JRockit for remote management

To enable a JRockit JVM for remote management, the external management agent must be started. It can either be started with the -Xmanagement command-line switch, or JRCMD can be used. JRCMD is discussed in detail in Chapter 11.

The following example starts up a JRockit JVM with a simple test program and enables it for remote monitoring on port 4712. Authentication and SSL support for the connection are turned off.

```
JROCKIT_HOME/bin/java
  -Xmanagement:ssl=false,authenticate=false,port=4712 -cp . HelloJRMC
```

For now, let's ignore the security flags and focus on the port. Examples of how to set up JRockit Mission Control with security turned on will be shown in the section *Running in a Secure Environment*, later in this chapter.

As mentioned, the default management agent uses the JMX over RMI protocol for communication. This has been a source of some grief to people trying to establish connections through firewalls as RMI usually requires communication over an anonymous port. A full discussion on RMI is outside the scope of the book, but this is how it used to work in versions prior to R28:

- `-Xmanagement:port=<port>` opens up a single entry, read only, RMI registry on the specified port (default 7091)
- The RMI registry contains a single entry: `jmxrmi` — the stub for communicating with the RMI server
- The port of the RMI server is anonymous with no way to override it

In R28, things have improved. The RMI registry and the RMI server ports are the same by default, making firewall configuration much easier.

The JRockit Discovery Protocol

The JRockit JVM comes with a network auto discovery feature called **JRockit Discovery Protocol (JDP)**. The JDP Server works like a beacon that broadcasts the presence of the JRockit instance to the network. This makes it easier for JRockit Mission Control to automatically discover remote JVMs. The following example shows how to enable auto discovery.

```
JROCKIT_HOME/bin/java
  -Xmanagement:ssl=false,authenticate=false,port=4712,
  autodiscovery=true -cp . HelloJRMC
```

The following table lists the various system properties that can be used to control the JDP server in R28. Use the standard `-D` syntax for setting system properties on the command line when starting up the JRockit JVM.

For example:

```
-Dcom.oracle.management.autodiscovery.period=2500
```

System property	Explanation
`com.oracle.management.autodiscovery.period`	Time between broadcasts (milliseconds). Default is `5000`.
`com.oracle.management.autodiscovery.ttl`	Time to live for the broadcast packages. Default is `1` hop.
`com.oracle.management.autodiscovery.address`	The multicast address to use for autodiscovery. Default is `232.192.1.212`.

System property	Explanation
`com.oracle.management.autodiscovery.targetport`	Override the port used to broadcast autodiscovery information. Default is 7095.
`com.oracle.management.autodiscovery.name`	Hierarchical name. See the following example.

 To use the properties in the previous table for JRockit versions prior to R28, the `com.oracle.management.autodiscovery` namespace in the properties must be replaced by `jrockit.managementserver.discovery`, as it was called earlier.

When a JDP server transmits the location of a running JRockit JVM, the **JVM Browser** in the JRockit Mission Control client can use the hierarchical name in three different ways.

- **Simple name:**

  Example: `-Djrockit.managementserver.discovery.name=MyJVM`

  Result: The name of the connection when it appears in the browser will be `MyJVM`.

- **Full path:**

  Example: `-Djrockit.managementserver.discovery.name=/MyJVMs/MyJVM`

  Result: The connection will appear under a `MyJVMs` folder in the browser, and the name will be `MyJVM`.

- **Path ending with path delimiter:**

  Example: `-Djrockit.managementserver.discovery.name=/MyJVMs/`

  Result: The connection will appear under `MyJVMs`, the name will be the result of a reverse DNS lookup of the host reported by the JDP packet.

 Advanced tip for plug-in developers

System properties starting with the string `com.oracle.management.autodiscovery.property` will be automatically picked up by the JDP server and broadcast to the client. For the R28.0.0 version, no such extra properties are actually used by the client. The properties will, however, be present in the `IConnectionDescriptor` of the Mission Control client—a fact that can be used by authors of plug-ins for Mission Control.

For reference, the following table lists the various –Xmanagement arguments in JRockit R28:

Flag	Explanation	Default
port = <int>	The port of the RMI registry.	7091
ssl = [true|false]	Enables secure monitoring over SSL. Note that this only enables server-side SSL. If you also want clients to authenticate themselves, set com.sun.management.jmxremote.ssl. need.client.auth=true. Also note that SSL communication with the registry will not be enabled by default. See *registry.ssl*.	true
registry.ssl = [true|false]	Binds the RMI connector stub to an RMI registry protected by SSL.	false
authenticate = [true|false]	If this is set to false, JMX does not use passwords or access files—all users are allowed full access.	true
autodiscovery = [true|false]	Enables autodiscovery service for the remote JMX connector. Autodiscovery allows other machines on the same subnet to automatically detect a JVM with remote management enabled. Note that the autodiscovery service will only start if remote JMX management is enabled.	false
local = [true|false]	Explicitly enables or disables the local management agent.	true
rmiserver.port = <int>	Binds the RMI server to the specified port. Default behavior is to bind to the same port as the RMI registry if possible. However, if the RMI server is using SSL and the registry is not, an arbitrary free port will instead be selected.	Same as port
remote = [true|false]	Explicitly enables or disables the remote management agent.	false
config.file = <path>	Specifies a file from which to load additional management configuration properties.	JRE_HOME/lib/ management/ management. properties

There are also system properties available in JRockit R28 for controlling specific settings. The following table lists the relevant system properties with their default values:

Property	Explanation	Default
com.oracle.management.jmxremote = [true|false]	Enables JMX local monitoring through a JMX connector. The connector is published on a private interface used by local JMX clients through the Attach API (see the Java Documentation for com.sun.tools.attach). Clients can use this connector if it is started by the same user as the one that started the agent. No password or access files are checked for requests coming through this connector. If explicitly set to false, no local connector is started even if jmxremote.port is specified.	true
com.oracle.management.jmxremote.port = <int>	Same as -Xmanagement:port=<int>	7091
com.oracle.management.jmxremote.rmiserver.port = <int>	Same as -Xmanagement:rmiserver.port=<int>	7091
com.oracle.management.jmxremote.ssl = [true|false]	Same as -Xmanagement:ssl=[true|false]	true
com.oracle.management.jmxremote.registry.ssl = [true|false]	Same as -Xmanagement:registry.ssl=[true|false]	false
com.oracle.management.jmxremote.ssl.enabled.protocols = <values>	A comma-delimited list of SSL/TLS protocol versions to enable. Used in conjunction with the SSL flags.	Default SSL/TLS protocol version.
com.sun.management.jmxremote.ssl.enabled.cipher.suites = <values>	A comma-delimited list of SSL/TLS cipher suites to enable. Used in conjunction with the SSL flags.	Default SSL/TLS cipher suites.

Property	Explanation	Default

`com.oracle.management.`
`jmxremote.ssl.`
`need.client.auth =`
`[true|false]`
	If this property is `true` and `SSL` is enabled, client authentication will be performed.	`false`

`com.oracle.management.`
`jmxremote.authenticate`
`= [true|false]`
	Same as –
	`Xmanagement:authenticate =`
	`[true|false]`
		`true`

`com.oracle.management.`
`jmxremote.password.file`
`= <path>`
	Specifies the location of the password file. If `com.sun.`
	`management.jmxremote.`
	`authenticate` is `false`, this property and the password and access file are ignored. Otherwise, the password file must exist and be in the valid format. If the password file is empty or nonexistent, no access is allowed.
		`JRE_HOME/lib/`
		`management/`
		`jmxremote.`
		`password`

`com.oracle.management.`
`jmxremote.access.file =`
`<path>`
	Specifies the location for the access file. If `com.sun.management.`
	`jmxremote.authenticate` is `false`, then this property and the password and access file are ignored. Otherwise, the access file must exist and be in the valid format. If the access file is empty or nonexistent, no access is allowed.
		`JRE_HOME/lib/`
		`management/`
		`jmxremote.`
		`access`

`com.oracle.management.`
`jmxremote.login.config`
`= <config entry>`
	Specifies the name of a **Java Authentication and Authorization Service (JAAS)** login configuration entry to use when the JMX agent authenticates users. When using this property to override the default login configuration, the named configuration entry must be in a file that is loaded by JAAS. In addition, the login modules specified in the configuration should use the name and password callbacks to acquire the user's credentials. For more information, see the API documentation for `javax.`
	`security.auth.callback.`
	`NameCallback` and `javax.`
	`security.auth.callback.`
	`PasswordCallback`
		Default login configuration is file-based password authentication

Property	Explanation	Default
`com.oracle.management.jmxremote.config.file`	Same as `-Xmanagement:config.file=<file name>`	`JRE_HOME/lib/management/management.properties`
`com.oracle.management.snmp.port = <int>`	Enables the built-in SNMP agent on the specified port.	No default
`com.oracle.management.snmp.trap = <int>`	Remote port to which the built-in SNMP agent sends traps.	`162`
`com.oracle.management.snmp.acl = [true|false]`	Enables **Access Control Lists (ACL)** for the built-in SNMP agent.	`true`
`com.oracle.management.snmp.acl.file = <path>`	Path to a valid ACL file. After the agent has started, modifying the ACL file has no further effect.	`JRE_HOME/lib/management/snmp.acl`
`com.oracle.management.snmp.interface=<inetaddress>`	The `inetAddress` of the local host. This is used to force the built-in SNMP agent to bind to the given `inetAddress`. This is for multi-home hosts if one wants to listen to a specific subnet only.	No default
`com.oracle.management.autodiscovery = [true|false]`	Same as `-Xmanagement:autodiscovery=true`	`false`

Running in a secure environment

The best way to ensure a secure environment with JRockit Mission Control is to first use standard networking techniques, such as firewalls, to ensure that only a very limited set of machines are allowed to even attempt a connection to the management agent. Setting up routers and firewalls is beyond the scope of this book.

In versions prior to the JRockit R28, using firewalls with the management agent was complicated, as communication with the RMI server was done on an anonymous port. That is, after establishing a connection with the RMI registry, there was no way of influencing on what port the communication with the RMI server would take place. In R28, the same port is used for the registry and the server by default, which makes firewall configuration much easier.

For secure communication, the management agent should be configured to only allow SSL encrypted connections. The management agent can be configured to use SSL both for the RMI registry and the RMI server. For a secure environment, both should use SSL. By default, secure server authentication over SSL is enabled, but client authentication is not.

Following is an example of the options used to enable SSL on the server and the registry, as well as for enabling secure client authentication:

```
JROCKIT_HOME\bin\java -Xmanagement:ssl=true,registry.ssl=true,port=4711
  -Dcom.oracle.management.jmxremote.ssl.need.client.auth=true MyApp
```

For SSL to work, **certificates** must be set up. In most Java environments, a **keystore** is used to store the private keys, and a **truststore** to store the trusted certificates.

> For more information on using keystores, please see the *J2SE SDK Documentation*, on the Internet, especially the JSSE section on creating keystores.

Next, authentication and **roles** need to be configured to ensure that only authorized entities have access to sensitive functionality. Access rights are controlled by the `jmxremote.password` and `jmxremote.access` files. These are normally placed in the directory `JROCKIT_HOME/jre/lib/management/`. The **password file** contains the passwords for the different roles, and the **access file** specifies the access rights of each role. A role must have an entry in both files in order to work.

To facilitate easy setup, there is a `jmxremote.password` template file included with the JRockit JRE. To get started with this template, copy the file `JROCKIT_HOME/jre/lib/management/jmxremote.password.template` to `JROCKIT_HOME/jre/lib/management/jmxremote.password`.

> To be able to initiate JMXMAPI, which is necessary for all Mission Control tools to work, the user must have the permission to create the `JRockitConsole` MBean.

Following is an example of granting permission to create the `JRockitConsole` MBean to the **control role** (see the `jmxremote.access` file):

```
controlRole readwrite \
create oracle.jrockit.management.JRockitConsole
```

The `JRockitConsole` MBean will in turn initiate the rest of JMXMAPI.

In a multi-user environment, that is, in an environment where different users will use the same Java installation, the custom is to copy the `jmxremote.password` file to each user's home directory and use the `com.sun.management.jmxremote.password.file` system property to specify the location of the file.

As the password file contains unencrypted passwords, Java will rely on the file permissions of the underlying operating system to ensure that the file can only be read by the user executing the JVM. If an error is shown about the password file not being restricted, steps must be taken to ensure that the password file is only readable by the user that is executing the Java process. On a *NIX system, this can be done by executing something like `chmod 600 <password file name>` from a shell. On a Windows system, the process is slightly more complicated.

> There is a good guide for setting file access permissions on Windows in the *Java 1.5.0 documentation*, available at `http://java.sun.com/j2se/1.5.0/docs/guide/management/security-windows.html`.

To top things off, all communication can be done over an encrypted SSH tunnel, instead of by opening an additional port in the firewall. Access to the SSH tunnel is commonly enabled through a port on `localhost`. The stub transmitted when a connection to the JMX agent is established normally contains the address of the computer to connect to. We want to trick the computer running the agent into transmitting a stub containing the loopback address or `localhost` instead. This can either be done by editing the `hosts` file, or by setting the `java.rmi.server.hostname` system property on startup. Both these techniques should be used with caution, as they may cause problems for other software running in the system and/or on the same JVM.

Troubleshooting connections

If you are having problems connecting to locally discovered JRockit JVMs, you should check:

- If you are running on Windows, verify that the system temporary directory is on a file system that supports file permissions (for example NTFS). This is required. Local connections will create artifacts that rely on file permissions to work, and will simply fail if running on a FAT file system.

- Are you really attempting to connect to a JRockit JVM, and is the Mission Control client (or Eclipse, if running in Eclipse) running on a JRockit JVM?

- If a local connection is attempted, are both your JRockit Mission Control Client and the JRockit JVM that you are attempting to connect to, using a JDK version of 1.5 or later?

- Is the JVM you are trying to connect to executing as your user?

 To connect to a locally executing 1.4 version of the JRockit JVM, create a connection manually in the JRockit Mission Control **JVM Browser**. Then start the management agent explicitly on the JRockit JVM that you want to monitor. This is because 1.4 versions of the JVM really do not have a platform MBean server. JRockit 1.4 versions did, however, implement a proprietary management protocol called RMP that is translated to JMX on the client. Starting the agent can either be done by using the command-line options as described earlier, or by using the JRCMD tool, described in Chapter 11.

If you are having problems connecting to an external management agent (usually, but not necessarily, one running on a remote machine) you should check:

- Is the connection properly configured? There is a test button in the connection wizard that will verify the settings for you. If you are trying to connect to a JDK 1.4 version of the JRockit JVM, you should be using a 3.x client.

- Is the correct version of the client being used? The easiest way to be sure is to use the version that came with the JVM. If attempting to connect to a JDK 1.4 version of the JRockit JVM, a 3.x version should be used.

- Is the 1.4/1.5 setting correct in the Connection Wizard?

- Is the firewall configured to let the traffic through on the appropriate ports?

- If SSL is being used, are the SSL settings correct on both the server and the client?

- If authentication is enabled, is the `jmxremote.access` file properly set up, as described in the Java SE documentation?

- Verify the `hosts` file of the machine to which you are trying to connect.

While troubleshooting connections to the remote management agent, first make sure that the connection works with SSL and that authentication is turned off. If that works, make sure that all the steps in the *Running in a Secure Environment* section have been followed, that the certificate is valid, that the keystore password is correct, and that the `password.properties` file has been properly configured.

If the Management Console tells you that a certain MBean, for instance the Profiling MBean, cannot be found, it may be due to a misconfigured `jmxremote.access` file. To be able to initialize JMXMAPI, the user must have authorization to create the `JRockitConsole` MBean that, in turn, will initialize the rest of the JMXMAPI. See the *Running in a Secure Environment* section for more information.

Hostname resolution issues

Trouble connecting Mission Control to a remote machine can sometimes stem from the hostname resolving to the wrong address, for example to `127.0.0.1` (or `localhost`). An exception looking something like this would normally be shown in such a case:

```
Could not open Management Console for sthx6454:7094.
  java.rmi.ConnectException: Connection refused to host:
    127.0.0.1; nested exception is: java.net.ConnectException:
    Connection refused: connect
  at sun.rmi.transport.tcp.TCPEndpoint.newSocket(TCPEndpoint.java:574)
  at sun.rmi.transport.tcp.TCPChannel.createConnection
    (TCPChannel.java:185)
  at sun.rmi.transport.tcp.TCPChannel.newConnection(TCPChannel.java:171)
  at sun.rmi.server.UnicastRef.invoke(UnicastRef.java:94)
  at javax.management.remote.rmi.RMIServerImpl_Stub.newClient
    (Unknown Source)
  at javax.management.remote.rmi.RMIConnector.getConnection
    (RMIConnector.java:2239)
  at javax.management.remote.rmi.RMIConnector.connect
    (RMIConnector.java:271)
  at javax.management.remote.rmi.RMIConnector.connect
    (RMIConnector.java:229)
  at com.jrockit.console.rjmx.RJMXConnection.setupServer
    (RJMXConnection.java:504)
```

The RMI registry exports a stub relying on a hostname to establish a connection to the RMI server. In the previous example, we have successfully connected to the RMI registry and retrieved a stub for connecting to the RMI server. However, the default behavior when creating the stub is to use `InetAddress.getLocalHost().getHostAddress()`, to find out what host name to use. This will of course be a problem if the machine is multi-homed (that is, has several network interfaces) or if it is badly configured. In the previous example, the information provided in the stub tells us to connect to `localhost` instead of `sthx6454`.

The most common problem is that the `hosts` file (`/etc/hosts` on Linux systems, `%SYSTEMROOT%\system32\drivers\etc\hosts` on Windows) is not properly configured. On a Linux system, `hostname -i` can be used to see what the hostname resolves to.

A workaround is to set the `java.rmi.server.hostname` system property on the server to whatever name the client should use to locate the machine. Note that this can affect other applications running on the JVM.

Another workaround is to use SSH tunneling where the fact that the hostname resolves to `localhost` can be used to an advantage. This workaround is only possible using JRockit R28, where the RMI server port can be explicitly specified.

The Experimental Update Site

Since JRockit Mission Control 3.1, there is an Experimental Update Site from which plug-ins for Mission Control can be installed. The plug-ins either extend JRockit Mission Control, or facilitate building extensions for JRockit Mission Control. The homepage for the update site for 3.1 versions of JRockit Mission Control can be found here:

```
http://www.oracle.com/technology/software/products/jrockit/
missioncontrol/updates/experimental/3.1.0/eclipse/index.html
```

The update site for the 4.0 release can be found here:

```
http://www.oracle.com/technology/software/products/jrockit/
missioncontrol/updates/experimental/4.0.0/eclipse/index.html
```

When using the update site URLs in Eclipse, the ending `index.html` must be removed.

Both the JRockit and reference J2SE distributions contain a reference JMX console called JConsole. The 3.1.0 release of the update site included a plug-in that allowed JConsole plug-ins to be run within JRockit Mission Control. It also contained a set of **Plug-in Development Environment** (PDE) plug-ins that allows the development of custom plug-ins for the JRockit Mission Control Console. More information on creating plug-ins for JRockit Mission Control can be found at the end of *Chapter 7* (*The Management Console*), in *Chapter 9* (*The Flight Recorder*), and in *Chapter 10* (*The Memory Leak Detector*).

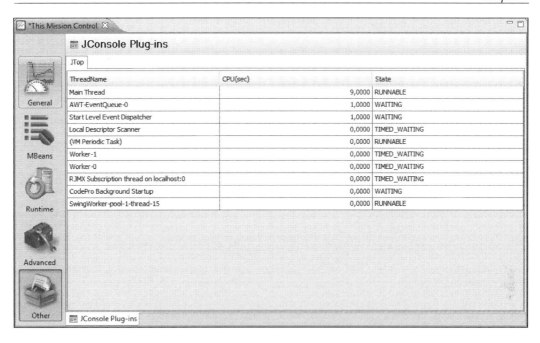

After the 4.0 release of JRockit Mission Control, Oracle plants to make additional plug-ins for Mission Control available. New experimental plug-ins will be announced on the blog at `http://blogs.oracle.com/hirt`.

Debugging JRockit Mission Control

JRockit Mission Control can be started in debugging mode to provide more information. Simply add the `-debug` flag when launching the `jrmc` executable. Starting in debug mode will cause various subsystems to behave differently. For example, the console charts will start showing rendering information and log levels will be changed to display more verbose output.

To view the log messages sent to the console on Windows systems, `stderr` must be redirected somewhere. This is because the `jrmc` launcher is derived from the `javaw` launcher. Following is an example:

```
D:\>%JROCKIT_HOME%\bin\jrmc -consoleLog -debug 2>&1 | more
```

To only change the logging levels, select a Logging settings file in the **Preferences**. The logging settings file is a file on standard `java.util.logging` format. After changing the logging settings, JRockit Mission Control must be restarted.

The following example shows the debug settings used when starting with
the –debug flag:

```
###########################################################
# JRockit Mission Control Logging Configuration File
#
# This file can be overridden by setting the path to another
# settings file in the Mission Control preferences.
###########################################################


###########################################################
# Global properties
###########################################################


# "handlers" specifies a comma separated list of log Handler
# classes. These handlers will be installed during ApplicationPlugin
# startup.
# Note that these classes must be on the system classpath.
handlers= java.util.logging.FileHandler,
  java.util.logging.ConsoleHandler


# Default global logging level.
# This specifies which kinds of events are logged across
# all loggers.  For any given facility this global level
# can be overridden by a facility specific level
# Note that the ConsoleHandler also has a separate level
# setting to limit messages printed to the console.
.level= ALL


###########################################################
# Handler specific properties.
# Describes specific configuration info for Handlers.
###########################################################


# Default file output is in user's home directory.
java.util.logging.FileHandler.pattern = %h/mc_%u.log
java.util.logging.FileHandler.limit = 50000
```

```
java.util.logging.FileHandler.count = 1

java.util.logging.FileHandler.formatter =
  java.util.logging.SimpleFormatter

java.util.logging.FileHandler.level = FINE


java.util.logging.ConsoleHandler.formatter =
  java.util.logging.SimpleFormatter

java.util.logging.ConsoleHandler.level = FINE


############################################################
# Facility specific properties.
# Provides extra control for each logger.
# For example setting the warning level for logging from the
# JRockit Browser, add the following line:
# com.jrockit.mc.browser.level = INFO
############################################################
sun.rmi.level = INFO

javax.management.level = INFO
```

Summary

This chapter explained how to get started with the JRockit Mission Control tools suite. We briefly went over the background for the product and its various subcomponents—the Management Console, the Memory Leak Detector, and the Flight Recorder. For completeness, we also mentioned JRCMD, the command-line tool that is part of the JRockit JDK.

We showed how to run both the standalone version of Mission Control and the plug-in version for the Eclipse IDE. We explained how to enable the JRockit management agent for remote management and how to troubleshoot the connection when Mission Control fails to connect. Additional tips and tricks on how to debug the Mission Control client were also presented.

We outlined how to secure access to the server-side Mission Control components. Finally, the Experimental Update Site, where additional content for Mission Control can be found, was introduced.

The next few chapters will focus on the various tools in the JRockit Mission Control suite.

7

The Management Console

The oldest tool in the JRockit Mission Control tools suite is the JRockit Management Console. The Management Console can be used to monitor the JRockit JVM and any application running in the JVM. It can also be used to alter the runtime state of certain parameters in JRockit. This chapter assumes some prior familiarity with **Java Management Extensions (JMX)** and the JMX terminology.

 For more information on JMX go to `http://java.sun.com/javase/` `technologies/core/mntr-mgmt/javamanagement/`

The Management Console relies on the JMX standard and provides a way to monitor any application that exposes manageability features through JMX, including the JRockit JVM.

In this chapter you will learn:

- How to start up the Management Console
- How to monitor and plot arbitrary MBean attributes
- How to invoke arbitrary MBean operations
- How to create trigger rules
- How to enable deadlock detection
- How to perform per-thread memory allocation and CPU profiling
- About the diagnostic commands
- How to extend the Management Console

A JMX Management Console

The JRockit Management Console predates the JRockit Mission Control tools suite. It even predates JMX.

The first few versions of JRockit were made available as "Virtual Machines for Java", not JVMs. The key difference is that only a virtual machine certified by Sun (now Oracle) to be compliant with the Java standard is allowed to be called a JVM. Furthermore, if the VM is not certified, it may not use the Java trademark. At that time, in order to be accepted as a Sun certified JVM, a key differentiator, known as "value add" was required. In our first attempt to become a proper Java licensee, we had specified "superior performance" as our value add. While technically true, it was not deemed to be a valid value add, so we exposed some of the online manageability aspects of the JVM instead. This is what became the JRockit Management Console.

The primary use of the Management Console is to provide detailed monitoring of one or more JRockit instances. As each monitored JVM has its own Management Console (editor), more than a few JVM instances are rarely monitored at a time. To monitor large installations for longer periods of time, a distributed solution that scales well over large amounts of JVMs should be used, such as **Oracle Enterprise Manager**.

The Management Console and JRockit use standard JMX technology for communication. As of Java 5.0, some aspects of using JMX to expose manageability features of the JVM are standardized through JSR-174.

JSR-174 enhanced the manageability of the JVM by adding the `java.lang.management` classes and providing the platform MBean server.

For more information on the platform MBean server, see the Java *APIs and Documentation on SDN* on the Internet and search for **java.lang.management.ManagementFactory.getPlatformMBeanServer()**

Since the advent of JSR-174 and the platform MBean server, most Java applications and frameworks are publishing their monitoring and management MBeans to the platform MBean server, which in effect means that the Management Console can monitor most parts of the software stack running in the JVM.

As JRockit had a Management Console well before the start of JSR-174, the JRockit Management Console can also connect to pre 1.5.0 versions of JRockit. In these setups, everything still looks like JMX to the client, but underneath a proprietary protocol is used.

The rest of this chapter is dedicated to discussing the JRockit Mission Control Console and its various uses. The chapter is divided into sections corresponding to the different tabs in the Management Console, so that it can also be used as a reference to quickly check on details for a specific tab.

Using the console

Starting a JRockit Management Console is quite easy—simply select the JVM to connect to from the **JVM Browser** and either click on the Management Console button from the toolbar, or click on **Start Console** from the context menu.

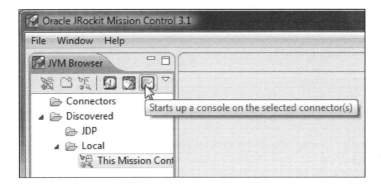

There is a trick available for starting the console—connections can be dragged and dropped into the editor area. The default action for dragging a connection to the editor area is to open up the Console on the connection. Recollect from *Chapter 6*, *JRockit Mission Control*, that connections are either remote or local—the difference being that the local connections are automatically discovered JVMs running on the local machine. This particular trick does not work with local connections, as they cannot be used as sources in drag-and-drop operations.

For more information on the different types of connections and how to establish remote connections, see the previous chapter.

General

The tabs in the Management Console are grouped into different tab groups, the first one being the **General** tab-group. The different tab groups are accessible through the vertical toolbar to the left in the Management Console editor, as shown in the following screenshot:

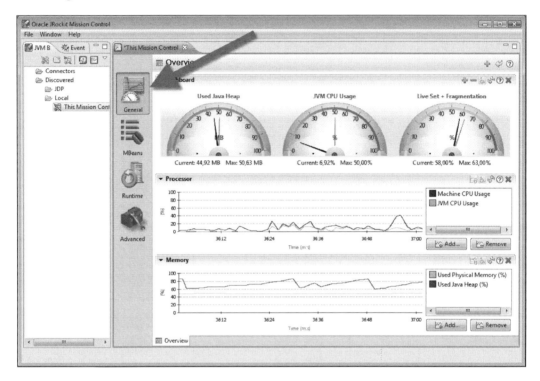

The **General** tab group only contains one tab—the **Overview**. The tab folder where the visible tab can be changed is located at the bottom of the JRockit Mission Control editor.

The Overview

This tab shows an overview of some key characteristics of the JVM and its operating environment. The tab is highly configurable and should you require other information than the chosen key characteristics; it can be adapted to your needs.

The following screenshot shows the **Overview** tab of the JRockit Management Console:

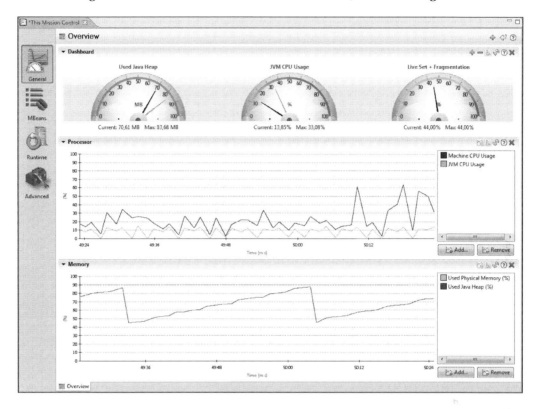

The tabs in JRockit Mission Control are divided into section parts. At the top of the **Overview** tab is a section part called **Dashboard**. The **Dashboard** contains an array of dials. Each dial can plot the current and maximum value obtained for an attribute that is being monitored. The lighter of the two indicators in a dial shows the **watermark**, which indicates the maximum value attained since a subscription to the attribute started. The darker indicator shows the current value. Both the current and maximum values are also shown as numbers below the dial.

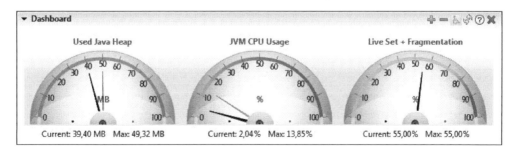

In the Management Console, most section parts can be folded away to allow more space for the other sections in the same tab. Simply click on the little triangle (▾) at the top left of the section part to fold it. The section parts also contain a toolbar with various actions. Some commonly used actions are:

- **Accessibility mode toggle**: Toggles the contents of the section part between the default graphical representation and an alternative, text-based representation.

- **Updates toggle**: Toggles updates for the contents of the section part.

- **Help**: Provides context sensitive help for the section part when clicked.

- **Remove:** Removes the section part altogether.

- **Add**: Adds a component of the kind that the section part contains. In the case of a dial section part, a dial will be added.

- **Delete**: Deletes one of the enclosed components from the section part.

- **Table settings**: This action provides a dialog for configuring a table. Most tables only show a selection of columns by default, and more columns can be made visible, as needed, by using the table configuration dialog.

It is possible to revert any changes by clicking the **Reset to default** button (⟳) in the upper right corner of the toolbar for the tab.

The **Dashboard** can be reconfigured in various ways. It is possible to add dials, remove dials, and change the attributes that each dial displays. The entire dial section part can be removed altogether. As the dial has a resettable watermark that shows the maximum value attained for an attribute, dials are useful for attributes that may peak very intermittently, but that you still want to keep an eye on.

 Changes made to automatically discovered connections are not saved. If you suspect you will want to keep the adjustments made in the console user interface, make sure that you use a **user-defined connection** as described in the previous chapter.

The default attributes shown in the dial dashboard are the Current and Max values for heap usage, the CPU usage of the JVM process, and the live set and fragmentation as a percentage of the heap size. The last value is a good measure of how full the heap is and it is only calculated and updated on every garbage collection. If no indicator is shown for the **Live Set + Fragmentation** dial, it means that no garbage collection has taken place yet.

One way to force a garbage collection is to press the little garbage can icon (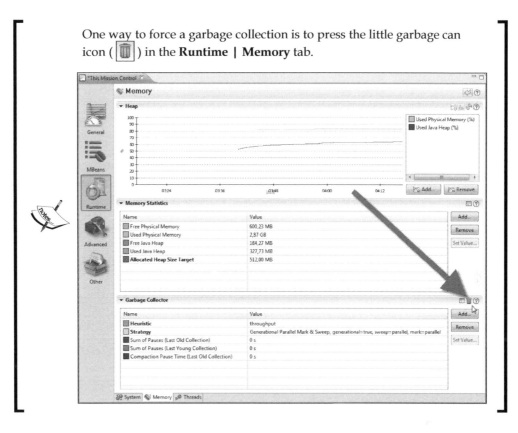) in the **Runtime | Memory** tab.

A JVM process that is constantly saturating the CPU (maxing out the CPU load) can be a good thing. For instance, for a batch application that is computationally bound, it would normally be a best case scenario for it to complete as soon as possible. Normally, however, some over-provisioning is needed to keep an application responsive. If the CPU usage is very high, you may want to invest in better hardware, or look over the data structures and algorithms employed by the application. One very good way to proceed is to capture a JRockit Flight Recording to find out where all those cycles are being spent.

Having a very large percentage of the heap filled with live objects will increase the garbage collector overhead, as GCs will have to be run more frequently. If the **Live Set + Fragmentation** dial remains steady on a high level and garbage collection performance is an issue, increasing the heap size will improve performance. If the trend is for the **Live Set + Fragmentation** dial instead to steadily increase over time, there is probably a memory leak in the application. We will give memory leaks more attention in *Chapter 10, The Memory Leak Detector*.

As any attribute available in the platform MBean server can be subscribed to. This includes attributes from any domain, such as application server MBeans or even your own MBeans that you have registered in the platform MBean server. An example of such an attribute is the `OpenSessionsCurrentCount` in WebLogic Server.

> WebLogic Server does not use the platform MBean server by default. However, if you wish to monitor the WebLogic Server MBeans together with the MBeans provided by the rest of the platform, it may be convenient to make WebLogic Server add the MBeans to the platform MBean server. Consult your WebLogic Server documentation for information on how to do this.
>
> The recommendation from WebLogic Server is to not use the platform MBean server, as there are potential security implications, especially if the applications running in the JVM cannot be trusted. If you use the platform MBean server, make sure you understand the security implications, as all code running in the JVM will have access to the WebLogic MBeans.

The two charts under the **Dashboard** show CPU usage information and memory information, one below the other. The CPU usage is listed as a percentage of full CPU saturation and is an average across all available cores. It is shown for both the entire machine and the JVM process. For the memory chart, the used heap is shown as a percentage of the total heap size and used physical memory is shown as a percentage of the total physical memory available.

One way to track the live set and fragmentation is to check how the heap usage changes over time in the memory chart.

Consider the following screenshot. An imaginary line is drawn through each point in time where a garbage collection has finished and where memory has been reclaimed. This gives us a good indication as to what is happening to the live set.

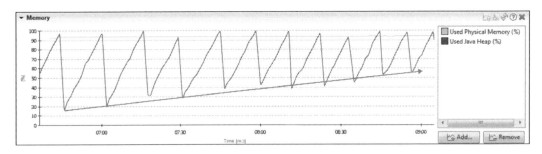

An even better way to watch live set and fragmentation is of course to simply add the **Live Set + Fragmentation** attribute to the chart, as shown in the following screenshot.

As can be seen from the growing live set in the screenshot, the monitored application probably has a memory leak. If left unchecked, the application will eventually throw an `OutOfMemoryError`.

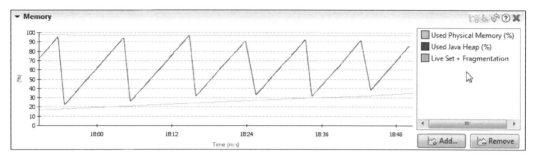

The charts can also be configured. It is possible to add or remove attributes to subscribe to. The colors used to visualize attributes, the text labels, and various other properties can also be changed.

Another useful, but often overlooked, feature is that additional info can be gained when the chart is frozen. If a chart is frozen by toggling the updates button ( ), context sensitive tooltips will be shown with detailed information when the pointer is hovered near a point in a data series. This is shown in the following screenshot:

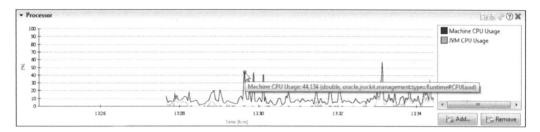

A chart will automatically be frozen when zooming in on a selection. To make a selection in a chart, simply left click and drag with the mouse to select the time period to zoom in on. To zoom in, select **Zoom | Selection** from the context menu.

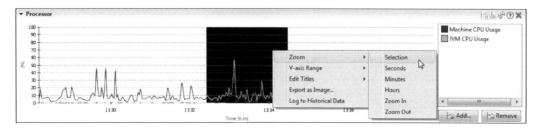

The default value range selected for the Y-axis of new charts and most of the default charts in the user interface is between **0** and **100**. This setting must be changed when adding an attribute that has values outside this range. In the following screenshot, the **Total Loaded Class Count** attribute has been added. It will always be outside the **0** to **100** range. To configure the Y-axis range to automatically select the correct range, select one of the auto range alternatives, for instance **Y-axis Range | Auto, always show zero**, from the context menu.

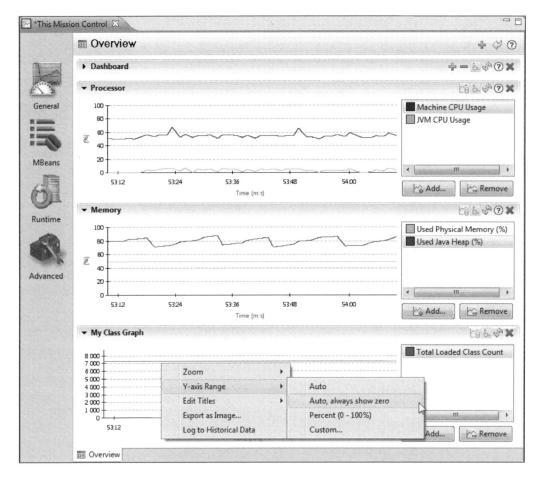

None of the range choices will alter the input data in any way. The **Percent** range will simply set the range to **0-100%** and add a percent sign to the Y-axis title. An attribute value of **1** will not be rendered as **100%**.

An attribute that has a value range of **0** to **1** can still be rendered correctly in the **Percent (0-100%)** range by adding a **pre-multiplier** to the attribute. Both CPU usage attributes have a pre-multiplier setting of **100**. To change the pre-multiplier, right click on the attribute and then, click on **Edit Pre-multiplier** as shown in the following screenshot:

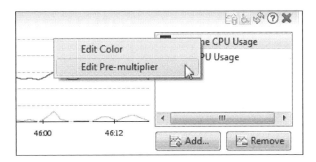

The charts are quite useful and there are more options available for charts than described here. A tip (certainly valid for most components in JRockit Mission Control) is to examine the choices available in the context menus for a component.

MBeans

The **MBeans** tab group contains tabs with general tools for viewing, manipulating, subscribing, and creating trigger rules for various aspects of the MBeans. It contains two tabs—the **MBean Browser** that can be used for browsing the different attributes in the MBeans registered in the platform MBean server, and the **Triggers** tab that can be used to create rules that trigger when user specified conditions occur.

MBean Browser

The first tab in the MBeans tab group is the **MBean Browser**. This is where all the attributes available in the platform MBean server can be browsed. Primitive values as well as collections, arrays, composite data, and tabular data can be viewed. To make it easier to view large collections, the **MBean Browser** will automatically group values into subgroups. How the values are grouped can be controlled by changing the preferences.

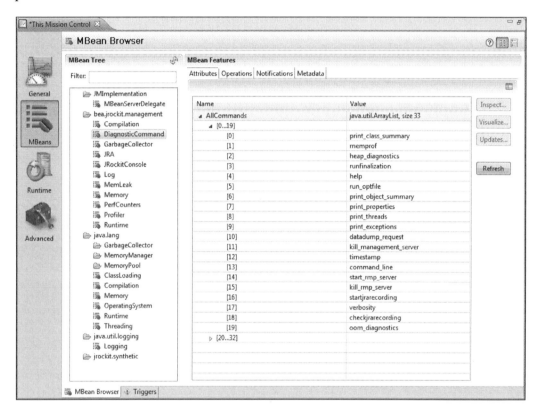

If an attribute in the list is rendered in a bold faced font, it means it is writable. Simple MBean attributes can be changed directly in the MBean browser table. It is, for example, possible to go to the **GarbageCollector** MBean under the **oracle.jrockit. management** domain and change the allocated heap size of JRockit. Simply double click on the **AllocatedHeapSizeTarget**, and change the value. Don't worry if the value of the **AllocatedHeapSize** does not follow suit immediately, as JRockit may have to choose another heap size for various reasons, including memory alignment and currently occupied memory.

The attribute table in the **MBean Browser** contains more information than is shown by default. In the following screenshot, the table settings have been updated to show the update interval for the attributes:

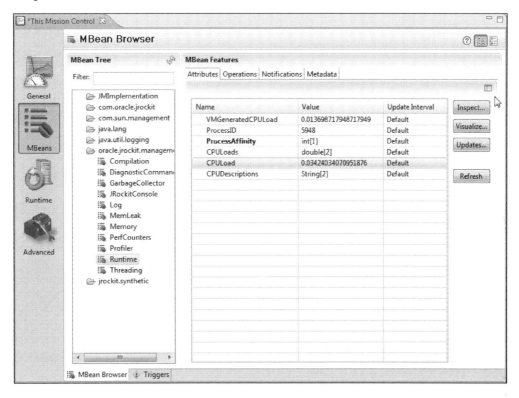

The default update interval is once every second (1,000 milliseconds). To change the default update interval for an attribute, select the attribute in the table and click on the **Updates...** button.

This will open the update interval dialog, where the appropriate update interval can be selected, as shown in the following screenshot:

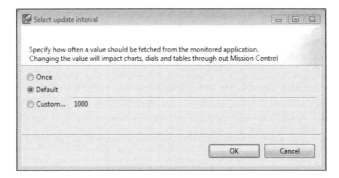

The update interval for an attribute can be set to:

- **Once:** The attribute will only be fetched once if subscribed to. This is good for attributes that are not expected to change, such as the number of CPUs.

- **Default:** The default update interval setting. The default update interval is normally set to 1,000 milliseconds, but that can be changed in the preferences.

- **Custom:** A custom update interval specified in milliseconds.

In the following screenshot, the update interval has been changed for the CPU load—it will only be fetched once every two seconds:

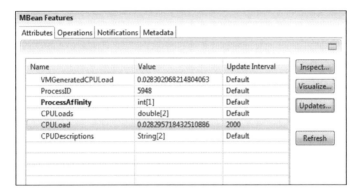

The **MBean Browser** can also be used to invoke MBean operations dynamically. This feature is very useful when prototyping a JMX API or when simply trying out someone's else's JMX API.

For example:

A **diagnostic command** can be invoked by browsing to the **DiagnosticCommand** MBean under the **oracle.jrockit.management** domain. Diagnostic commands are explained in detail later in this chapter, as well as in *Chapter 11, JRCMD*.

Select the **Operations** tab and then select the **execute(String p1)** operation and click on **invoke**. Click on the **p1** button to set the parameter and enter `print_threads`. Click on **OK** to set the parameter and then **OK** again to execute the operation. You should now see a thread stack dump. There is, of course, a much easier way to do this. Simply use the **Diagnostic Commands** tab under the **Advanced** tab group.

One thing that sets aside the Mission Control Management Console from other JMX consoles is that it is able to subscribe to many different kinds of values, or even part of values. It is, for instance, possible to subscribe to sub-values of a composite data attribute.

For example:

1. Go to the **java.lang | MemoryPool | Old Space MBean** (The `java.lang:type=MemoryPool:name=Old Space` MBean to be precise).
2. Expand the **Usage** attribute and select a key in the composite data, for instance **# used.**
3. Right click and select **Visualize....**
4. Select a chart to add the attribute to, or click on **Add Chart** to add a new chart.

Go back to **Overview** to check out your chart. Remember to change the Y-axis to **auto**, as the chart defaults to a fixed range between **0** and **100**.

The subscription engine can also handle subscriptions based on JMX notifications and **synthetic attributes**. Synthetic attributes have a corresponding, client side, class that implement the value retrieval. As the class can be implemented in whatever way the implementer desires, it can be used to retrieve the value from any source at all, not even necessarily JMX. The **LiveSet** attribute is an example of a synthetic attribute that relies on the notification-based GC attribute and some additional calculations. There is also a **Notification** tab, where you will find the JMX notifications available on the selected MBean. Most MBeans do not have notifications.

For example:

1. Go to the **GarbageCollector** MBean under the **oracle.jrockit.management** domain.
2. Select the **Notifications** tab.
3. Check the **Subscribe** check box.
4. Go to the **Operations** tab.
5. Invoke the **gc** operation.
6. Go back to the **Notifications** tab and check the result.

Depending on which garbage collector you have selected and which version of JRockit you are using, you may have one or several notifications listed in notifications tab.

For other examples on notifications available, see the Java documentation on `java.lang.management.MemoryPoolMXBean` and the `java.lang:Memory` MBean.

The **Notification** tab is not very interesting—it is mostly meant for trying out notification-based JMX APIs. It is much more useful to weave the notifications into the subscription service in the Management Console, so that they can participate in the attribute visualization framework.

> There is, unfortunately, currently no officially documented way of adding your own synthetic or notification based attributes. To see how it works today, search the `attributes.xml` file in the `com.jrockit.mc.rjmx` plugin for `flavour="synthetic"` and `flavour="Notification"` respectively. If you would like to see official support for this, please let the authors know.

Triggers

With the Management Console, rules can be built that trigger when a certain user-defined condition occurs. Such a rule consists of three different parts:

1. **A trigger condition**: This specifies when to trigger. An example of a trigger condition can be that CPU Load exceeds 90 percent.

2. **An action**: The action defines what to do when the rule triggers. An example of an action is to send an e-mail with information about the condition that caused the rule to trigger.

3. **A set of constraints**: This is a set of constraints that, in addition to the trigger condition, must be fulfilled for the rule to trigger. An example of such a set of constraints can be a day and a time, for instance "only weekdays" and "between 9:00 AM and 6:00 PM".

In the **Triggers** tab, you can add, remove, activate, deactivate, and edit such rules. As of JRockit Mission Control 3.1, these rules can be added to a set of rules that can be exported and imported.

As shown in the following screenshot, the rules already defined are listed in the **Trigger Rules** tree to the left, and the details for a selected rule are shown to the right:

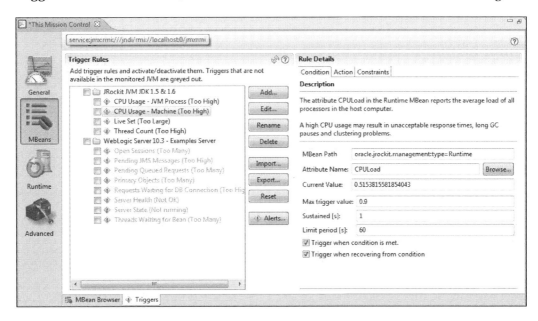

Note that simple modifications to an existing rule, such as changing what action to take, or changing the trigger value, can be done by directly editing the rule in the **Rule Details** section. In the earlier example, no trigger rule is currently active. To activate a rule, simply click on the check box next to rule name in the **Trigger Rules** tree.

For example:

JRockit Mission Control comes pre-packaged with various example rules. For the sake of clarity, let's create a duplicate rule of one of the pre-existing ones.

1. Click on **Add....** This will bring up the **Add New Rule** Wizard.

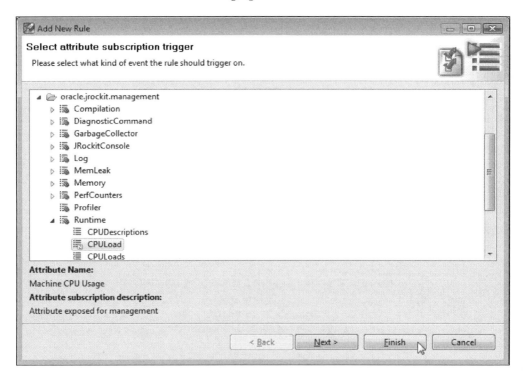

2. Expand the **oracle.jrockit.management | Runtime** MBean.
3. Select the **CPULoad** attribute.

    The little N ( ) in the icon indicates that this is a numeric attribute. It is possible to build rules that are not based on numeric attributes; for string attributes there is a string matching expression instead of a numeric evaluator.

4. Click on **Next** and choose the **Max trigger value** – this is the boundary value upon which the trigger will take action. In this case we can, for example, choose **0.25**. Triggers operate on the raw value from the subscription, so the pre-multiplier will not be active. The **CPULoad** attribute gives us the CPU load as a fraction, and so **0.25** would mean 25 percent. With the default settings, this means that action will be taken once the CPU load passes 25 percent and once when the trigger recovers and goes below 25 percent.

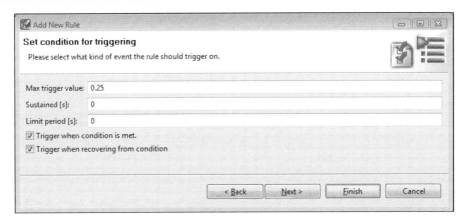

5. There are other options available to us, that we won't change for this example:

    ° **Sustained [s]**: This decides for how long the value must be sustained above the threshold before triggering.

    ° **Limit period [s]**: The period after which to throttle the events, that is events will not trigger more often than this. Events that do trigger more often will simply be discarded.

    ° **Trigger when condition is met**: In our case, when the attribute goes from less than **0.25** to greater than or equal to **0.25**.

    ° **Trigger when recovering from condition**: In our case, when the attribute goes from greater than or equal to **0.25** to less than **0.25**.

6. Click on **Next** and select the **Application alert** action.

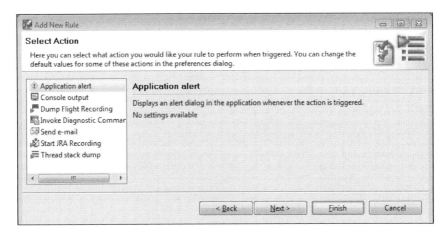

The **Application alert** action requires no settings. When a rule triggers with the application alert action, the triggered event is logged and optionally displayed in a log dialog window. There are a few default actions available, but the fun part is that it is possible to write your own actions. We'll show you how at the end of this chapter.

7. Click on **Next** and optionally select one or more constraints.

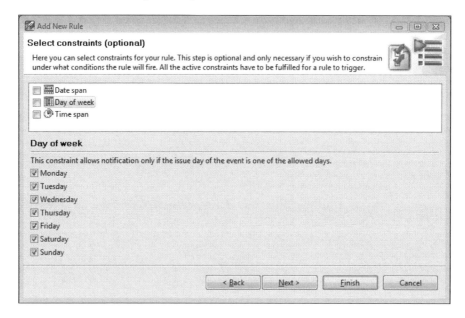

For this example, it really isn't necessary, but it is nice to be able to have constraints that limit when the rule may trigger, such as only on weekdays. You can write your own constraints too. It works pretty much the same way as the actions.

8. Click on **Next** and review the group and rule names.

It is usually a good idea to put in an informative description of the rule as well as to explain in a little more detail what the rule does and how it is supposed to be used. You can use the standard `<b>`, `</b>`, and `<br/>` HTML tags in your description for formatting.

9. Click on **Finish**.

10. Enable the new rule by checking the check box next to the rule name in the **Trigger Rules** tree.

11. Add some CPU load to make the rule trigger. You can usually peak the load by forcing the UI to redraw itself a lot, for example by frantically resizing the UI for a little while.

The **Trigger Alerts** dialog should pop up and show you the details of why one of your rules triggered, as shown in the following screenshot:

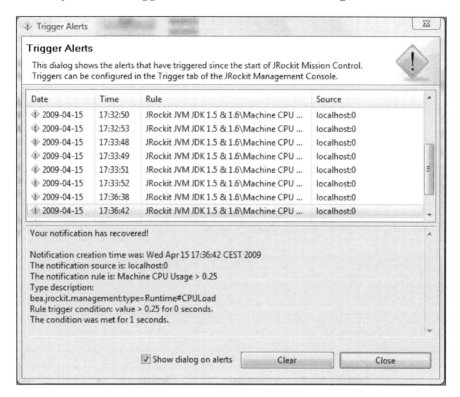

It is possible to extend the Management Console with custom-made actions and constraints. This is done by creating custom-made plug-ins that use a few well-defined extension points. Please see the end of this chapter for details on how to do this.

Runtime

The **Runtime** tab group contains a few tabs that visualize information about the JRockit runtime. The first tab in the **Runtime** tab group is the **System** tab.

System

The most useful thing in this tab is the filterable **System Properties** table. System properties can either be filtered by key or by property. For example, to show the properties that start with java.vm, simply write **java.vm** in the filter text box.

It is possible to use regular expressions in the JRockit Mission Control filter textboxes by prefixing the filter string with "regexp:". For example, to filter out all properties starting with "sun." and ending with "path", the following expression can be used: regexp:sun\..*path

Some useful default properties have been added to an attribute table named **System Statistics**. Most tables in JRockit Mission Control only show a few selected columns by default. To show more columns, either select the column to show from the table context menu (**Visible Columns | <column name>**), or click on the little table icon in the section toolbar ( ) to bring up the **Table Settings** dialog. In the previous screenshot, the **Updated** column has been added to the table, which shows when the attribute was last updated. Note that different tables will have different information available.

As you can see from the example, different attributes may have different update policies. Attributes that are not likely to change very often will be requested less often than other attributes. The JVM version can be expected to not change at all. The number of CPUs in the machine will also probably not change during a particular run. How often an attribute is to be updated can be changed in the **MBean Browser**.

Memory

This tab contains memory-related information. At the top is the familiar memory chart from the **Overview** tab, followed by two attribute tables. The first attribute table contains memory statistics, and the second one GC-related attributes. The most interesting part here is that there are actually a few of these that can be changed at runtime—the allocated heap size, the garbage collector strategy, and the garbage collector heuristic.

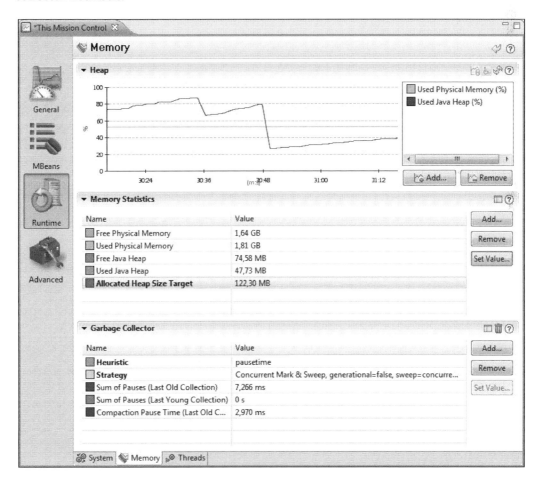

The GC **heuristic** is the rule set that the garbage collector currently uses to adaptively alter the GC strategy and other GC parameters. Such a heuristic can, for instance, be `throughput` that optimizes for maximum memory system throughput or `pausetime`, that optimizes for lowest possible pause times.

The rules for valid heuristic changes are somewhat different for different releases of JRockit. The rules for changing GC heuristic in R28 are quite versatile. Heuristics can be changed freely with one exception—it is not possible to change another heuristic to `deterministic`. This is because a lot of special data structures and configuration settings are created at JVM startup when starting with the deterministic garbage collector (JRockit Real Time).

The garbage collection **strategy** is defined by nursery, mark strategy and sweep strategy. The nursery can either be present or not present. The mark and sweep phases can either be concurrent or parallel, using the terms as defined in Chapter 3.

The strategy can also be changed freely in R28, with one exception—if JRockit was started explicitly with the `singlepar` strategy (`-Xgc:singlepar`), the strategy cannot be changed at all. However, if starting with any other strategy, it is possible to change back and forth from `singlepar`.

An example of a complete strategy name is `Concurrent Mark & Sweep, generational=false, sweep=concurrent, mark=concurrent`. The names are unfortunately quite long and also a bit redundant. As was mentioned in Chapter 3, when explicitly setting the same strategy with the `-Xgc` command-line option, the same strategy is simply named `singlecon`. The best way to get the input value right when attempting to change these attributes is to first look it up in the `oracle.jrockit.management:GarbageCollector` MBean. There is one attribute for strategies and and one for heuristics. Each contains an array of `CompositeData`, and each `CompositeData` entry contains a name and description. Each name value is valid input to change the corresponding `Strategy` or `Heuristic` attribute.

It is worth noting that changing strategies can implicitly change the heuristic as well. A change to any strategy with a concurrent part will result in a change to the heuristic `pausetime`. Any purely parallel strategy will result in a change to `throughput`. Changing the heuristic can, in the same manner, result in an implicit strategy change.

Also worth noting is that changing to a new heuristic or strategy will not exactly be the same thing as starting with that heuristic or strategy because of the following reasons:

- Changing the heuristic to `pausetime` will not set up some necessary data structures for abortable compaction, if it wasn't previously enabled. Abortable compaction will not be available to the garbage collector.

- TLA sizes will be calculated based on the startup arguments. They will not be recalculated upon strategy or heuristic change.

Threads

The **Threads** tab contains information about the running threads. All available threads are listed in a table, together with information related to each thread, such as the thread state. If a thread is selected, the stack trace for the thread will appear in the trace tree, as shown in the following screenshot. **CPU profiling, deadlock detection**, and **allocation profiling** can be enabled by checking the appropriate checkboxes. As usual, more information can be enabled in the table by clicking on the table properties icon in the section toolbar.

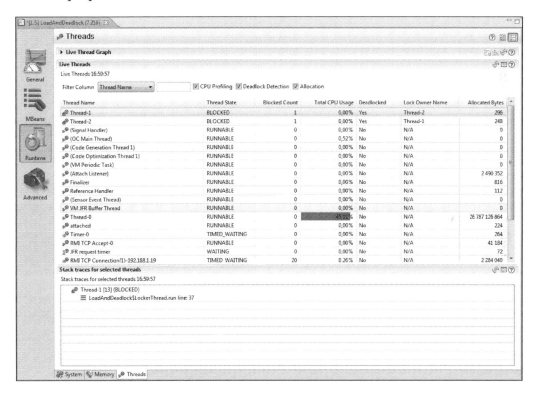

In the previous screenshot, we've added the **Lock Owner Name** attribute to the table, and enabled **Deadlock Detection**.

> **Deadlock detection** is a very useful feature in the JRockit Management Console, which can make debugging parallel programs easier.

As can be seen, the icon used for deadlocked threads (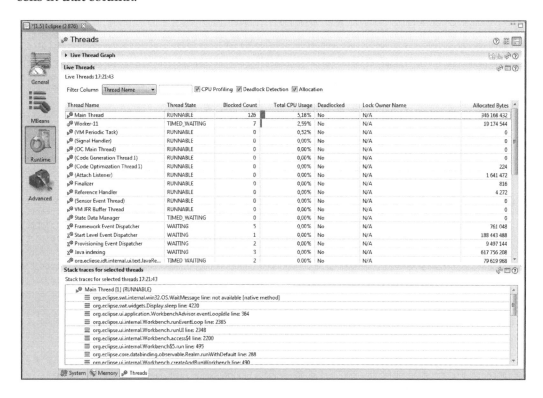) is different. We can infer that two of the threads are in a deadlock, waiting for each other.

Another easy-to-miss feature in the **Threads** tab is the CPU profiling check box. When it is enabled, the total CPU usage per thread will be shown in the **Total CPU Usage** column, and a normalized bar chart will be shown in the background of the cells in that column.

Enabling **allocation profiling** will show how much memory has been allocated in each thread. Note that this value is the amount of memory that has been allocated by the thread in total since it started, not how much memory the thread is currently keeping live.

Advanced

The **Advanced** tab group contains tabs that can be somewhat complex to use as they may either have performance implications, or require knowledge about the JRockit JVM internals. After reading this book, you should be able to put most of the tabs in the **Advanced** tab group to good use.

Method Profiler

The **Method Profiler** in the JRockit Management Console can be used to do exact method profiling, for a selected set of methods. This is not the same thing as **sample based method profiling. Exact method profiling** means that the profiler will report exact invocation counts for the selected methods and the total time spent executing them. Sample-based method profiling will be discussed in *Chapter 8, The Runtime Analyzer* and *Chapter 9, The Flight Recorder*.

To add a method for profiling, first make sure that the profiler is turned off. Then select a template to which to add the method, or create a new template by clicking on the **Add...** button in the **Templates** section. The templates are very useful, not only for saving commonly profiled methods for easy access later, but also to quickly turn on and off profiling for groups of methods in the method profiler.

Next click on the **Add...** button in the methods section for the selected template (**My New Template** in the following screenshot). In the dialog box, select the class that declares the method you want to profile.

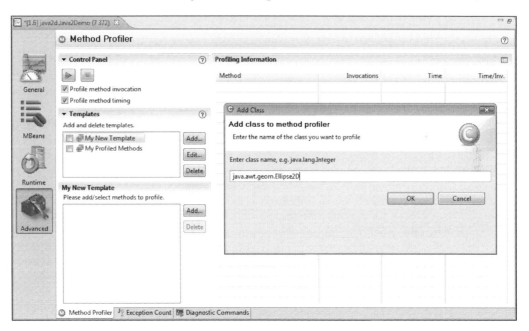

The **Method Profiler** will fetch information about the class from the JVM that the console is connected to, and display the methods available for profiling in the method tree as shown in the following screenshot:

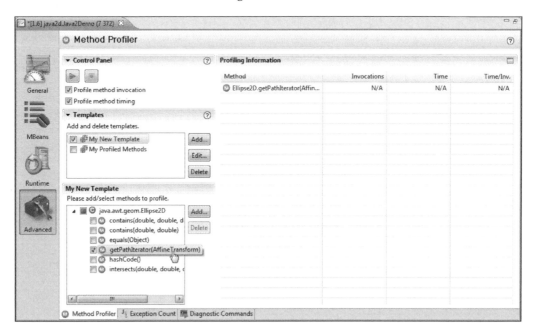

If the template to which the method was added is active, it should now show up in the **Profiling Information** table to the right in the **Method Profiler** tab. If it is not, simply activate it by checking the check box next to the template name in the **Templates** section.

To start the profiler, simply press the play (▷) button.

To stop the profiler, press the stop (■) button.

The following screenshot shows a few of the methods on the critical path in one of the Java2D demos that come with the JDK (located in the `demo/jfc` folder):

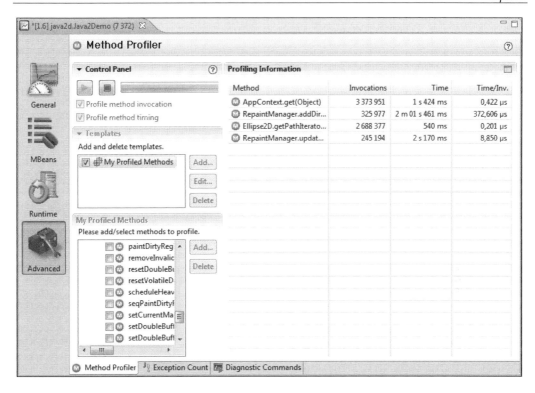

There are a few caveats worth mentioning when using the **Method Profiler** in the Management Console. These are the top three culprits:

- **The profiler requires you to select the exact set of methods you want to profile:** This is somewhat of a chicken and egg problem, as it's hard to know which methods to profile until you've done some profiling. And once you've done that profiling (for example using JRockit Flight Recorder), you usually have the answers you were looking for anyway.

- **The overhead of gathering the exact profiling information is hard to estimate:** This particular **Method Profiler** is not sampling-based, like the one in the JRockit Flight Recorder. The overhead, especially for a method that does not take long to execute and that is being executed a lot, such as the hot parts of a rendering engine, may be hard to predict. This is especially true for method timing information. If all hot methods in the system are profiled, the overhead can be quite large.

- **There is currently no class loader information available when selecting the class**: The profiler will use the first matching class it can find. So, there is no way to know which is the exact version of the class that is being profiled if it has been loaded by multiple class loaders.

We have been at various customer sites and customer meetings when developers have been certain a particular method is the main performance bottleneck. Usually, plenty of exact measurements on that particular method have been made, and after optimization it runs a magnitude faster. Unfortunately, the performance of the application as such, has still not been improved. After performing a JRockit Flight Recording, before and after the change, it is usually concluded that the method in question is not even among the top 50 hot spots in the application, and that, in practice, the optimization effort was a waste of time.

When profiling an application, the JRockit Flight Recorder is usually the best place to start. If you still believe there is a need for online exact method profiling after doing a recording, you should convince yourself that the need is valid. Maybe you have already done a recording so that you know that the method you are spending time on tuning is worth the effort. You may be curious as to how the timing information changes for a certain optimization (fully realizing that, if the method is on the critical path, the difference in overhead of the measurements themselves may actually change after the optimizations have been implemented). Or perhaps you are simply wondering if a certain method is called at all. This is probably, in the authors' humble opinion, one of the most valid reasons for using the method profiler in the Management Console.

Exception Count

The exception tab can be used to count the number of exceptions thrown. You can either count all the exceptions of a specific type or count the exceptions of a specific type including subclasses of that type.

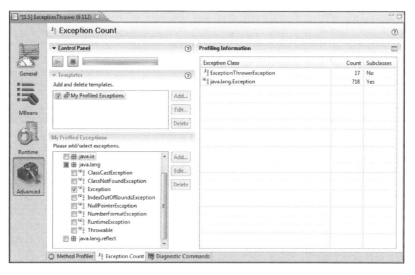

The functionality is somewhat limited, as it will not show the stack traces for the exceptions. If you not only want to know how many exceptions are thrown, but also where they are thrown, you should instead use JRockit Flight Recorder or enable verbose logging for exceptions. For more information on JRockit Flight Recorder, see Chapter 9. For more information on how to do verbose logging, please see *Chapter 5, Benchmarking and Tuning* or *Chapter 11, JRCMD*.

Diagnostic Commands

The Mission Control Console also provides a tab that facilitates access to the **diagnostic commands** in JRockit. The diagnostic commands is a set of commands that can be sent to JRockit through the JRockit Management APIs and the command-line tool JRCMD.

 For more information on individual diagnostic commands and on JRCMD, see Chapter 11. For more information about the management APIs, see *Chapter 12, Using the JRockit Management APIs*.

The list in the upper left corner of the **Diagnostic Commands** tab shows the available commands classified in three different groups—normal, advanced, and internal. The ones in the "normal" class are usually the easiest to understand. They are also the ones that can be executed without any risk of affecting the runtime in adverse ways. Of course, no truth without exceptions, for example invoking the **runsystemgc** command over and over again may incur a performance overhead. The **print_object_summary** command can also be fairly expensive as it will, in effect, cause a garbage collection (gathering info on all objects on the heap requires traversing the heap).

The diagnostic commands in the "advanced" group are more complicated; they are either more complex, requiring a lot of low level JRockit or JVM knowledge, or have security or performance implications. For example, the **heap_diagnostic** command can be expensive to execute and there may be security implications of starting up the external management agent with **start_management_server**.

The filter box above the command list helps finding specific commands, and to the right of the command list the parameters of a selected command can be configured.

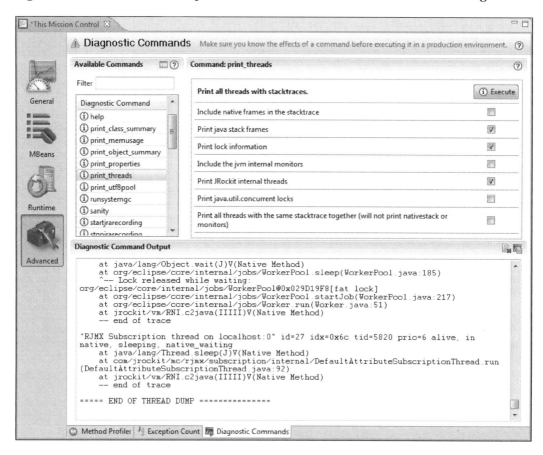

Clicking on the **Execute** button invokes the diagnostic command in the JVM that the Management Console is connected to. When the command completes, the result is displayed in the **Diagnostic Command Output** box at the bottom of the tab. Note that not all commands have output, but some of them simply instruct the JRockit runtime to take some action.

The output of several commands can be appended by clicking on the **Append result** button in the **Diagnostic Command Output** section toolbar.

Other

The last tab group is the **Other** group. This tab group will only be visible if you have installed custom tabs—either your own, or custom tabs from the experimental update site. As the **JConsole Meta Plug-in tab** is easily installed from the experimental update site, we will briefly explain it here.

JConsole

In the JDK, a JMX management console named JConsole is included. In 6.0 versions of the JDK, JConsole has its own plug-in interface, through which additional tabs can be added. The JConsole plug-in for JRockit Mission Control allows such plug-ins to run inside the JRockit Management Console, as shown in the following screenshot:

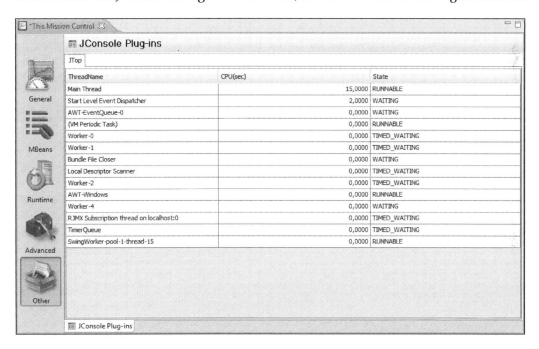

To be able to run the JConsole plug-in, JRockit Mission Control (or Eclipse, if using the plug-in version of JRockit Mission Control), must be running on a JDK 6.0 version of JRockit. The plug-in will automatically attempt to find the JTop plug-in delivered with the JDK (located in the `demo/management/JTop` folder), and to use that folder as the **JConsole plug-in directory**. Any `jar` file containing a JConsole plug-in found in the JConsole plug-in directory will be added under its own tab in the JConsole plug-ins tab.

The JConsole plug-in directory and update interval, that is how often the plug-ins should be refreshed, can be changed in the Console preferences (**Window | Preferences**), as shown in the following screenshot:

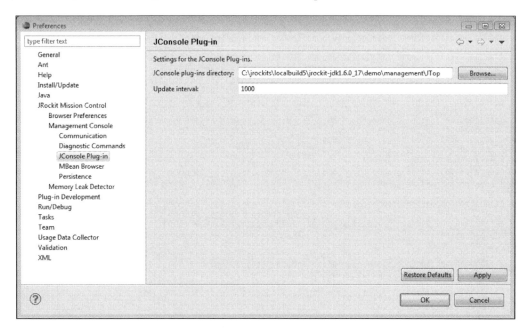

Extending the JRockit Mission Control Console

This section is for developers interested in extending the JRockit Mission Control Management Console with custom tabs. It assumes some familiarity with the Eclipse platform and terminology, such as **extension point** and **form page**.

There is an extension point available for the console that can be used to implement custom tabs. This extension point was, for instance, used when creating the **JConsole** plug-in tab available from the JRockit Mission Control experimental update site. See the previous chapter for more information on the experimental update site.

The easiest way to get started building your own JRockit Mission Control Console plug-in is to use the PDE wizard available from the experimental update site. First make sure that Eclipse for RCP/Plug-in Developers (Eclipse 3.5/Ganymede or later versions) is installed. Next install the JRockit Mission Control Plug-in into Eclipse. Finally install the **PDE Integration Plug-in** from the experimental update site.

PDE is short for **Plug-in Development Environment**, which is a set of tools built into Eclipse to help create, develop, test, debug, build, and deploy Eclipse plug-ins. The PDE Integration Plug-in from the experimental update site provides specialized wizards and templates that make it easier to write plug-ins for JRockit Mission Control.

The available console PDE wizards can be used to generate the boilerplate code needed to contribute custom tabs to the JRockit Mission Control Console. They also serve as examples on how custom tabs can be implemented.

There are two different wizards for creating JRockit Mission Control tabs available in the PDE plug-in—simple and advanced. The simple wizard will generate an example tab that shows a label with the CPU load. The advanced wizard will use various components built into the JRockit Mission Control console to show three selected attributes in various different ways.

This section walks you through how to create a new tab project:

1. Select **File | New | Project...**

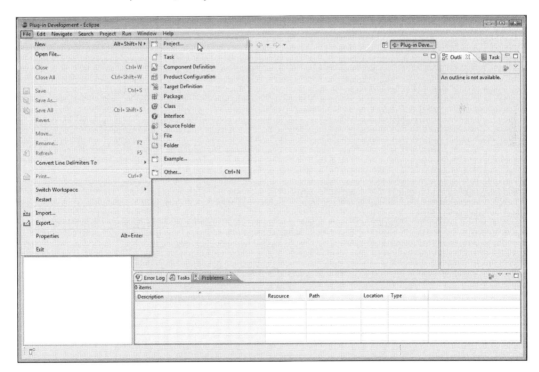

2.   In the **New Project** dialog box, select **Plug-in Project** and click on **Next**.

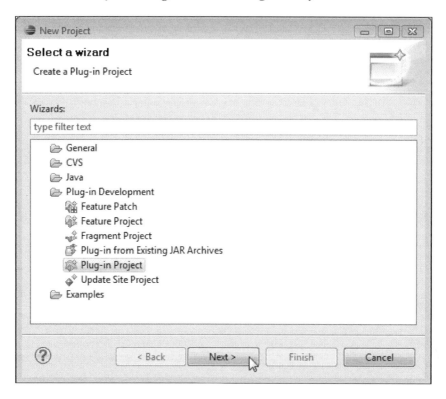

3.   Name your project. It is common practice to name the plug-in project after the main package of your plug-in, for example `com.example.mc.console.myplugin`.

4. Ensure that the correct target platform is selected (Eclipse 3.4 for JRockit Mission Control 3.1 and Eclipse 3.5 for JRockit Mission Control 4.0).

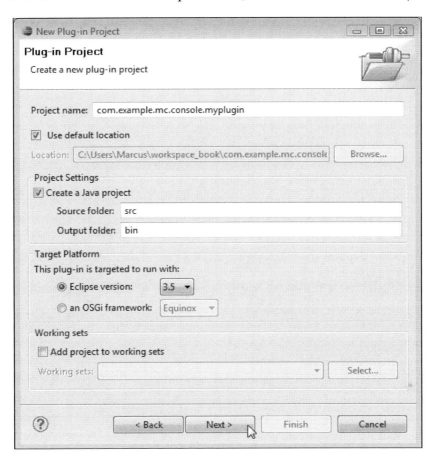

5. Click on **Next** and optionally change plug-in property details. When satisfied, click on **Next** again.

6. If the PDE plug-in is correctly installed, you should now be presented with numerous templates, two of which should be the advanced and simple console tab ones. Select either the advanced or the simple one and then click on **Next**.

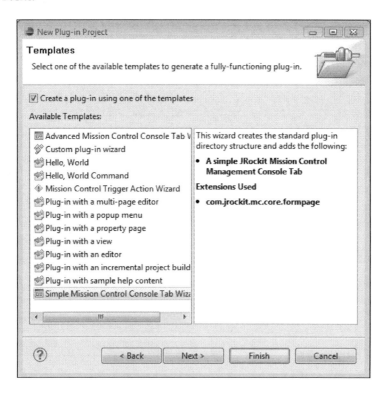

7. Change the details to match your plug-in and then click on **Finish**.

The end result should be a plug-in project with all the necessary code for an additional tab in the JRockit Mission Control Console. To try out your new tab, simply go to **Run | Run Configurations...** In the **Run Configurations Dialog,** right click on **Eclipse Application** and select **New**. This will create a new run configuration for launching Eclipse. By default, it should be using the Eclipse in which you are developing as a target platform and include all the plug-ins in your workspace. As your Eclipse includes the JRockit Mission Control plug-in, everything should be fine. Select the new configuration and press the **Run** button in the lower right corner.

A new Eclipse should be launched with your brand new plug-in deployed. Open up the Mission Control perspective the way you normally would and start the console. Your tab will show up under the **Other** tab group.

If the advanced wizard was used, a class containing the code for creating a tab looking much like the standard **Overview** tab should have been created. It displays three different attributes in various different ways.

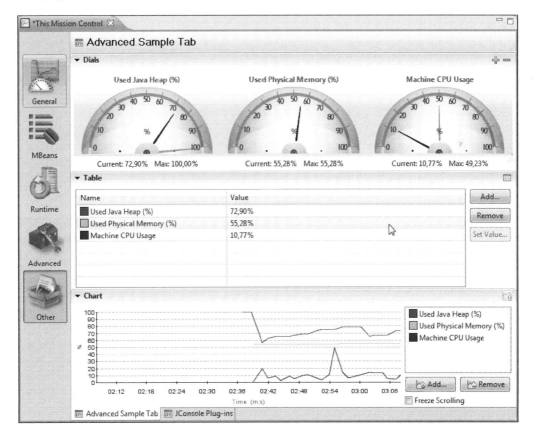

Setting up the tab is done programmatically and the code for it is rather simple. The extension point only requires us to subclass `org.eclipse.ui.forms.editor.FormPage`. So, there are really no dependencies on JRockit or JRockit Mission Control specific classes for the extension point itself. The editor input from the form page can be adapted to an `IMBeanService`, which is a communication helper service for the console available in the `com.jrockit.mc.rjmx.core` package.

```
private IMBeanService getMBeanService() {
  return (IMBeanService)
    getEditorInput().getAdapter(IMBeanService.class);
}
```

This allows access to the JRockit Mission Control specific MBean layer residing in the `com.jrockit.mc.rjmx*` plug-ins. RJMX provides, among other things, access to the subscription engine and the proxy layer in JRockit Mission Control.

The proxy layer can be used to access JRockit specific attributes and operations in a version neutral way with respect to the API. Use `getMBeanService().getProxyNames()` for the attributes and `getMBeanService().getProxyOperations()` for the operations.

For example, the location of the attribute for the CPU load is different in JRockit versions R26.4 , R27.x, and R28.x. To get the location of the CPU load, regardless of JRockit version, the proxy layer can be used like this:

```
getMBeanService().getProxyNames().
  getAttributeDescriptor(IProxyNames.Key.OS_CPU_LOAD);
```

This will return an attribute descriptor containing the MBean `ObjectName` and attribute name needed to locate the attribute. Most of RJMX makes use of attribute descriptors that are objects encapsulating the MBean `ObjectName` and the attribute name.

This is how we create an attribute descriptor directly pointing to the CPU load where it is located in R28 versions of JRockit:

```
new AttributeDescriptor(
  "oracle.jrockit.management:type=Runtime","CPULoad");
```

To invoke a garbage collection, regardless of JRockit version, the proxy layer can be used in the following way:

```
getMBeanService().getProxyOperations().gc();
```

As can be seen from the advanced template code, adding a table for a collection of attributes is very easy.

```
builder.setProperty(
   AttributeVisualizerBuilder.TITLE, "Chart");
builder.setProperty(
   AttributeVisualizerBuilder.TITLE_AXIS_Y, "%");
builder.setProperty(
   AttributeVisualizerBuilder.TITLE_AXIS_X, "Time");
   addAttributesToVisualizer(builder.createChart());
```

The simple template is actually a little bit more complex than it seems, as it uses the different services directly and does not rely on the standard Mission Control GUI components. The resulting GUI is, however, much simpler. The tab generated from the simple template provides a good example for how to use the RJMX subscription service. The subscription service allows subscribing to the values of one or more attributes using the same subscription mechanism as the rest of the console. Adding a subscription to the CPU load is done by using the `SubscriptionService`.

```
getMBeanService().getAttributeSubscriptionService()
   .addAttributeValueListener(getMBeanService().getProxyNames().
     getAttributeDescriptor(IProxyNames.Key.OS_CPU_LOAD),
     new LabelUpdater(valueLabel));
```

The `LabelUpdater` is a simple implementation of the `IAttributeValueListener` interface defined in the `com.jrockit.mc.rjmx.subscription` package. Each time a new value is retrieved, the `valueChanged` method is called with an event containing the value. Note that there are no guarantees as to which thread is delivering the event. In the current implementation, it will either be the subscription thread (most events) or the JMX subsystem (notification based events). It will very likely never be the GUI thread, which means that any updates to the GUI will need to be posted to the GUI thread, as done by using `DisplayToolkit.safeAsyncExec` in the `LabelUpdater` example code:

```
public static class LabelUpdater
implements IAttributeValueListener {
  private final Label label;

  public LabelUpdater(Label label) {
    this.label = label;
  }

  public void valueChanged(final AttributeValueEvent event) {
    DisplayToolkit.safeAsyncExec(label, new Runnable(){
      public void run() {
        Double latestValue = (Double) event.getValue();
```

```
            label.setText("CPU Load is: "
              + (latestValue.doubleValue() * 100) + "%");
        }
      });
    }
  }
```

Creating an extension for a trigger action is done in the same way. Simply select the **Mission Control Trigger Action Wizard** template from the plug-in project wizard in step 6.

Summary

This chapter has demonstrated how to use the Management Console to monitor any application running on JRockit. The information and functionality available in the different tabs of the JRockit Management Console was described together with examples and various use cases.

We have also shown how the Management Console can easily be extended with custom tabs with specialized user interfaces as well as custom actions to be used with the trigger rules.

The next chapter will explain how to use the JRockit Runtime Analyzer to profile and diagnose both the JRockit runtime as well as the applications running in JRockit.

8

The Runtime Analyzer

The JRockit Runtime Analyzer, or JRA for short, is a JRockit-specific profiling tool that provides information about both the JRockit runtime and the application running in JRockit. JRA was the main profiling tool for JRockit R27 and earlier, but has been superseded in later versions by the JRockit Flight Recorder. Because of its extremely low overhead, JRA is suitable for use in production.

In this chapter you will learn:

- Different ways to create a JRA recording
- How to find the hot spots in your application
- How to interpret memory-related information in JRA
- How to hunt down latency-related problems
- How to detect indications of a memory leak in an application
- How to use the operative set in the JRA latency analyzer component

This chapter is mainly targeted at R27.x/3.x versions of JRockit and Mission Control. The next chapter covers performing and analyzing runtime recordings in R28/4.0 using JRockit Flight Recorder. As several of the components for recording analysis in Mission Control are similar in R28, they are introduced in this chapter. Where applicable, the next chapter covers new components and the most important differences between R27.x/3.x and R28/4.0.

The need for feedback

In order to make JRockit an industry-leading JVM, there has been a great need for customer collaboration. As the focus for JRockit consistently has been on performance and scalability in server-side applications, the closest collaboration has been with customers with large server installations. An example is the financial industry. The birth of the JRockit Runtime Analyzer, or JRA, originally came from the need for gathering profiling information on how well JRockit performed at customer sites.

One can easily understand that customers were rather reluctant to send us, for example, their latest proprietary trading applications to play with in our labs. And, of course, allowing us to poke around in a customer's mission critical application in production was completely out of the question. Some of these applications shuffle around billions of dollars per week. We found ourselves in a situation where we needed a tool to gather as much information as possible on how JRockit, and the application running on JRockit, behaved together; both to find opportunities to improve JRockit and to find erratic behavior in the customer application. This was a bit of a challenge, as we needed to get high quality data. If the information was not accurate, we would not know how to improve JRockit in the areas most needed by customers or perhaps at all. At the same time, we needed to keep the overhead down to a minimum. If the profiling itself incurred significant overhead, we would no longer get a true representation of the system. Also, with anything but near-zero overhead, the customer would not let us perform recordings on their mission critical systems in production.

JRA was invented as a method of recording information in a way that the customer could feel confident with, while still providing us with the data needed to improve JRockit. The tool was eventually widely used within our support organization to both diagnose problems and as a tuning companion for JRockit.

In the beginning, a simple XML format was used for our runtime recordings. A human-readable format made it simple to debug, and the customer could easily see what data was being recorded. Later, the format was upgraded to include data from a new recording engine for latency-related data. When the latency data came along, the data format for JRA was split into two parts, the human-readable XML and a binary file containing the latency events. The latency data was put into JRockit internal memory buffers during the recording, and to avoid introducing unnecessary latencies and performance penalties that would surely be incurred by translating the buffers to XML, it was decided that the least intrusive way was to simply dump the buffers to disk.

To summarize, recordings come in two different flavors having either the `.jra` extension (recordings prior to JRockit R28/JRockit Mission Control 4.0) or the `.jfr`

(JRockit Flight Recorder) extension (R28 or later). Prior to the R28 version of JRockit, the recording files mainly consisted of XML without a coherent data model. As of R28, the recording files are binaries where all data adheres to an event model, making it much easier to analyze the data.

To open a JFR recording, a JRockit Mission Control of version 3.x must be used. To open a Flight Recorder recording, JRockit Mission Control version 4.0 or later must be used.

Recording

The recording engine that starts and stops recordings can be controlled in several different ways:

- By using the JRCMD command-line tool. For more information on JRCMD, see *Chapter 11, JRCMD*.

- By using the JVM command-line parameters. For more information on this, see the -XXjra parameter in the JRockit documentation.

- From within the JRA GUI in JRockit Mission Control.

The easiest way to control recordings is to use the JRA/JFR wizard from within the JRockit Mission Control GUI. Simply select the JVM on which to perform a JRA recording in the **JVM Browser** and click on the JRA button in the **JVM Browser** toolbar. You can also click on **Start JRA Recording** from the context menu. Usually, one of the pre-defined templates will do just fine, but under special circumstances it may be necessary to adjust them. The pre-defined templates in JRockit Mission Control 3.x are:

- **Full Recording**: This is the standard use case. By default, it is configured to do a five minute recording that contains most data of interest.

- **Minimal Overhead Recording**: This template can be used for very latency-sensitive applications. It will, for example, *not* record heap statistics, as the gathering of heap statistics will, in effect, cause an extra garbage collection at the beginning and at the end of the recording.

- **Real Time Recording**: This template is useful when hunting latency-related problems, for instance when tuning a system that is running on JRockit Real Time. This template provides an additional text field for setting the **latency threshold**. The latency threshold is explained later in the chapter in the section on the latency analyzer. The threshold is by default lowered to 5 milliseconds for this type of recording, from the default 20 milliseconds, and the default recording time is longer.

- **Classic Recording**: This resembles a classic JRA recording from earlier versions of Mission Control. Most notably, it will not contain any latency data. Use this template with JRockit versions prior to R27.3 or if there is no interest in recording latency data.

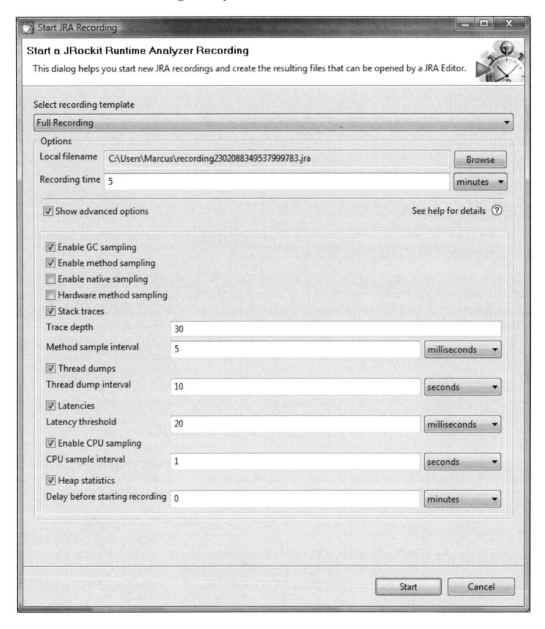

All recording templates can be customized by checking the **Show advanced options** check box. This is usually not needed, but let's go through the options and why you may want to change them:

- **Enable GC sampling**: This option selects whether or not GC-related information should be recorded. It can be turned off if you know that you will not be interested in GC-related information. It is on by default, and it is a good idea to keep it enabled.

- **Enable method sampling**: This option enables or disables method sampling. Method sampling is implemented by using sample data from the JRockit code optimizer. If profiling overhead is a concern (it is usually very low, but still), it is usually a good idea to use the **Method sample interval** option to control how much method sampling information to record.

- **Enable native sampling**: This option determines whether or not to attempt to sample time spent executing native code as a part of the method sampling. This feature is disabled by default, as it is mostly used by JRockit developers and support. Most Java developers probably do fine without it.

- **Hardware method sampling**: On some hardware architectures, JRockit can make use of special hardware counters in the CPU to provide higher resolution for the method sampling. This option only makes sense on such architectures. *Chapter 2, Adaptive Code Generation* discusses hardware-based sampling to a greater extent.

- **Stack traces**: Use this option to not only get sample counts but also stack traces from method samples. If this is disabled, no call traces are available for sample points in the methods that show up in the **Hot Methods** list.

- **Trace depth**: This setting determines how many stack frames to retrieve for each stack trace. For JRockit Mission Control versions prior to 4.0, this defaulted to the rather limited depth of 16. For applications running in application containers or using large frameworks, this is usually way too low to generate data from which any useful conclusions can be drawn. A tip, when profiling such an application, would be to bump this to 30 or more.

- **Method sampling interval**: This setting controls how often thread samples should be taken. JRockit will stop a subset of the threads every **Method sample interval** milliseconds in a round robin fashion. Only threads executing when the sample is taken will be counted, not blocking threads. Use this to find out where the computational load in an application takes place. See the section, *Hot Methods* for more information.

- **Thread dumps**: When enabled, JRockit will record a thread stack dump at the beginning and the end of the recording. If the **Thread dump interval** setting is also specified, thread dumps will be recorded at regular intervals for the duration of the recording.

- **Thread dump interval**: This setting controls how often, in seconds, to record the thread stack dumps mentioned earlier.

- **Latencies**: If this setting is enabled, the JRA recording will contain latency data. For more information on latencies, please refer to the section *Latency* later in this chapter.

- **Latency threshold**: To limit the amount of data in the recording, it is possible to set a threshold for the minimum latency (duration) required for an event to actually be recorded. This is normally set to 20 milliseconds. It is usually safe to lower this to around 1 millisecond without incurring too much profiling overhead. Less than that and there is a risk that the profiling overhead will become unacceptably high and/or that the file size of the recording becomes unmanageably large. Latency thresholds can be set as low as nanosecond values by changing the unit in the unit combo box.

- **Enable CPU sampling**: When this setting is enabled, JRockit will record the CPU load at regular intervals.

- **Heap statistics**: This setting causes JRockit to do a heap analysis pass at the beginning and at the end of the recording. As heap analysis involves forcing extra garbage collections at these points in order to collect information, it is disabled in the low overhead template.

- **Delay before starting a recording**: This option can be used to schedule the recording to start at a later time. The delay is normally defined in minutes, but the unit combo box can be used to specify the time in a more appropriate unit—everything from seconds to days is supported.

Before starting the recording, a location to which the finished recording is to be downloaded must be specified. Once the JRA recording is started, an editor will open up showing the options with which the recording was started and a progress bar. When the recording is completed, it is downloaded and the editor input is changed to show the contents of the recording.

Analyzing JRA recordings

Analyzing JRA recordings may easily seem like black magic to the uninitiated, so just like we did with the Management Console, we will go through each tab of the JRA editor to explain the information in that particular tab, with examples on when it is useful.

Just like in the console, there are several tabs in different tab groups.

General

The tabs in the **General** tab group provide views of key characteristics and recording metadata. In JRA, there are three tabs—**Overview**, **Recording**, and **System**.

Overview

The first tab in the **General** tab group is the **Overview** tab. This tab contains an overview of selected key information from the recording. The information is useful for checking the system health at a glance.

The first section in the tab is a dial dashboard that contains CPU usage, heap, and pause time statistics.

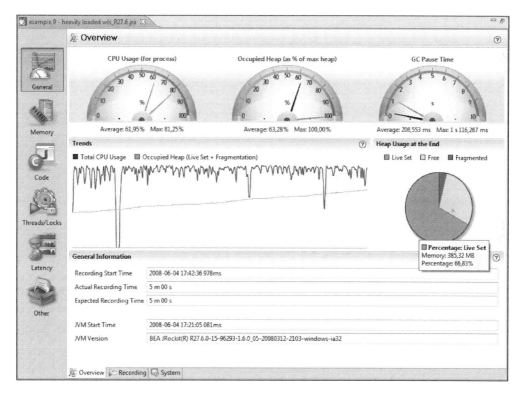

What to look for depends on the system. Ideally the system should be well utilized, but not saturated. A good rule of thumb for most setups would be to keep the **Occupied Heap (Live Set + Fragmentation)** to half or less than half of the max heap. This keeps the garbage collection ratio down.

All this, of course, depends on the type of application. For an application with very low allocation rates, the occupied heap can be allowed to be much larger. An application that does batch calculations, concerned with throughput only, would want the CPU to be fully saturated while garbage collection pause times may not be a concern at all.

The **Trends** section shows charts for the CPU usage and occupied heap over time so that trends can be spotted. Next to the **Trends** section is a pie chart showing heap usage at the end of the recording. If more than about a third of the memory is fragmented, some time should probably be spent tuning the JRockit garbage collector (see *Chapter 5, Benchmarking and Tuning* and the *JRockit Diagnostics Guide* on the Internet). It may also be the case that the allocation behavior of the application needs to be investigated. See the *Histogram* section for more information.

At the bottom of the page is some general information about the recording, such as the version information for the recorded JVM. Version information is necessary when filing support requests.

In our example, we can see that the trend for **Live Set + Fragmentation** is constantly increasing. This basically means that after each garbage collection, there is less free memory left on the heap. It is very likely that we have a memory leak, and that, if we continue to let this application run, we will end up with an `OutOfMemoryError`.

Recording

This tab contains meta information about the recording, such as its duration and the values of all the recording parameters used. This information can, among other things, be used to check if information is missing from a recording, or if that particular piece of information had simply been disabled for the recording.

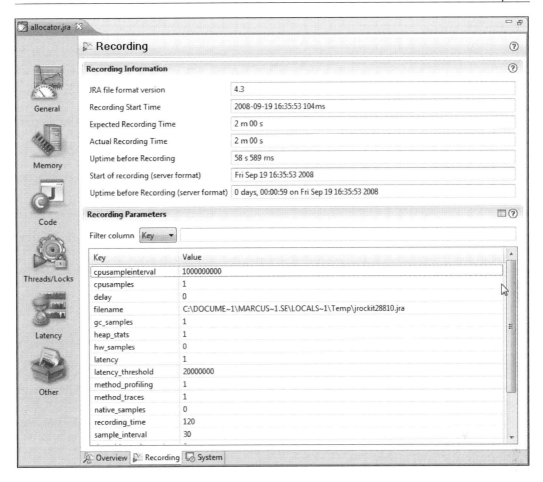

System

This tab contains information about the system the JRockit JVM was running on, such as the OS. The JVM arguments used to start the JVM can also be viewed here.

Memory

The **Memory** tab group contains tabs that deal with memory-related information, such as heap usage and garbage collections. In JRA there are six such tabs, **Overview**, **GCs**, **GC Statistics**, **Allocation**, **Heap Statistics**, **Heap Contents**, and **Object Statistics**.

Overview

The first tab in the **Memory** tab group is the **Overview** tab. It shows an overview of the key memory statistics, such as the physical memory available on the hardware on which the JVM was running. It also shows the **GC pause ratio**, i.e. the time spent paused in GC in relation to the duration of the entire recording.

If the GC pause ratio is higher than 15-20%, it usually means that there is significant allocation pressure on the JVM.

At the bottom of the **Overview** tab, there is a listing of the different garbage collection strategy changes that have occurred during recording. See *Chapter 3, Adaptive Memory Management,* for more information on how these strategy changes can occur.

GCs

Here you can find all the information you would ever want to know about the garbage collections that occurred during the recording, and probably more.

With the GCs tab, it is usually a good idea to sort the **Garbage Collections** table on the attribute **Longest Pause**, unless you know exactly at what time from the start of the JVM you want to drill down. You might know this from reading the application log or from the information in some other tab in JRA. In the following example, the longest pause also happens to be the first one.

It is sometimes a good idea to leave out the first and last garbage collections from the analysis, depending on the recording settings. Some settings will force the first and last GC in the recording to be full garbage collections with exceptional compaction, to gather extra data. This may very well break the pausetime target for deterministic GC. This is also true for JRockit Flight Recorder

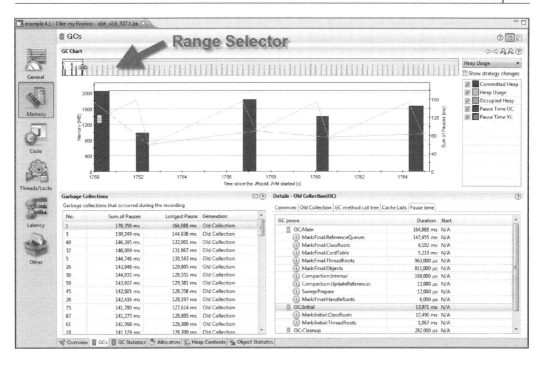

At the top of the screen is the **Range Selector**. The **Range Selector** is used to temporally select a set of events in the recording. In this case, we have zoomed in on a few of the events at the beginning of the recording. We can see that throughout this range, the size of the occupied heap (the lowest line, which shows up in green) is around half the committed heap size (the flat topmost line, which shows up in blue), with some small deviations.

In an application with a very high pause-to-run ratio, the occupied heap would have been close to the max heap. In that case, increasing the heap would probably be a good start to increase performance. There are various ways of increasing the heap size, but the easiest is simply setting a maximum heap size using the –Xmx flag on the command line. In the example, however, everything concerning the heap usage seems to be fine.

In the **Details** section, there are various tabs with detailed information about a selected garbage collection. A specific garbage collection can be examined more closely, either by clicking in the **GC chart** or by selecting it in the table.

Information about the reason for a particular GC, reference queue sizes, and heap usage information is included in the tabs in the **Details** section. Verbose heap information about the state before and after the recording, the stack trace for the allocation that caused the GC to happen, if available, and detailed information about every single pause part can also be found here.

In the previous screenshot, a very large portion of the GC pause is spent handling the reference queues. Switching to the **References and Finalizers** chart will reveal that the finalizer queue is the one with most objects in it.

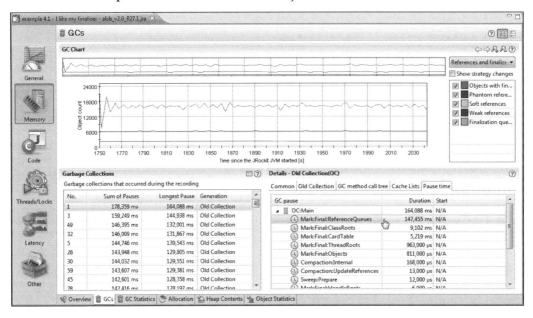

One way to improve the memory performance for this particular application would be to rely less heavily on finalizers. This is, as discussed in Chapter 3, always a good idea anyway.

The recordings shown in the **GCs** tab examples earlier were created with JRockit R27.1, but are quite good examples anyway, as they are based on real-life data that was actually used to improve a product. As can be seen from the screenshot, there is no information about the start time of the individual pause parts. Recordings made using a more recent version of JRockit would contain such information. We are continuously improving the data set and adding new events to recordings. JRockit Flight Recorder, described in the next chapter, is the latest leap in recording detail.

Following is a more recent recording with an obvious finalizer problem. The reasons that the pause parts differ from the previous examples is both that we are now using a different GC strategy as well as the fact that more recent recordings contain more detail. The finalizer problem stands out quite clearly in the next screenshot.

The data in the screenshot is from a different application, but it nicely illustrates how a large portion of the garbage collection pause is spent following references in the finalizers. Handling the finalizers is even taking more time than the notorious synchronized external compaction. Finalizers are an obvious bottleneck.

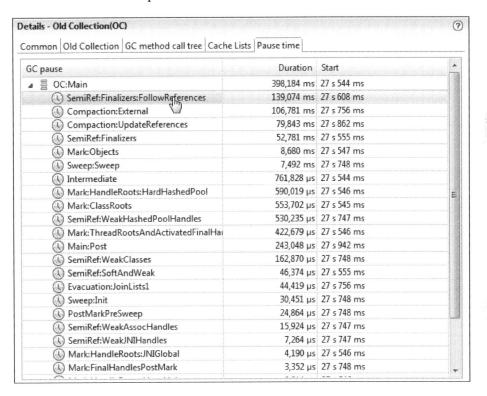

To make fewer GCs happen altogether, we need to find out what is actually causing the GCs to occur. This means that we have to identify the points in the program where the most object allocation takes place. One good place to start looking is the **GC Call Trees** table introduced in the next section. If more specific allocation-related information is required, go to the **Object Allocation** events in the **Latency** tab group.

For some applications, we can lower the garbage collection pause times by tuning the JRockit memory system. For more about JRockit tuning, see Chapter 5.

GC Statistics

This tab contains some general statistics about the garbage collections that took place during the recording. One of the most interesting parts is the **GC Call Trees** table that shows an aggregated view of the stack traces for any garbage collection. Unfortunately, it shows JRockit-specific internal code frames as well, which means that you may have to dig down a few stack frames until the frames of interest are found—i.e., code you can affect.

Prior to version R27.6 of JRockit, this was one of the better ways of getting an idea of where allocation pressure originated. In more recent versions, there is a much more powerful way of doing allocation profiling, which will be described in the *Histogram* section.

In the interest of conserving space, only the JRockit internal frames up to the first non-internal frame have been expanded in the following screenshot. The information should be interpreted as most of the GCs are being caused as the result of calls to `Arrays.copyOf(char[], int)` in the Java program.

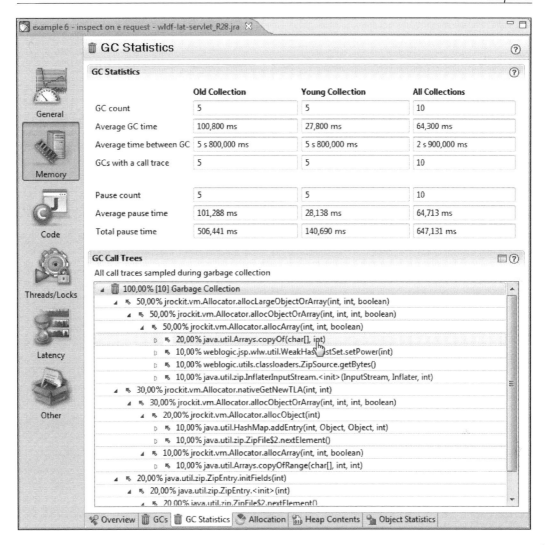

Allocation

The **Allocation** tab contains information that can be used mainly for tuning the JRockit memory system. Here, relative allocation rates of large and small objects are displayed, which affects the choice of the **Thread Local Area** (TLA) size. TLAs are discussed to a great extent in Chapter 3 and Chapter 5. Allocation can also be viewed on a per-thread basis, which can help find out where to start tuning the Java program in order to make it stress the memory system less.

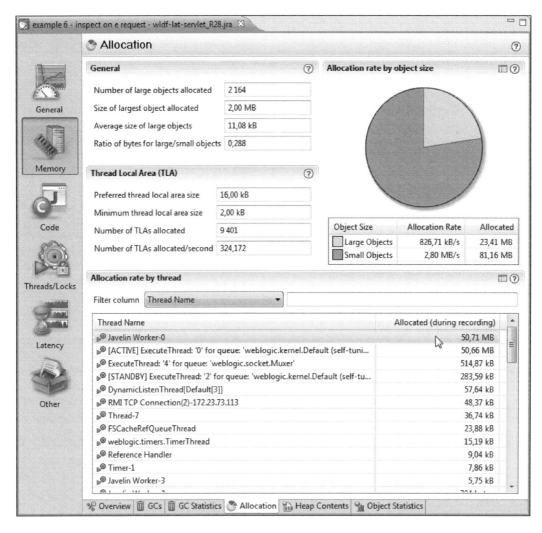

Again, a more powerful way of finding out where to start tuning the allocation behavior of a Java program is usually to work with the **Latency | Histogram** tab, described later in this chapter.

Heap Contents

Information on the memory distribution of the heap can be found under the **Heap Contents** tab. The snapshot for this information is taken at the end of the recording. If you find that your heap is heavily fragmented, there are two choices—either try to tune JRockit to take better care of the fragmentation or try to change the allocation behavior of your Java application. As described in Chapter 3, the JVM combats fragmentation by doing compaction. In extreme cases, with large allocation pressure and high performance demands, you may have to change the allocation patterns of your application to get the performance you want.

Object Statistics

The **Object Statistics** tab shows a histogram of what was on the heap at the beginning and at the end of the recording. Here you can find out what types (classes) of objects are using the most memory on the heap. If there is a large positive delta between the snapshots at the beginning and at the end of the recording, it means that there either is a memory leak or that the application was merely executing some large operation that required a lot of memory.

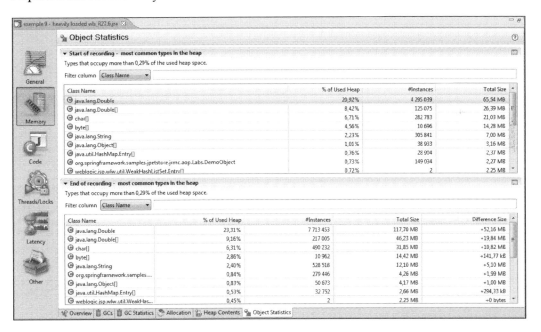

In the previous example, there is actually a memory leak that causes instances of `Double` to be held on to forever by the program. This will eventually cause an `OutOfMemoryError`.

The best way to find out where these instances are being created is to either check for **Object Allocation** events of `Double` (see the second example in the *Histogram* section) or to turn on allocation profiling in the Memory Leak Detector. The Memory Leak Detector is covered in detail in *Chapter 10, The Memory Leak Detector*.

Code

The **Code** tab group contains information from the code generator and the method sampler. It consists of three tabs—the **Overview**, **Hot Methods**, and **Optimizations** tab.

Overview

This tab aggregates information from the code generator with sample information from the code optimizer. This allows us to see which methods the Java program spends the most time executing. Again, this information is available virtually "for free", as the code generation system needs it anyway.

For CPU-bound applications, this tab is a good place to start looking for opportunities to optimize your application code. By CPU-bound, we mean an application for which the CPU is the limiting factor; with a faster CPU, the application would have a higher throughput.

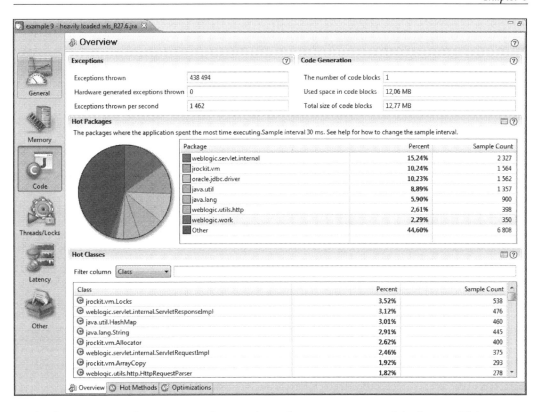

In the first section, the amount of exceptions thrown per second is shown. This number depends both on the hardware and on the application—faster hardware may execute an application more quickly, and consequently throw more exceptions. However, a higher value is always worse than a lower one on identical setups. Recall that exceptions are just that, rare corner cases. As we have explained, the JVM typically gambles that they aren't occurring too frequently. If an application throws hundreds of thousands exceptions per second, you should investigate why. Someone may be using exceptions for control flow, or there may be a configuration error. Either way, performance will suffer.

In JRockit Mission Control 3.1, the recording will only provide information about how many exceptions were thrown. The only way to find out where the exceptions originated is unfortunately by changing the verbosity of the log, as described in Chapter 5 and Chapter 11. As the next chapter will show, exception profiling using JRockit Flight Recorder is both easier and more powerful.

An overview of where the JVM spends most of the time executing Java code can be found in the **Hot Packages** and **Hot Classes** sections. The only difference between them is the way the sample data from the JVM code optimizer is aggregated. In **Hot Packages**, hot executing code is sorted on a per-package basis and in **Hot Classes** on a per-class basis. For more fine-grained information, use the **Hot Methods** tab.

As shown in the example screenshot, most of the time is spent executing code in the `weblogic.servlet.internal` package. There is also a fair amount of exceptions being thrown.

Hot Methods

This tab provides a detailed view of the information provided by the JVM code optimizer. If the objective is to find a good candidate method for optimizing the application, this is the place to look. If a lot of the method samples are from one particular method, and a lot of the method traces through that method share the same origin, much can potentially be gained by either manually optimizing that method or by reducing the amount of calls along that call chain.

In the following example, much of the time is spent in the method `com.bea.wlrt.adapter.defaultprovider.internal.CSVPacketReceiver.parseL2Packet()`. It seems likely that the best way to improve the performance of this particular application would be to optimize a method internal to the application container (WebLogic Event Server) and not the code in the application itself, running inside the container. This illustrates both the power of the JRockit Mission Control tools and a dilemma that the resulting analysis may reveal—the answers provided sometimes require solutions beyond your immediate control.

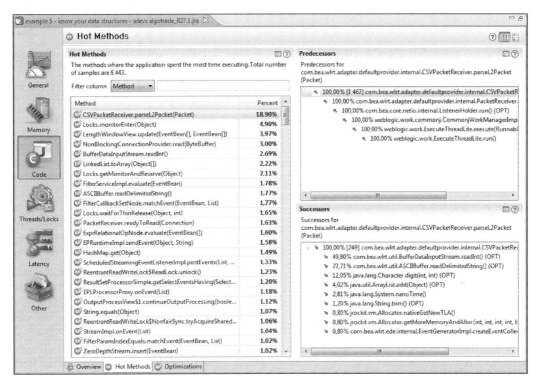

Sometimes, the information provided may cause us to reconsider the way we use data structures. In the next example, the program frequently checks if an object is in a `java.util.LinkedList`. This is a rather slow operation that is proportional to the size of the list (time complexity $O(n)$), as it potentially involves traversing the entire list, looking for the element. Changing to another data structure, such as a `HashSet` would most certainly speed up the check, making the time complexity constant ($O(1)$) on average, given that the hash function is good enough and the set large enough.

Optimizations

This tab shows various statistics from the JIT-compiler. The information in this tab is mostly of interest when hunting down optimization-related bugs in JRockit. It shows how much time was spent doing optimizations as well as how much time was spent JIT-compiling code at the beginning and at the end of the recording. For each method optimized during the recording, native code size before and after optimization is shown, as well as how long it took to optimize the particular method

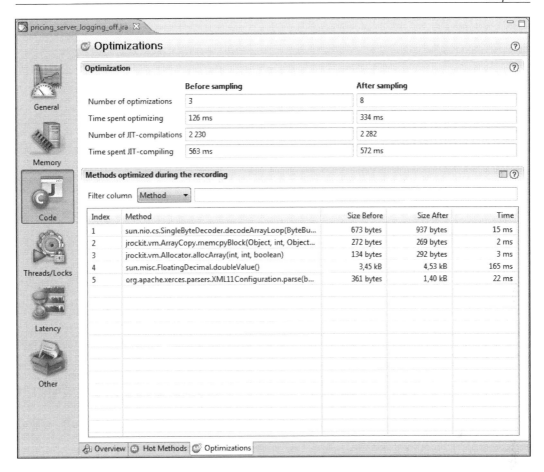

Thread/Locks

The **Thread/Locks** tab group contains tabs that visualize thread- and lock-related data. There are five such tabs in JRA—the **Overview, Thread, Java Locks, JVM Locks,** and **Thread Dumps** tab.

Overview

The **Overview** tab shows fundamental thread and hardware-related information, such as the number of **hardware threads** available on the system and the number of context switches per second.

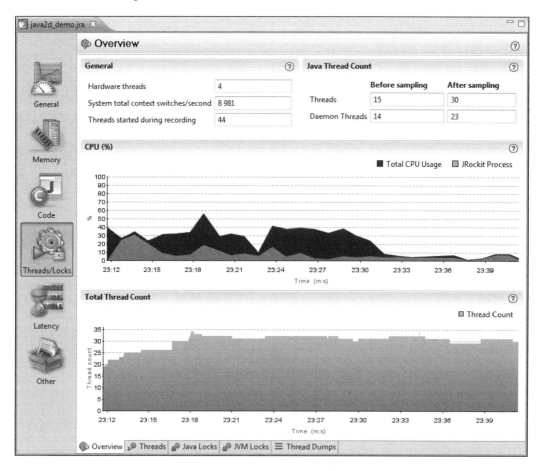

A dual-core CPU has two hardware threads, and a hyperthreaded core also counts as two hardware threads. That is, a dual-core CPU with hyperthreading will be displayed as having four hardware threads.

A high amount of context switches per second may not be a real problem, but better synchronization behavior may lead to better total throughput in the system.

There is a CPU graph showing both the total CPU load on the system, as well as the CPU load generated by the JVM. A saturated CPU is usually a good thing — you are fully utilizing the hardware on which you spent a lot of money! As previously mentioned, in some CPU-bound applications, for example batch jobs, it is normally a good thing for the system to be completely saturated during the run. However, for a standard server-side application it is probably more beneficial if the system is able to handle some extra load in addition to the expected one.

> The hardware provisioning problem is not simple, but normally server-side systems should have some spare computational power for when things get hairy. This is usually referred to as **overprovisioning**, and has traditionally just involved buying faster hardware. Virtualization has given us exciting new ways to handle the provisioning problem. Some of these are discussed in *Chapter 13, JRockit Virtual Edition*.

Threads

This tab shows a table where each row corresponds to a thread. The tab has more to offer than first meets the eye. By default, only the start time, the thread duration, and the Java thread ID are shown for each thread. More columns can be made visible by changing the table properties. This can be done either by clicking on the **Table Settings** icon, or by using the context menu in the table.

As can be seen in the example screenshot, information such as the thread group that the thread belongs to, allocation-related information, and the platform thread ID can also be displayed. The platform thread ID is the ID assigned to the thread by the operating system, in case we are working with native threads. This information can be useful if you are using operating system-specific tools together with JRA.

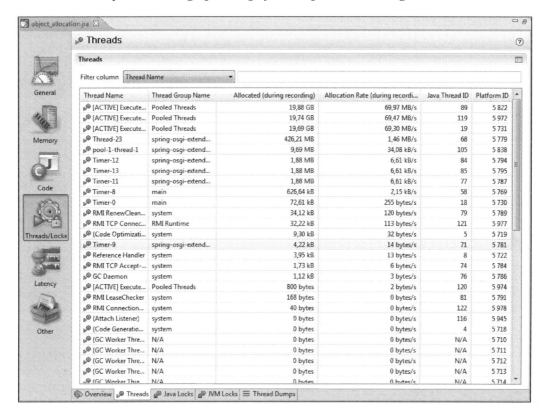

Java Locks

This tab displays information on how Java locks have been used during the recording. The information is aggregated per type (class) of monitor object. For more information regarding the different kind of locks, please refer to *Chapter 4, Threads and Synchronization*.

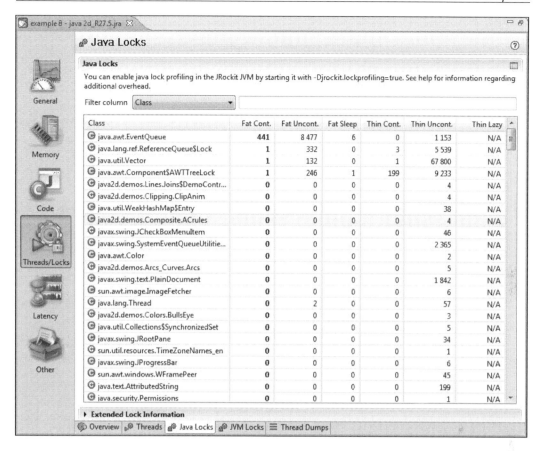

This tab is normally empty. You need to start JRockit with the system property `jrockit.lockprofiling` set to `true`, for the lock profiling information to be recorded. This is because lock profiling may cause anything from a small to a considerable overhead, especially if there is a lot of synchronization.

With recent changes to the JRockit thread and locking model, it would be possible to dynamically enable lock profiling. This is unfortunately not the case yet, not even in JRockit Flight Recorder.

For R28, the system property `jrockit.lockprofiling` has been deprecated and replaced with the flag `-XX:UseLockProfiling`.

JVM Locks

This tab contains information on JVM internal native locks. This is normally useful for the JRockit JVM developers and for JRockit support.

> Native locks were discussed to some extent in Chapter 4. An example of a native lock would be the code buffer lock that the JVM acquires in order to emit compiled methods into a native code buffer. This is done to ensure that no other code generation threads interfere with that particular code emission.

Thread Dumps

The JRA recordings normally contain thread dumps from the beginning and the end of the recording. By changing the **Thread dump interval** parameter in the JRA recording wizard, more thread dumps can be made available at regular intervals throughout the recording.

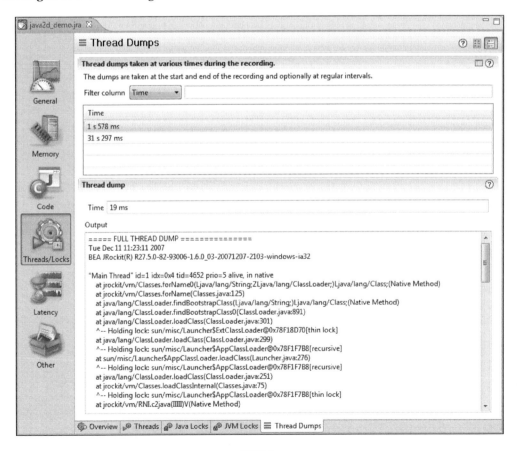

Latency

The latency tools were introduced as a companion to JRockit Real Time. The predictable garbage collection pause times offered by JRockit Real Time made necessary a tool to help developers hunt down latencies introduced by the Java application itself, as opposed to by the JVM. It is not enough to be able to guarantee that the GC does not halt execution for more than a millisecond if the application itself blocks for hundreds of milliseconds when, for example, waiting for I/O.

When working with the tabs in the **Latency** tab group, we strongly recommend switching to the **Latency perspective**. The switch can be made from the menu **Window | Show Perspective**. In the latency perspective, two new views are available to the left—the **Event Types** view and the **Properties** view. The **Event Types** view can be used to select which latency events to examine and the **Properties** view shows detailed information on any selected event.

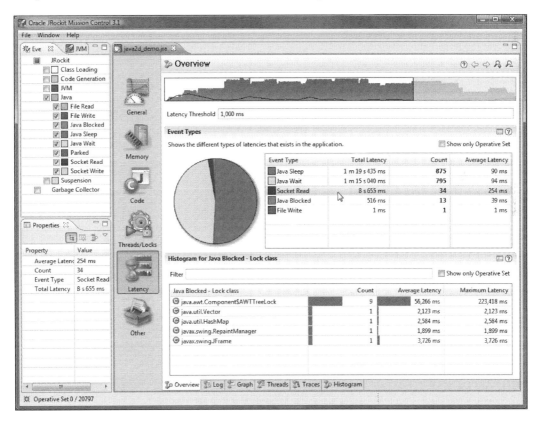

Similar to in the GCs tab, at the top of all the latency tabs is the **Range Selector**. The range selector allows you to temporarily select a subset of the events and only examine this subset. Any changes either to the **Event Types** view or the range selector will be instantly reflected in the tab. The graph in the backdrop of the range selector, normally colored red, is the normalized amount of events at a specific point in time. The range selector also shows the CPU load as a black graph rendered over the event bars. It is possible to configure what should be displayed using the range selector context menu.

The **operative set** is an important concept to understand when examining latencies and subsets of latencies. It is a set of events that can be added to and removed from, by using the different tabs in the latency tab group. Think of it as a collection of events that can be brought from one tab to another and which can be modified using the different views in the different tabs. Understanding and using the operative set is very important to get the most out of the latency analysis tool.

Overview

The **Overview** tab provides an aggregated view of the latency events in the recording. At the top, just under the range selector, the **Latency Threshold** used during the recording can be seen. As potentially very large volumes of data can be recorded, the **Latency Threshold** is normally used to limit the amount of events so that only the ones longer than a certain threshold are actually recorded. The default is to only record latency events that are longer than 20 milliseconds.

A **latency event** is any time slice longer than a preset value that the JVM spends *not executing* Java code. For example, it may instead be waiting for data on a socket or performing a phase of garbage collection that stops the world.

The **Event Types** histogram and accompanying pie chart show breakdowns per event type. This is useful to quickly get a feel for what kind of events were recorded and their proportions. Note that the pie chart shows the *number of events* logged, not the total time that the events took. A tip for finding out where certain types of events are occurring is to use the context menu in the **Event Types** histogram to add the events of a certain type to the operative set. This causes the events of that type to be colored turquoise in the range selector.

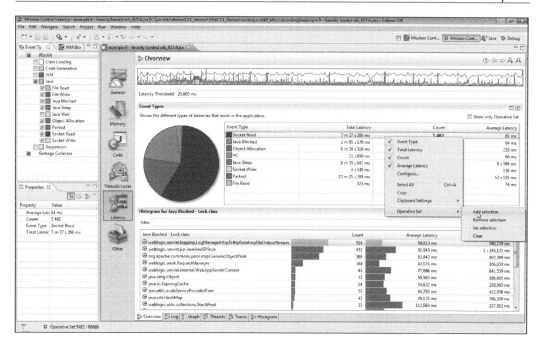

Another tip is to go to the **Traces** view and click on **Show only Operative Set**, to see the stack traces that led up to the events of that particular type.

Log

The latency **Log** tab shows all the available events in a table. The table can be used for filtering events, for sorting them, and for showing the events currently in the operative set. It is mostly used to quickly sort the events on duration to find the longest ones. Sometimes, the longest latencies may be due to socket `accept`s or other blocking calls that would actually be expected to take a long time. In such cases, this table can be used to quickly find and remove such events from the operative set, concentrating only on the problematic latencies.

Graph

The latency **Graph** tab contains a graph where the events are displayed, aggregated per thread. In the following example, we only show the events from the Java and Garbage Collector event types. The normal rendering procedure for the graph is that each event producer gets its own per-thread **lane** where the events for that particular producer are displayed. For each thread, only one event can occur in a lane at any given time. Garbage collection events are drawn in a slightly different way — they are always shown at the top of the latency event graph, and each GC is highlighted as a backdrop across all the other threads. This is useful for seeing if a certain latency event was caused by a garbage collection. If part of a lane in the latency graph is green, it means that the thread is happily executing Java code. Any other color means that a latency event is taking place at that point in time. To find out what the color means, either hover the mouse over an event and read the tooltip, or check the colors in the **Event Types** view.

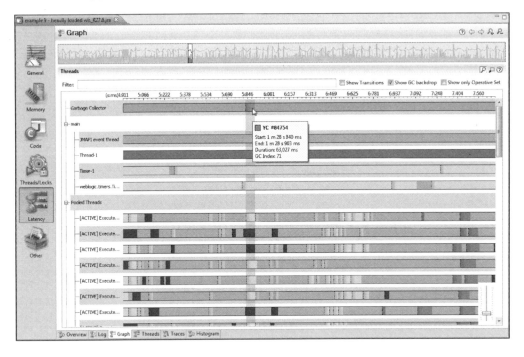

The latency **Graph** can also show thread transitions. The application in the next screenshot has an exaggerated pathological behavior, where all threads in an application are sharing a logger through a static field, and where the logger is using a synchronized resource for writing log data. As can be seen, the worker threads are all waiting on the shared resource. The worker threads that are there to execute parts of the work in parallel, rely on the shared logger. This actually causes the entire application to execute the work in a sequential fashion instead.

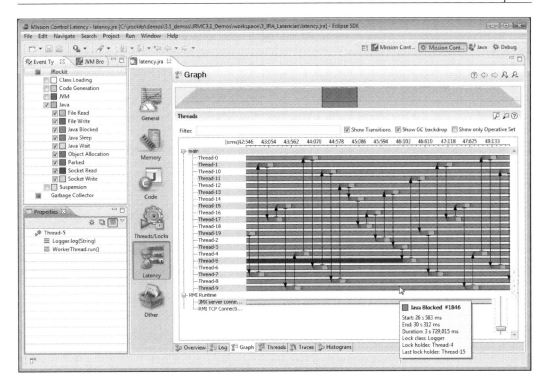

If you see an event that you want to get more information on, you can either select it in the graph and study it in the properties view, hover the mouse pointer over it and read the tooltip that pops up, or add it to the operative set for closer examination in one of the other views.

To summarize, the **Graph** view is good for providing an overview of the latency and thread behavior of the application.

Threads

The **Threads** tab is basically a table containing the threads in the system, much like the threads tab in the Management Console, as described in Chapter 7. The most useful properties in this table tend to be the event **Count** and the **Allocation Rate** per thread.

This view is mainly used to select a specific thread, either based on an attribute, such as the one with highest allocation rate, or for finding a specific thread by name. The operative set is then used to select the events for that particular thread, so that the events can be studied in the other views. Sets of threads can also be selected.

Traces

This is where the stack traces for sets of events get aggregated. For instance, if the operative set contains the set of allocation events for `String` arrays, this is the tab you would go to for finding out where those object allocations take place. In the next example, only the traces for the operative set are visible. As can be seen, the **Count** and **Total Latency** columns have bar chart backdrops that show how much of the max value, relative to the other children on the same level, the value in the cell corresponds to. Everything is normalized with respect to the max value.

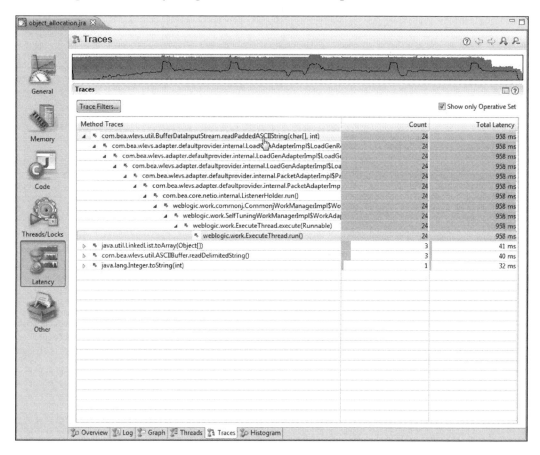

Normally, while analyzing a recording, you end up in this tab once you have used the other tabs to filter out the set of events that you are interested in. This tab reveals where in the code the events are originating from.

Histogram

This very powerful tab is used to build histograms of the events. The histogram can be built around any event value. A few examples of useful ones are:

- **Object Allocation | Class Name**: For finding out what types of allocations are most common

- **Java Blocked | Lock Class**: For finding out which locks are most frequently blocking in the application

- **Java Wait | Lock Class**: For finding out where the application spends the most time in `wait()`

Once the interesting events have been found, they are usually added to the **operative set** and brought to another tab for further investigation.

Using the Operative Set

Sadly, one of the most overlooked features in JRA is the **operative set**. This example will explain how the operative set can be used to filter out a very specific set of events to solve a specific problem. In this example, we have been given a JRA recording from another team. The team is unhappy with the garbage collections that take place in an application. Garbage collections seem to be performed too frequently and take too long to complete. We start by looking at the **GCs** tab in the **Memory** section.

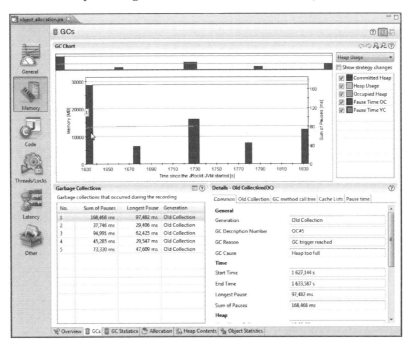

The initial reaction from examining the garbage collections is that they are indeed quite long, tens of milliseconds, but they do not happen all that often. For the duration of the recording only five GCs took place. We could probably ask the clients to switch to deterministic GC. This would cause more frequent but much shorter garbage collections. However, as we are curious, we would like to get back to them with more than just a GC strategy recommendation. We would still like to know where most of the pressure on the memory system is being created.

As this is an example, we'll make this slightly more complicated than necessary, just to hint at the power of JRA. We switch to the latency data thread tab and look for the most allocation intensive threads. Then we add these events to the **Operative Set**. It seems that almost all allocation is done in the top three threads.

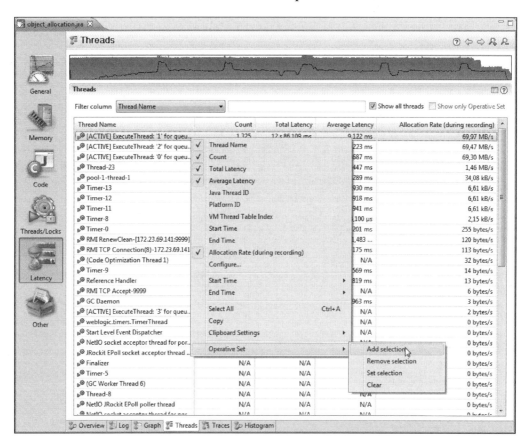

We have now added all the events for the three threads to our **Operative Set**, but we are only interested in studying the allocation behavior. In order to do this, we move to the **Histogram** tab and build a histogram for the allocation events in our **Operative Set**.

Note that object allocations are weird latency events, as we are normally not interested in their duration, but rather the number of occurrences. We therefore sort them on event count and see that most of the object allocation events in our three threads are caused by instantiating Strings. As we're eager to find out where these events take place, we limit the **operative set** to the String allocation events.

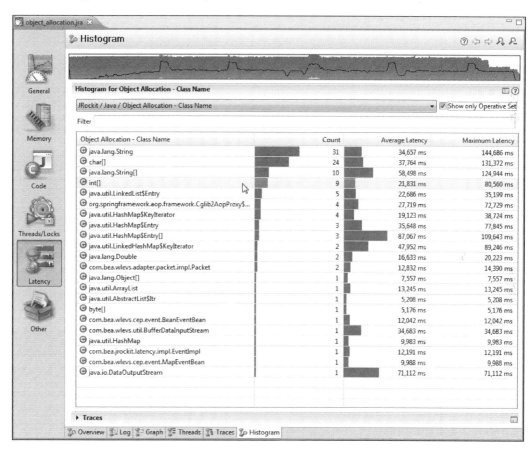

We proceed to the **Traces** view with our trimmed **Operative Set**, and once again check the **Show only Operative Set** button.

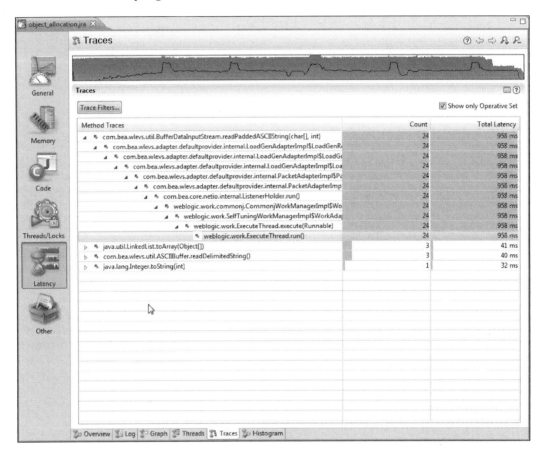

We quickly see that almost all the String instances in our three most allocation-intensive threads are allocated by the same method —readPaddedASCIIString(char [], int). If we also add char arrays, we can see that the char arrays are mostly created as a result of allocating the String objects in the same method. This makes sense as each String wraps one char array.

We can now recommend the team not only to change GC strategies, but we can also say for sure, that one way to drastically reduce the pressure on the memory system in this particular application would be to either create less strings in the method at the top in the **Traces** view, or to reduce the number of calls along the path to that method.

Troubleshooting

Sometimes, there will be no data in the **Code | Hot methods** tab, even if the method sampling was enabled. The most common reason is that the application did not generate enough load to provide the method sampler with data. The method sampler only samples threads that are actively running Java code. If the recording is short and the threads are spending most of their time waiting and doing nothing, chances are that no samples will be recorded at all. If you aren't profiling a production system, try to stress your application during profiling, if possible in a manner that is close to the real deployment scenario.

When using native method sampling, all samples will be stored. Normally, only the samples for threads executing Java will be stored. Don't be surprised if you find almost all of the native samples to be in some native method, such as `ntdll.dll#KiFastSystemCallRet`, even when the system is mostly idle.

Summary

In this chapter, we showed how to use the JRockit Runtime Analyzer to analyze the behavior of the JRockit runtime and the application running in JRockit.

We showed various different ways to create recordings. We also discussed the information available in JRA recordings with examples.

Several use cases were demonstrated, such as:

- How to find methods that would make good candidates for manual optimization, also known as hot spots
- How to interpret memory-related information, such as the live set, garbage collection-related information, fragmentation, the object summary, and the heap histogram
- How to hunt down latency-related problems

We also provided an example on how to use the Operative Set in the latency analyzer to quickly narrow down the amount of data being studied and to focus on the data of interest.

The next chapter covers JRockit Flight Recorder, which has superseded JRA as of JRockit R28 and JRockit Mission Control 4.0. Most of what has been covered in this chapter works in similar ways and is still applicable.

9
The Flight Recorder

The overhead of using JRA proved so low that we started considering the notion of always having it enabled when the JVM is running. The project to implement such a recording engine was internally first known as **continuous JRA**. In the R28 version of JRockit, this has finally been productized and named **JRockit Flight Recorder**.

As near-zero overhead data is continuously stored about JVM behavior, the JRockit Flight Recorder allows us to go back in time and analyze the behavior of the application and the JVM even *after* something has gone wrong. This is a very powerful feature for JVM and application forensics—the recording being the "black box" that contains information on all events leading up to a problem. Naturally, the framework still works well as a profiling and instrumentation tool, which will likely remain the most common use case.

In this chapter, you will learn:

- How JRockit Flight Recorder works
- About the Flight Recorder event model
- How to start a continuous recording
- How to start a JRA-style recording
- How recordings interact in JRockit Flight Recorder
- How to configure the various aspects of JRockit Flight Recorder
- The main differences between JRockit Flight Recorder and the JRockit Runtime Analyzer
- How to record custom events
- How to design custom extensions to the JRockit Flight Recorder client
- About future tools, APIs, and projects around JRockit Flight Recorder

The evolved Runtime Analyzer

Just like the JRockit Runtime Analyzer, the JRockit Flight Recorder consists of two parts—a recording engine built into the JRockit JVM and an analysis tool built into the JRockit Mission Control client. The recording engine produces a recording file that can be analyzed. The file does not require an active connection; the format is self describing, that is, all metadata that the recording needs is part of the recording and can be saved for later or sent to a third party for further analysis.

 Throughout this chapter, we will use the terms JRockit Flight Recorder and Flight Recorder interchangeably.

With JRockit Flight Recorder, recordings are no longer in XML format. Everything is recorded as time-stamped events in internal memory buffers and written to a binary file, which constitutes the recording. There is also a public Java API available for providing custom events to the JRockit recording engine, and a **design mode** that allows the creation of custom designed user interfaces from within the analysis tool itself.

 Recall from *Chapter 8, The Runtime Analyzer*, that a JRA recording is in XML format and the files are suffixed .jra. With Flight Recorder, the files are suffixed .jfr and are in a binary format. Because of the immense amount of events produced, there is a need to avoid unnecessary overhead and consequently to store events in a more compact way. JRA recordings are not forward-compatible and cannot be opened with JRockit Flight Recorder.

A word on events

As mentioned, data is recorded as **events**. An event is simply data recorded at a specific time.

There are four different types of events:

- **Duration events**: Duration events are events that last over a duration of time or, in other words, events with a start time and an end time. The **Garbage Collection event** is an example of a duration event.

- **Timed events**: The timed events are duration events for which a **threshold** can be set. The concept of a threshold is discussed in detail later in this chapter. The **Java Wait** and **Java Sleep** events are examples of timed events.

- **Instant events**: Instant events have no duration, only a start time. The **Exception** and the **Event Settings Changed** events are examples of instant events.

- **Requestable events**: Requestable events can be configured to be polled periodically by the recording engine. The event implements a callback that a separate thread in the recording engine will call at specified intervals. An example of a requestable event is the **CPU Load Sample event**.

Events are produced by **event producers**. An event producer defines the types of events being produced, also known as **event types**, as well as the actual events. An event type contains metadata that describes how the events of that type will look. The metadata contains information such as what attributes (also known as **fields**) the event contains, of what types the attributes are, and human-readable descriptions of the attributes. Every recording file contains information about its event producers.

An event producer with the imaginative and thought-provoking name "JRockit JVM" is already built into JRockit. The main advantage of the JRockit JVM producer, just as with JRA, is that it cheaply records information that the runtime already needs to collect as part of doing its job. Using the Java API, which will be discussed later, anyone can contribute events to bring additional context to the lower level events created by the JRockit JVM producer.

The recording engine

The recording engine, also known as the **recording agent**, is part of the JVM itself and provides highly optimized services for the event producers. A few examples are:

- **A recording facility**: Of course, the main purpose of the recording engine is to record events. It does this highly efficiently by providing thread local buffers where the events are recorded and a scheme to transfer these to a global buffer when the thread local buffers are full. Once the global buffer is full, it is either emitted to disk in the previously mentioned compact binary format, or reused in a circular fashion depending on the configuration. See the next figure.

- **Stack traces**: If the event producer sets the appropriate options, the stack trace that generated the event will be recorded along with the event. This is useful for finding where, in the source code of a Java application, an event originated.

- **Threshold**: The recording engine can be configured to only include duration events that last longer than a specified amount of time. This is used to both limit the amount of data in the recording, and to filter out data that would be of no interest anyway. The threshold can be configured per event type.

- **Highly optimized time stamping of events**: As was briefly discussed in *Chapter 5, Benchmarking and Tuning,* using `System.currentTimeMillis()` for getting the system time can be a much more expensive operation than one would think. The recording engine provides a highly optimized native implementation for timestamping events.

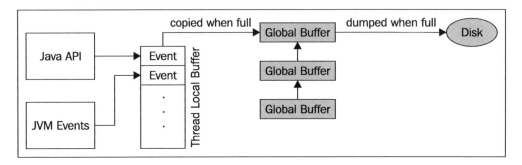

As JRockit R28 is released as part of a patch release of the application stack, it was decided that enabling the default recording was too big a change. The recording engine is enabled in R28, but there is no recording running from the start of the JVM. Both the recording engine and the JRockit JVM event producer have been designed and tested for always being enabled. As a matter of fact, all of the testing, including the stress testing of JRockit R28, was performed with the default recording enabled. The default recording will most likely be enabled out of the box in future releases of JRockit.

Ongoing recordings in the JVM have an associated recording ID, which is unique, and a recording name, which does not have to be. The recording ID is automatically assigned to the recording when it is created, and can be used for identifying a recording. The recording ID can, for example, be used when referring to a recording from JRCMD.

To enable the Flight Recorder and to configure it to continuously record data with the default settings, simply start JRockit with the following option:

```
-XX:FlightRecorderOptions=defaultrecording=true
```

This will create a recording with recording ID 0 and the name `JRockit default`.

There can be an arbitrary amount of recordings running in JRockit Flight Recorder at any given time. If more than one recording is active, the recorded data will contain events from the union of the enabled event types and use the threshold found for each type. For users new to the Flight Recorder, this can be quite confusing, as there may actually be more events in the recording than asked for.

To configure the engine to record more detailed information, you can either change the **event settings** of the default recording, or start a new recording with different settings. To record less information, the event settings of any ongoing recording must be changed.

Startup options

There are various ways to configure the different aspects of the recording engine, some of which are only available from the command line when starting the JVM.

There are two main command-line parameters. As previously mentioned, the first one turns on (+) or off (-) the Flight Recorder altogether:

    -XX:[+|-]FlightRecorder

The second is for controlling the Flight Recorder:

    -XX:FlightRecorderOptions=parameter1=value1[,parameter2=value2]

The available parameters are:

Parameter	Description
`settings=[name|filepath]`	Loads additional event settings from this server-side template. The default templates available under `JROCKIT_HOME/jre/lib/jfr` can be referred to by name. More information on server-side templates is available after this table.
`repository=[dir]`	The base directory where the Flight Recorder will emit chunks of data. This can be seen as the temporary directory of the Flight Recorder. The default is a directory under `java.io.tmpdir` with a name generated in the format `yyyy_mm_dd_hh_mm_ss_pid`. For example, a repository created at the time of writing for a process with a process ID of `4711` would have the repository base directory name `2010_04_21_16_28_59_4711`.

Option	Description
threadbuffersize=[size]	The size to use for the thread local buffers. The default is 5 KB.
globalbuffersize=[size]	The size to use for a single global buffer. The default is 64 KB.
numglobalbuffers=[num]	There may be more than one global buffer. This sets the number of global buffers to use. The default is 8.
maxchunksize=[size]	The maximum size of a single data chunk in the repository. The default is 12 MB.
continuous=[true|false]	Enable the default continuous recording, that is the built-in continuous recording with recording ID 0. This does not enable or disable continuous recording as a concept. No matter what value this attribute has, continuous recordings can still be started from JRockit Mission Control as long as the Flight Recorder engine itself is enabled. As mentioned, the default recording is disabled in JRockit R28.0, but is likely to be enabled by default in future versions of JRockit.
disk=[true|false]	Emit data to disk. This is disabled by default, meaning that circular in-memory buffers will be used instead. The contents of the buffers can be dumped to disk, either from Mission Control or by using JRCMD.
maxage=[nanotime]	Defines the maximum age of the data kept on disk. Data younger than this is retained. The time is specified in nanoseconds by default. The default value is 0, which means the age check is ignored and that all data is retained.
maxsize=[size]	The maximum size of the data to keep on disk. The default value is 0, which means the size check is ignored.

When using either JRCMD or the command-line options, specifying what information will actually be recorded is done through JSON-based template files. The JRockit distribution comes with several example templates available under JROCKIT_HOME/jre/lib/jfr. These templates are also known as **server-side templates**, as they differ from the ones used by the JRockit Mission Control client. The templates in the JRockit distribution serve as good examples, should you want to create your own server-side template.

An in-depth discussion on the server-side templates is beyond the scope of this book. See the example templates for further information on server-side templates and *Chapter 11, JRCMD*, for information about using JRCMD to control the recording life cycle.

Starting time-limited recordings

Just like with JRA, it is possible to use command-line options to start time-limited recordings. In the Flight Recorder, the parameter is called -XX:StartFlightRecording. This parameter is useful when wanting to do several recordings and compare them. It is for instance possible to delay a recording to give the application and the JVM time to warm up. The following example starts a recording after two minutes. The recording will last for one minute and will be named MyRecording. The resulting recording file ends up as C:\tmp\ myrecording.jfr. Just like with -XX:FlightRecorderOptions, a server-side template can be referred to by name. The example uses the profile.jfs template.

```
-XX:StartFlightRecording=delay=120s,duration=60s,
  name=MyRecording,filename=C:\tmp\myrecording.jfr,settings=profile
```

See the command-line reference for JRockit R28 for more information about the available parameters to the StartFlightRecording option.

The rest of this chapter focuses on using the JRockit Mission Control client for controlling the Flight Recorder and for viewing recordings.

Flight Recorder in JRockit Mission Control

The easiest way to both control the life cycle of recordings and transfer whole or parts of recordings to JRockit Mission Control, is to do everything from inside the JRockit Mission Control client.

Starting a JRA-style time-bound recording is quite similar to how it was done in previous JRockit versions, using JRA—simply right click on the JVM in the **JVM Browser**, and then click on **Start Flight Recording....**

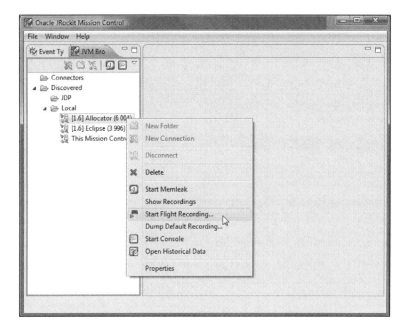

In JRockit Mission Control 4.0, two things will happen:

1. The **Start Flight Recording** wizard dialog box will open.
2. The **Flight Recorder Control** view will open.

The **Flight Recorder Control** view is new for JRockit Mission Control 4.0. It shows the recordings available for one or more connections, and can also be used for controlling the recordings. It is quite useful for checking if any recordings are already running in the JVM. In the following screenshot, the continuous recording is already running:

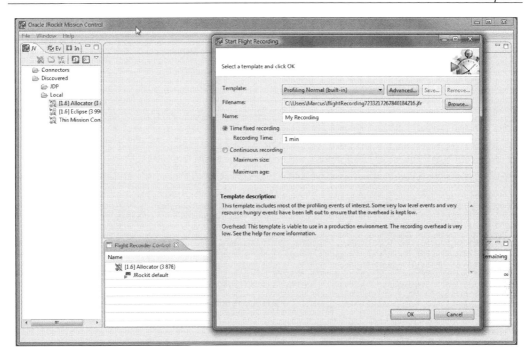

Similar to JRA, this wizard contains a few built-in templates to choose from, and if none of the provided templates records the information of interest, new templates can be created. These templates differ from the server-side templates in that they are fully resolved (no wildcards anywhere), and in that they support metadata for the user interface.

The default built-in client-side templates are:

- **Default Profiling**: A good, general-purpose profiling template with low profiling overhead.
- **Profiling with Locks**: Same as the previous one, but with lock profiling enabled. This requires the JRockit instance that is to be profiled to be started with `-XX:+UseLockProfiling`. This, in turn, causes some additional overhead, even when not recording.

- **Profiling with Exceptions**: Same as the **Default Profiling** template, but with exception profiling enabled. For most applications, the overhead of this template will not be different from that of the **Default Profiling** template. However, for some pathological applications, where a large number of exceptions are thrown, the overhead can be considerable.

- **Real-Time**: Focuses on garbage collection related events, but leaves out some of the most resource hungry events.

Worth noting is that both the default client-side and server-side templates omit exception events by default, as it is difficult to estimate their performance impact on a pathological application. To include exception profiling, select the built-in **Profiling with Exceptions** template. Exception profiling will be further discussed later in this chapter.

Once a suitable template is selected, a destination file must be specified, and an appropriate name chosen. Some event producers, such as the ones from the WebLogic Diagnostics Framework, have their own recordings running. In a large system, there can be quite a few recordings running in parallel. Naming the recording properly will make it easier to find it later.

 Not only the JVM can record events in the Flight Recorder. There are already event producers for the **Oracle WebLogic Diagnostics Framework (WLDF)** and the **Oracle Dynamic Monitoring System (DMS)**. We expect more Oracle products to provide producers in the future, such as JRockit Virtual Edition.

It is possible to perform either a time-limited recording or a continuous one. For a time-limited recording, a duration must be chosen. In order to limit the resource usage of continuous recordings, it is possible to limit the amount of data to store, either by time, size, or both.

Once the recording wizard is filled out, clicking on **Continue** will start the recording.

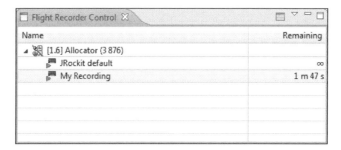

The **Flight Recorder Control** view is updated to show the newly started recording. For time-limited recordings, the remaining time until the recording is done is shown and periodically updated. Continuous recordings show an infinity (∞) sign instead of the remaining time.

Note that there is a table settings action (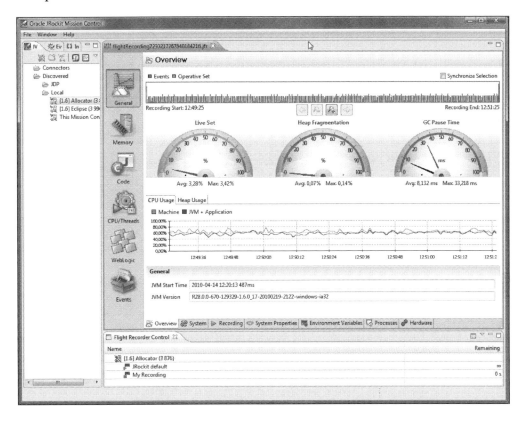) in the toolbar of the Flight Recorder control view. The table can be configured to show more information, if needed.

For a time-limited recording, the recording will be downloaded automatically once it is complete.

As can be seen in the previous screenshot, recordings are left on the server by default when completed, even after they have been downloaded. In the screenshot, **My Recording** has just been downloaded. It is also displayed as being finished ( ) in the **Flight Recorder Control** view, with no time remaining. Such finished recordings can be removed by right clicking on the recording in the **Flight Recorder Control** view and then clicking on **Close**.

As mentioned, it is possible to see the recording activities of more than one JVM at a time in the **Flight Recorder Control** view. To add a connection to monitor, simply right click on the connection in the **JVM Browser** and then click on **Show Recordings**. The following screenshot shows the recordings for three different JVMs at once:

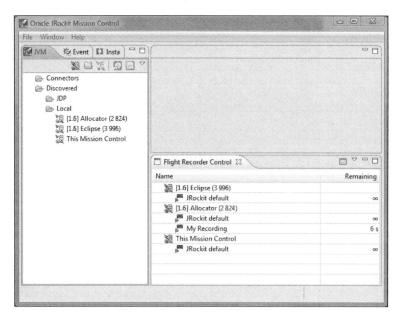

To use the control view to dump data from an ongoing recording, simply right click on it and select **Dump....** This brings up the **Dump Recording** dialog, as shown in the following screenshot:

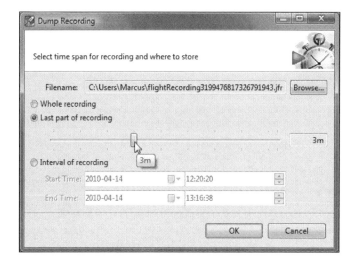

There are three different ways to select what part of the recording to dump:

- **Whole recording**: Dumps all available data.

- **Last part of recording**: Dumps the last data in the recording, given a specified period of time. Note that it is possible to get more data than was specified, as only whole data chunks will be dumped.

- **Interval of recording**: Dumps recording data for a specified interval of time. Note that the time is specified in server time. If the client is running in Stockholm and the server in Tokyo, make sure you specify the correct time. If there is no data within the specified time, an error message is displayed.

Again, what is actually dumped may be more than you were asking for.

The data is dumped in whole data chunks of a fixed size. Each chunk of data contains a constant pool that the events in the chunk use to resolve the data. For instance, there is a pool containing the stack traces for the events. When an event contains a stack trace, the event will refer to the stack trace by index in the pool. This way, the format can be streamed and used on a per-chunk basis, each chunk being self-contained.

Advanced Flight Recorder Wizard concepts

The Flight Recording Wizard lets you create custom templates. Clicking on the **Advanced...** button next to a template name brings up a dialog box where the template settings can be edited.

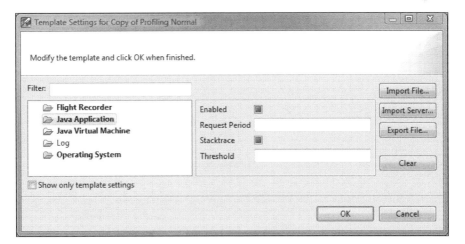

To the left in the wizard is an event type tree similar to the one in the **Event Types** view. Selecting a parent node will allow the settings to be changed recursively for all the descendants of that node. If there are different settings for the different children, no value is shown for that of the parent node. For example, in the previous screenshot, the settings for the events under the **Java Application** node vary, so no values are shown for the **Request Period** and **Threshold**. Also, it would seem that some events in the selection are disabled as well, as there is no check mark in the check box for **Enabled**. To enable all of the **Java Application** events, click on the **Enabled** check box.

In our example, the check box under the event type tree has been unchecked to allow event types that are not a part of the current template to be shown. Nodes with children that are part of a template are rendered in a bold faced font. Consequently, we can see that no event types under **Log** are part of the current template.

The event types shown in the tree depend both on what application is running in the JVM (the application may also utilize the Flight Recorder API) and on the settings in the template. This allows the user to change settings for event types originating in producers other than the default JRockit JVM producer. In the following example, an event producer with event types with a path beginning with **Log** is available in the running JVM.

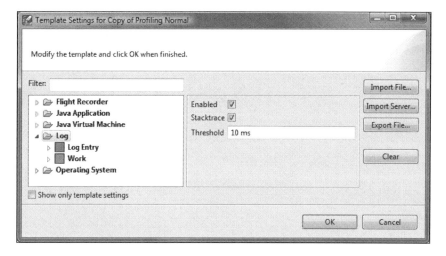

Updating the settings for event types will make them bold, indicating that they are now part of the template.

It is possible to import server-side templates from the advanced wizard. A good idea when doing so is to first clear the template from any interfering settings. To clear the template of all settings, click on the **Clear** button. The import functionality is additive, as the server-side templates are meant to be used in an additive fashion. This means that it is possible to, for example, start out with the settings for a default recording and then add lock profiling, by first importing the **default** template, and then importing the **locks** template. The next screenshot shows the import dialog:

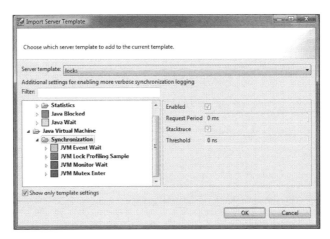

Entering the advanced dialog creates a temporary working copy of the template. Clicking on **OK** will save the settings to this temporary copy. An asterisk (*) next to the template name indicates that the copy has not yet been stored. If the changes to the template were done for only this particular recording, the template changes need probably not be stored.

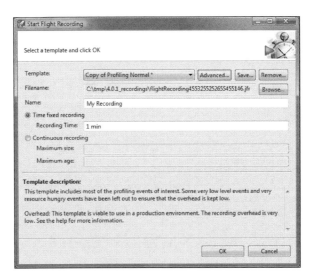

Simply clicking on **OK** in the **Start Flight Recording** dialog box allows the recording to commence without the template first being saved. The template will be available for the rest of the session, but gone the next time that JRockit Mission Control is started.

To save the template and give it a name and description, click on **Save....**

Once the recording is saved, it can be reused, even on JVMs that do not support all the event types for which the template has settings. For instance, when connecting to a JVM not supporting the log event types, a template containing settings for the log event types will render the log event types in italics, as shown in the following screenshot. As the template can be applied anyway, it is easy to store your favorite settings for a lot of different producers and scenarios in a small set of templates.

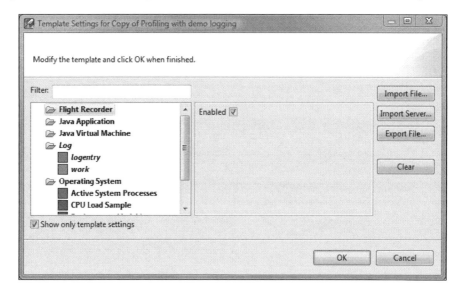

Differences to JRA

Due to the change to an event-based data model, some things are radically different compared to JRA. For instance, almost every tab now has a range selector. As everything now is an event, it almost always makes sense to be able to filter out data for a specific period of time. Another major change is that the data in general is much more fine-grained and there is a large number of new data sources.

We will discuss some of the more fundamental differences in detail.

The range selector

The following screenshot shows the **General | Overview** tab in the Flight Recorder GUI. This can be compared with the way it looked in JRA, as introduced in *Chapter 8, The Runtime Analyzer*.

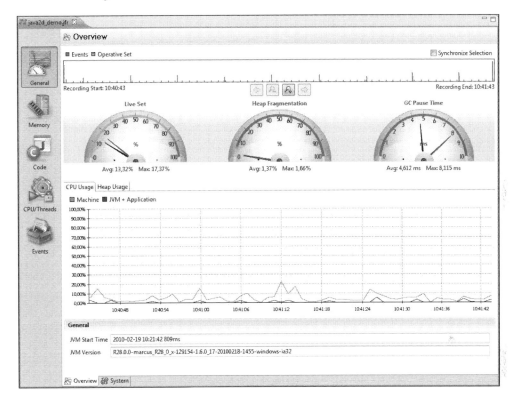

As mentioned, the range selector (available at the top of the window) can now be found in almost every tab in the Flight Recorder. The backdrop for the range selector in a tab normally shows the amount of events active during the time of recording for the events used in that particular tab. For example, the **Overview** tab uses various heap, garbage collection, CPU usage, and general information events.

One effect of the event-based data model is that it is possible to select a range that does not include an event where such data is available. Recall from Chapter 8 that some of the general information is written at the end of the recording. In the Flight Recorder, some events are written at the end of a chunk. If a range is selected that does not include the needed event, **N/A** is displayed, as shown in the following screenshot. Thus, care should be taken when modifying the range so that events of interest are actually included for the active view.

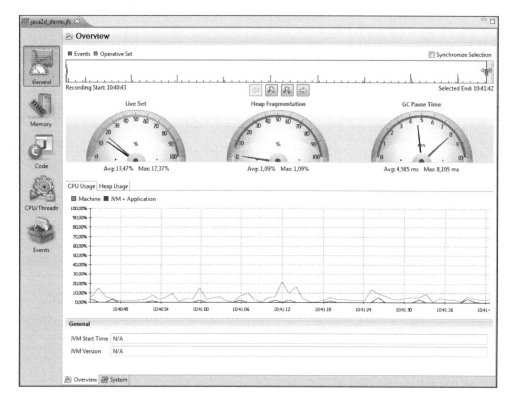

As the range selector is used in so many places, it is now possible to synchronize the selected range between all range selectors in all tabs. Check the **Synchronize Selection** check box to make the other range selectors follow the selection made.

Just as before, in JRA, the **Operative Set** will be highlighted in turquoise if any of the events are added to the **Operative Set**.

The Operative Set

The **Operative Set** has also been improved. It is now possible to manipulate the **Operative Set** from most views, even the ones mimicking the old JRA-style tabs.

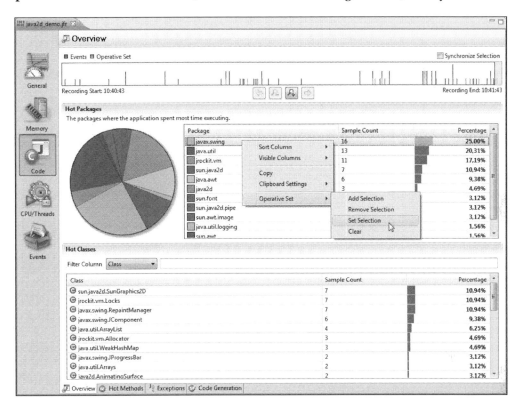

In the screenshot, we are adding the code samples found in the `javax.swing` package that, in this case, is the hottest package to the operative set. The corresponding events are highlighted in the range selector.

The relational key

Event attributes can now have a **relational key**. The relational key is globally unique, and is used to associate events of different types with each other. One such example is the GCID of the GC events. The GCID is specified to have the relational key `http://www.oracle.com/jrockit/jvm/vm/gc/id`. This makes it easy to find all events that are related to a specific garbage collection.

The relational key is on an URI format, much like name spaces in XML.

The user interface provides menu alternatives on the **Operative Set** context menu for events having attributes with relational keys. In the next screenshot, we do this for garbage collection number 239:

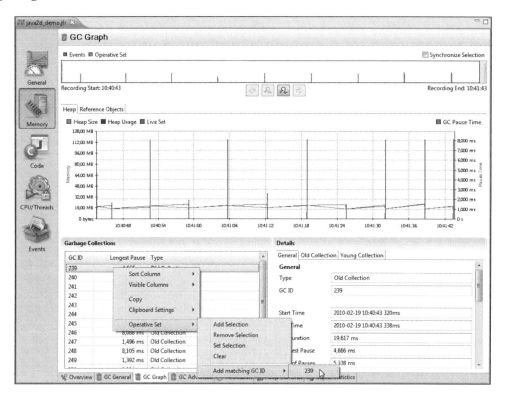

Third-party event producers use the relational key to associate events across producers. For instance, WLDF and DMS use the **Execution Context ID (ECID)** relational key to associate events across probes and producers all over WebLogic Server. It is, for example, possible to add all the events associated with a certain database call to the **Operative Set**.

These producers also provide relational keys for other attributes. The following example screenshot uses the experimental **WebLogic Tab Pack** to illustrate this by adding all the events with a matching SQL statement to the operative set.

The experimental plug-ins used in some of the examples in this book, such as the WebLogic Tab Pack, are only available for JRockit Mission Control 4.0.1 or later. Chances are that this book is published before the release of 4.0.1, and that the plug-ins will not be available for a little while. The good news is that the experimental plug-ins are available for download from within the JRockit Mission Control 4.0.1 GUI. As soon as version 4.0.1 (or later) of Mission Control is out, the authors' advice is to upgrade immediately.

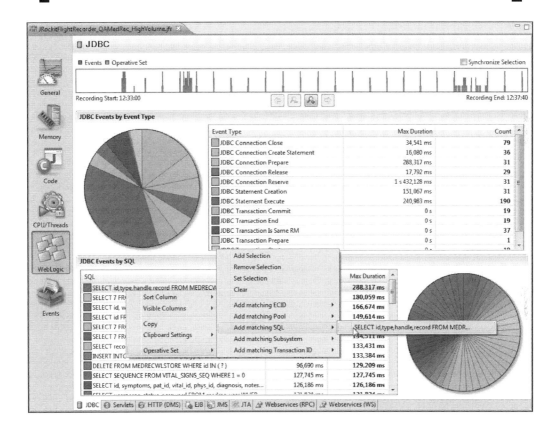

What's in a Latency?

Now that everything is an event, it is no longer wise to assume that all events are latency-related, as was the case in JRA. By **latency-related,** we mean any event directly involved in stalling the execution of a thread. There are specific tabs in the Flight Recorder GUI that deal with latency-related events, and latency-related Java events may still be used in a fashion similar to the old latency analyzer in JRA.

The **Events** tab group now contains general-purpose tabs for visualizing events, similar to how the **Latency** tab group was used in JRA. The following screenshot shows a synchronization problem:

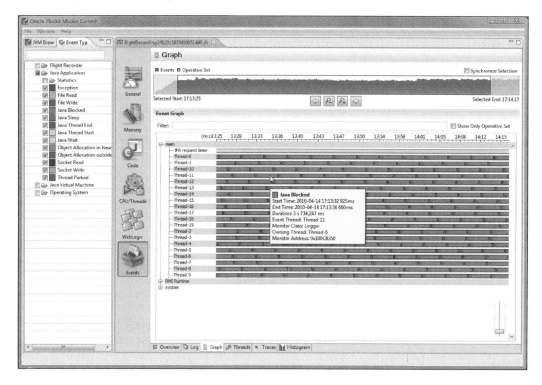

If only the Java Application events are selected in the **Event Types** view, the result will be very similar to the way things looked in the old latency analyzer in JRA.

The specialized tabs related to latencies can be found under the **CPU | Threads** tab group. There are new tabs in the Flight Recorder that aggregate the latency-related events in several interesting ways. The **Latencies** tab will, for instance, show an aggregation per event type, and the aggregated stack traces for the selected event type. In the next example, which is a recording from the Java 2D demo shipped with the JDK, we can see that the threads are mostly halted by (explicit/voluntary) sleeps.

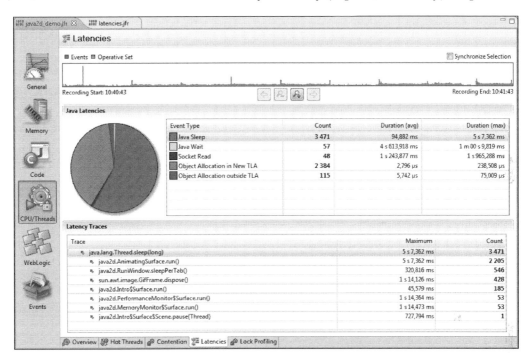

This is as would be expected, as there is probably a lot of thread sleeps going on between each rendering pass in the rendering loops. Note that the pie chart to the left is based on the *event count*, and not on the max duration, on which the table is sorted.

 In Mission Control 4.0.0, the pie chart is bound to a pre-defined column. It is possible to change which column by using the design mode, as is explained later in this chapter. In the next minor version of the Flight Recorder, we're exploring the option to bind the pie chart to whichever numerical column was sorted last.

The **Contention** tab, introduced in JRockit Flight Recorder, is specialized for showing the **Java Blocking** (threads blocked, waiting on acquiring monitors) events. In the example recording from WebLogic Server shown in the next screenshot, we can see that the longest total time a thread had to wait for acquiring a monitor was spent waiting on an instance of `weblogic.servlet.internal.HttpServer`, trying to execute the method `loadWebApp(...)`.

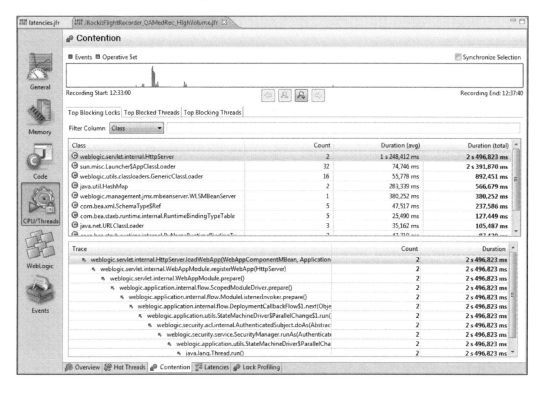

It is also possible to see which threads were blocked the most, as well as which threads were blocking other threads the most.

Just like in JRA, it is possible to enable very detailed lock profiling, and just like in JRA, lock profiling comes with a small additional runtime overhead, even when not recording. To enable lock profiling, start JRockit with the flag `-XX:+UseLockProfiling` and use the **Profiling with Locks** template. More information on the lock profiling flags was given in *Chapter 4, Threads and Synchronization*.

Exception profiling

In JRA, the only available exception profiling information was the total number of exceptions being thrown. The only way to correlate that to where in the code the exceptions were thrown, was to change the log settings for the JVM to enable the logging of exceptions. For example, through JRCMD or by restarting the JVM with `-Xverbose:exceptions=debug`, and then checking the output. With the Flight Recorder, there are now events containing the necessary information, and a tab that allows for easy browsing. Remember to use the **Profiling with Exceptions** template when creating a recording that is to use exception profiling. The tab is located under **Code | Exceptions**.

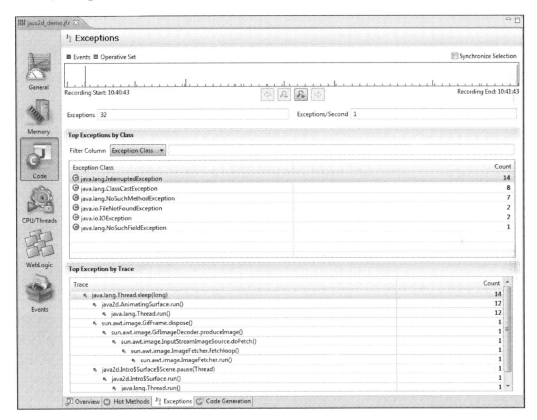

In the example recording from the Java 2D demo, we can see that most of the exceptions are `InterruptedExceptions` thrown from `java2d.AnimatingSurface.run()`. The range selector shows us two main bursts of exceptions, one at the beginning of the recording and one at the end. The burst of exceptions at the beginning of the recording is mostly due to `ClassCastExceptions`, and the burst at the end is due to `NoSuchMethodExceptions`. This can easily be determined by using the range selector to home in on the peaks, as shown in the following screenshot:

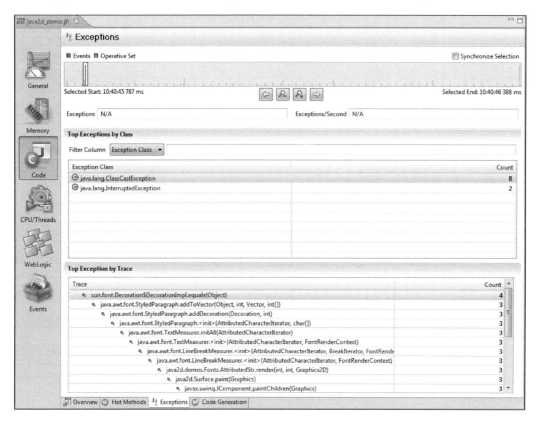

The Java 2D demo does not throw that many exceptions, so the exception data in the recording merely serves as an example on how to use the user interface. If an application throws more than several hundred exceptions per second, the cause should be investigated.

Memory

Even though the memory tabs, and the information in them, are quite similar to the old JRA layout there are a few things worth pointing out.

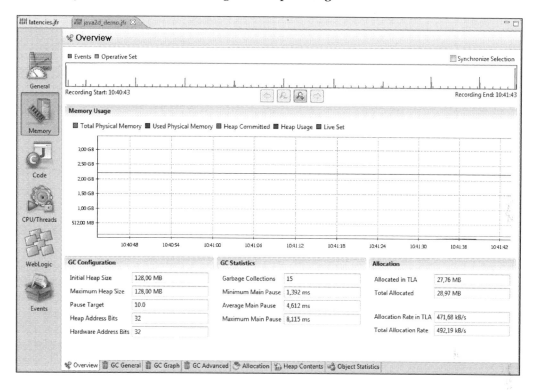

In the **Memory | Overview** tab, the **Total Physical Memory** and **Used Physical Memory** both refer to the physical memory on the machine and *not* the Java process! In the Java2D Demo recording earlier, the recording was done on a machine with 4 GB of physical memory, and at the point of recording, approximately 2.2 GB was in use. The committed Java heap was as small as 128 MB, as can be seen from both the graph and the **GC Configuration** section part. To see graphs of the Java heap usage, use the **Heap Contents** tab.

In the **Heap Contents** tab are two graphs, one focusing on the contents of the heap, and one focusing on how the free space of the heap is distributed. Worth noting in the **Heap Contents** tab, is that what was previously referred to as dark matter is now called **Fragmentation**, which is a more descriptive name.

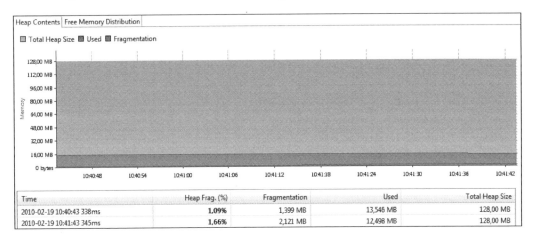

Time	Heap Frag. (%)	Fragmentation	Used	Total Heap Size
2010-02-19 10:40:43 338ms	**1.09%**	1,399 MB	13,546 MB	128,00 MB
2010-02-19 10:41:43 345ms	**1.66%**	2,121 MB	12,498 MB	128,00 MB

The used memory is simply rendered grey in the **Free Memory Distribution** chart, with a line delimiting the used and fragmented parts. The charts in the example show a very healthy heap, with lots of free memory and with fragmentation under control. In the following screenshot, most of the free contiguous heap blocks are huge. If the heap were instead made up of a lot of smaller free blocks, an allocation of, for example, a large array would fail and cause the garbage collector to need to perform costly compactions and possibly stop the world.

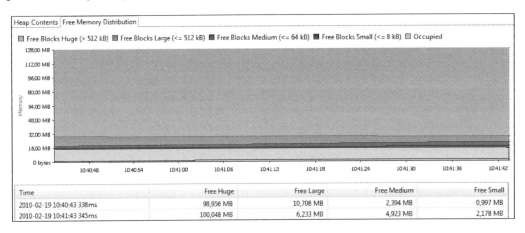

Time	Free Huge	Free Large	Free Medium	Free Small
2010-02-19 10:40:43 338ms	98,956 MB	10,708 MB	2,394 MB	0,997 MB
2010-02-19 10:41:43 345ms	100,048 MB	6,233 MB	4,923 MB	2,178 MB

In the next screenshot, a recording from the memory leaking demo application further studied in Chapter 10 is shown. As can be seen, the live set is steadily increasing over time and the free parts of the heap are split into smaller free blocks:

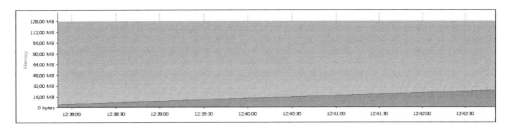

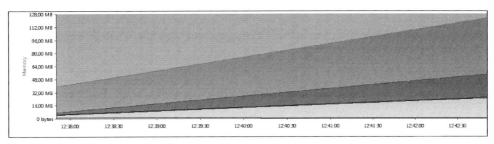

Adding custom events

There is a simple Java API that can be used to contribute custom events to flight recordings. It is located under the package `com.oracle.jrockit.jfr` and is distributed as part of the JRockit JDK. It is located in the JRockit `rt.jar`.

> The `com.oracle.jrockit.jfr` API is under development, and not currently supported outside Oracle. Some internal Oracle products, like WebLogic Server already use it to plug into JRockit Flight Recorder.

To create a custom event using the API, first decide what kind of event is needed. You may recall from the start of this chapter that there are four main event types. Depending on what kind of event is needed, a different event class will need to be extended. There are four different ones, each corresponding to a different kind of event:

- `com.oracle.jrockit.jfr.InstantEvent`
- `com.oracle.jrockit.jfr.DurationEvent`
- `com.oracle.jrockit.jfr.TimedEvent`
- `com.oracle.jrockit.jfr.RequestableEvent`

Events can also be created dynamically, which will be discussed later.

Our next example creates a simple event that will be logged every time a hypothetical logging service is called. We choose to make this a timed event, as we want to know the duration of the logging calls. We also want to be able to set a threshold so that only the longest lasting events are logged.

Creating the event is easy. Following is the full source code:

```
import com.oracle.jrockit.jfr.EventDefinition;
import com.oracle.jrockit.jfr.TimedEvent;
import com.oracle.jrockit.jfr.ValueDefinition;

@EventDefinition(name = "logentry")
public class LogEvent extends TimedEvent {
  @ValueDefinition(name = "message")
  private String text;

  public LogEvent(String text) {
    this.text = text;
  }

  public String getText() {
    return text;
  }
}
```

To use the event from our Java application, we simply create a new event instance, and use it like this in our logging method:

```
public synchronized void log(String text) {
  LogEvent event = new LogEvent(text);
  event.begin();
  // Do logging here
  event.end();
  event.commit();
}
```

Before we can use the event, however, we need to create and register an event producer:

```
private static Producer registerProducer() {
  try {
    Producer p;
    p = new Producer("Log Producer (Demo)",
```

```
          "A demo event producer for the demo logger.",
          "http://www.example.com/logdemo");
      p.addEvent(LogEvent.class);
      p.register();
      return p;
   } catch (Exception e) {
      // Add proper exception handling.
      e.printStackTrace();
   }
   return null;
}
```

The `Producer` reference that is returned needs to be kept alive for as long as we want the producer to be available.

That is really all that is needed. However, the previous code is not very efficient. Whenever one of our events is created, a lookup is implicitly made to find the corresponding event type. The `addEvent()` call when registering our event with our producer actually returns an event token that, if provided to the event constructor, avoids these global lookups altogether.

We would also like the recording engine to provide stack traces and thread information for each event. Also, to be a good event producing citizen, the event should be self documenting. Consequently, we modify the event slightly as follows:

```java
import com.oracle.jrockit.jfr.EventDefinition;
import com.oracle.jrockit.jfr.EventToken;
import com.oracle.jrockit.jfr.TimedEvent;
import com.oracle.jrockit.jfr.ValueDefinition;

@EventDefinition(path = "log/logentry", name = "Log Entry",
   description = "A log call in the custom logger.",
   stacktrace = true, thread = true)
public class LogEvent extends TimedEvent {
   @ValueDefinition(name = "Message", description =
      "The logged message.")
   private String text;

   public LogEvent(EventToken eventToken, String text) {
      super(eventToken);
      this.text = text;
   }

   public String getText() {
      return text;
   }
}
```

This means we would need to save the event token when registering the producer:

```
static EventToken token;
static Producer producer;

static {
  registerProducer();
}

static void registerProducer() {
  try {
    producer = new Producer("Log Producer (Demo)",
      "A demo event producer for the demo logger.",
      "http://www.example.com/logdemo");
    token = producer.addEvent(LogEvent.class);
    producer.register();
  } catch (Exception e) {
    // Add proper exception handling.
    e.printStackTrace();
  }
}
```

And then use the stored event token like this:

```
public synchronized void log(String text) {
  LogEvent event = new LogEvent(token, text);
  event.begin();
  // Do logging here
  event.end();
  event.commit();
}
```

Also, if the event is guaranteed to only be used in a thread safe manner, the text attribute can be made writable, and the event instance stored and reused like this.

```
private LogEvent event = new LogEvent(token);

public synchronized void log(String text) {
  event.reset();//clear the instance for reuse
  event.setText(text);
  event.begin();
  // Do logging here
  event.end();
  event.commit();
}
```

The events are disabled by default. To start recording the events, remember to enable them in the template used to start the recording. It is also possible to enable the events programmatically by creating a recording with the event enabled. The following code snippet shows how to enable all events for a producer with the URI PRODUCER_URI (for our example, that would be http://www.example.com/logdemo/) by creating a recording and then enabling the events for the recording:

```
FlightRecorderClient fr = new FlightRecorderClient();
FlightRecordingClient rec = fr.createRecordingObject("tmp");

for (CompositeData pd : fr.getProducers()) {
  if (!PRODUCER_URI.equals(pd.get("uri"))) {
    continue;
  }

  CompositeData events[] = (CompositeData[]) pd.get("events");
  for (CompositeData d : events) {
    int id = (Integer) d.get("id");
    rec.setEventEnabled(id, true);
    rec.setStackTraceEnabled(id, true);
    rec.setThreshold(id, 200);
    rec.setPeriod(id, 5);
    System.out.println("Enabled event " + d.get("name"));
  }
}

rec.close();
```

Extending the Flight Recorder client

The Flight Recorder contains a GUI builder that allows anyone to modify the Flight Recorder user interface, as well as creating and exporting custom-designed user interfaces. This functionality was used by the Mission Control team to radically reduce development time and turn-around time for bugfixes when developing the Flight Recorder user interface.

The current GUI builder was designed by the JRockit Mission Control team to be "good enough" for Oracle internal use. It is not intended for use outside of Oracle in JRockit R28. Thus, using the GUI builder is unsupported in R28/4.0. We mean it! You are on your own. We are planning on supporting the GUI builder at some point, but the exact release date for this has not been decided yet.

Even though the GUI builder is unsupported, it can be quite useful for modifying the things you want to change the most in the user interface. It can also be used to add custom tabs for your own event producers. The best part is that any customizations can be exported directly from within the user interface. Such plug-ins can easily be shared with colleagues by simply dropping the plug-in into the JROCKIT_HOME/ missioncontrol/plug-in folder of a JRockit installation.

To gain access to the GUI builder, JRockit Mission Control must be started with the **designer option**, JROCKIT_HOME\bin\jrmc -designer.

This will enable the **Designer View** under the **Window | Show View** menu, as shown in the following screenshot. The view appears in the same view folder as the **JVM Browser** view and the **Event Types** view by default.

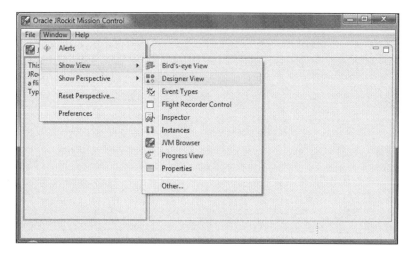

Once a flight recording is opened, the **Designer View** enables switching back and forth between **design mode** and **run mode**.

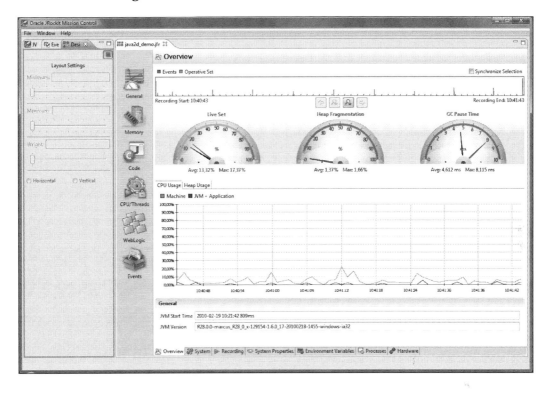

When in run mode, the only available operation is to stop the recording and enter design mode. To stop and enter design mode, simply click on the red rectangular stop button (▦).

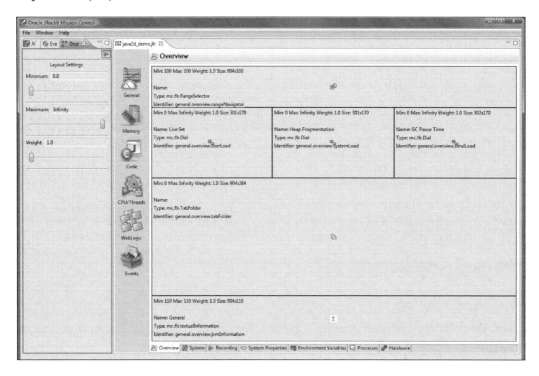

When in the design mode, any part of the Flight Recorder user interface can be modified, even the tabs that were delivered as part of the Flight Recorder. This is quite powerful, but also means it is potentially very easy to mess up pretty much every part of the Flight Recorder user interface. Fortunately, it is simple to reset the user interface to factory settings. In **Window | Preferences** under Flight Recorder, there is a button for resetting the user interface.

Reverting to factory settings through the GUI is only available in JRockit Mission Control 4.0.1 or later. This can be accomplished in 4.0.0 by erasing the <user.home>/.jrmc folder. However, this will unfortunately also erase any other custom JRockit Mission Control settings you may have.

Once satisfied with the changes, press the play button (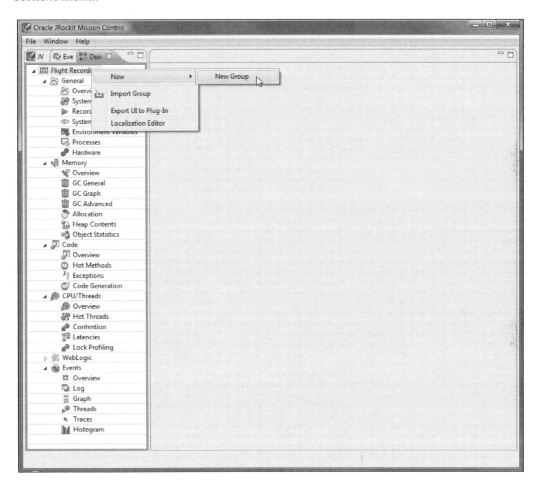) to see how the changes play out in the recording. To add new tabs and tab groups, the recording must first be closed. This will change the design view to show a tree of available tabs, as illustrated in the next screenshot.

To add a new group, right click on the root and select **New | New Group** from the context menu.

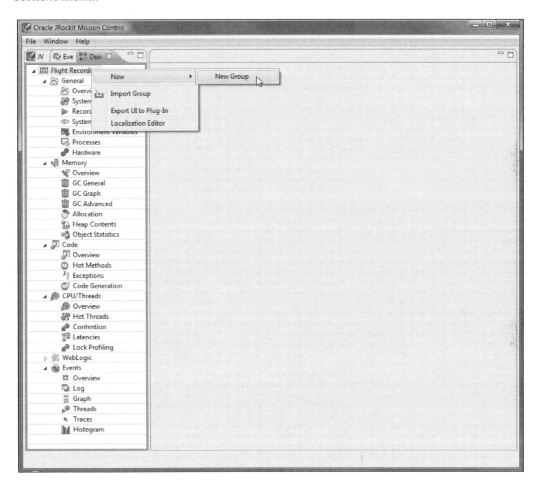

The tab group **Placement Path**, in the **Properties Tab Group**, is used to determine where on the toolbar the tab group will appear. Two icons are needed—the smaller one is used when there is not enough space for the larger one.

New tabs are created by right clicking on the tab group under which the tab shall be created, and selecting **New | New Tab**.

To design the newly-created tab, first load a recording containing events of the kind you want to visualize. As an example, we will design a new tab for examining the total amount of memory allocation in the JVM.

First navigate to the tab to design. Since it currently is empty, it will be blank and show an **Unknown Component** message in the upper left corner.

Now, we take care of the layout of our tab. We want a standard range selector at the top, and a chart under the range selector.

To add a space for a range selector at the top, do the following:

1. Vertically split the area by right clicking in the editor and selecting **Vertical Split** from the context menu.

2. Use the sliders in the **Design View** to set the minimum and maximum size of the topmost area to **100** pixels. All range selectors are exactly 100 pixels high.

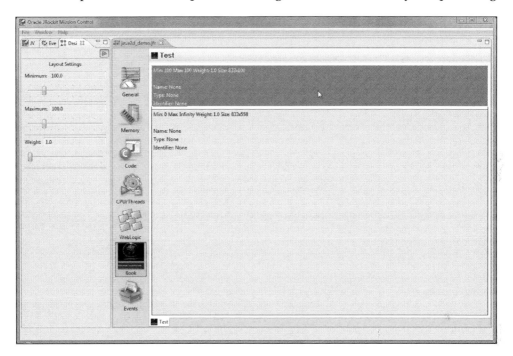

Next, we want to add a chart to the large remaining area below the range selector. Right click on this area and select **Assign Component | Graphics | Chart** from the context menu. This brings up the chart configuration dialog box. To add a total allocation attribute to the chart, do the following:

1. Select the tab for the axis with which to associate the attribute. In this case, we select the **Left Y Axis**.

2. Select the **Data Series** tab to configure the data series that is to be shown.

3. Click the **Add...** button to open the attribute browser dialog box. For the 4.0.0 version of JRockit Mission Control, all attributes are listed in a flattened hierarchy of event types (in human-readable form) with all attributes for a certain event type listed as children.

4. Select the attribute to use. In this case, **Allocated by All Threads/ Total Allocated**.

That is all that is required. The chart can be configured to look better by selecting various options. In the following screenshot, the content type for the axis was modified to "Memory". Fill colors for the data series were also chosen, and the axis was given a name.

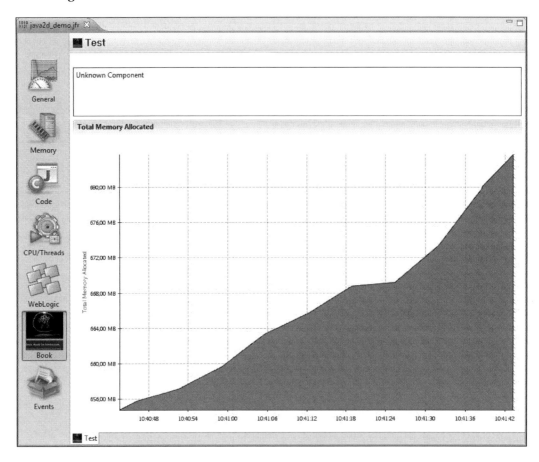

Creating the range selector for the custom tab is slightly more complicated. Start by assigning the correct component to the topmost area by selecting **Assign Component | Other | Range Selector** from the context menu.

This brings up a dialog box where the properties for the range selector can be configured. The range selector contains a chart, so configuring it is quite similar to configuring a standard chart. If we want it to look like the other range selectors, we must remove the tick marks and the visibility for each axis by unchecking the corresponding check boxes.

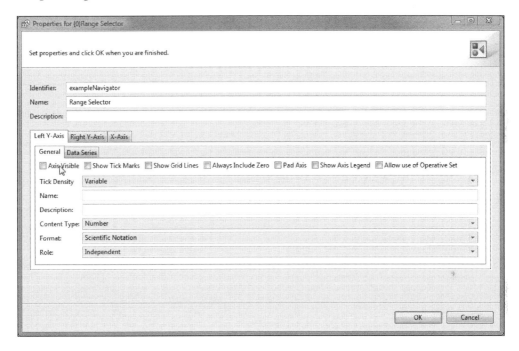

As we want a backdrop of events to make up the tab, we need to configure it to show the number of ongoing events. We do this by adding the **duration** attribute for the event types used in our other components. In this case, this is the same event type as in the chart. We use the **Integrating Point Density** style. The range selectors actually contain two stacked series with different colors for each event attribute being shown—one for the events in the operative set, and one for the ones that are not in the operative set. This is to allow visual feedback when events used in the tab are included in the operative set. We must therefore add the attribute twice, with different colors and with **In Operative Set** set to **No** and **Yes** respectively.

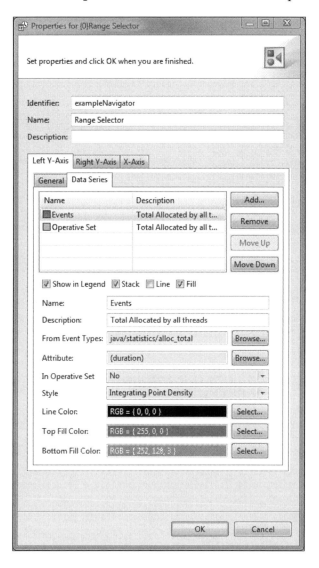

This concludes the example. The resulting tab can be seen in the following screenshot, with a few of the events added to the operative set:

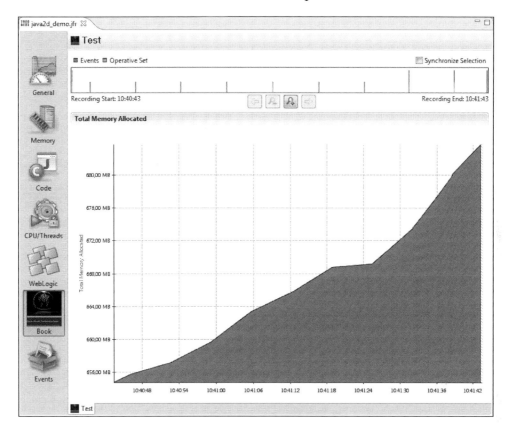

 The easiest way to find out how to use other components available in the Flight Recorder designer is to enter design mode and see how they are being used in the original Flight Recorder user interface.

To export the newly designed tab to a plug-in, so that it can be shared with others, first close the tab. This will make the tree view of the different tabs visible again.

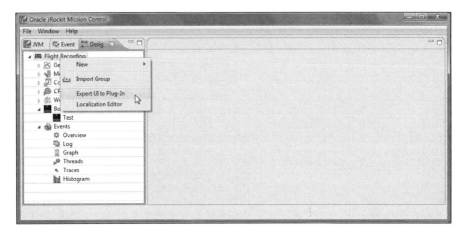

From the root node, select **Export UI to Plug-In**. This brings up a dialog where the tabs available for export are listed.

Normally, only the tabs changed and/or added should be selected. In our example, we will only add the **Test** tab. After clicking **OK**, we will be presented with a dialog where the plug-in ID and version can be selected. Take care to always increase the plug-in version for newer releases of your additions, as they will otherwise be overridden by older versions.

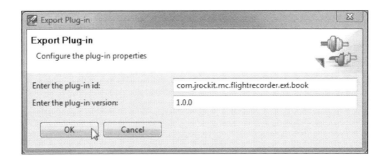

After clicking on **OK**, a file dialog will be presented where you can choose where to store the new plug-in. The plug-in will be saved as a jar file.

The resulting jar file can be shared with friends and colleagues, either through an update site, or by simply dropping the file in the `JROCKIT_HOME/missioncontrol/ plugins` folder.

Summary

In this chapter, JRockit Flight Recorder was introduced. The new data model and the notion of events and data producers were explained. It was shown how to capture flight recordings, and various ways to control the Flight Recorder itself were explained. Advanced concepts in the flight recording wizard were shown, such as how to control the enablement and the options of any single event type. The main differences to the old JRockit Analyzer were discussed, such as:

- The new range selector
- New event types such as the exception event
- Changes to the operative set
- The relational key
- How to do old JRA (LAT) style latency analysis in Flight Recorder
- Changes to some of the memory-related tabs

We also explained how anyone can add custom events to flight recordings through a standard Java API available in the JRockit runtime jar.

Finally, the unsupported design mode was introduced, where the user interface of the Flight Recorder can be customized and even extended. We also showed how to use the design mode to export customizations to plug-ins that can be shared with others.

In the next chapter, we will discuss how the JRockit Mission Control Memory Leak Detection Tool can be used for hunting down memory leaks in Java applications.

10
The Memory Leak Detector

As described in the chapter on memory management, the Java runtime provides a simplified memory model for the programmer. The developer does not need to reserve memory from the operating system for storing data, nor does he need to worry about returning the memory once the data is no longer in use.

Working with a garbage collected language could easily lead to the hasty conclusion that resource management is a thing of the past, and that memory leaks are impossible. Nothing could be further from the truth. In fact, memory leaks are so common in Java production systems that many IT departments have surrendered. Recurring scheduled restarts of Java production systems are now all too common.

In this chapter, you will learn:

- What we mean by a Java memory leak
- How to detect a memory leak
- How to find the cause of a memory leak using the JRockit Memory Leak Detector

A Java memory leak

Whenever allocated memory is no longer in use in a program, it should be returned to the system. In a garbage collected language such as Java, quite contrary to static languages such as C, the developer is free from the burden of doing this explicitly. However, regardless of paradigm, whenever allocated memory that is no longer in use is not returned to the system, we get the dreaded **memory leak**. Eventually, enough memory leaks in a program will cause it to run out of memory and break.

Memory leaks in static languages

In static languages, memory management may be even more complex than just recognizing the need to explicitly free allocated memory. We must also know when it is possible to deallocate memory without breaking other parts of the application. In the absence of automatic memory management, this can sometimes be difficult. For example, let's say there is a service from which address records can be retrieved. An address is stored as a data structure in memory for easy access. If modules A, B, and C use this address service, they may all concurrently reference the same address structure for a record.

If one of the modules decides to free the memory of the record once it is done, all the other modules will fail and the program will crash. Consequently, we need a firm allocation and deallocation discipline, possibly combined with some mechanism to let the service know once every module is done with the address record. Until this is the case, it cannot be explicitly freed. As has been previously discussed, one approach is to manually implement some sort of reference counting in the record itself to ensure that it can be reclaimed once all modules are finished with it. This may in turn require synchronization and will add complexity to the program. To put it simply, sometimes, in order to achieve proper memory hygiene in static languages, the programmer may have to implement code that behaves almost like a garbage collector.

Memory leaks in garbage collected languages

In Java, or any garbage collected language, this complexity goes away. The programmer is free to create objects and the garbage collector is responsible for reclaiming them. In our hypothetical program, once the address record is no longer in use, the garbage collector can reclaim its memory. However, even with automatic memory management, there can still be memory leaks. This is the case if references to objects that are no longer used in the program are still kept alive.

The authors once heard of a memory leak in Java being referred to as an **unintentional object retention**. This is a pretty good name. The program is keeping a reference to an object that should not be referenced anymore. There are many different situations where this can occur.

Perhaps the leaked object has been put in a cache, but never removed from the cache when the object is no longer in use. If you, as a developer, do not have full control over an object life cycle, you should probably use a weak reference-based approach. As has previously been discussed, the `java.util.WeakHashMap` class is ideal for caches.

Be aware that weak references is not a one-size-fits-all answer to getting rid of memory leaks in caches. Sometimes, developers misuse weak collections, for instance, by putting values in a `WeakHashMap` that indirectly reference their keys.

In application containers, such as a J2EE server, where multiple classloaders are used, special care must be taken so that classes are not dependency injected into some framework and then forgotten about. The symptom would typically show up as every re-deployment of the application leaking memory.

Detecting a Java memory leak

It is all too common to find out about a memory leak by the JVM stopping due to an `OutOfMemoryError`. Before releasing a Java-based product, it should generally be tested for memory leaks. The standard use cases should be run for some duration, and the live set should be measured to see that no memory is leaking. In a good test setup, this is automated and tests are performed at regular intervals.

We got overconfident and failed to heed our own advice in JRockit Mission Control 4.0.0. Normally, we use the Memory Leak Detector to check that editors are reclaimed properly in JRockit Mission Control during end testing. This testing was previously done by the developers themselves, and had failed to find its way into the formal test specifications. As a consequence, we would leak an editor each time a console or a Memleak editor was opened. The problem was resolved, of course, using the Memory Leak Detector.

A memory leak in Java can typically be detected by using the Management Console to look at the **live set attribute**. It is important to know that a live set increase over a shorter period of time does not necessarily have to be indicative of a memory leak. It could be the case that the load of the Java application has changed, that the application is serving more users than before, or any other reason that may trigger the need to use more memory. However, if the trend is consistent, there is very likely a problem that should be investigated.

There are primarily two different ways of doing detailed heap analysis:

- Online heap analysis, using the JRockit Memory Leak Detector
- Offline heap analysis from a heap dump

For online analysis, **trend analysis** data is collected by piggybacking on the garbage collector. This is virtually without overhead since the mark phase of a GC already needs to traverse all live objects on the heap. The resulting heap graph is all the data we need to do a proper trend analysis for object allocation.

The heap dump format used by JRockit is the same as produced by the **Java Virtual Machine Tool Interface (JVMTI)** based heap profiler HPROF, included with the JDK. Consequently, the dumps produced by JRockit can be analyzed in all tools supporting the HPROF format. For more information about HPROF, see the following file in the JRockit JDK:

`JROCKIT_HOME/demo/jvmti/hprof/src/manual.html`

For more information about JVMTI, see the JDK Documentation:

`http://java.sun.com/javase/6/docs/platform/jvmti/`
`jvmti.html`

Memleak technology

The JRockit Mission Control Memory Leak Detector, or Memleak for short, is a dynamic tool that can be attached to a running JRockit instance. Memleak can be used to track how heap memory usage in the Java runtime changes over time for each type (class) in the system. It can also find out which types have instances pointing to a certain other type, or to find out which instances are referring a certain other instance. **Allocation tracing** can be enabled to track allocations of a certain type of object. This all sounds complicated, but it is actually quite easy to use and supported by a rich graphical user interface. Before we show how to use it to resolve memory leaks, we need to discuss some of the architectural consequences of how Memleak is designed.

- **Trend analysis is very cheap**: Data is collected as part of the normal garbage collection mark phase. As mentioned, this is a surprisingly fast operation. When the tool is running, every normal garbage collection will collect the necessary data. In order to ensure timely data collection, the tool will also, by default, trigger a garbage collection every ten seconds if no normal garbage collection has taken place. To make the tool even less intrusive, this setting can be changed in the preferences.

- **Regardless of client hardware, you will be able to do the analysis**: Connecting to a server with a multi-gigabyte heap from a puny laptop is not a problem.

- **Events and changes to the heap can be observed as they happen**: This is both a strength and a weakness. It is very powerful to be able to interact with the application whilst observing it, for example to see which operation is responsible for certain behavior, or to introspect some object at the same time as performing operations on it. It also means that objects can become eligible for garbage collection as they are being studied. Then further operations involving the instances are impossible.

- **No off-line analysis is possible**: This can be a problem if you want to get a second opinion on a memory leak from someone who can't be readily given access to your production system. Fortunately, the R28 version of JRockit can do standard HPROF heap dumps that can be analyzed in other tools, such as Eclipse MAT, if required.

 Note that HPROF dumps contain the contents of the heap. If the system from which the HPROF dump was generated contains sensitive data, that data will be readily accessible by anyone getting access to the dump. Be careful when sharing dumps.

Tracking down the leak

Finding the cause of memory leaks can be very tricky, and tracking down complex leaks frequently involves using several tools in conjunction. The application is somehow keeping references to objects that should no longer be in use. What's worse, the place in the code where the leaked instance was allocated does not necessarily have to be co-located with the place in the code pertaining to the leak. We need to analyze the heap to find out what is going on.

To start Memleak, simply select the JVM to connect to in the **JVM Browser** and choose **Memleak** from the context menu.

 Only one Memleak instance can be connected to any given JVM at a time.

In Memleak, the **trend table** can help detect even slow leaks. It does this by building a histogram by type (class), and by collecting data points about the number of instances of every type over time. A least squares approximation on the sizes over time is then calculated, and the corresponding growth rate in bytes per second is displayed.

In JRockit Mission Control 4.1.0, this algorithm will be a little bit more sophisticated, as it will also incorporate the correlation to the size of the live set over time. The types that have the highest tendency to grow as the live set is growing are more likely to be the ones causing a leak.

The trend table can usually be helpful in finding good candidates for memory leaks. In the trend table, classes with a high growth rate are colored red—higher color intensity means higher growth rate. We can also see how many instances of the class there are, and how much memory they occupy.

In the program being analyzed in the following example, it would seem that char arrays are leaking. Not only are they colored deep red and at the top of the trend analysis table, signifying a suspected memory leak, but they also have the one of the highest growth rates of any type in the system.

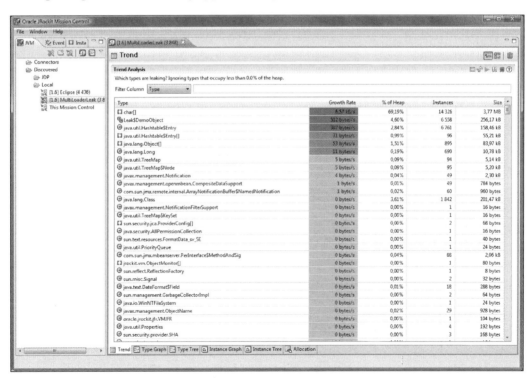

It would also seem, to a lesser extent, that classes related to the types `Leak$DemoObject` and `Hashtable` are leaking.

In total, we seem to be leaking about 7.5 KB per second.

$(6.57*1{,}024+512+307+71+53+11)/1{,}024 \approx 7.5$

The JVM was started with a maximum heap size of 256 MB, and the used live set was about 20 MB (the current size of the live set was checked with the Management Console).

$(256 – 20) *1{,}024 / 7.5 \approx 32{,}222$ seconds ≈ 537 minutes ≈ 22 hours

If left unchecked, this memory leak would, in about 22 hours, result in an `OutOfMemoryError` that would take down the JVM and the application it is running.

This gives us plenty of time to find out who is holding on to references to the suspected leaking objects. To find out what is pointing to leaking `char` arrays, right click on the type in the trend table and click on **Add to Type Graph**, as shown in the following screenshot:

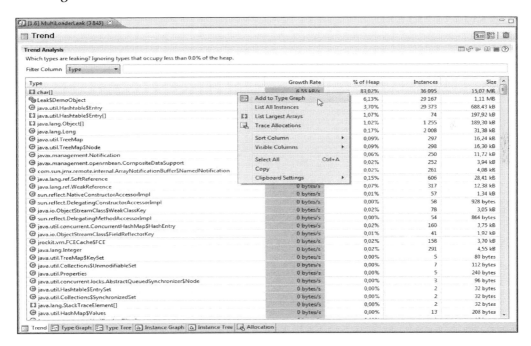

This will add the selected class to the **Type Graph** tab and automatically switch to that tab. The tab is not a type graph in the sense of an inheritance hierarchy, but rather a graph showing how instances of classes point to other classes. The **Type Graph** will appear with the selected class, as shown in the following screenshot:

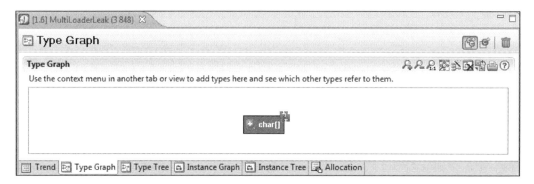

Clicking on the little plus sign ( ) to the left of the class name will help us find out what other types are referring to this type. We call this **expanding the node**. Every click will expand another five classes, starting with the ones that leak the most memory first.

In the **Type Graph**, just like in the trend table, types that are growing over time will be colored red—the redder, the higher the leak rate.

As we, in this example, want to find out what is ultimately holding on to references to the character arrays, we expand the **char[]** node.

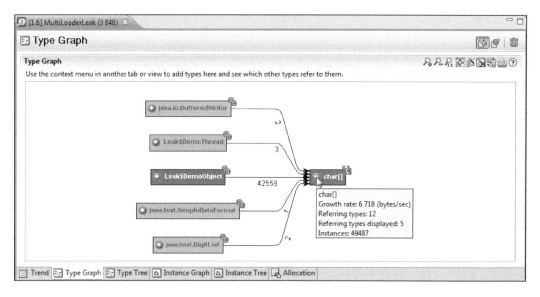

Expanding the **char[]** node reveals that there is only one other type (or rather instances of that type) that also seem to be leaking and have references to char arrays—the inner class DemoObject of the conspicuously named Leak class.

Expanding the **Leak$DemoObject** node until we don't seem to be finding any more leaking types reveals that the application seems to be abusing some sort of Hashtable, as shown in the next screenshot:

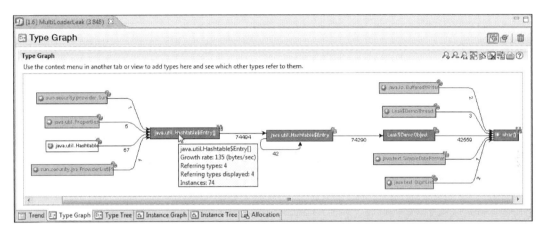

The next step would be to find the particular instance of Hashtable that is being misused. This can be done in different ways. In this example, it would seem that the leaking of the char arrays is due to the leaking of the Leak$DemoObjects. We would therefore like to start by listing the Hashtable$Entry instances that point to Leak$DemoObject.

> Classes declared inside other classes in Java, for example the Entry class in Hashtable, have the naming format OuterClass$InnerClass in the bytecode, and this is the way they show up in our profiling tools—in our example, Hashtable$Entry and Leak$DemoObject. This is because when inner (nested) classes were introduced in the Java language, Sun Microsystems didn't want to change the JVM specification as well.

To list instances that are part of a particular relationship, simply right click on the relation and select **List Referring Instances**, as shown in the following screenshot:

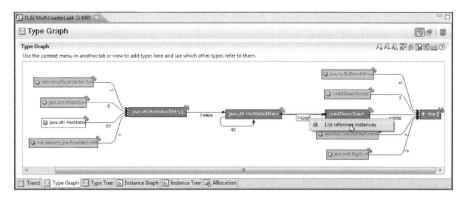

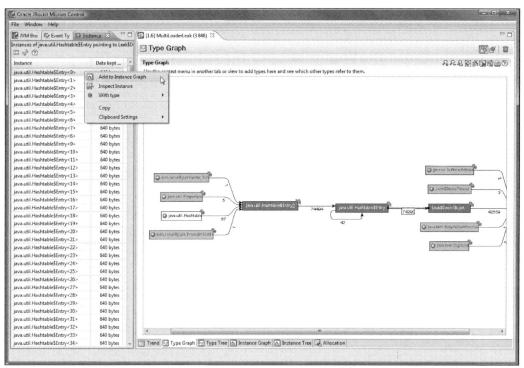

This brings up the **instances view,** to the left of the Memleak editor, where the instances pointing from Hashtable entries to demo objets are listed. An instance can be added to the **instance graph** by right clicking on the instance, and selecting **Add to Instance Graph** from the context menu. This will bring up a graph similar to the **Type Graph,** but this time showing the reference relationships between instances.

Once the **Instance Graph** is up, we need to find out what is keeping the instance alive. In other words, who is referring the instance, keeping it from being garbage collected? In previous versions of Memleak, this was sometimes a daunting task, especially when searching in large object hierarchies. As of JRockit Mission Control 4.0.0, there is a menu alternative for letting JRockit automatically look for the path back to the **root referrer**. Simply right click on the instance and click on **Expand to Root**, as shown in the next screenshot. This will expand the graph all the way back to the root.

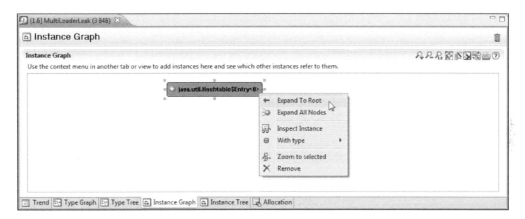

As shown in the following screenshot, expanding to root for our example reveals that there is a thread named `Thread-2` that holds on to an instance of the inner class `DemoThread` of the class `Leak`. In the `DemoThread` instance, there is a field named `table` that refers to a `Hashtable` containing our leaked `DemoObject`.

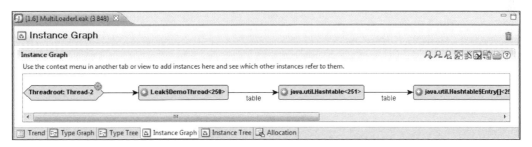

When running in Eclipse, it is possible to view the code that manipulates the `table` field, by selecting **View Type Source** from the context menu on the **Leak$DemoThread** nodes. In this example, we'd find a programming error:

```
for (int i = 0; i <= 100; i++) {
  put(total + i);
}

for (int i = 0; i < 100; i++) {
  remove(total + i);
}
```

As an equals sign is missing from the second loop header, more objects are placed in the `Hashtable` than are removed from it. If we make sure that we call `remove` as many times as we call `put`, the memory leak would go away.

[The complete examples for this chapter can be found in the code bundle that comes with this book.]

To summarize, the text book recipe for hunting down memory leaks is:

1. Find one of the leaking instances.
2. Find a path to the root referrer from the leaking instance.
3. Eliminate whatever is causing the reference to be kept alive.
4. If there still is a leak, start over from 1.

Of course, finding an instance that is unnecessarily kept alive can be quite tricky. One way to home in on unwanted instances is to only look at instances participating in a certain reference relationship. In the previous example, we chose to look at char arrays that were only being pointed to by `DemoObjects`. Also, the most interesting relationships to look for are usually found where leaking types and non-leaking types meet. In the **Type Graph** for the example, we can see that once we expand beyond the `Hastable$Entry` array, object growth rates are quite neutral. Thus, the leak is quite likely due to someone misusing a `Hashtable`.

It is common for collection types to be misused, thereby causing memory leaks. Many collections are implemented using arrays. If not dealt with, the memory leak will typically cause these arrays to grow larger and larger. Therefore, another way of quickly homing in on the offending instance is to list the largest arrays in the system. In the example, we can easily find the `Hashtable` holding on to the `DemoObjects` by running the leaking application for a while. Use the **List Largest Arrays** operation on the array of `Hashtable` entries, as shown in the next screenshot.

If all else fails, statistics will be on your side the longer you wait, as more and more heap space will be occupied by the leaking objects.

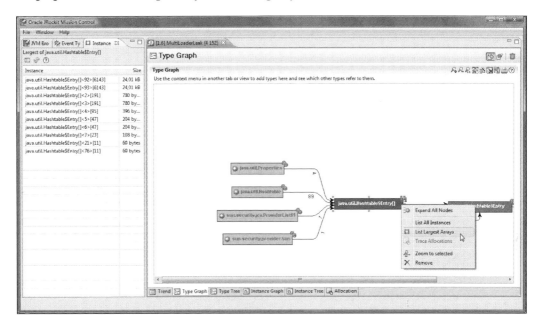

Both of the largest `Hashtable$Entry` arrays are leaking. Adding any one of them to the **Instance Graph** and expanding it to the root referrer will yield the same result, implicating the instance field `table` in the `Leak$DemoThread` class. This is illustrated in the following screenshot:

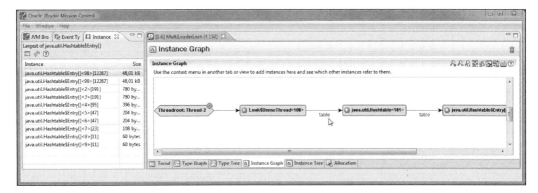

A look at classloader-related information

In our next example, there are actually three different classloaders running almost the same code—two with the memory leak and one that actually behaves well. This is to illustrate how things can look in an application server, where different versions of the same application can be running. In Memleak, just like with the other tools in JRockit Mission Control, the tables can be configured to show more information. To see classloader-related information in the table, edit the **Table Settings** as shown in the following screenshot:

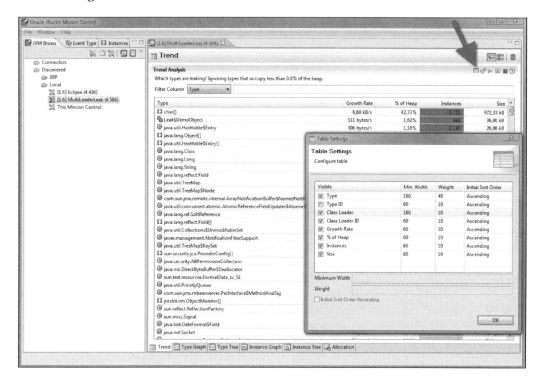

Memleak will, by default, aggregate classes with the same name in the same row. To make Memleak differentiate between classes loaded by different classloaders, click on the **Individually show each loaded class** ( ) button.

In the next screenshot, the trend table is shown for all classes with names containing the string Demo. As can be seen, there are three classloaders involved, but only two of them are leaking instances of Leak$DemoObject.

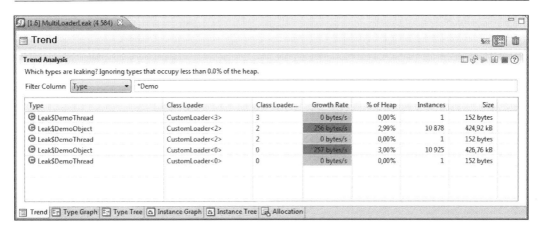

The option of splitting the classes per classloader is also available in the **Type Graph**. The **Type Graph** can be configured to use a separate node for each loaded class, when expanding a node. Simply click on the **Use a separate node for each loaded class** icon (⚙) in the **Type Graph**. Following is a screenshot showing the first expansion of the **char[]** node when using separate nodes for each class. The bracket after the class name contains the classloader ID.

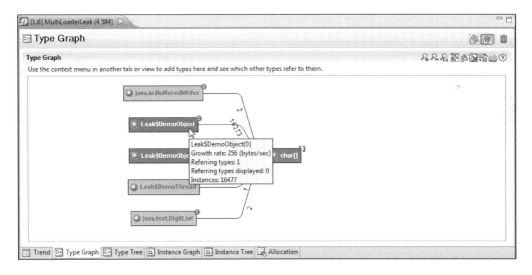

It is possible to switch back to aggregating the nodes again by clicking on the **Combine classes with same class name** button (⚙). Note that the setting will not change the state of the currently visible nodes. Only nodes that are expanded after changing the setting are affected.

Interactive memory leak hunting

Another way of using the Memleak tool is to validate a hypothesis about memory management in an application. Such a hypothesis could for example be "when I remove all contacts from my contact list, no `Contact` objects should be left in the system". Because of the interactive nature of the Memleak tool, this is a very powerful way of finding leaks, especially in an interactive application. A huge amount of such scenarios can be tested without interruptions caused by, for example, dumping heaps to files. If done well and with enough systems knowledge, finding the leaks can be a very quick business.

For example, consider a simple address book application. The application is a self-contained Swing application implemented in a single class named `AddressBook`. The class contains a few inner classes, of which one is the representation of a contact—`AddressBook$Contact`. In the application, we can add and remove contacts in the address book. One hypothesis we may want to test is that we do not leak contacts.

The Memleak tool normally only shows types that occupy more than 0.1 percent of the heap, or the amount of data in the general case would be overwhelming. We are normally not interested in types not heavily involved in leaks, and as time passes, the interesting ones tend to occupy quite a lot of the heap anyway. However, most leaks usually only occupy a tiny fraction of the heap until the leaking application has run for quite some time. In order to detect memory leaks earlier, this setting can be changed to **0** so that all types are shown, regardless of their used heap space. This can be done in the preferences, as shown in the following screenshot:

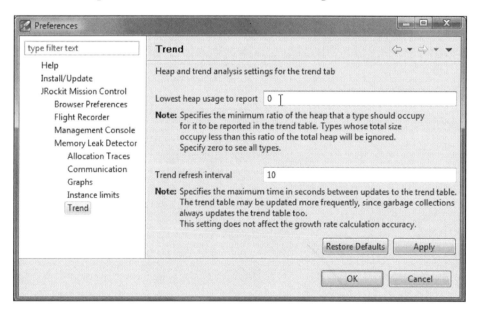

We then filter out the classes related to the hypothesis that we want to test and watch how they behave while we run the application.

 Remember from *Chapter 7, The Management Console,* that the filter boxes in JRockit Mission Control can use regular expressions by entering the prefix `regexp`.

In the following screenshot, three addresses have been removed from the `AddressBook`, but the number of `Contact` instances remain at the original eight:

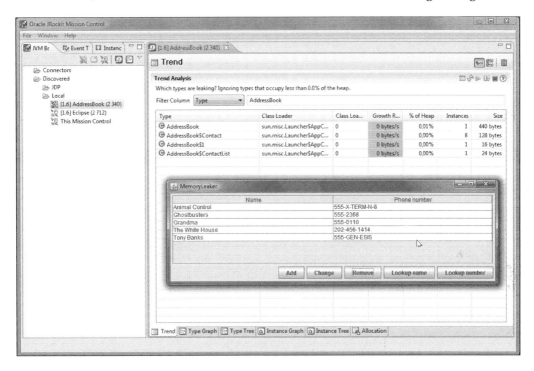

Removing all of them will still leave all eight of the original `AddressBook$Contact` instances in the system. There is indeed a memory leak.

 To get the Memleak tool to react faster to the changes on the heap, the **trend refresh interval** (shown in the preference screenshot earlier) can be lowered.

Now, as all the remaining instances are unintentionally retained, drilling down into any of them will be sufficient for tracking down the leak. Simply click on **List all instances** from the context menu in the trend table and then add any of the instances to the **Instance Graph**. The path to root referrer in the example reveals that the contacts are retained in some sort of index map named `numberToContact`. The developer of the application should be familiar with this structure and know where to look for it in the code. If we ensure that we remove the `Contact` objects from the index map as well as from the contact list, the leak will go away.

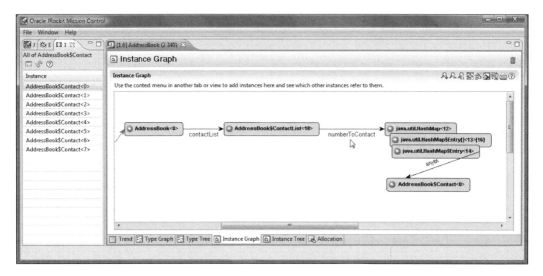

The recipe for interactively testing for memory leaks is:

1. Formulate a hypothesis, such as "When I close my Eclipse PHP Editor, I expect the editor instance and the instances associated with it to go away".

2. Filter out the classes of interest in the trend table.

3. See how they are freed and allocated as the hypothesis is tested.

4. If a memory leak is found, it is usually quite easy to find a leaking instance and locate the problem by tracing the path to the root referrer.

The general purpose heap analyzer

Yet another way to use the Memleak tool is as a general purpose heap analyzer.
The **Types** panel shows relationships between the types (classes) on the Java heap.
It can also list the specific instances in such a relationship. In the next example, we've
found a peculiar cycle in our **Type Graph**. We can see that there are instances of
`Hashtable` entries that are actually pointing back to their `Hashtable`. To list just
the instances of `Hashtable$Entry` pointing to `Hashtable`, we simply right click on
the number in the reference relation (see the following screenshot), and select **List
referring instances**.

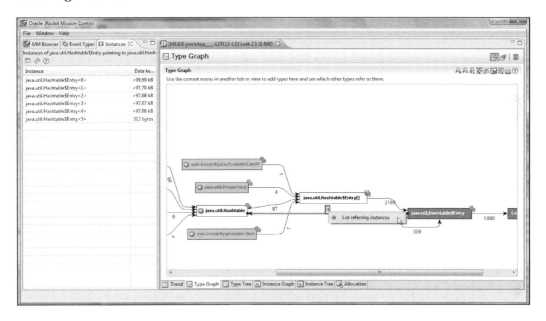

We have now, with a few clicks, been able to list all the `Hashtable` instances in the
system that contain `Hashtable`s. It is also easy to determine exactly where they are
located in the system. Simply select an instance, add it to the **Instance Graph** and
trace the shortest path back to the root referrer. Doing this for the first instance will
reveal that it is located in the `com.sun.jmx.mbeanserver.RepositorySupport`. Of
course, having `Hashtable`s that contain `Hashtable`s is not a crime; this merely serves
as an example of the versatility of the Memleak tool.

You need a 1.5-based JDK to see the `Hashtable`s containing `Hashtable`s
for this example. In a 1.6-based JDK, the design has changed.

Any instance can be inspected in Memleak. Next, we inspect the instance of `com.sun.jmx.mbeanserver.RepositorySupport` to verify that it indeed contains `Hashtable` instances.

Allocation traces

The last major feature in Memleak to be discussed in this book, is the ability to turn on allocation tracing for any given type. To, for instance, find out where the `Leak$DemoObject`s are being allocated in our previous example, simply right click on the type and then click on **Trace Allocations**. The example has been tailored to do allocations in the vicinity of the code that causes the actual leak (note that this is normally not the case).

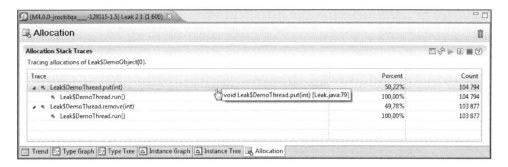

As can be readily seen from the screenshot, we are invoking `put` more often than
`remove`. If we are running Memleak from inside Eclipse, we can jump directly
to the corresponding line in the `Leak` class by right clicking on the stack frame
and then clicking on **Open Method** from the context menu.

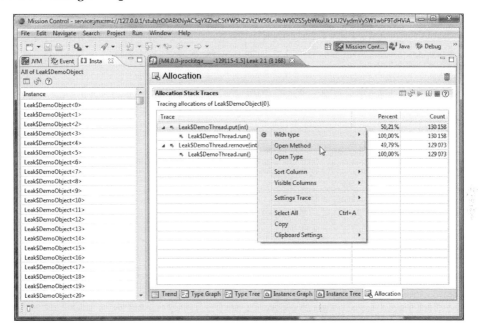

Allocation traces can only be enabled for one type (class) at a time.

 A word of caution: Enabling allocation traces for types with a
high allocation pressure can introduce significant overhead. For
example, it is, in general, a very bad idea to enable allocation traces
for `java.lang.Strings`.

Troubleshooting Memleak

If you have trouble connecting to your JVM with Memleak, it is probably due to
Memleak requiring an extra port. Communication using Memleak, unlike other tools
in the JRockit Mission Control suite, is only *initiated* over JMX. Memleak requires the
internal **MemLeak Server (MLS)** to be running in the JVM.

When starting Memleak, a run request is sent over JMX. The MLS will then be started
and a communication port is returned. The client stops communicating over JMX
after startup and instead uses the proprietary **Memory Leak Protocol (MLP)** over the
communication port.

The MLS was built as a native server in JRockit, as the original idea was to be able to run the MLS when running out of Java heap, similar to the way that a heap dump can be triggered when running out of memory. We wanted to introduce a flag that would suspend the JVM on OutOfMemoryErrors and then launch the MLS. This was unfortunately never implemented.

It is possible to specify which port to use for MLS in the initial request over JMX. This can be set in the preferences, as shown in the following screenshot:

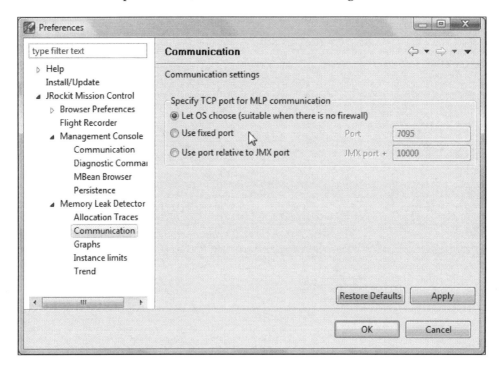

Also worth noting is:

- There can only be one client connected to MLS at any given time
- When a client disconnects, the MLS will automatically shut down

Summary

In this chapter, we have shown how to use the JRockit Mission Control Memory Leak Detector to detect and find the root cause for Java memory leaks. We have also discussed the advantages and disadvantages of the Memory Leak Detector in various use cases.

It has been demonstrated how the Memory Leak Detector can be used to detect even quite slow memory leaks. We have also shown how the Memory Leak Detector can be used in an interactive manner to quickly test particular operations in an application that may be prone to memory leaks.

We have explained how the Memory Leak Detector can also be used as an interactive general purpose heap analyzer to both find relationships between different types on the heap, as well as for inspecting the contents of any instance on the heap.

Finally, we showed how to troubleshoot the most common problems associated with using the tool.

11
JRCMD

This chapter is dedicated to JRCMD—one of the simplest tools in the JRockit distribution. JRCMD is a small command-line tool that can be used to interact with a running JRockit instance. It can also be used to list all running instances of the JRockit JVM on a system.

In this chapter, you will learn:

- How to use JRCMD to list the locally running JVMs on your machine
- How to use JRCMD to execute diagnostic commands on one or all JVMs running locally on your machine
- How to override the SIGQUIT signal handler to make JRockit run diagnostic commands of your choice instead of printing stack dumps, which is the default action
- How to utilize JRCMD to solve various tasks such as:
  - Heap analysis
  - Exception profiling
  - Native memory tracking
  - Controlling the management server lifecycle
  - Controlling JRockit Flight Recorder from the command line

The last part of this chapter is in a format that makes it usable as a JRCMD reference. The reference part lists the various diagnostic commands in alphabetical order, complete with examples.

Introduction

Sometimes a command-line utility is exactly the right tool for the job. You may want to send commands to JVMs in batch scripts, or you may be operating in a very secure environment and only have a command line at your disposal through SSH. Whatever the reason, JRCMD is a small and powerful tool for sending commands to locally running instances of the JRockit JVM from the command line.

The basic usage pattern is to first execute JRCMD with no arguments to list the JVMs currently running on the system. The JVMs will be listed by operating system **Process ID (PID)** followed by the class name of the main class of the Java application running in the JVM.

For example:

```
C:\>JROCKIT_HOME\bin\jrcmd
2416 com.jrockit.mc.rcp.start.MCMain
19344 jrockit.tools.jrcmd.JrCmd
```

In the previous example, there were two JVM instances running when JRCMD was executed—an instance running JRockit Mission Control and, as JRCMD is a Java application too, the JVM running JRCMD itself.

The JRockit instance on which to execute the command is selected by passing its PID as the first argument to JRCMD. A special case is passing PID 0, in which case JRCMD will attempt to execute the command on all the JVMs it can find. As different versions of JRockit may be running at the same time and may support different sets of commands, not all commands may be available for all versions of JRockit. Normally, a specific PID should be selected. In addition, two instances of the same JRockit version may also export different sets of diagnostic commands depending on command-line parameters and configuration.

To list the commands available in a specific instance of JRockit, the help command is used, as illustrated by the following example:

```
C:\>JROCKIT_HOME\bin\jrcmd 2416 help
2416:
The following commands are available:
        kill_management_server
        start_management_server
        print_object_summary
        memleakserver
        ...
For more information about a specific command use 'help <command>'.
Parameters to commands are optional unless otherwise stated.
```

The following examples assume that the `bin` directory in `JROCKIT_HOME` is on the path.

The commands that JRCMD can execute are commonly referred to as the **JRockit Diagnostic Commands**, as that is what they are called when accessed through the **JRockit Management API (JMAPI)** or the custom **JRockit JMX MBeans (JMXMAPI)**.

The diagnostic commands can be invoked in several different ways. JMAPI and JMXMAPI can be used to invoke them programmatically, from Java. This will be discussed in *Chapter 12, Using the JRockit Management APIs*.

Overriding SIGQUIT

Diagnostic commands can also be invoked by overriding the default behavior of the SIGQUIT process signal. Recollect from Chapter 4 that the default behavior of a JVM receiving a SIGQUIT is to write a thread dump containing the current state of all the threads to the console. One way of sending a SIGQUIT signal to the JVM process is to press *Ctrl + Break* (Windows), or *Ctrl + * (Linux), in the shell where the Java process was started. On *NIX-systems, executing `kill -3 <PID>` or `kill -QUIT <PID>` from a shell is an alternative way of issuing a SIGQUIT to a process with a given ID.

To override the SIGQUIT behavior of JRockit with a custom command sequence; put the list of commands to be executed in a plain text file and name it `ctrlhandler.act`. The file needs to be placed into the `lib` folder of JRockit distribution or the current directory of the JVM process. The presence of a `crtlhandler.act` file overrides the behavior of the SIGQUIT signal and makes it execute your diagnostic commands instead of producing the normal thread stack dump. Following is an example of a `ctrlhandler.act` file:

```
version
print_threads
print_object_summary
```

A `ctrlhandler.act` file can be passed to JRCMD using the `-f` option. This option causes JRCMD to read the commands to execute from the `ctrlhandler.act` file.

 The diagnostic commands were originally dubbed "control break handlers".

Following is an example using the -f option with the ctrlhandler.act file from the previous example:

```
C:\>jrcmd 7736 -f c:\tmp\ctrlhandler.act
7736:
Oracle JRockit(R) build R28.0.0-670-129329-1.6.0_17
  -20100219-2122-windows-ia32,
compiled mode
GC mode: Garbage collection optimized for short pausetimes,
  strategy: genconcon

===== FULL THREAD DUMP ===============
Mon Mar 01 15:53:40 2010
Oracle JRockit(R) R28.0.0-670-129329-1.6.0_17-20100219-2122-windows-ia32

"Main Thread" id=1 idx=0x4 tid=7420 prio=6 alive, in native
  at org/eclipse/swt/internal/win32/OS.WaitMessage()Z(Native Method)
  at org/eclipse/swt/widgets/Display.sleep(Display.java:4220)
  at org/eclipse/ui/application/WorkbenchAdvisor.eventLoopIdle
    (WorkbenchAdviso
r.java:364)
  at org/eclipse/ui/internal/Workbench.runEventLoop(Workbench.java:2385)
  at org/eclipse/ui/internal/Workbench.runUI(Workbench.java:2348)

  -- end of trace

===== END OF THREAD DUMP ===============

--------- Detailed Heap Statistics: ---------
39.1% 8232k    140800  +8232k [C
13.5% 2840k    121192  +2840k java/lang/String
10.1% 2135k      2933  +2135k [Ljava/util/HashMap$Entry;
 5.5% 1161k     49568  +1161k java/util/HashMap$Entry
 4.2%  889k      8136   +889k java/lang/Class
 4.1%  869k     18430   +869k [I
 4.0%  841k     15322   +841k [Ljava/lang/Object;
 2.0%  414k       299   +414k [B
 1.3%  281k     12015   +281k java/util/ArrayList
 1.2%  256k      4698   +256k org/eclipse/core/internal
    /registry/ReferenceMap$Soft
Ref
 1.1%  241k      1843   +241k [[C
 0.6%  136k      2907   +136k java/util/HashMap
 0.6%  130k       275   +130k [Ljava/util/Hashtable$Entry;
 0.6%  116k      2407   +116k [Ljava/lang/String;
    21054kB total ---

--------- End of Detailed Heap Statistics ---
```

Special commands

Not all the diagnostic commands are available by default. There are, for example, commands to force JRockit to crash (and dump core) and for instantiating any class in the system implementing the `java.lang.Runnable` interface and then calling the `start` method of the instances. For added security, these kinds of commands are disabled by default and must be enabled by setting command-specific system properties in JRockit on startup.

A command can be enabled by specifying the system property `jrockit.ctrlbreak.enable<command>=[true|false]`. For example:

```
-Djrockit.ctrlbreak.enableforce_crash=true
-Djrockit.ctrlbreak.enablerun_class=true
```

Limitations of JRCMD

The `tools.jar` in the JDK contains an API for attaching to a running JVM—the **Java Attach API**. This is the API used by Mission Control to automatically detect the locally running JVMs. The same framework is also utilized by JRCMD to invoke diagnostic commands.

When a JVM is started, an entry will be created in the temporary directory of the user starting the JVM process. These entries can then be used by JRCMD, through the Java Attach API, to find the JVMs started by the same user as the one running JRCMD. For this to be secure, the Attach API relies on a properly set up temporary directory on a file system with per-file access rights. This means that if the folder is on an insecure file system, such as FAT; JRCMD will not work. It also means that the user running JRCMD and the user running the Java process must be the same. Another implication is that a Java process running as a service on Windows will not be reachable from a JRCMD started from the desktop—they are running in different environments.

When a JRockit process is started as root and then has its ownership changed to a less privileged user, JRCMD will not be able to communicate properly with that process anymore due to security restrictions. Root will be able to list the process, but any attempt to send a command will be interpreted as a SIGQUIT and print a thread dump instead. The less privileged user will not be able to list the process, but if the PID of the process is known, commands can still be sent to it.

The rest of this chapter is dedicated to explaining some commonly used diagnostic commands.

JRCMD command reference

The commands are presented in alphabetical order to make it easier to use the following section as a standalone reference. If a command is specific to either JRockit R28 or JRockit R27, its section header is annotated with version information. No version information is given for commands that work on both R27 and R28.

check_flightrecording (R28)

This command is used to check the state of the JRockit Flight Recorder engine. For more information on JRockit Flight Recorder, see *Chapter 8, The Runtime Analyzer*, and *Chapter 9, The Flight Recorder*. The corresponding command for R27 is `checkjrarecording`. This command normally always returns at least one ongoing recording. This is because most versions of R28 run with a low overhead recording always enabled. As there can be multiple recordings running in parallel, the command takes as argument the ID of the recording for which to retrieve the status. If `-1` or no argument is supplied, the status of all ongoing recordings will be shown. The recordings can also be referenced by name through the `name` parameter. The continuously running recording, where available, can for example be referred to by the name `continuous`.

For example:

```
C:\>jrcmd 6328 check_flightrecording name=continuous verbose=true
6328:
Recording : id=0 name="continuous" duration=0s (running)
http://www.oracle.com/jrockit/jvm/:
java/alloc/accumulated/thread : disabled period=1000
java/alloc/accumulated/total : enabled period=0
java/alloc/object/in_new_tla : disabled threshold=10000000
java/alloc/object/outside_tla : disabled threshold=10000000
java/exception/stats : enabled period=1000
java/exception/throw : disabled period=1000
java/file/read : disabled threshold=10000000
java/file/write : disabled threshold=10000000
java/monitor/enter : disabled threshold=10000000
java/monitor/profile : disabled period=1000
java/monitor/wait : disabled threshold=10000000
java/socket/read : disabled threshold=10000000
java/socket/write : disabled threshold=10000000
```

```
java/thread/end : enabled period=0

java/thread/park : disabled threshold=10000000

java/thread/sleep : disabled threshold=10000000

java/thread/start : enabled period=0

vm/class/load : disabled threshold=10000000

vm/class/memory/free : enabled threshold=0
```

If the `verbose` argument is set to `false`, the listing simply consists of one line per recording, with recording id, `name`, and `duration`. The verbose listing, as shown in this example, lists all the active event producers, and for each producer the status for each event type. The listing starts with the recording `name` and the status for the recording. In the previous example, it can be seen that the continuous recording is active and that its ID is 0. We can see that for the http://www.oracle.com/ jrockit/jvm/ producer, there are quite a few event types available, and that only some of them are enabled.

See *start_flightrecording*, *stop_flightrecording* and *dump_flightrecording*.

checkjrarecording (R27)

This is a very simple command that is useful together with the `startjrarecording` command. It is used for checking if there is already an active ongoing recording in a JRockit instance. If a JRA recording is currently in progress, the options used when that recording was initiated will be shown. The following example shows the result of running the `checkjrarecording` command nine seconds into a JRA recording.

```
C:\>jrcmd 5516 checkjrarecording

5516:

JRA is running a recording with the following options:

filename=D:\myrecording.jra, recordingtime=120s, methodsampling=1,
gcsampling=1, heapstats=1, nativesamples=0, methodtraces=1,
  sampletime=5,zip=1, hwsampling=0, delay=0s, tracedepth=64
  threaddump=1, threaddumpinterval=0s, latency=1,
  latencythreshold=20ms, cpusamples=1, cpusampleinterval=1s

The recording was started 9 seconds ago.

There are 111 seconds left of the recording.
```

The JRA recording was started using the command line from the `startjrarecording` example, given later in this chapter

See *startjrarecording* and *stopjrarecording*.

command_line

Sometimes it can be useful to be able to examine the command line that launched a particular JVM. Perhaps a JVM subsystem, like the garbage collector, is behaving peculiarly because a parameter was set to a suboptimal value at startup. Or maybe we want to find out how the management agent was initialized on the command line—for example, was SSL really enabled, and if so, was the keystore really the right one?

The `command_line` command shows the parameters a JVM was started with. Note that the command line is reconstructed from what was actually supplied to the JVM from the launcher, and may include parameters that were not explicitly passed to the JVM by the user.

Following is an example of what can be shown if the command is executed on an instance of JRockit running JRockit Mission Control, with some additional parameters set:

```
C:\>jrcmd 2416 command_line

2416:

Command Line: -Denv.class.path=.;C:\Program Files\
  Java\jre6\lib\ext\QTJava.zip -Dapplication.home=C:\jrockits\R28.0.0_
  R28.0.0-547_1.6.0 -client -Djrockit.ctrlbreak.enableforce_crash=true
  -Dsun.java.launcher=SUN_STANDARD com.jrockit.mc.rcp.start.MCMain
  -Xmx512m -Xms64m -Xmanagement:port=4712,ssl=false,authenticate=false
```

dump_flightrecording (R28)

This command is useful for retrieving the contents of an ongoing recording without having to halt it. The idea is to never stop the continuous recording that is enabled by default in the JVM (for most versions of R28). The command basically clones the recording, stops the cloned recording, and writes it to disk.

For example:

```
C:\>jrcmd 7420 dump_flightrecording recording=0
  copy_to_file=my_continuous_snapshot.jfr.gz compress_copy=true
```

This example takes the JRockit Flight Recorder recording with ID 0, clones it, stops the clone, and writes the contents to the file `my_continous_snapshot.jfr.gz`, as specified by the `copy_to_file` argument. The recording with ID 0 is normally the continuous recording that is always running in the JVM. The recording to clone can also be specified by name using the `name` parameter, in this case, we would use `name=continuous`. As the `compress_copy` argument was set to true, the resulting file will be **gzip compressed**.

See *start_flightrecording*, *stop_flightrecording*, and *check_flightrecording*.

heap_diagnostics (R28)

The `heap_diagnostics` command provides detailed information about the heap usage in a virtual machine, including information on reference object usage. Executing the command triggers a full garbage collection during which the information is gathered. The command takes no arguments and returns the diagnostic information.

The output contains three main sections.

The first section in the diagnostic dump lists some general information about the system, such as available memory and heap usage.

```
C:\>jrcmd 7420 heap_diagnostics

7420:

Invoked from diagnosticcommand

======== BEGIN OF HEAPDIAGNOSTIC =========================


Total memory in system: 3706712064 bytes

Available physical memory in system: 1484275712 bytes

-Xmx (maximal heap size) is 1073741824 bytes

Heapsize: 65929216 bytes

Free heap-memory: 8571400 bytes
```

The next section, `Detailed Heap Statistics`, is basically the same output as from the `print_object_summary` command, but without the optional points-to information. Also, there is no cut-off for this summary—all classes in the system will be listed, so expect the result to be quite long. There is one line of output per class in the system.

- The first column is how large a part of the heap all instances of the class occupies.
- The second column is the amount of memory in kilobytes that instances of this class take up.
- The third column is the total number of instances of the class currently live in the system.
- The fourth column is the delta from the last invocation of the command.
- The fifth and last column is the name of the class. In our example, most of the heap is occupied by char arrays (`[C`).

```
--------- Detailed Heap Statistics: ---------
25.9% 3179k      37989      +0k [C
 9.6% 1178k       2210      +0k [I
 7.4%  912k      38943      +0k java/lang/String
 7.4%  906k        265      +0k [B
 6.2%  764k       6994      +0k java/lang/Class
. . .

     12257kB total ---


--------- End of Detailed Heap Statistics ---
```

The next section, `Reference Objects statistics`, contains detailed information on the use of reference objects, such as **weak references**. The reference objects are also listed per type (class). Under each type, there is a listing grouped by what objects they point to, or in the case of finalizers, their declaration type.

- The first column states how many instances there are in total.

- The second column states how many instances are still reachable.

- The third column shows how many instances are unreachable and thus eligible for garbage collection.

- The fourth column states how many reference objects were activated, or found non-reachable, during this GC.

- The fifth column shows how many reference objects were activated before this GC. This usually refers to the last GC before the one triggered by the command, but if the reference objects are put in reference queues, they can hang around for quite some time and will remain in this group until removed from the queue.

- The sixth column shows how many instances are pointing to `null`.

- The seventh and last column shows what type of instances the reference object is pointing to, or in the case of finalizers, where the finalizer was declared.

```
----- Reference Objects statistics separated per class -----
    Total Reach Act PrevAct Null

    ----- ----- --- ------- ----

Soft References:
     637    81   0       4  552 Total for all Soft References
java/lang/ref/SoftReference =>
     559     7   0       0  552 Total
     552     0   0       0  552 => null
       2     2   0       0    0 => [Ljava/lang/reflect/Constructor;
       1     1   0       0    0 =>
```

```
org/eclipse/osgi/internal/baseadaptor/DefaultClassLoader
        1     1     0          0       0 => [Ljava/lang/String;
        1     1     0          0       0 => java/util/jar/Manifest
        1     1     0          0       0 => java/lang/StringCoding$StringDecoder
        1     1     0          0       0 => sun/font/FileFontStrike


java/util/ResourceBundle$BundleReference =>
       44    42     0          2       0 Total
       31    31     0          0       0 => java/util/ResourceBundle$1
       11    11     0          0       0 => java/util/PropertyResourceBundle
        2     0     0          2       0 => null


org/eclipse/core/internal/registry/ReferenceMap$SoftRef =>
       21    20     0          1       0 Total
       20    20     0          0       0 =>
  org/eclipse/osgi/framework/internal/core/BundleHost
        1     0     0          1       0 => null


sun/misc/SoftCache$ValueCell =>
        1     0     0          1       0 Total
        1     0     0          1       0 => null


Weak References:
     3084  2607     0        236     241 Total for all Weak References


java/lang/ref/WeakReference =>
     1704  1463     0          0     241 Total
      765   765     0          0       0 => java/lang/String
      330   330     0          0       0 => java/lang/Class
      241     0     0          0     241 => null


Phantom References:
        6     6     0          0       0 Total for all Phantom References
```

```
java/lang/ref/PhantomReference =>
        6       6    0         0      0 Total
        5       5    0         0      0 => java/lang/Object
        1       1    0         0      0 => sun/dc/pr/Rasterizer


Cleared Phantom:
        9       9    0         0      0 Total for all Cleared Phantom


jrockit/vm/ObjectMonitor =>
        9       9    0         0      0 Total
        2       2    0         0      0 =>
    org/eclipse/osgi/framework/eventmgr/EventManager$EventThread
        1       1    0         0      0 => java/util/TaskQueue


Finalizers:
      197     197    0         0      0 Total for all Finalizers
       88      88    0         0      0 => java/util/zip/ZipFile
       55      55    0         0      0 => java/util/zip/Inflater
       18      18    0         0      0 => java/awt/Font
       14      14    0         0      0 => java/lang/ClassLoader$NativeLibrary


Weak Handles:
    12309 12309    0         0      0 Total for all Weak Handles
     9476  9476    0         0      0 =>
    org/eclipse/osgi/internal/baseadaptor/DefaultClassLoader
     1850  1850    0         0      0 => java/lang/String


Soft reachable referents not used for at least 198.332 s cleared.

4 SoftReferences were soft alive but not reachable
  (when found by the GC),
  0 were both soft alive and reachable, and 633 were not soft alive.

----- End of Reference Objects statistics -----

======== END OF HEAPDIAGNOSTIC =========================
```

In this example, we can see that most of the weak references in the system point to Strings. The weak references are the ones referenced by java.lang.ref. WeakReference. There are in total 3,084 weak references in the system, of which 2,607 are reachable. For soft references, we can see that the current objects pointed out by soft references survived for at least 198 seconds.

The `heap_diagnostics` command is quite useful for doing coarse grained analysis of the use of reference objects and for getting statistics on heap usage. However, it is usually easier to use the JRockit Mission Control Memleak Tool and/or JRockit Flight Recorder.

See *print_object_summary*.

hprofdump (R28)

Sometimes it can be useful to dump the heap for offline analysis, as opposed to the online analysis available through the Memleak tool in JRockit Mission Control. As of version R28, JRockit can produce heap dumps in the popular **HPROF** format. There are quite a few memory analysis tools available that operate on HPROF dumps, for instance the excellent **Eclipse Memory Analyzer Tool** (**MAT**).

For example:

```
C:\>jrcmd 7772 hprofdump filename=mydump.hprof
  segment_threshold=2G segment_size=1G
7772:
Wrote dump to mydump.hprof
```

The `segment_threshold` and `segment_size` arguments can be used to split the dump into several smaller files whenever the heap usage is larger than convenient. In the previous example, the split would occur if the heap usage was more than two gigabytes, and JRockit would then attempt to dump the memory in several one gigabyte chunks.

 Note that the `segment_threshold` and `segment_size` arguments should only be used with a tool that supports JAVA PROFILE 1.0.2 HPROF dumps.

The files will be written to the `JROCKIT_HOME` directory. The filename is optional — if no filename is provided, a date-stamped file name will be provided, for example:

```
C:\>jrcmd 7772 hprofdump
7772:
Wrote dump to heapdump_Tue_Sep_22_19_09_16_2009
```

See *memleakserver* and *oom_diagnostics*.

kill_management_server

This command is used to shut down the external management server. Note that the command is not called "stop_management_server". This is purely for legacy reasons. Once upon a time any command name that began with "stop" was interpreted as a command to stop parsing the `ctrlhandler.act` file.

The `kill_management_server` command takes no arguments.

```
C:\>jrcmd 7772 kill_management_server
7772:
```

See *start_mangement_server*.

list_vmflags (R28)

Certain JVM parameters can be set on the command line using the `-XX:<Flag>=<value>` syntax. As explained in Chapter 1, these parameters are known as **VM flags**, and can be listed using the `list_vmflags` command.

For example:

```
C:\>jrcmd 7772 list_vmflags describe=true alias=true

Global:
  UnlockDiagnosticVMOptions = false (default, writeable)
    - Enable processing of flags relating to field diagnostics
  UnlockInternalVMOptions = false (default)
    - Enable processing of internal, unsupported flags
Class:
  FailOverToOldVerifier = true (default, writeable)
    - Fail over to old verifier when split verifier fails
  UseVerifierClassCache = true (default)
    - Try to cache java.lang.Class lookups for old verifier.
  UseClassGC = true (default)
    (Alias: -Xnoclassgc)
    - Allow GC of Java classes
...
Threads:
  UseThreadPriorities = false (default)
    - Use native thread priorities
  DeferThrSuspendLoopCount = 4000 (default, writeable)
    - Number of iterations in safepoint loop until we try blocking
...
```

There are quite a lot of flags available, so only a short subset is shown in this example. Some of the flags are writable and can be changed at runtime using the set_vmflag command. Other VM flags can only be set at startup.

 For advanced users, access to JVM internal flags can be enabled by adding -XX:UnlockInternalVMOptions=true to the JVM startup parameters. Use at your own risk.

See *set_vmflag*.

lockprofile_print

This command is only available if the JVM is running with lock profiling enabled, by using -XX:UseLockProfiling=true and/or -XX:UseNativeLockProfiling=true, as described in Chapter 4. It outputs a lock profile similar to the one available in JRockit Mission Control.

```
C:\>jrcmd 1442 lockprofile_print
1442:
Class, Lazy Banned, Thin Uncontended, Thin Contended, Lazy Reservation,
   Lazy lock, Lazy Reverted, Lazy Coop-Reverted, Thin Recursive, Fat
   Uncontended, Fat Contended, Fat Recursive, Fat Contended Sleep,
   Reserve Bit Uncontended, Reserve Bit Contended
[B, false, 0, 0, 1, 0, 0, 0, 0, 0, 0, 0, 0, 0, 0
java/lang/Thread, false, 11, 0, 3, 0, 0, 0, 0, 0, 0, 0, 0, 0, 0
java/security/Permissions, false, 0, 0, 2, 2, 0, 0, 0, 0, 0, 0, 0, 0, 0
java/util/Hashtable, false, 0, 0, 34, 524, 1, 0, 0, 0, 0, 0, 0, 0, 0
java/lang/Class, false, 0, 0, 24, 77, 2, 0, 0, 0, 0, 0, 0, 0, 0
java/lang/Object, false, 1, 0, 11, 139572, 1, 0, 0, 1, 0, 0, 0, 6, 0
java/lang/StringBuffer, false, 0, 0, 137, 773, 0, 0, 0, 0, 0, 0, 0, 0, 0
sun/nio/cs/StandardCharsets,
   false, 0, 0, 1, 0, 0, 0, 0, 0, 0, 0, 0, 0, 0
java/util/Properties, false, 0, 0, 5, 479, 0, 0, 0, 0, 0, 0, 0, 0, 0
java/lang/ThreadGroup, false, 0, 0, 3, 16, 1, 0, 0, 0, 0, 0, 0, 0, 0
java/lang/ref/Reference$ReferenceHandler,
   false, 0, 0, 1, 0, 0, 0, 0, 0, 0, 0, 0, 0, 0
sun/security/provider/Sun,
   false, 0, 0, 39, 5589, 0, 0, 0, 0, 0, 0, 0, 0, 0
java/io/PrintStream, false, 0, 0, 7, 7818, 0, 0, 0, 0, 0, 0, 0, 0, 0
java/net/URL, false, 0, 0, 70, 68, 0, 0, 0, 0, 0, 0, 0, 0, 0
java/io/ByteArrayInputStream,
```

```
  false, 0, 0, 47, 1115, 0, 0, 0, 0, 0, 0, 0, 0, 0
java/util/logging/Logger, false, 0, 0, 2, 18, 0, 0, 0, 0, 0, 0, 0, 0, 0
jrockit/vm/CharBufferThreadLocal,
  false, 0, 0, 2, 0, 1, 0, 0, 0, 0, 0, 0, 0, 0
java/security/Provider$Service,
  false, 0, 0, 1, 0, 0, 0, 0, 0, 0, 0, 0, 0, 0
java/lang/Runtime, false, 0, 0, 1, 0, 0, 0, 0, 0, 0, 0, 0, 0, 0
java/lang/reflect/Field, false, 0, 0, 8, 8, 0, 0, 0, 0, 0, 0, 0, 0, 0
java/util/Random, false, 0, 0, 6, 18556549, 1, 0, 0, 0, 0, 0, 0, 0, 0
```

See *lockprofile_reset*.

lockprofile_reset

This command is only available if the JVM is running with lock profiling enabled, by using -XX:UseLockProfiling=true and/or -XX:UseNativeLockProfiling=true, as described in Chapter 4. It resets all profile counters to zero for the current lock profile.

See *lockprofile_print*.

memleakserver

This command is for starting and stopping the native **Memory Leak Server (MLS)**. The JRockit Memory Leak Detector uses its own native server, the MLS, for communication. This server is normally automatically started over JMX, but sometimes it may make sense to start the server explicitly. It may, for instance, be necessary to start only the MLS without starting the JMX agent. The memleakserver command can be used to control the lifecycle of the MLS. The command works as a toggle; executing the command twice will first start the MLS and then shut it down.

The following example starts the MLS on port 7899:

```
C:\>jrcmd 5516 memleakserver port=7899
5516:
Memleak started at port 7899.
```

Executing the command again will shut down the server.

```
C:\>jrcmd 5516 memleakserver port=7899
5516:
```

Stopping the server does not produce any output.

See *hprofdump*.

oom_diagnostics (R27)

This command was renamed `heap_diagnostics` in R28.

See *heap_diagnostics*.

print_class_summary

Sometimes it can be helpful to know if a certain class has been loaded by the JVM. For example, dynamic class loading may be used with an SPI framework, and when it fails to work as expected, a useful start may be to find out if the classes that should have been contributed by the framework were even loaded at all. One way of finding this out would be to have the JVM dump the names of all the loaded classes in the system and `grep` for the specific class being sought. Executing `print_class_summary` simply dumps the names of the classes like this:

```
C:\>jrcmd 5516 print_class_summary
5516:
 - Class Summary Information starts here
class java/lang/Object
*class java/util/Vector$1
*class sun/util/calendar/CalendarUtils
*class sun/util/calendar/ZoneInfoFile$1
*class sun/util/calendar/ZoneInfoFile
*class sun/util/calendar/TzIDOldMapping
*class java/util/TimeZone$1
*class java/util/TimeZone
**class java/util/SimpleTimeZone
**class sun/util/calendar/ZoneInfo
*class sun/util/calendar/CalendarDate
**class sun/util/calendar/BaseCalendar$Date
***class sun/util/calendar/Gregorian$Date
*class sun/util/calendar/CalendarSystem
**class sun/util/calendar/AbstractCalendar
***class sun/util/calendar/BaseCalendar
****class sun/util/calendar/Gregorian

...
```

As can be seen from the previous example, the output is sorted in the form of an inheritance tree, with the stars denoting the depth in the tree. The following example shows how to find all loaded classes containing the string LoadAnd on a *NIX system:

```
$ jrcmd 5516 print_class_summary | grep LoadAnd
*class LoadAndDeadlock
**class LoadAndDeadlock$LockerThread
**class LoadAndDeadlock$AllocThread
```

print_codegen_list

This command shows the length of the code generation queue and the optimization queue in a JVM at the current time. An optional boolean argument, list, can be given to also show the contents of the queues, i.e. a list of methods and their generation order for the optimizer and the JIT.

```
C:\>jrcmd 1442 print_codegen_list list=true
1442:
--------------------------------------------------------
     format: <position> <directive no> <method description>
     strategies: q=quick, n=normal, o=optimize
        JIT queue: 0 methods in queue
        OPT queue:
  0: 1 java/math/BigDecimal.<init>(Ljava/math/BigInteger;JII)V
  1: 1 java/math/BigDecimal.add
        (Ljava/math/BigDecimal;)Ljava/math/BigDecimal;
  2: 1 java/lang/String.<init>([C)V
  3: 1 java/util/TreeMap$NavigableSubMap.size()I
  4: 1 java/util/TreeMap$NavigableSubMap.setLastKey()V
  5: 1 jrockit/vm/Strings.compare(Ljava/lang/String;Ljava/lang/String;)I
  6: 1 com/sun/org/apache/xerces/internal/dom/CharacterDataImpl.
        setNodeValueInternal(Ljava/lang/String;Z)V
  7: 1 com/sun/org/apache/xerces/internal/dom/
        CoreDocumentImpl.changed()V
  8: 1 java/lang/String.getChars(II[CI)V
  9: 1 com/sun/org/apache/xerces/internal/dom/NodeImpl.appendChild
        (Lorg/w3c/dom/Node;)Lorg/w3c/dom/Node;
 10: 1 spec/jbb/Warehouse.getAddress()Lspec/jbb/Address;
 11: 1 jrockit/vm/ArrayCopy.copy_checks_done2
        (Ljava/lang/Object;ILjava/lang/Object;II)V
 12 methods in queue
```

print_memusage (R27)

As has been explained in previous chapters, JRockit uses memory for things other than just the Java heap. Sometimes, when too much memory is in use by the Java heap, JRockit can run out of native memory. The print_memusage command is very useful for finding out how JRockit is utilizing system memory. Here is an example of the memory usage for a JRockit JVM running an Eclipse instance:

```
C:\>jrcmd 484536 print_memusage
484536:
[JRockit] memtrace is collecting data...
[JRockit] *** 0th memory utilization report
(all numbers are in kbytes)
Total mapped                    ;;;;;;;;1298896
; Total in-use                  ;;;;;; 438768
;;   executable                 ;;;;;  28460
;;;    java code                ;;;;   5952;    20.9%
;;;;     used                   ;;;    5647;    94.9%
;;   shared modules (exec+ro+rw) ;;;;;  35912
;;   guards                     ;;;;;    528
;;   readonly                   ;;;;;  25936
;;   rw-memory                  ;;;;; 376392
;;;    Java-heap                ;;;; 262144;    69.6%
;;;    Stacks                   ;;;;   3472;     0.9%
;;;    Native-memory            ;;;; 110775;    29.4%
;;;;     java-heap-overhead     ;;;    8206
;;;;     codegen memory         ;;;     896
;;;;     classes                ;;;   43008;    38.8%
;;;;;      method bytecode       ;;    4477
;;;;;      method structs        ;;    3895      (#83104)
;;;;;      constantpool          ;;   18759
;;;;;      classblock            ;;    1596
;;;;;      class                 ;;    3041      (#8403)
;;;;;      other classdata       ;;    8280
;;;;;      overhead              ;;      34
;;;;     threads                ;;;      24;     0.0%
;;;;     malloc:ed memory       ;;;   22647;    20.4%
;;;;;      codeinfo              ;;    1231
```

```
;;;;;      codeinfotrees                   ;;      429
;;;;;      exceptiontables                 ;;      125
;;;;;      metainfo/livemaptable           ;;     5883
;;;;;      codeblock structs               ;;        2
;;;;;      constants                       ;;       14
;;;;;      livemap global tables           ;;      994
;;;;;      callprof cache                  ;;        0
;;;;;      paraminfo                       ;;      146      (#1979)
;;;;;      strings                         ;;     8376      (#148622)
;;;;;      strings(jstring)                ;;        0
;;;;;      typegraph                       ;;     2009
;;;;;      interface implementor list      ;;       40
;;;;;      thread contexts                 ;;       19
;;;;;      jar/zip memory                  ;;     5378
;;;;;      native handle memory            ;;       19
;;;;    unaccounted for memory             ;;;    36017;    32.5%;1.59
--------------------!!!
```

From the listing, we can see that the JRockit process has reserved more than a gigabyte of memory. This may sound excessive, but JRockit is only using less than 429 MB of the allocated gigabyte. Out of those, around 60 percent is used for the Java heap.

The listing is hierarchical—each allocation node has sub-nodes (for example "malloc:ed memory" is used for native structure inside the JVM: livemaps, the type graph, and so on). The percentage notation listed in the margin may seem a little bit confusing at first, as it is calculated as a percentage of the total of the parent node. There is no percentage calculated for the topmost nodes—the 60 percent used by the Java heap mentioned in the previous example was calculated manually and not given by the printout (262,144/438,768 * 100 = 59.7%)

This command may come in handy for tracking down a native memory leak. Such a memory leak can, for example, be caused by a native agent like a third party JVMTI agent.

print_memusage (R28)

Similar to the R27 version of this command, `print_memusage` in R28 is used for finding out how JRockit is utilizing its memory. In R28, the command has been improved.

This command is very useful to find out why the JRockit process is running out of memory. The cause is usually unintentional object retention, as described in Chapter 10, but sometimes the reason is not directly related to objects on the Java heap. Mismanagement of native resources can also cause leaks. Common examples are having an excessive number of `java.util.zip.GZIPOutputStreams` open, class loaders holding on to classes, or leaks in third-party JNI code

For example:

```
C:\>jrcmd 7772 print_memusage
7772:
Total mapped                    1281284KB       (reserved=1002164KB)
-               Java heap       1048576KB       (reserved=932068KB)
-               GC tables         35084KB
-            Thread stacks        11520KB       (#threads=27)
-            Compiled code         5696KB       (used=5490KB)
-                 Internal          840KB
-                       OS        67712KB
-                    Other        48048KB
-            JRockit malloc        29184KB       (malloced=27359KB #275574)
- Native memory tracking           1024KB       (malloced=537KB #11)
-           Java class data       33600KB       (malloced=33471KB #41208)
```

The first column contains the name of a memory space and the second column shows how much memory is mapped for that space. The third column contains details. In the previous example, we can conclude that most of the memory is occupied by the Java heap, which would normally be the case.

When tracking native memory leaks, it is useful to look at how much the memory usage changes over time. The argument `baseline` is used to establish a point from which to start measuring.

The `scale` argument modifies the unit of the amounts of memory in the printout. The default is kilobytes.

For example, use `scale=M` to get the units in megabytes instead:

```
C:\>jrcmd 7772 print_memusage scale=M baseline
7772:
Total mapped                    1252MB          (reserved=978MB)
-               Java heap       1024MB          (reserved=910MB)
-               GC tables         34MB
-            Thread stacks        11MB          (#threads=27)
-            Compiled code         5MB          (used=5MB)
-                 Internal         0MB
-                       OS        66MB
```

-	Other	47MB		
-	JRockit malloc	28MB		(malloced=26MB #275601)
- Native memory tracking		1MB		(malloced=0MB #11)
-	Java class data	32MB		(malloced=32MB #41208)

The baseline argument can be used to perform differential analysis. Once print_
memusage is executed with the baseline argument, subsequent calls will include
differentials against the baseline. For example:

```
C:\>jrcmd 7772 print_memusage scale=M
7772:
```

Total mapped		1282MB	+30MB	(reserved=984MB +6MB)
-	Java heap	1024MB		(reserved=910MB)
-	GC tables	34MB		
-	Thread stacks	14MB	+3MB	(#threads=35 +8)
-	Compiled code	6MB	+1MB	(used=6MB)
-	Internal	0MB		
-	OS	70MB	+4MB	
-	Other	49MB	+2MB	
-	JRockit malloc	41MB	+13MB	(malloced=34MB +8MB #330019 +54418)
- Native memory tracking		2MB		(malloced=1MB #21 +10)
-	Java class data	38MB	+6MB	(malloced=38MB +6MB #48325 +7117)

In this case we can see that, after the baseline was set, the process mapped in
another 30 MB of memory, of which six more were reserved. We added another
eight threads, and JRockit allocated an additional 8 MB. There is now in total 330,019
malloc objects on the JRockit native heap, an increase of 54,418. This resulted in a 13
MB increase in virtual memory usage.

A **malloc object** is the result of a native memory allocation mechanism
from within the JVM similar to the malloc system call. For example,
code like the following might create a malloc object on the native heap,
increasing the number of malloc objects by one.

```
void * foo = malloc(512);
```

Symmetrically, a call like free(foo) will decrease the number of
malloc objects by one, thus returning the number of malloc objects to the
original count.

To reset `baseline` and continue getting the readouts without the comparisons, the `reset` argument is used:

```
C:\>jrcmd 7772 print_memusage reset
```

The argument `trace_alloc_sites` enables tracing of allocation sites where native allocations are made. Set `trace_alloc_sites` to `1` to enable tracing, and to `0` to disable it. To trace all allocations, even the ones occurring during startup of the JVM, the environment variable `TRACE_ALLOC_SITES` can be set to `1`, as an override.

Once tracing has been enabled, memory allocations can then be displayed with different levels of detail using the `level` argument. If a `baseline` has been set, only the sites where changes have occurred are listed. For example:

```
C:\>jrcmd 5784 print_memusage level=1

5784:
Total mapped                1300092KB  +25040KB (reserved=
                                                 1090888KB -7496KB)

-              Java heap    1048576KB            (reserved=
                                                 1008068KB -11020KB)

-              GC tables      35084KB

-           Thread stacks    14336KB   +3840KB (#threads=32 +9)

-           Compiled code     4928KB   +1152KB (used=4774KB +1209KB)

-                Internal     1416KB    +256KB

-                      OS     83040KB   +2048KB

-                   Other     50312KB   +2448KB

-          JRockit malloc     27200KB   +7424KB (malloced=25807KB
                                                 +6236KB #266150 +63919)

                  balance       44KB      +9KB (#23 +5)
              breakpoints        9KB      -8KB (#37 -255)
              breaktable         8KB      +2KB (#13 +3)
                codealloc       56KB     +25KB (#1037 +502)
                codeblock      143KB     +39KB (#2567 +686)
                 codeinfo     1224KB    +351KB (#22300 +6404)
             codeinfotree      400KB    +126KB (#74 +18)
                 dynarray      116KB     +30KB (#2058 +392)
             finalhandles        3KB      +2KB (#14 +7)
                hashtable       32KB     +32KB (#5 +3)
               implchange      982KB    +354KB (#20920 +7556)
                 javalock      279KB    +266KB (#4477 +4092)
```

```
            libcache         245KB      +47KB  (#9473  +1840)
      libconstraints          22KB       +3KB  (#464  +75)
           lifecycle          14KB       +4KB  (#33  +9)
      livemap_system        1083KB     +305KB  (#25117  +5207)
      memleak_trends         544KB     +544KB  (#5809  +5809)
        memleakserver          96KB      +96KB  (#2906  +2906)
            metainfo        7669KB    +1916KB  (#21935  +6416)
```

In the previous example, the JRockit Mission Control Memleak tool was started on a JVM monitoring itself between the invocations of the command. It can be seen how the Memleak modules have allocated a small amount of native memory. Raising the level to 4, even the source code lines in the JVM responsible for the allocations can be determined:

```
C:\>jrcmd 5784 print_memusage level=4

5784:
Total mapped      1310708KB      +35656KB    (reserved=1083664KB  -14720KB)
-                 Java heap     1048576KB    (reserved=1002572KB  -16516KB)
-                 GC tables       35084KB
108KB
    +32KB (#27 +8)
    update_trends                   memleak_trends.c: 364          592KB
    +592KB (#3612 +3612)
    update_trends                   memleak_trends.c: 365           84KB
    +84KB (#3612 +3612)
    create_id_from_object           memleakserver.c: 170            25KB
    +25KB (#1 +1)
    create_id_from_classp           memleakserver.c: 217           116KB
```

Finally, the print_memusage command can be used to display a memory map of various JVM subsystems and libraries that are loaded, including third-party libraries. This is done by passing the displayMap argument.

```
C:\>jrcmd 5784 print_memusage displayMap
5784:
Total mapped                 1311220KB  +36168KB (reserved=1083664KB -
                                                  14720KB)
-              Java heap     1048576KB            (reserved=1002572KB -
                                                  16516KB)
-              GC tables       35084KB
```

```
-              Thread stacks    14592KB    +4096KB (#threads=33 +10)

-              Compiled code     5824KB    +2048KB (used=5634KB +2069KB)

-                   Internal     1160KB

-                         OS    83180KB    +2188KB

-                      Other    52660KB    +4796KB

-              JRockit malloc   30464KB   +10688KB (malloced=29618KB
                                                  +10047KB #302842 +100611)

- Native memory tracking        2112KB    +1088KB (malloced=1035KB
                                                  +582KB #672 +308)

-            Java class data    37568KB   +11264KB (malloced=37537KB
                                                  +11243KB #45413 +14104)


+++++++++++++++++++++++++++++++++++++++++++++++++++++++++++++++++++++++++


  CODE                 Compiled code  rwx 0x0000000007ef0000 (128KB)

...

  MSP        JRockit malloc (179/266)  rw  0x0000000008150000 (64KB)
THREAD                  Stack 6952  rwx 0x0000000008d80000 (12KB)

...

  INT              TLA memcache  rw  0x000000000e330000 (64KB)

  HEAP                  Java heap  rw  0x0000000010040000 (46004KB)

  HEAP         Java heap reserved      0x0000000012d2d000.(1002572KB)

   OS                    *awt.dll r x 0x000000006d0b1000

...

+++++++++++++++++++++++++++++++++++++++++++++++++++++++++++++++++++++++++


Lowest accessible address 00010000

Highest accessible address 7FFEFFFF

Amount free virtual memory 786016KB

     6 free vm areas in range    4KB -    8KB totalling > 24KB

     7 free vm areas in range    8KB -   16KB totalling > 76KB

    24 free vm areas in range   16KB -   32KB totalling >528KB

   281 free vm areas in range   32KB -   64KB totalling > 15MB

     3 free vm areas in range   64KB - 128KB totalling >236KB

     9 free vm areas in range  128KB - 256KB totalling >  1MB

     5 free vm areas in range  256KB - 512KB totalling >  1MB

     7 free vm areas in range  512KB -   1MB totalling >  4MB

     8 free vm areas in range    1MB -   2MB totalling > 11MB
```

```
     2 free vm areas in range    2MB -    4MB totalling >   4MB
     5 free vm areas in range    4MB -    8MB totalling > 30MB
     1 free vm areas in range    8MB -   16MB totalling > 11MB
     5 free vm areas in range   16MB -   32MB totalling >103MB
     1 free vm areas in range   32MB -   64MB totalling > 51MB
     1 free vm areas in range   64MB - 128MB totalling > 67MB
     1 free vm areas in range  128MB - 256MB totalling >135MB
     1 free vm areas in range  256MB - 512MB totalling >326MB
```

As can be seen in the previous example, the chunks of memory are categorized as:

- THREAD: Thread related, for example thread stacks.
- INT: Internal use, for example pointer pages.
- HEAP: Chunk used by JRockit for the Java heap.
- OS: Mapped directly from the operating system, such as third party DLLs or shared objects.
- MSP: Memory space. A memory space is a native heap with a specific purpose, for example native memory allocation inside the JVM.
- GC: Garbage collection related, for example live bits.

print_object_summary

This command shows how memory on the heap is used on a per-class basis. It can be used as a simple memory leak detection tool. Of course, the JRockit Mission Control Memory Leak Detector is far superior to this command, but it can still be useful when it, for some reason, is not feasible to use the Memory Leak Detector. There could, for instance, be a policy restriction which forbids the opening of an MLS server (see *Chapter 10, The Memory Leak Detector*).

The print_object_summary command prints a histogram of all the instances on the heap on a per-class basis, together with a differential value of how the memory usage has changed since the last invocation of the command.

```
C:\>jrcmd 6328 print_object_summary
6328:
--------- Detailed Heap Statistics: ---------
22.1% 2697k      34813   +2697k [C
14.3% 1744k        373   +1744k [B
14.2% 1736k       3220   +1736k [Ljava/lang/Object;
11.8% 1443k       2177   +1443k [I
```

```
6.9%   839k     35833   +839k java/lang/String
5.6%   682k      6240   +682k java/lang/Class
2.6%   314k     13429   +314k java/util/HashMap$Entry
2.0%   242k      3218   +242k [Ljava/util/HashMap$Entry;
1.2%   149k      3185   +149k java/util/HashMap
1.0%   126k      5406   +126k java/util/Hashtable$Entry
0.9%   106k      2844   +106k [Ljava/lang/String;
0.8%    98k      1396    +98k java/lang/reflect/Field
0.5%    65k       844    +65k java/lang/reflect/Method
0.5%    64k       190    +64k [S
       12192kB total ---


--------- End of Detailed Heap Statistics ---
```

The output contains one line per class that has instances on the heap.

- The first column shows how large a part of the heap all instances of the class occupies.
- The second column lists the total size occupied by the instances of the specific class.
- The third column lists the number of instances of the specific class.
- The fourth column shows the change in size from the first invocation of the command. For the first invocation, the second and fourth columns should be the same.
- The fifth column contains the name of the class.

The types are listed in the formal Java descriptor format. For more information on this format, please see *The Java Language Specification* on the Internet.

Normally, only types occupying more than 0.5 percent of the heap will be listed. To change this cutoff value, set the `cutoff` option to a value equal to the percentage value times 1,000. For example, to set it to 1.2 percent, set the cutoff to 1,200.

The `print_object_summary` command can do other tricks. The "points-to" parameters can be used to find out who is referring to all those `char` arrays in the previous example. A maximum of eight "points-to" parameters specifying different types are supported. They are somewhat unimaginatively named `name1` through `name8`, and are called "points-to" as the type entered as argument will list the types having instances that in turn points to the argument type.

The following example lists all the types that have instances that point to `char` arrays and strings that occupy more than 0.1 percent of the heap:

```
C:\>jrcmd 6352 print_object_summary cutoffpointsto=100
  name1=[C name2=java/lang/String
```

The result would look something like this:

```
--------- Detailed Heap Statistics: ---------
42.0% 10622k    116820      +0k [C
11.3% 2851k     121648      +0k java/lang/String
 6.0% 1520k       3676      +0k [Ljava/util/HashMap$Entry;
 4.1% 1033k      18906     +12k org/eclipse/core/internal/
   registry/ReferenceMap$SoftRef
 3.5%  890k      38001      +0k java/util/HashMap$Entry
 3.2%  800k       7323      +0k java/lang/Class
 3.0%  747k      19820      +0k [Ljava/lang/String;
 2.9%  741k      10063      +0k [I
 2.9%  738k      15765      +0k org/eclipse/core/internal/
   registry/ConfigurationElement
 2.8%  699k      15469      +0k [Ljava/lang/Object;
 1.1%  284k        262      +0k [B
 1.0%  241k       4411      +1k org/eclipse/osgi/internal/
   resolver/ExportPackageDescriptionImpl
 0.7%  173k       7408      +0k org/osgi/framework/Version
 0.7%  171k       3653      +0k java/util/HashMap
 0.6%  148k        734      +0k [Ljava/util/Hashtable$Entry;
 0.5%  129k          2      +0k [Lorg/eclipse/core/internal/
   registry/ReferenceMap$IEntry;
     25273kB total ---


  [C is pointed to from:
     99.6%     121713 java/lang/String
      0.2%        270 [[C


  java/lang/String is pointed to from:
     37.2%      98288 [Ljava/lang/String;
     15.6%      41274 java/util/HashMap$Entry
     11.9%      31530 org/eclipse/core/internal/registry/
ConfigurationElement
      7.2%      19067 [Ljava/lang/Object;
--------- End of Detailed Heap Statistics ---
```

In the previous example, we can see that most of our `char` arrays are being referenced by strings, and that our strings are mostly being referenced by string arrays. No surprise there.

This command is usually employed to give an idea of the heap usage distribution. It can also be used to keep track of the types growing over time and for doing points-to analysis on such growing types to find memory leaks. However, if possible, the JRockit Mission Control Memory Leak Detector (Memleak) should be used for this kind of analysis, being both easier and more powerful to use.

See *heap_diagnostics*.

print_properties

This command prints the initial properties from when the JVM was started, a set of JRockit specific VM properties, and the current state of the system properties. The output is in three sections, one for each property type. Each section has a header and a footer. Following is an example:

```
C:\>jrcmd 6012 print_properties
6012:
=== Initial Java properties: ===
java.vm.specification.name=Java Virtual Machine Specification
java.vm.vendor.url.bug=http://edocs.bea.com/
  jrockit/go2troubleshooting.html
java.home=D:\demos_3.1\jrmc_3.1\jre
java.vm.vendor.url=http://www.bea.com/
java.vm.specification.version=1.0
file.encoding=Cp1252
java.vm.info=compiled mode
...
=== End Initial Java properties ===


=== VM properties: ===
jrockit.alloc.prefetch=true
jrockit.alloc.redoprefetch=true
jrockit.vm=D:\demos_3.1\jrmc_3.1\jre\bin\jrockit\jvm.dll
jrockit.alloc.pfd=448
jrockit.alloc.pfl=64
jrockit.alloc.cs=512
jrockit.vm.dir=D:\demos_3.1\jrmc_3.1\jre\bin\jrockit
jrockit.alloc.cleartype=0
=== End VM properties ===
```

```
=== Current Java properties: ===
java.vm.vendor.url.bug=http://edocs.bea.com/
  jrockit/go2troubleshooting.html
java.runtime.name=Java(TM) 2 Runtime Environment, Standard Edition
sun.boot.library.path=D:\demos_3.1\jrmc_3.1\jre\bin
java.vm.version=R27.6.3-40_o-112056-1.5.0_17-20090318-2104-windows-ia32
java.vm.vendor=BEA Systems, Inc.
java.vendor.url=http://www.bea.com/
path.separator=;
java.vm.name=BEA JRockit(R)
file.encoding.pkg=sun.io
user.country=SE
...
=== End Current Java properties ===
```

 Duplicates may be found when using grep or similar tools to filter out properties. This is because the sought property may be in both the initial and current section.

print_threads

This is the default SIGQUIT handler. It prints the stack trace for all threads. There are many different tools in the market for analyzing such thread dumps, but the most powerful way to analyze thread latency and blocking behavior is to either use the Latency Analysis part of the JRockit Runtime Analyzer or JRockit Flight Recorder. Even the JRockit Management Console can be used for simple analysis and for discovering deadlocked threads and information about them. This was covered in the previous chapters.

For example:

```
C:\>jrcmd 7420 print_threads
7420:

===== FULL THREAD DUMP ===============
Mon Sep 28 00:08:56 2009
Oracle JRockit(R) R28.0.0-547-121310-1.6.0_14-20090918-2121-windows-ia32
```

```
"Main Thread" id=1 idx=0x4 tid=7776 prio=6 alive, in native
   at org/eclipse/swt/internal/win32/OS.WaitMessage()Z
      (Native Method) [optimized]
   at org/eclipse/swt/widgets/Display.sleep(Display.java:4220)[inlined]
   at org/eclipse/ui/application/WorkbenchAdvisor.eventLoopIdle
      (WorkbenchAdvisor.java:364) [optimized]
   at org/eclipse/ui/internal/Workbench.runEventLoop(Workbench.java:2385)
   at ...
      -- end of trace


"State Data Manager" id=13 idx=0x38 tid=7596
   prio=5 alive, sleeping, native_waiting, daemon
   at java/lang/Thread.sleep(J)V(Native Method) [optimized]
   at org/eclipse/osgi/internal/baseadaptor/
      StateManager.run(StateManager.java:297)
   at java/lang/Thread.run(Thread.java:619)
   at jrockit/vm/RNI.c2java(IIIII)V(Native Method) [optimized]
   -- end of trace


...


"JFR request timer" id=34 idx=0x84 tid=2624
   prio=5 alive, waiting, native_blocked, daemon
   -- Waiting for notification on: java/util/
      TaskQueue@0x1202F238[fat lock]
   at jrockit/vm/Threads.waitForNotifySignal
      (JLjava/lang/Object;)Z(Native Method) [optimized]
   at java/lang/Object.wait(J)V(Native Method)
   at java/lang/Object.wait(Object.java:485)
   at java/util/TimerThread.mainLoop(Timer.java:483)
   ^-- Lock released while waiting: java/util/
      TaskQueue@0x1202F238[fat lock]
   at java/util/TimerThread.run(Timer.java:462)
   at jrockit/vm/RNI.c2java(IIIII)V(Native Method) [optimized]
   -- end of trace
===== END OF THREAD DUMP ================
```

The default version of the command prints the normal thread stack dump, that is a stack dump with no native frames. To include native frames in the thread dumps, pass the argument `nativestack=true`. To include information about locks implemented by classes in the `java.util.concurrent` package, pass the argument `concurrentlocks=true`.

print_utf8pool

This command lists all the UTF-8 constants currently in the JVM, for example class names, method names and string constants.

The following example lists the URLs in the constant pool.

```
$ jrcmd 3824 print_utf8pool | grep http
"http://www.w3.org/TR/xinclude": refs=2, len=29
"http://apache.org/xml/properties/internal/
  symbol-table": refs=12, len=54
```

`refs` is the number of references to the constant and `len` is the length of the constant in bytes.

print_vm_state

The `print_vm_state` command outputs the state of the JVM in a format similar to the dump file that is normally emitted when a JRockit instance crashes.

For example:

```
C:\>jrcmd 7420 print_vm_state
7420:
Uptime        : 0 days, 02:35:53 on Tue Sep 22 19:14:39 2009
Version       : Oracle JRockit(R) R28.0.0-547-121310
                -1.6.0_14-20090918-2121-windows-ia32
CPU           : Intel Core 2 SSE SSE2 SSE3 SSSE3 SSE4.1 Core Intel64
Number CPUs   : 2
Tot Phys Mem  : 3706712064 (3534 MB)
OS version    : Microsoft Windows Vista version 6.0 Service Pack 2
                (Build 6002) (32-bit)
Thread System: Windows Threads
Java locking  : Lazy unlocking enabled (class banning) (transfer banning)
State         : JVM is running
Command Line  : -Denv.class.path=.;C:\Program Files\
                Java\jre6\lib\ext\QTJava.zip -Dapplication.home=C:\
jrockits\R28.0.0_R28.0.0-547_1.6.0 -client -
  XX:UnlockInternalVMOptions=true -Dsun.java.launcher=
```

```
    SUN_STANDARD com.jrockit.mc.rcp.start.MCMain
java.home    : C:\jrockits\R28.0.0_R28.0.0-547_1.6.0\jre
j.class.path : C:\jrockits\R28.0.0_R28.0.0-
    547_1.6.0/missioncontrol/mc.jar
j.lib.path   : C:\jrockits\R28.0.0_R28.0.0-
...
StackOverFlow: 0 StackOverFlowErrors have occured
OutOfMemory  : 0 OutOfMemoryErrors have occured
C Heap       : Good; no memory allocations have failed
GC Strategy  : Mode: pausetime, with strategy: singleconcon
               (basic strategy: singleconcon)
GC Status    : OC is not running. Last finished OC was OC#369.
Heap         : 0x10040000 - 0x17207000  (Size: 113 MB)
Compaction   : (no compaction area)
CompRefs     : References are 32-bit.

Loaded modules:
0000000000400000-000000000043afff  C:\jrockits\
  R28.0.0_R28.0.0-547_1.6.0\bin\jrmc.exe
0000000077d30000-0000000077e56fff  C:\Windows\
  system32\ntdll.dll
00000000763f0000-00000000764cbfff  C:\Windows\system32\kernel32.dll
0000000077a30000-0000000077accfff  C:\Windows\system32\USER32.dll
0000000077400000-000000007744afff  C:\Windows\system32\GDI32.dll
0000000077ea0000-0000000077f65fff  C:\Windows\system32\ADVAPI32.dll
...
00000000764e0000-00000000765a2fff  C:\Windows\system32\RPCRT4.dll
000000006d3e0000-000000006d3fefff  C:\jrockits\
  R28.0.0_R28.0.0-547_1.6.0\jre\bin\java.dll
```

The dump contains diagnostic information about the state of the JVM, such as version information, locking paradigm, thread system, various paths, and the addresses of the loaded modules and libraries.

See *heap_diagnostics*.

run_optfile (R27)

As described in the code generation chapter, directive files can be used to start the JVM with a set of directives to the JVM optimization manager. The directive files can also be applied at run time by issuing the `run_optfile` diagnostic command. The command takes a single argument, `filename`—the file name of the directive file to be loaded. The directive file format for R27 differs from the one in R28. The R27 format is undocumented, and the only use case scenario where you are likely to encounter the `run_optfile` command in R27 is in interaction with JRockit support.

run_optfile (R28)

The R28 version of `run_optfile` for R28 can take several arguments. The most important one is the `filename` argument that specifies a directive file for the JVM as in R27. The directive file format for R28 is undocumented and subject to change without notice. Some limited examples of how to use directive files are given in Chapter 2, but this should by no means be considered complete.

The `run_optfile` command can also be used to re-compile selected methods with a given compilation strategy.

The following example will re-generate the `java.util.ArrayList.get` method using the optimized code generation strategy:

```
C:\>jrcmd 7736 run_optfile method=java.util.ArrayList.get*
  strategy=opt disass=false
```

runfinalization

This command forces the JVM to execute a call to `java.lang.System.runFinalization()`, that is, hints to the runtime that any available finalizers should be run.

runsystemgc

This command forces a full garbage collection.

Forcing a garbage collection is very rarely necessary. The JVM is good at deciding when to garbage collect. If the user interferes, the most probable result is a performance penalty. There are, however, rare cases when explicitly invoking the garbage collector may be helpful. Such cases may, for example, include using verbose GC logs to look at memory usage or live set usage, and not wanting to wait for a GC to occur.

If executed with no arguments, the `runsystemgc` command defaults to performing only a nursery collection. No compaction of the heap will take place.

To do a full garbage collection, the `full` argument needs to be set to true, as shown in the following example. When forcing a full garbage collection, an exceptional compaction will take place, which means that the entire heap will be compacted.

```
C:\>jrcmd 4748 runsystemgc full=true
4748:
```

The `runsystemgc` command does not return any result.

set_vmflag (R28)

This command sets an individual VM flag. It takes the name of the VM flag and its new value.

For example:

```
C:\>jrcmd 7772 set_vmflag flag=DumpOnCrash value=false
7772:
```

Upon successful completion, the command does not return any message. Only writeable VM flags can be changed this way. If an attempt to change the value of a read-only flag is made, an error message is returned. For example:

```
C:\>jrcmd 7772 set_vmflag flag=DisableAttachMechanism value=true
7772:
Not a writeable flag "DisableAttachMechanism"
```

To set the value of a VM flag that is not writeable at runtime, use the -XX:<Flag>=<value> syntax when starting the JVM.

See *list_vmflags*.

start_flightrecording (R28)

The start_flightrecording command starts a JRockit Flight Recorder recording. It can be used to start a continuous recording, that is a recording with no end time, or a timed recording that lasts for a specific duration. The recording can be configured using a number of named templates located in the JROCKIT_HOME/jre/lib/jfr folder. The files are in JSON format and can be copied and altered to create new templates.

For example:

```
C:\>jrcmd 7420 start_flightrecording name=MyRecording settings=
  jra.jfs duration=30s filename=my_recording.jfr.gz compress=true
7420:
Started recording 5
```

The previous example starts a recording using the jra.jfs template. The recording will last for 30 seconds, after which a file will be emitted to the JROCKIT_HOME directory, named my_recording.jfr.gz. The file will be gzip compressed.

Using the `check_flightrecording` command to check on the recording after it has started, should look something like this:

```
C:\>jrcmd 7420 check_flightrecording
7420:
Recording : id=0 name="continuous" duration=0s (running)
Recording : id=5 name="MyRecording" duration=30s
  dest="my_recording.jfr.gz" compress=true (running)
```

Once the 30 seconds have passed, the state of the recording will go from running to stopped and the recording file will be emitted.

Some templates are meant to be additive, that is they contain settings that are supposed to be used in addition to one of the base templates. The only way to identify such a template is currently by looking at the comment at the top of the file. If it starts with "Additional settings", the file is meant to be used together with one of the base settings. For instance, using the default template with additional lock information would look like this:

```
C:\>jrcmd 7420 start_flightrecording name=DefaultAndLocks
  settings=default.fls settings=lock.fls duration=30s
  filename=defaultAndLocks.jfr.gz compress=true
```

The simplest way of starting, configuring, and retrieving JRockit Flight Recorder (JFR) recordings for analysis is to use the JRockit Mission Control client. For more information on how to do this, please refer to *Chapter 9, The Flight Recorder*.

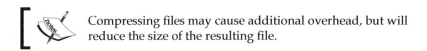

Compressing files may cause additional overhead, but will reduce the size of the resulting file.

See *check_flightrecording*, *dump_flightrecording*, and *stop_flightrecording*

start_management_server

This command starts the external management agent without having to edit startup scripts and then restarting the JVM. It works almost exactly the same way as the `-Xmanagement` JVM parameters used to start up the management agent.

Starting up an application server and deploying a J2EE application can take a considerable amount of time. There is usually a warm-up period involved to get everything properly optimized. Once everything is up and running, it is usually very annoying to realize that the necessary flags to start up the management agent were forgotten in the startup script. If the server is running in production, the next opportunity to take the server offline to restart it with a modified set of startup parameters may be quite far away.

The following example starts up the external management agent on port `4711` with SSL and authentication turned off and autodiscovery (JDP) turned on. Note that for SSL and authentication to work properly with this command, the `password.` `properties` file and a key store must be set up in advance. Please see the document *Monitoring and Management Using JMX Technology* on the *Oracle Sun Developer Network website*.

```
C:\>jrcmd 473528 start_management_server ssl=false
  authenticate=false port=4711 autodiscovery=true
2416:
```

If everything goes well, this command will produce no output.

 The `start_management_server` command will always start the local management agent, and the local management agent cannot be shut down once it has been started.

See *kill_management_server*.

startjrarecording (R27)

The simplest way of starting and retrieving JRockit Runtime Analyzer (JRA) recordings for analysis is to use the JRockit Mission Control client. For more information on how to do this, please see *Chapter 8, The Runtime Analyzer*.

Sometimes, however, using the JRockit Mission Control client may not be an option. The environment may not allow JMX connections, or perhaps a JDK 1.4 based version of JRockit is used. In those cases, the `startjrarecording` diagnostic command is very useful. The following example starts a JRA-recording on the JRockit process with PID `5516`. The duration of the recording will be two minutes and it will start after an initial delay of 30 seconds.

When sampling an application that utilizes a large framework or runs in an enterprise container, such as WebLogic Server, call stack depths can be quite large. In such cases, increasing the trace depth is usually a good idea. The trace depth in the following example has been increased to 64.

The `sampletime` option denotes how often the threads should be sampled. As this is a relatively short recording, the sample time has been compressed to every five milliseconds. The latency recording has been turned on to provide latency events.

```
C:\>jrcmd 5516 startjrarecording filename=C:\myrecording.jra
  recordingtime=120 delay=30 tracedepth=64 sampletime=5 latency=true
5516:
JRA recording started.
```

When the recording command has been sent, the JVM upon which the recording has been started should print something like the following to the console (`stdout`):

```
[INFO ][jra    ] Delaying JRA recording for 30 seconds.
[INFO ][jra    ] Starting JRA recording with these options:
filename=D:\myrecording.jra, recordingtime=120s, methodsampling=1,
  gcsampling=1, heapstats=1, nativesamples=0, methodtraces=1,
  sampletime=5, zip=1, hwsampling=0 delay=30s, tracedepth=64
  threaddump=1, threaddumpinterval=0s, latency=1,
  latencythreshold=20ms, cpusamples=1, cpusampleinterval=1s
```

Once the recording is done, it should print something similar to this:

```
[INFO ][jra    ] Zipped the recording file.
[INFO ][jra    ] Finished recording. Results written to
  C:\myrecording.jra.
```

See *checkjrarecording* and *stopjrarecording*.

stop_flightrecording (R28)

This command stops an ongoing JRockit Flight Recorder recording. The recording to stop can either be identified by name (`name`) or ID (`recording`).

For example:

```
C:\>jrcmd 7420 stop_flightrecording recording=10
7420:
```

By default, the data will be saved to file when the recording is stopped. If the data is unwanted, pass the argument `discard=true`. The `stop_flightrecording` command will remove the recording from the listed recordings in `check_flightrecording`. So, the command can be used to clean out information about old recordings that are no longer of interest.

See *check_flightrecording, dump_flightrecording, start_flightrecording*.

timestamp

This command prints a timestamp for a JVM and displays how long it has been running.

```
C:\>jrcmd 6012 print_properties
6012:
==== Timestamp ==== uptime: 0 days, 00:04:39 time:
  Sun Jan 24 15:47:42 2010
```

verbosity

This is a command for controlling the logging for the different logging modules in JRockit. The command can be used to change the logging level for a specific module, to redirect the output stream of the logger and to decorate the logging output. Running the `verbosity` command without arguments will list all the available logging modules with their current status.

```
C:\demos_3.1>jrcmd 4504 verbosity
4504:
Current logstatus:
        jrockit : level=WARN, decorations=201, sanity=NONE
        memory (gc) : level=WARN, decorations=201, sanity=NONE
        nursery (yc) : level=WARN, decorations=201, sanity=NONE
        model : level=WARN, decorations=201, sanity=NONE
        devirtual : level=WARN, decorations=201, sanity=NONE
        codegen (code) : level=WARN, decorations=201, sanity=NONE
        native (jni) : level=WARN, decorations=201, sanity=NONE
        thread : level=WARN, decorations=201, sanity=NONE
        opt : level=WARN, decorations=201, sanity=NONE
```

The first word on a line is the module name. The word in parenthesis after the module name, if there is one, is an alias that can also be used to refer to the module.

The following example shows how to enable verbose logging for the code generator in a similar fashion as described at the end of Chapter 2. This is equivalent to the output generated by starting the JVM with the flag -Xverbose:codegen.

```
C:\>jrcmd 5556 verbosity set=codegen=INFO
5556:
Current logstatus:
        jrockit : level=WARN, decorations=201, sanity=NONE
        memory (gc) : level=WARN, decorations=201, sanity=NONE
        nursery (yc) : level=WARN, decorations=201, sanity=NONE
        model : level=WARN, decorations=201, sanity=NONE
        devirtual : level=WARN, decorations=201, sanity=NONE
        codegen (code) : level=INFO, decorations=201, sanity=NONE
```

As can be seen from the previous example, `verbosity` responds by listing the new log status.

The `verbosity` command can also be used to do exception profiling. Exception profiling is used to find out where the exceptions in an application occur.

Prior to the R28 version of JRockit and the exception profiling capabilities of the Flight Recorder, logging was the only possible, if somewhat tedious, way of doing exception profiling. As can be realized, this is just a somewhat more flexible way of running JRockit with `-Xverbose:exceptions` as described in Chapter 5.

The following example shows how to enable and disable exception profiling. It also shows how to use decorations. Leaving decorations empty will default to decorating the output with timestamp, module, and PID.

```
C:\>jrcmd 6064 verbosity set=exceptions=info decorations=module
6064:
Current logstatus:
```

The resulting log for the JRockit process on which the diagnostic command is executed will contain an entry for every exception thrown. The example simply throws an `ExceptionThrowerException` every now and then with the message "Throw me!".

```
[excepti] ExceptionThrowerException: Throw me!
[excepti] ExceptionThrowerException: Throw me!
```

JRockit can also display the stack traces for thrown exceptions. Simply set the logging level to `debug` as shown in the following command-line execution:

```
D:\>jrcmd 6064 verbosity set=exceptions=debug decorations=module
6064:
Current logstatus:
```

This will result in each exception line being followed by the stack trace showing exactly where the exception was thrown. This is the same behavior as is achieved by running JRockit with `-Xverbose:exceptions=debug`.

```
[excepti] ExceptionThrowerException: Throw me!
  at jrockit/vm/Reflect.fillInStackTrace0
    (Ljava/lang/Throwable;)V(Native Method)
  at java/lang/Throwable.fillInStackTrace()
    Ljava/lang/Throwable;(Native Method)
  at java/lang/Throwable.<init>(Throwable.java:196)
  at java/lang/Exception.<init>(Exception.java:41)
```

```
    at ExceptionThrowerException.<init>(ExceptionThrowerException.java:5)
    at ExceptionThrower.throwMe(ExceptionThrower.java:24)
    at ExceptionThrower.doStuff(ExceptionThrower.java:20)
    at ExceptionThrower.loop(ExceptionThrower.java:11)
    at ExceptionThrower.main(ExceptionThrower.java:4)
    at jrockit/vm/RNI.c2java(IIIII)V(Native Method)
--- End of stack trace
```

This can be done at runtime, even in production systems. If log level is reverted to its original form after the analysis is complete, no overhead will remain.

version

This command is quite useful when there is a need to find out what exact version of JRockit an application is running on, without having to restart it. When, for example, the JRockit JVM has been started as a service, and no console is available, this command is probably one of the easiest ways to find out the version number. The version command takes no arguments.

```
C:\>%JAVA_HOME%\bin\jrcmd 2416 version
2416:
BEA JRockit(R) (build R27.6.2-20_o-108500-1.6.0_05-
  20090120-1116-windows-ia32, compiled mode)
```

Summary

This chapter showed how the JRCMD command-line utility can be used for listing and sending diagnostic commands to one or more locally running instances of the JRockit JVM.

Examples introducing basic usage patterns as well as detailed examples for the most common commands were presented.

Most of this chapter can readily be employed as an alphabetical reference guide to the JRCMD commands.

12
Using the JRockit Management APIs

There are various ways to access the JRockit management features programmatically, all of them more or less unsupported. As the APIs in question are unsupported, they are subject to change between JRockit releases or even to disappear entirely. This means that dependencies on these APIs may break between releases of JRockit. Because the APIs can be quite useful, this chapter will nevertheless show a few different ones, with their applications.

In this chapter, you will learn:

- How to use the **JRockit Management API (JMAPI)** to access runtime information in the JRockit JVM

- How to instantiate and access the **JMX-based JRockit Management API (JMXMAPI)** for various versions of JRockit

JMAPI is partly deprecated as of JRockit R28 and JMXMAPI is unsupported in all JRockit versions. This chapter is for informational purposes only — illustrating that having the power of the JVM at your fingertips can be great fun.

JMAPI

The first API we will discuss is called JMAPI, short for the JRockit Management API. It is a lightweight Java-only API which provides in-process access to various management features. This API has existed since very early versions of JRockit. However, parts of the API were marked as deprecated in R28.0.0 and its future is uncertain.

JMAPI was the JVM-side API that enabled the functionality of the earliest versions of the JRockit Management Console. In fact, even today, if a connection is established to a 1.4 version of JRockit, a proprietary internal protocol called the **Rockit Management Protocol (RMP)** will be used. This protocol will, in turn, use JMAPI to gather data and change the various runtime parameters of the JVM.

The next few pages contain various examples of things that can be done using JMAPI. The easiest way to compile the examples is to use the JRockit JDK. This requires no special configuration, as the necessary classes are available in the JRockit `rt.jar` that is part of the JRockit JDK. The examples can also be compiled by including `jmapi.jar`, that contains all the interface declarations, in your class path. The `jmapi.jar` is not part of the JDK, but is distributed by Oracle on request.

Using JMAPI for simple tasks is very easy. Use the `com.bea.jvm.JVMFactory` class to get an instance implementing the JVM interface. From the JVM interface a number of different subsystems can be reached.

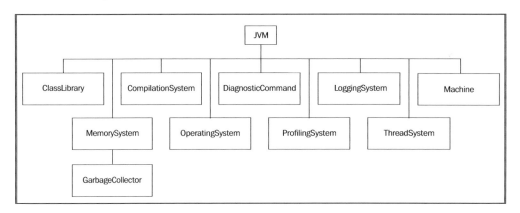

For readers who reacted on the `com.bea` part in the package name—JMAPI predates the 2008 Oracle acquisition of BEA Systems, and is used in other Oracle products as well as in third-party products. As JMAPI was supported in JRockit R27 and earlier releases, the package name cannot be changed without breaking existing products utilizing JMAPI.

Let us begin with a simple example that writes the current CPU load on the console ten times with a one second delay between each printout:

```
import com.bea.jvm.JVMFactory;

public class JMAPITest {
  public static void main(String[] args) throws InterruptedException {
```

```
      for (int i = 0; i < 10; i++) {
        System.out.println(
          String.format("CPU load is %3.2f%%",
          JVMFactory.getJVM().getMachine().getCPULoad() * 100.0));
        Thread.sleep(1000);
      }
    }
  }
```

Access permissions to JMAPI are very coarse-grained; access is either permitted or not allowed at all. If the code needs access to JMAPI when a security manager is active, it must be granted the `com.bea.jvm.ManagementPermission` `"createInstance"`.

The following security policy statement grants access to JMAPI for all code:

```
grant {
  permission com.bea.jvm.ManagementPermission "createInstance";
};
```

For more information on how to use permissions and policies, see: `http://java.sun.com/j2se/1.5.0/docs/guide/security/permissions.html`

JMAPI examples

JMAPI can be used to gather a lot of information about the operating environment. The following code example prints some information about the available network interfaces:

```
for (NIC nic : JVMFactory.getJVM().getMachine().getNICs()) {
  System.out.println(
    nic.getDescription() + " MAC:" +
    nic.getMAC() + " MTU:" + nic.getMTU());
}
```

It is also possible to change various aspects of the runtime parameters using JMAPI. The following piece of code will attempt to change the JRockit process affinity to only one CPU:

```
private static void bindToFirstCPU(JVM jvm) {
  Collection<CPU> cpus = jvm.getProcessAffinity();
  CPU cpu = cpus.iterator().next();
  Collection<CPU> oneCpu = new LinkedList<CPU>();
  oneCpu.add(cpu);
  jvm.suggestProcessAffinity(oneCpu);
}
```

This can be compared to using the command-line flag –XX:BindToCPUs, for controlling CPU affinity. The flag was introduced in *Chapter 5, Benchmarking and Tuning*.

Other aspects such as the pause time target, the heap size, and the nursery size can also be changed as follows:

```
MemorySystem ms = JVMFactory.getJVM().getMemorySystem();
ms.suggestHeapSize(1024*1024*1024);
ms.getGarbageCollector().setPauseTimeTarget(30);
ms.getGarbageCollector().setNurserySize(256*1024*1024);
```

Some features in JMAPI are a result of direct demands from customers with specialized setups. There is, in particular, one peculiar feature that comes to mind—it is possible to force the JRockit process to instantly terminate if it runs out of memory, instead of throwing an OutOfMemoryError.

```
ms.setExitOnOutOfMemory(true);
```

It is also possible to do simple method profiling using JMAPI. The following example enables profiling for the method java.io.StringWriter.append(CharSequence). The example executes it for a number of String instances, after which the number of invocations and the average time it took to invoke the method will be printed.

```
import java.io.StringWriter;
import java.lang.reflect.Method;

import com.bea.jvm.JVMFactory;
import com.bea.jvm.MethodProfileEntry;
import com.bea.jvm.ProfilingSystem;

public class MethodProfilerExample {
  public static void main(String[] args) throws Exception {
    String longString = generateLongString();
    ProfilingSystem profiler = JVMFactory.getJVM()
      .getProfilingSystem();
    Method appendMethod = StringWriter.class.getMethod(
      "append", CharSequence.class);
    MethodProfileEntry mpe = profiler
      .newMethodProfileEntry(appendMethod);
    mpe.setInvocationCountEnabled(true);
    mpe.setTimingEnabled(true);

    String total = doAppends(10000, longString);
    long invocationCount = mpe.getInvocations();
    long invocationTime = mpe.getTiming();
```

```
      System.out.println("Did " + invocationCount
        + " invocations");
      System.out.println("Average invocation time was "
        + (invocationTime * 1000.0d)
        / invocationCount + " microseconds");
      System.out.println("Total string length "
        + total.length());
  }

  private static String doAppends(int count, String longString) {
    StringWriter writer = new StringWriter();
    for (int i = 0; i < count; i++) {
      writer.append(longString);
    }
    return writer.toString();
  }

  private static String generateLongString() {
    StringWriter sw = new StringWriter(1000);
    for (int i = 0; i < 1000; i++) {
      // Build a string containing the characters
      // A to Z repeatedly.
      sw.append((char) (i % 26 + 65));
    }
    return sw.toString();
  }
}
```

The previous example is slightly simplified. Normally, profiling could already have been enabled for the method, and thus the counter and timing information already available in the MethodProfileEntry should be stored before the profiling run is started and subtracted from the total when it is finished.

Recall the diagnostic commands that were introduced in *Chapter 7, The Management Console* and *Chapter 11, JRCMD*. All diagnostic commands are available through JMAPI, and can be accessed through the DiagnosticCommand subsystem. Here is an example that prints the object summary histogram on stdout, in effect programmatically executing the diagnostic command print_object_summary:

```
import com.bea.jvm.DiagnosticCommand;
import com.bea.jvm.JVMFactory;

public class ObjectSummary {
  public static void main(String[] args)
  throws InterruptedException {
    DiagnosticCommand dc = JVMFactory.getJVM()
      .getDiagnosticCommand();
    String output = dc.execute("print_object_summary");
```

```
        System.out.println(output);
    }
}
```

Finally, JMAPI also contains powerful class pre-processing and redefinition features. The following example redefines the bytecode of the classes as they are loaded, by calling `transformByteCode` for each class:

```
ClassLibrary cl = JVMFactory.getJVM().getClassLibrary();
cl.setClassPreProcessor(new ClassPreProcessor() {
  @Override
  public byte[] preProcess(ClassLoader cl,
    String className,
    byte[] arg) {
    System.out.println("Pre-processing class " + className);
    return transformByteCode(arg);
  }
});
```

There can only be one active preprocessor in use at any given time. By using the method `redefineClass` in the class library, it is also possible to redefine already loaded classes.

> JMAPI can be used for much more than the examples listed here. In the interest of not spending too much time on describing deprecated and unsupported features, we have chosen to keep this chapter short. The full javadocs for JMAPI can be requested by Oracle customers.

JMXMAPI

The other management API available in JRockit is JMXMAPI. JMXMAPI can be seen as a JMX-based version of JMAPI, even though there is not a one-to-one mapping between the two. JMXMAPI is currently not supported and is subject to change between releases, without notice.

The name space (domain) of the MBeans for JMXMAPI has changed with every major JRockit release. With R28, it was changed once again due to the Oracle acquisition. Even though it is highly unlikely that Oracle will be acquired, as we have the luxury of not yet supporting the API, expect it to continue to change for a while. The JMXMAPI MBeans were originally co-located with the `java.lang.management` MBeans (see Chapter 7) in R26.x, but were later relocated to the `bea.jrockit.management` domain and finally moved to the `oracle.jrockit.management` domain. The best version-independent way to access a certain feature of JMX is by using the RJMX proxy layer introduced at the end of the Management Console chapter.

To access JMXMAPI, the `JRockitConsoleMBean` must first be loaded. This can easily be done programmatically, by using the `MBeanServerConnection`.

For R27.x versions of JRockit:

```
someMBeanServerConnection.createMBean
    ("bea.jrockit.management.JRockitConsole", null);
```

For R28.x versions of JRockit:

```
someMBeanServerConnection.createMBean
    ("oracle.jrockit.management.JRockitConsole", null);
```

With the Management Console proxy layer, this is done automatically.

The set of MBeans are organized as one per functional area. For the R28 version of JRockit, MBeans are also dynamically created for each ongoing JRockit Flight Recording.

Following is a table describing the different MBeans available:

JMXMAPI MBeans	
MBean name	**Description**
Compilation	Information from the JIT compiler.
DiagnosticCommand	Enables access to the JVM internal diagnostic commands, see *Chapter 11, JRCMD*.
GarbageCollector	Information from the garbage collector, allows some degree of control over the garbage collector.
JRockitConsole	Functionality specifically for the Management Console, such as the "dump heap" operation. Creating this MBean will instantiate and register the rest of the API.
Log	Controlling and getting information from the JRockit logging subsystem.
Memleak	For controlling the Memleak server.
Memory	For accessing information about physical memory.
PerfCounters	A dynamically generated MBean listing all of the internally available performance counters, described later in this chapter.
Profiler	For controlling the method profiler.
Runtime	For reading CPU information, CPU load, and for controlling CPU affinity.
Threading	Thread-related information. Currently only contains MBean operations, that is no MBean attributes.

In R28, there is also a supported JMX-based API for starting and controlling JRockit Flight Recordings. This is located under `com.oracle.jrockit`. The entry point for that API is the `FlightRecorder` MBean. This API is not part of JMXMAPI.

The JRockit internal performance counters

Most of JMXMAPI exposes MBeans implementing static interfaces. There is however one that is dynamically generated—the `PerfCountersMBean`. JRockit uses a number of internal performance counters for profiling and diagnostic purposes. The `PerfCountersMBean` contains an attribute for every internal performance counter in JRockit.

 As JMXMAPI is not yet supported, the dynamically generated `PerfCountersMBean` is not supported either. However, there is an internal distinction between the counters. The `jrockit.*` counters can be considered to be even less supported than the `oracle.*` counters.

The following table describes some of the most important counters available in 4.0/R28.x (at the time of writing, there are 139 different counters available):

Counter	Description
`java.cls.loadedClasses`	The number of classes loaded since the start of the JVM.
`java.cls.unloadedClasses`	The number of classes unloaded since the start of the JVM.
`java.property.java.class.path`	The class path of the JVM.
`java.property.java.endorsed.dirs`	The endorsed dirs. See the *Endorsed Standards Override Mechanism* on the Internet at `http://java.sun.com/javase/6/docs/technotes/guides/standards/index.html`.
`java.property.java.ext.dirs`	The extension dirs that are searched for JAR files that should be automatically put on the classpath. See the Java Documentation for `java.ext.dirs`. More information on the Extension Mechanism can be found here: `http://java.sun.com/j2se/1.4.2/docs/guide/extensions/spec.html`
`java.property.java.home`	The root of the JDK or JRE installation.
`java.property.java.library.path`	The library path used to find user libraries.

Counter	Description
`java.property.java.vm.version`	The JRockit version.
`java.rt.vmArgs`	The list of VM arguments.
`java.threads.daemon`	The number of running daemon threads.
`java.threads.live`	The total number of running threads.
`java.threads.livePeak`	The peak number of threads that have been running since JRockit was started.
`java.threads.nonDaemon`	The number of non-daemon threads running.
`java.threads.started`	The total number of threads started since the start of JRockit.
`jrockit.gc.latest.heapSize`	The current heap size in bytes.
`jrockit.gc.latest.nurserySize`	The current nursery size in bytes.
`jrockit.gc.latest.oc.compaction.time`	How long, in ticks, the last compaction lasted. Reset to 0 if compaction is skipped.
`jrockit.gc.latest.oc.heapUsedAfter`	Used heap at the end of the last OC, in bytes.
`jrockit.gc.latest.oc.heapUsedBefore`	Used heap at the start of the last OC, in bytes.
`jrockit.gc.latest.oc.number`	The number of OCs that have occurred so far.
`jrockit.gc.latest.oc.sumOfPauses`	The pause time for the last OC, in ticks.
`jrockit.gc.latest.oc.time`	The time the last OC took, in ticks.
`jrockit.gc.latest.yc.sumOfPauses`	The pause time for the last YC, in ticks.
`jrockit.gc.latest.yc.time`	The time the last YC took, in ticks.
`jrockit.gc.max.oc.individualPause`	The longest OC pause so far, in ticks.
`jrockit.gc.max.yc.individualPause`	The longest YC pause so far, in ticks.
`jrockit.gc.total.oc.compaction.externalAborted`	Number of aborted external compactions so far.
`jrockit.gc.total.oc.compaction.internalAborted`	Number of aborted internal compactions so far.
`jrockit.gc.total.oc.compaction.internalSkipped`	Number of skipped internal compactions so far.
`jrockit.gc.total.oc.compaction.time`	The total time spent doing compaction so far, in ticks.

Counter	Description
`jrockit.gc.total.oc.ompaction.externalSkipped`	Number of skipped external compactions so far.
`jrockit.gc.total.oc.pauseTime`	The sum of all OC pause times so far, in ticks.
`jrockit.gc.total.oc.time`	The total time spent doing OC so far, in ticks.
`jrockit.gc.total.pageFaults`	The number of page faults that have occurred during GC so far.
`jrockit.gc.total.yc.pauseTime`	The sum of all YC pause times, in ticks.
`jrockit.gc.total.yc.promotedObjects`	The number of objects that all YCs have promoted.
`jrockit.gc.total.yc.promotedSize`	The total number of bytes that all YCs have promoted.
`jrockit.gc.total.yc.time`	The total time spent in YCs, in ticks.
`oracle.ci.jit.count`	The number of methods JIT compiled.
`oracle.ci.jit.timeTotal`	The total time spent JIT compiling, in ticks.
`oracle.ci.opt.count`	The number of methods optimized.
`oracle.ci.opt.timeTotal`	The total time spent optimizing, in ticks.
`oracle.rt.counterFrequency`	Used to convert ticks values to seconds.

Many of these counters are excellent choices for attributes to plot in the Management Console. Also, be aware that many values are in **ticks**. To convert them to seconds, divide by the value in the `oracle.rt.counterFrequency` counter.

To find out which counters are in ticks, enable the **Description** column in the **MBean Browser** by editing the table properties as shown in the following screenshot:

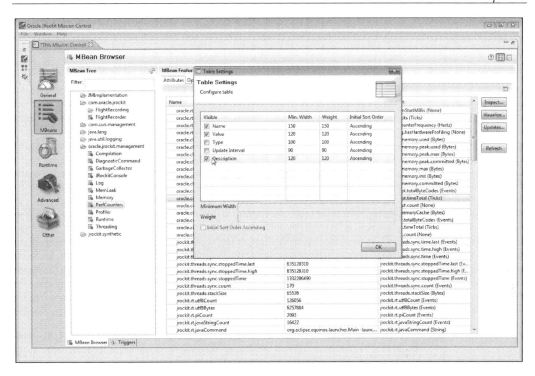

The unit will be listed at the end of the description, as can be seen (you may need a magnifier) in the rightmost column in the attribute table behind the **Table Settings** dialog in the screenshot.

An example—building a remote version of JRCMD

JMXMAPI is accessed through standard JMX mechanisms (as described in Chapter 7). Consequently, the API is easily accessed remotely through the platform MBean server and the standard remote JMX agent. As described in Chapter 11, a limitation of JRCMD is that it can only attach to JRockit instances running locally on the same machine as where JRCMD is executed. It can also only access JRockit instances running as the same user as the one invoking JRCMD. Using JMXMAPI, we can write a remote version of JRCMD that overcomes these limitations.

```
import java.lang.management.ManagementFactory;
import java.net.MalformedURLException;
import java.util.HashMap;
import java.util.Iterator;
import java.util.Map;
```

```java
import javax.management.Attribute;
import javax.management.InstanceNotFoundException;
import javax.management.MBeanAttributeInfo;
import javax.management.MBeanServerConnection;
import javax.management.ObjectName;
import javax.management.remote.JMXConnector;
import javax.management.remote.JMXConnectorFactory;
import javax.management.remote.JMXServiceURL;


/**
 * Simple code example on how to execute
 * ctrl-break handlers remotely.
 *
 * Usage:
 * RemoteJRCMD -host -port -user -pass -command []
 *
 * All arguments are optional. If no command is
 * specified, all performance counters and their
 * current values are listed.
 *
 * @author Marcus Hirt
 */
public final class RemoteJRCMD {
  private final static String KEY_CREDENTIALS =
    "jmx.remote.credentials";
  private final static String JROCKIT_PERFCOUNTER_MBEAN_NAME =
    "oracle.jrockit.management:type=PerfCounters";
  private final static String JROCKIT_CONSOLE_MBEAN_NAME =
    "oracle.jrockit.management:type=JRockitConsole";
  private final static String[] SIGNATURE =
    new String[] {"java.lang.String"};
  private final static String DIAGNOSTIC_COMMAND_MBEAN_NAME =
    "oracle.jrockit.management:type=DiagnosticCommand";

  public static void main(String[] args)
    throws Exception {
      HashMap<String, String> commandMap =
        parseArguments(args);
      executeCommand(
        commandMap.get("-host"),
        Integer.parseInt(commandMap.get("-port")),
        commandMap.get("-user"),
        commandMap.get("-password"),
        commandMap.get("-command"));
  }
```

```java
private static HashMap<String, String> parseArguments(
  String[] args) {
    HashMap<String, String> commandMap =
      new HashMap<String, String>();
    commandMap.put("-host", "localhost");
    commandMap.put("-port", "7091");
    for (int i = 0; i < args.length; i++) {
      if (args[i].startsWith("-")) {
        StringBuilder buf = new StringBuilder();
        int j = i + 1;
        while (j < args.length && !args[j].startsWith("-")) {
          buf.append(" ");
          buf.append(args[j++]);
        }
        commandMap.put(args[i], buf.toString().trim());
        i = j - 1;
      }
    }
    return commandMap;
}


@SuppressWarnings("unchecked")
public static void executeCommand(
  String host, int port, String user,
  String password, String command)
  throws Exception {
    MBeanServerConnection server = null;
    JMXConnector jmxc = null;
    Map<String, Object> map = null;
    if (user != null || password != null) {
      map = new HashMap<String, Object>();
      final String[] credentials = new String[2];
      credentials[0] = user;
      credentials[1] = password;
      map.put(KEY_CREDENTIALS, credentials);
    }
    // Use same convention as Sun. localhost:0 means
    // "VM, monitor thyself!"
    if (host.equals("localhost") && port == 0) {
      server = ManagementFactory.getPlatformMBeanServer();
    } else {
      jmxc = JMXConnectorFactory.newJMXConnector(
        createConnectionURL(host, port), map);
      jmxc.connect();
```

```
    server = jmxc.getMBeanServerConnection();
}


System.out.println("Connected to " + host+ ":" + port);

try {
  server.getMBeanInfo(new ObjectName(
    JROCKIT_CONSOLE_MBEAN_NAME));
} catch (InstanceNotFoundException e1) {
    server.createMBean(
      "oracle.jrockit.management.JRockitConsole", null);
}

if (command == null) {
  ObjectName perfCounterObjectName = new ObjectName(
    JROCKIT_PERFCOUNTER_MBEAN_NAME);
  System.out.println("Listing all counters...");
  MBeanAttributeInfo[] attributes = server.getMBeanInfo(
    perfCounterObjectName).getAttributes();
  System.out.println("Counter\tValue\n=======\t====");

  String[] attributeNames = new String[attributes.length];
  for (int i = 0; i < attributes.length; i++) {
    attributeNames[i] = attributes[i].getName();
  }
  Iterator valueIter = server.getAttributes(
    perfCounterObjectName,
    attributeNames).iterator();
  while (valueIter.hasNext()) {
    Attribute attr = (Attribute) valueIter.next();
    System.out.println(attr.getName() + "\t=\t"
      + attr.getValue());
  }
} else {
  System.out.println("Invoking the ctrl-break command '"
    + command + "'...");
  ObjectName consoleObjectName = new ObjectName(
  DIAGNOSTIC_COMMAND_MBEAN_NAME);
  Object[] params = new Object[1];
  params[0] = command;
  System.out.println("The CtrlBreakCommand returned: \n"
    + server.invoke(consoleObjectName,
```

```
        "execute", params,
        SIGNATURE));
    }

    if (jmxc != null) {
      jmxc.close();
    }
  }

  private static JMXServiceURL createConnectionURL(
    String host, int port)
    throws MalformedURLException {
      return new JMXServiceURL("rmi", "", 0,
        "/jndi/rmi://" + host + ":"
        + port + "/jmxrmi");
    }
  }
```

The command uses the following syntax:

```
java RemoteJRCMD -command <command string> -host <host>
  -port <port>
```

Where:

- `<command string>` is the diagnostic command as you would write it using JRCMD, for example `"start_flightrecording name=MyRecording duration=30s"`.

- `<host>` is the name of the host where the JVM that we want to connect to is running, for instance `localhost`.

- `<port>` is the port number on the JRockit machine where the remote JMX agent (the RMI Registry) is listening. See the section *Starting JRockit for remote management* in *Chapter 6, JRockit Mission Control*. The default port is `7091`.

The following command-line example would list all the performance counters and their values on `localhost` using the default port (`7091`):

`java RemoteJRCMD`

The following command-line example would list all available commands on a JRockit running on the host `bitsy`, using port `4711`:

`java RemoteJRCMD -command help -host bitsy -port 4711`

The following command-line example would start a 30 second flight recording on a JRockit running on `localhost` on the default port (`7091`), writing the resulting recording to the designated file:

```
java RemoteJRCMD -command start_flightrecording
  name=myrecording filename=c:\tmp\myrecording.jfr
  duration=30s
```

Summary

In this chapter, two of the JRockit internal management APIs were described. Both APIs grant access to internal JRockit functionality, such as performance metrics. They also make it possible to programmatically manipulate a running JRockit JVM.

JMAPI is a local Java API that was fully supported in JRockit versions prior to R28. Parts of JMAPI was deprecated in R28, and the future of JMAPI is undecided at the time of this writing.

JMXMAPI is an unsupported JMX-based API consisting of several MBeans deployed in the platform MBean server. As the API is JMX-based, standard JMX mechanisms can be used to allow remote access.

Even though the APIs are currently (mostly) unsupported, there are situations where they can be quite useful. An example implementing a remote version of JRCMD was demonstrated.

13
JRockit Virtual Edition

Virtualization, the practice of running software on emulated hardware, has emerged rapidly as an important concept in the last few years. The main benefits of virtualization are that hardware resource utilization can be maximized and that resource management is made simpler. However, as virtualization is yet another abstraction layer between the application and the actual hardware, it may also introduce extra overhead.

This chapter deals with the product JRockit Virtual Edition; a new piece of technology that is part of the JRockit product family. Throughout this chapter, the terms JRockit Virtual Edition and the short form JRockit VE are used interchangeably.

JRockit VE enables the user to run Java in a virtualized environment *without an operating system*, removing large amounts of the overhead typically associated with virtualization. JRockit VE is a separate product that contains the minimum components necessary to run a Java application in a virtualized environment—a small lightweight OS-like kernel and a JRockit JRE.

JRockit VE can run any Java application, but initially, the most likely way in which users will encounter JRockit VE is as part of the **WebLogic Server on JRockit Virtual Edition** product (WLS on JRockit VE). WLS on JRockit VE is basically a prepackaged instance of a WebLogic Server installation, in **virtual machine image** form. A virtual machine image is a binary image that contains a virtual machine configuration, software, and a file system. The image is intended for deployment on a specific virtualization platform, such as Oracle VM Server.

This chapter, being a technical introduction to JRockit VE, concentrates on the virtualization layer and the technology behind the JRockit VE product. It will not discuss specific software stacks built on top of JRockit VE.

As this is a chapter about recently productized or emerging technology, details, names, concepts, and implementations can be counted on to change more rapidly than technology covered in other chapters of this book. The chapter may also contain forward-looking statements that will not be implemented. The fundamental concepts, however, remain the same. Online documentation should always be consulted for the freshest information on any product.

From this chapter you will learn:

- About virtualization as a concept and some common terms used for different kinds of virtualization.

- What a hypervisor is, the different types of hypervisors, and the most important hypervisors in the market today.

- The advantages and disadvantages of virtualizing a software stack and how to get the most out of the advantages.

- About specific issues with virtualizing Java and how the JRockit Virtual Edition product simplifies the virtualization process and enhances performance.

- About the concept of virtual machine images.

- What the future has in store—can virtualization overhead be reduced further or even removed, making virtualization an even more powerful tool? Can a virtualized application even run faster than on physical hardware, given the right environment?

Introduction to virtualization

Virtualization is a word that has been used in many contexts over the years. However, it always concerns abstracting a physical resource as a virtual one. It is not a new concept. **Virtual memory** on a per-process basis is the main schoolbook example, present in all operating systems. Partitions on a single hard drive that each look like separate physical drives to an operating system are also technically virtualization. But the buzz the last few years has been about virtualizing *everything* in a physical machine. This is not a new concept either, it goes back at least as far as to IBM in the 1960s. Not until recently, however, has virtualization proven itself as a way to increase resource utilization and manageability in the server room.

Virtualization, for the purposes of this book, is the practice of running a platform (such as an operating system) or an individual application on **virtual hardware**, emulated in software. The virtual hardware typically looks like actual physical hardware to the running platform or application. An entity deployed on a virtual system is often referred to as a **guest**. The piece of software that enables multiple guests, for example operating systems, to run on a single system is called a **hypervisor**. A hypervisor can help the guest by, for example, supplying device drivers that are tailored to run in a virtualized environment and thus improve performance for the guest.

 What actually hides behind the physical hardware camouflage varies, depending on the type of resource being virtualized. For example, what looks like a physical hard drive is typically a file, or collection of files on a server somewhere. What looks like four available physical CPUs is actually an amount of timeshare on an unknown number of existing CPUs. What looks like 1 GB of memory is actually the claim to part of a larger amount of physical memory. Some hypervisors even allow the guests to **overcommit** memory within their limited allocation space. But to the guest this does not matter, it only sees what it believes to be physical hardware (with some exceptions).

Virtualization is becoming increasingly important, mainly because it makes it possible to use existing physical machines more efficiently. If the CPU on a physical machine is idle, for example while waiting for I/O, those CPU cycles that could have been used for execution are wasted in the idle time. Multiplexing several guests on the same hardware makes it possible for those idle CPU cycles to be used for other guests until the I/O request returns. Naturally, when several guests (for example operating systems) run at the same time, another performance penalty may result from additional context switching. However, it is an undeniable fact that virtualization makes more efficient use of the available hardware. This is attractive also from the power consumption angle, in a world that is becoming increasingly environmentally conscious.

Virtualization falls into several categories, mostly having to do with the layer of exposure to the underlying platform. While there is some confusion in terminology here, let us start by introducing some common concepts and explain how they will be used in this book. Virtualization is a complex area—the following is a simplified version of the world.

Full virtualization

Full virtualization means that all sensitive functionality of an underlying platform is emulated by the hypervisor—for example device interaction and memory mapping. This makes it possible to deploy any *unmodified* software as a guest, the guest believing that it is actually executing on physical hardware.

This is implemented on a platform that lacks explicit hardware support for virtualization, by letting the hypervisor trap sensitive (privileged) instructions executed by the guest and emulate them in a sandboxed environment.

Full virtualization can also be hardware-assisted, for example the Intel VT or AMD-V technologies have CPU-specific support for running several operating systems at once. Hardware-supported virtualization dramatically reduces the emulation overhead in a hypervisor. Lately, other pieces of hardware than the CPU have also been equipped with virtualization support. One example would be network cards with built-in hardware support for virtualization.

Large performance benefits to virtualization have been achieved with hardware support. This seems to indicate that full virtualization is rapidly becoming the main virtualization paradigm in the market.

Paravirtualization

Paravirtualization is used to refer to a virtualized environment where the guest needs to know about the underlying hypervisor. Typically, in a paravirtualized environment, privileged actions need to be explicitly requested by the guest through calls to a public hypervisor API. This means that the guest has to communicate with a lower abstraction layer and consequently needs to know that it is virtualized.

Paravirtualization removes some of the flexibility of virtualization, as the guest (for example an operating system) needs to be modified before virtual deployment. An advantage might be that unnecessary layers of abstraction can be scaled away, enabling additional performance improvements at the price of less flexibility. Also, the end user rarely has to worry about the implementation of the underlying hypervisor. For example, on Xen, which originally was a paravirtualization-only hypervisor, the main use case is to run pre-packaged operating systems that have already been modified for paravirtualization. The user typically deploys his application on top of these.

With the emergence of high-performance hardware support for full virtualization, it is the authors' opinion that paravirtualization is becoming less important.

Other virtualization keywords

There are several other keywords in the virtualization area that have many different meanings, for example **partial virtualization**. Partial virtualization and paravirtualization are sometimes used interchangeably, but partial virtualization may also mean virtualizing only specific parts of the underlying hardware. For example, the term has been used to describe binary translation tools such as Rosetta on the Macintosh, enabling software compiled for PowerPC to run on Intel hardware. Partial virtualization may or may not require hardware support. Concepts like virtual memory in an operating system can also fall under the category partial virtualization.

Operating system level virtualization is another term that pops up from time to time. This typically describes some kind of isolation mechanism built into an OS for dividing the OS into separate instances, protected from one another, making them look like they are running on different physical machines. Solaris Containers is probably the most well-known example.

Hypervisors

Recall that the hypervisor is the software layer that makes virtualization possible (optionally with the aid of explicit hardware support). The hypervisor provides an idealized view of a physical machine. All "dangerous operations" that would break the abstraction, such as device interaction and memory mapping, are trapped and emulated by the hypervisor.

Just as there are different types of virtualization, there are different types of hypervisors. Again, terminology is rather complicated. For the purposes of this book, we will discriminate only between **hosted hypervisors** and **native hypervisors**.

Hosted hypervisors

A hosted hypervisor typically runs as a standard process in an ordinary operating system. As mentioned earlier, sensitive (kernel mode) operations performed by the guest are typically emulated or JIT-interpreted by the hypervisor. User mode operations can often execute directly as part of the hosted hypervisor process, but may also be emulated or JIT-interpreted when applicable.

The main advantage with a hosted hypervisor is that it is typically very easy to install and use—just another application in your operating system. Usually, the performance of a hosted hypervisor is not up to server-side requirements, but this is not its main purpose.

Real world example—large parts of this book were developed and written on a Macintosh, where no JRockit version currently exists. For the purpose of producing JRockit examples, the author has used the hosted hypervisor VMware Fusion to run a Linux version of JRockit on his home computer.

VMware Player is an example of a simple hosted hypervisor. Oracle VirtualBox is another.

Native hypervisors

A native hypervisor requires no host operating system. It can be installed directly on physical hardware out of the box. Hardware device drivers can be provided by the hypervisor, either in a special virtual machine for isolation (for example in Oracle VM- and Xen-based solutions) or as part of the hypervisor itself (for example in VMware ESX).

Typically, a native hypervisor is much more efficient than a hosted hypervisor.

Oracle VM and the VMware ESX product suite are two examples of native hypervisors, who, although their approaches to virtualization are different, both fulfill the criterion that they install directly on physical hardware.

Hypervisors in the market

There are several mature hypervisors available in the quickly-changing market.

Xen is an open source hypervisor, originally developed at the University of Cambridge. Xen later turned into the company XenSource Inc., and was acquired by Citrix Corporation in 2007. Citrix release their own commercial server-grade Xen systems with extra APIs, along with several management tools. The Xen hypervisor itself continues to be available for free, under public open source license.

Xen has, because of its free nature, been widely used in several virtualization frameworks, and has been turned into native hypervisors, Oracle VM being one of them. Oracle VM is an Oracle Enterprise Linux-based operating system with Xen at the bottom, and a native hypervisor.

Xen was originally a paravirtualized solution. In other words, it required that the guests know that they are virtualized so that they can interact with the hypervisor. For example, Linux kernels that should run on paravirtualized Xen need to be specially compiled. The trend lately, however, seems to be that Xen is moving away from the paravirtualized metaphor towards an environment with support for unmodified guests. This requires hardware virtualization support.

VMware corporation, one of the first players in the virtualization field, has several virtualization products, both native and hosted hypervisors. Most notable are VMware Workstation (VMware Fusion on Macintosh), VMware ESX and VMware ESXi. These are commercial products. VMware also makes a stripped-down version of VMware Workstation available for free, called VMware Player that does not provide support for creating and configuring your own virtual machines, but allows you to run an existing virtual guest. VMware also has a hosted virtualization platform called VMware Server. It is available for free.

Microsoft corporation has developed the **Hyper-V virtualization framework**, designed to work with Windows Server that is already a widely adopted technology. Hyper-V requires hardware virtualization support.

KVM (Kernel-based Virtual Machine) is an open source hypervisor project, licensed under the GNU Public License, driven by RedHat.

Parallels Inc. produces desktop and server virtualization software for Macintosh, Windows, and Linux.

Also worth mentioning is **VirtualBox**, an independent virtualization package containing its own hypervisor. It is targeted at desktop, server, and embedded use. VirtualBox was originally developed by the German company Innotek, who were acquired by Sun Microsystems, who in turn are now part of Oracle Corporation.

Advantages of virtualization

The main advantage of virtualization is, as we have mentioned, more efficient resource utilization. Several guests can compete for all resources of one physical machine. When one guest is idle, another guest may run. Virtualization may substantially decrease the idle time in the server room.

Another advantage is that virtualization further enables the "cloud computing" metaphor. As virtualized guests may be suspended, migrated to other physical machines, and resumed, an entire machine park can be abstracted as a **cloud** of computational power, on which deployments of applications may be made. This is usually facilitated through different management frameworks.

Another, somewhat overlooked, but very important application for virtualization is keeping legacy applications alive. A common nightmare in IT is having to retire old hardware on which legacy applications with no forward compatibility are hosted. This requires porting the applications to new platforms, either requiring complete rewrites or ending up with Frankenstein-type solutions such as COBOL to (unreadable) Java converters. Virtualizing the old hardware instead will make it possible to continue running the legacy application for some time, while figuring out how to replace it in a less stressful manner.

Disadvantages of virtualization

The main problem with virtualization is, of course, the extra overhead introduced by another abstraction layer, the hypervisor, in the stack between application and hardware. While hardware resource usage indeed gets more optimal in a virtualized environment, there are costs associated both with running several guests at once on a piece of physical hardware as well as with the extra overhead incurred by the hypervisor abstraction layer.

Now consider the case of a Java application in a virtual environment. For a standard, non-virtualized local Java application, the JVM provides one layer of abstraction against the hardware. The operating system on which the JVM runs provides another. The hypervisor layer that is responsible for emulating the virtual hardware below the OS adds yet another zone of abstraction between the application and its actual execution as native code.

We can try to make each layer of abstraction as thin and efficient as possible, but we can't make them go away altogether. For example, using hardware support to implement the hypervisor will decrease the virtualization overhead. However, we are still dealing with emulating physical hardware for the virtualized application. This naturally incurs overhead anyway.

Virtualizing Java

Let us now discuss the implications of running an industrial strength Java application server in a virtualized environment. Consider the following figure that illustrates the entire stack from the application server down to the hardware. Between the Java application and the hardware on which it ultimately executes, we have a JVM, a general purpose OS (for example Oracle Enterprise Linux), and a Hypervisor (such as Oracle VM).

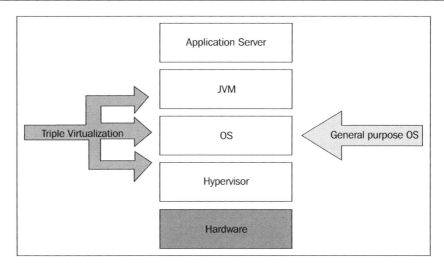

The application server, for example Oracle WebLogic, is a typical Java application that needs a JVM to execute. The JVM provides abstraction against the operating system on which the application server is deployed. This is obviously because the same WebLogic shipment should run equally as well on Linux as on Windows or Solaris—this is the whole point of Java. The price of the convenience of write once / run anywhere is thus paid for by the JVM abstraction layer.

Under the JVM is an operating system that the JVM must know how to interact with. This requires multiple JVM back-ends for multiple operating systems. For example, on *NIX-style operating systems, pages in memory are allocated differently than on Microsoft Windows, with different system calls (`mmap` versus `VirtualAlloc`). The thread API typically also differs between operating systems (POSIX threads versus Windows threads). Thus, the JVM needs OS-specific modules in order to facilitate the execution of the same Java application on different operating systems. Consequently, the operating system itself forms another abstraction layer under the virtual machine.

So, what is the role of a general purpose operating system? The OS abstracts the hardware, making it easier to interact with it programmatically. We can hardly expect a C++ application developer to implement his own synchronization for a particular chipset using atomic assembly instructions or to write his own thread representation. Instead, the OS provides library calls for these kinds of tasks. Thus, the OS forms a second level of abstraction under the JVM.

And finally, in a virtualized world, the hypervisor—while making it possible to run multiple sandboxed operating systems on the same machine—forms a third abstraction layer before we get to the actual hardware.

All these abstraction layers need to communicate with each other. There is overhead here, especially as talking to a lower layer usually requires some kind of privileged action that takes time, destroys caches, and preempts other tasks.

However, if the sole responsibility of the virtualized operating system is to run the JVM, whose sole responsibility in turn is to run the Java application server, don't the various levels of abstraction seem unnecessary and quite wasteful? Why would we need a full-fledged OS such as Microsoft Windows in the middle of our stack, when all we do is run a Java program? The Java program, assuming that it is 100 percent pure Java, doesn't know anything about Microsoft Windows and doesn't use any OS-specific mechanisms. If the Java program is an application server with no GUI, do we even need the functionality to display graphics on screen? If all users and access controls necessary to interact with the system are handled by a model inside the application server, do we even need an OS?

We can make the observation that a JVM is not so far removed from an OS as one might think. It implements JDK library calls to support threads and synchronization. It handles memory management and so on. Without stretching the metaphor too tightly, a JVM is just like a special-purpose virtual operating system.

Maybe a direct-to-hypervisor JVM isn't such a bad idea?

Introducing JRockit Virtual Edition

The case can be made that if there was a way to reap the benefits of virtualized Java without the overhead, much would be gained. If the layers between Java and hardware are kept small enough, there is not just performance to be had, but also the added benefit of simplicity and security. The solution proposed by the JRockit architects is the product JRockit Virtual Edition, or JRockit VE for short.

As a proof of concept back in 2005, we wrote a linker that told us what symbols a JVM deprived of its operating system was missing. The discovery that the list was really quite short was the start of the JRockit VE project.

JRockit VE consists of the JRockit JRE, a collection of pure Java services (for example an SSH daemon), and finally a thin OS-like layer that runs on top of the hypervisor. This layer provides all of the very limited amount of OS functionality that a JVM needs. It is known as the **JRockit VE kernel**.

JRockit VE is currently available only on x86 platforms.

The commercial versions of the JRockit VE virtualization framework currently only ship with support for running on top of the Oracle VM native hypervisor (and consequently on top of Xen). JRockit VE may, however, also support other hypervisors in the future.

It has always been our design philosophy, as it should be in a virtualization stack, that the target platform for the JRockit VE kernel is *hardware* and not a hypervisor. The JRockit VE kernel with a small built-in E1000 network driver can boot from a USB stick and run Java applications on any x86 machine out of the box (It is doubtful, however, why this demo, except for the fact that it is really cool, would illustrate any benefits of JRockit VE in cloud computing, but we'll get to that).

JRockit VE also comes with a tool for creating and manipulating Java applications that are to run in a virtualized environment, the **Image Tool**. When a Java application is virtualized and packaged for use with JRockit VE, it is referred to as a **virtual machine image**.

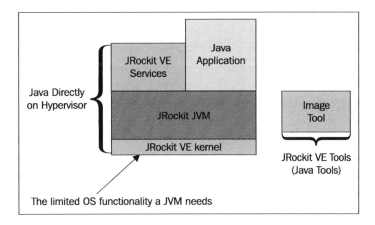

The previous figure illustrates the stack, as it looks for a Java application deployed on JRockit VE. Services like SSH run in Java land, along with the Java application. The JRockit JVM sits on top of the JRockit VE kernel layer that provides all OS functionality needed by the JVM.

Let us now look closely at the **JRockit VE kernel** to understand both why implementing it is a much smaller undertaking than writing a complete OS, and what functionality we need to make available to the layers above.

The JRockit VE kernel

JRockit Virtual Edition removes the need for an OS under the JVM and makes it possible to run Java directly on top of a hypervisor. Currently, an unmodified Linux version of the JRockit JVM can run directly on top of the JRockit VE kernel. This is, however, expected to change for future releases and the JRockit VE kernel is expected to turn into its own JVM platform, requiring a special version of the JVM. This is to further decrease the number of abstraction layers in the stack and to provide additional simplicity of implementation. The only reason that the JRockit VE kernel currently emulates a Linux API upwards has been the lack of development time to create an additional platform for the JRockit JVM.

 The fact that the JRockit JVM currently is a Linux distribution does not impact performance negatively or constrain it to Java-on-Linux levels. The JRockit VE kernel can do plenty with the OS layer to provide a much more ideal execution environment for the Linux JVM. With a specialized JVM, performance will improve even further.

The JRockit VE kernel is conceptually very much like an OS, but far from the real deal. It contains its own thread implementation, scheduler, support for file systems, memory allocation mechanisms, and so on, but is vastly less complex than an operating system.

For one thing, the JRockit VE kernel can run only one process—the JRockit JVM. Also, as a JVM is an inherently secure sandboxed execution environment, we do not need to worry about malicious Java code causing, for example, deliberate buffer overruns. Bytecode verification and all other security aspects of validating executing Java code is handled for us by the JVM already.

An important constraint here is that JRockit VE needs to disallow the execution of arbitrary native code, as there is no way to determine what it does. This is both a functionality and a security concern. Native code can contain operating system calls that only work on a standard operating system and it may also perform any, potentially insecure, task. Disallowing native code, however, tends to be a small price to pay in a modern Java-based server environment. Therefore, JNI is not supported on JRockit VE.

Another example of the limited functionality is the lack of advanced paging mechanisms that would be present in any general purpose OS. The JRockit VE kernel runs just one process and needs just one virtual address space.

The following figure illustrates the various modules in the JRockit VE kernel. They include, among other things, file system implementations, device driver stubs that communicate with the hypervisor, block cache mechanisms, a self-contained network stack, simple memory management systems, and a thread scheduler.

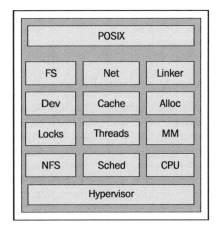

The JRockit VE kernel, in its exposed APIs is very *NIX-like. As stated, a distribution of JRockit for Linux can run unmodified on top of the JRockit VE kernel, but this only means that the very limited amount of Linux APIs that JRockit needs have been implemented in the kernel, not that the kernel is Linux-compatible in any way. Typically, the APIs available to the JVM look like POSIX system calls, but have less generic functionality. Given that future JRockit versions become JRockit VE aware, we could avoid most kludges caused by pretending to be Linux. One example of this would be not having to emulate parts of /proc file system in the kernel, as this is the way JRockit on Linux collects information on memory layout. We would also like to remove some OS calls, such as mmap, that look like POSIX calls in JRockit VE, but are not. The standard POSIX version of mmap is very complex, but in JRockit VE only the specific use cases that JRockit for Linux needs have to be implemented. Porting JRockit to an explicit JRockit VE platform would not be too complex an undertaking as all operating system calls in the JVM already exist in a well-defined platform abstraction layer.

In conclusion, it is important not to be taken aback by thinking about the concept of the JRockit VE kernel as a small lightweight OS. It is much less than that and large parts of the complexities required for an operating system are not needed in our kernel. The need to implement and maintain a set of device drivers, in operating systems such as Linux, which is a much larger task than maintaining the actual kernel code, is made unnecessary as JRockit VE requires a hypervisor to run on. The hypervisor will take care of device drivers where necessary and abstract physical hardware for us. The complete JRockit VE kernel module is only around 130,000 lines of C code, large parts making up the network stack.

The virtual machine image concept and management frameworks

The "virtual cloud" is a hot buzzword right now. It is a fairly simple concept to understand — a vast blob of Internet-connected computing resources that can be harnessed without the need to care about individual configurations and individual machines.

A Java application installed on a physical machine is also a well-known concept.

Most cloud solutions today use some kind of **management framework** that handles application deployments in the cloud, removing the need for individual machines through abstraction, which makes plenty of sense — "the cloud is the computer". Typically, management frameworks are used to deploy entire self-contained guest operating systems, for example virtual Linux distributions, in a server cloud.

 A concrete example of a management framework in cloud computing is the Oracle VM Manager software that is part of the Oracle VM native hypervisor. Oracle VM Manager allows the administrator to configure and group clusters of servers in the cloud and deploy virtual machine images on them.

JRockit Virtual Edition originally started out with an ambition to look like "local Java". This meant starting the virtual application and deploying it in the cloud with command line on a local machine. On the local machine, it would look like the virtual application was executing locally, instead of remotely. This was accomplished by, among other things, feeding back JVM console output to the local console. It turned out that this was a very complicated concept to understand and it also led to some degree of confusion: where is an application actually running?

After alpha releases, and user testing, the JRockit VE team decided to go the other way instead — local Java applications should be turned into **virtual machine images.** These are binary blobs ready for cloud deployment through existing management frameworks like Oracle VM Manager. Controlling the virtual machine image, such as changing its virtual hardware layout and migrating it across server pools, are examples of functionality provided already by the management framework.

Virtual machine images, in the general case, can contain any machine configuration with any operating system. A JRockit VE virtual machine image consists of a complete virtual machine specification and setup for a Java application along with a file system containing said Java application.

We can think of distributing a virtual machine image containing, for example, WebLogic Server to a customer, as shipping the customer a physical machine. On its hard disk is a preinstalled version of WebLogic Server good to go, and all the user needs to do is plug the machine into a power outlet, attach a network cable, and start it up. The main difference in the case of the virtual machine image is that we don't ship the physical machine along with the installed software. We only ship the *specification* of the machine—how much memory does it have, how many CPUs—and a cloned image of its hard disk. The cloud will provide the resources necessary for emulating the machine in order to run the application. This is what virtualization is all about.

Thus, virtual machine images also remove the need for installing software. Preinstalled software in virtual machines can be deployed directly. This is one of the reasons that virtualization can help reduce IT costs in an organization.

A virtual machine image can be generated from scratch, or **assembled**, by applying the Image Tool that ships with JRockit VE to a locally installed application. Instances of this image can then be deployed directly into your server cloud. We call this the "physical to virtual" use case. Another use case, however, is for the customer to run software that is shipped in the form of an already assembled virtual machine image (for example WLS on JRockit VE), available from an OEM or software vendor, and not create images of his own.

Many aspects of the machine specification for an existing virtual machine image, for example the amount of memory available to the virtual machine, can be manipulated offline with the JRockit VE Image Tool as well as from the management framework. The virtual machine environment for the virtualized application can vary from being very simple to very complex.

A JRockit VE virtual machine image with a minimum configuration can simply be auto-generated. Typically, the Image Tool only needs to know things like disk size, number of CPUs, and amount of memory in the virtual machine. The JRockit VE kernel requires at least one network interface to work. When booting, the kernel will try to use the DHCP protocol, if available, to configure networking. This makes setup very simple and portable. If DHCP is unavailable on your network, explicit configuration of the virtual network cards needs to be done.

The local file system in the virtual machine image is part of the generated disk image and available to the virtualized Java application once it runs.

The following example shows a very simple, but fully sufficient, configuration file for a JRockit VE virtual machine specification. It describes a virtual machine image that executes a `HelloWorld` Java program. The virtual machine image can be created using the Image Tool. Similar configuration files can be obtained by querying an existing virtual machine image for its specification.

The JRockit VE config file format is totally hypervisor agnostic.

```xml
<?xml version="1.0" encoding="UTF-8"?>

<!-- helloworld.xml -->
<jrockitve-imagetool-config xmlns:xsi="http://
  www.w3.org/2001/XMLSchema-instance"xsi:noNamespaceSchemaLocation=
  "jrockitve-imagetool-config.xsd" version="5.1">
  <jrockitve-config memory="512 MB" cpus="1">
    <storage>
      <disks>
        <disk id="root" size="256 MB"/>
      </disks>
      <mounts>
        <mount>
          <mount-point>/</mount-point>
          <disk>root</disk>
        </mount>
      </mounts>
    </storage>
    <vm-name>helloworld-vm</vm-name>
    <java-arguments>-Xmx256M HelloWorld</java-arguments>
    <network>
      <nics>
        <nic/>
      </nics>
    </network>
  </jrockitve-config>
  <jrockitve-filesystem-imports>
    <copy from="~/myLocalApp/HelloWorld/*" to="/"/>
  </jrockitve-filesystem-imports>
</jrockitve-imagetool-config>
```

The configuration describes a machine with 512 MB of RAM and one CPU. The machine contains one hard drive that is 256 MB in size. The virtual machine, once the image is deployed, will show up as `helloworld-vm` in various management frameworks. At boot time, the JRockit VE kernel will invoke JRockit. JRockit then executes the `HelloWorld` program, whose `.class` file (and possibly other resources) are placed in the root directory of the hard drive in the virtual machine. The virtual machine contains one network card (NIC). As no explicit configuration other than that which exists is given, the JRockit VE kernel will use DHCP to establish things like the IP address for the virtual machine when it boots.

Following are a few command-line examples, illustrating using the Image Tool to assemble a virtual machine image and to modify it before deployment. The default behavior is to create a standard Xen or Oracle VM configuration, consisting of a hypervisor-specific vm.cfg file and a system image, system.img, with the virtual hard drive containing the Java application, the JRockit JRE, and the JRockit VE kernel. The following example creates a virtual machine image from the previous specification:

```
hastur:marcus$ java -jar jrockitve-imagetool.jar


Usage: java -jar jrockitve-imagetool.jar [options]


-h,  --help                 [<option_name>]
-c,  --create-config        [<config_file.xml>] [<vm_name>]
     --create-full-config   [<config_file.xml>] [<vm_name>]
-r,  --reconfigure          <vm_cfg> <op> <field> [<parameter>]*
     --reconfigure-service  <vm_cfg> <service-name>
       <op> <field> [<parameter>]*
-f,  --file                 <vm_cfg> <operation> [<parameter>]*
     --get-log              <vm_cfg> [<output file>]
     --repair               <vm_cfg> [<auto|prompt|check>]
-p,  --patch                <vm_cfg> <patch_file>
-a,  --assemble             <config.xml> <output_dir> [<hypervisor>]
-d,  --disassemble          <vm_cfg> <output_dir>
-v,  --version              [<vm_cfg>|<jrockitve_image>]
-l,  --log (#)              <quiet|brief|verbose|debug>
     --force (#)


Options marked "#" are not standalone.
  They must be used together with other options


hastur:marcus$ java -jar jrockitve-imagetool.jar
  --assemble helloworld.xml /tmp/outputdir


Assembling the image...
```

```
|                              |
. . . . . . . . . . . . . . . . . . . . . . . . . .
Wrote 127 MB
Done


hastur:marcus$ ls -lart /tmp/outputdir/


total 327688
drwxrwxrwt  18 root          612         Aug 29 11:09
-rw-r--r--   1 marcus        270         Aug 29 11:10 vm.cfg
-rw-r--r--   1 marcus        268435456   Aug 29 11:10 system.img
drwxr-xr-x   4 marcus        136         Aug 29 11:10


hastur:marcus$ java -jar jrockitve-imagetool.jar
  --reconfigure /tmp/outputdir/vm.cfg get java-arguments


-Xmx256M HelloWorld


hastur:marcus$ cat /tmp/outputdir/vm.cfg


# OracleVM config file for 'helloworld-vm'.
# Can be used with 'xm <start|create> [-c] vm.cfg'
#
# note that Xen requires an absolute path to the image!


name="helloworld-vm"
bootloader="/usr/bin/pygrub"
memory=512
disk=['tap:aio:/OVS/seed_pool/helloworld-vm/system.img,sda1,w']
vif=['']
on_crash="coredump-destroy"
```

Given an assembled virtual machine image, we can use the JRockit VE Image Tool to query and reconfigure its virtual machine specification. In the following example, we retrieve and change the number of virtual CPUs that should be available in the virtual machine. This will cause changes to the underlying hypervisor specific config file and possibly to the contents of the image (in our example system.img). An assembled image is always uniquely identified by its hypervisor specific config file (in our case vm.cfg for Oracle VM or Xen).

```
hastur:marcus$ java -jar jrockitve-imagetool.jar
  --reconfigure /tmp/outputdir/vm.cfg get cpus


1


hastur:marcus$ java -jar jrockitve-imagetool.jar
  --reconfigure /tmp/outputdir/vm.cfg set cpus 4


Done


hastur:marcus$ cat /tmp/outputdir/vm.cfg


# OracleVM config file for 'helloworld-vm'.
# Can be used with 'xm <start|create> [-c] vm.cfg'
#
# note that Xen requires an absolute path to the image!


name="helloworld-vm"
bootloader="/usr/bin/pygrub"
memory=512
disk=['tap:aio:/OVS/seed_pool/helloworld-vm/system.img,sda1,w']
vif=['']
vcpus=4     #<--- we now have 4 virtual CPUs
on_crash="coredump-destroy"
```

 An assembled virtual machine image can also be reduced to its component parts and **disassembled** by the Image Tool, but this use case (virtual to physical), exactly like the assembly use case (physical to virtual), is not the only one available to end customers. We also assume that end customers, to some extent, will work with prepackaged virtual machine images that can be reconfigured and manipulated with the Image Tool.

Aside from manipulating a virtual machine image, the Image Tool can also be used to **patch** an image, with bugfixes or upgrades to the software within, such as the JRockit VE kernel or WebLogic Server. Thus, a pre-packaged virtual machine image can be upgraded by vendor fixes without the need for taking it apart.

The Image Tool can also be used for a number of other common offline manipulation tasks such as extracting log file information from the virtual application or enabling services such as SSH that come pre-installed in every JRockit VE image. Even though the patch framework fully supports patch version control and rollbacks, an implicit safety mechanism in patching machine images is apparent given that an image is just a couple of files on disk: backing up the image is just a matter of copying the files somewhere. Should anything go wrong, they can be easily restored.

Following is another example of querying a JRockit VE virtual machine image for its installed services and enabling one of them—the previously mentioned SSH daemon:

```
hastur:marcus$ java -jar jrockitve-imagetool.jar -r
  /tmp/outputdir/vm.cfg get installed-services

sshd (An SSH2 implementation with SCP and SFTP support)
jmxstat (JRockitVE kernel statistics MBean)
sysstat (JRockitVE kernel sysstat statistics)

hastur:marcus$ java -jar jrockitve-imagetool.jar -r
  /tmp/outputdir/vm.cfg get enabled-services

None

hastur:marcus$ java -jar jrockitve-imagetool.jar -r
  /tmp/outputdir/vm.cfg enable service sshd

Done

hastur:marcus$ java -jar jrockitve-imagetool.jar -r
  /tmp/outputdir/vm.cfg get enabled-services

sshd (An SSH2 implementation with SCP and SFTP support)
```

When the SSH service is enabled in a running virtual machine image, the virtual machine will answer SCP and SFTP requests, given some preconfigured authentication policy.

Finally, the Image Tool can be used to manipulate the file system of a virtual machine image, for example by allowing creation and removal of files and directories. The Image Tool also supports that files from a local file system can be placed in the image and conversely, that files from the image can be copied to a local file system.

```
hastur:marcus$ java -jar jrockitve-imagetool.jar
  --file /tmp/outputdir/vm.cfg ls /
 [Feb 04  2010]                      boot/

 [Feb 04  2010]                      jrockitve/

 [Feb 04  2010]                      lost+found/

 [Feb 04 16:00        498 bytes]     HelloWorld.class

 [Feb 04 16:00        358 bytes]     VERSION


Done


hastur:marcus$ java -jar jrockitve-imagetool.jar
  --file  /tmp/outputdir/vm.cfg get HelloWorld.* /tmp


Done


hastur:marcus$ ls -l /tmp/HelloWorld*


-rw-r--r-- marcus wheel 489 Feb 14 15:36 /tmp/HelloWorld.class
```

Benefits of JRockit VE

There are several advantages to using JRockit VE as a specialized virtualization solution for Java. The main ones are:

- Performance and better resource utilization
- Simplicity
- Manageability
- Security

We will discuss them in order.

Performance and better resource utilization

Increased performance in JRockit VE stems from two general areas, the first one being (as we have already mentioned), the removal of unnecessary abstraction layers. With a specialized Java environment for virtualization, some of the "triple virtualization" caused by a combination of JVM, OS, and hypervisor is removed.

The other side to virtual Java performance with JRockit VE is even more interesting—there are several areas where being the link between the hypervisor and the JVM can provide us with information that, if correctly used, may outperform standard virtualized operating systems or even in the right environment (although it might sound too good to be true), physical hardware. We will address these intriguing issues in the section *A look ahead — can virtual be faster than real* at the end of this chapter.

Getting rid of "Triple virtualization"

In a normal operating system, certain operations, such as system calls, need to run in more privileged modes on the hardware. Modern hardware typically has some kind of **hierarchical protection domains**. All code executes in one of these domains. They go from least privileged access (userland) to most privileged (kernel). On x86 hardware, these protection domains are referred to as **rings**, and a more privileged operation is said to be running in a ring with lower ring number. **Ring 0** is the most privileged level and corresponds to kernel access. Non-trusted user code, on the other hand, must run in a less privileged ring. As soon as the user code needs to execute a privileged operation, such as a system call, the CPU needs to change rings, which is a very expensive operation, requiring synchronization and potentially destroying all caches.

As the JRockit VE kernel contains OS-like subsystems of its own and because it relies on the hypervisor for hardware interaction, there is nothing stopping it from executing mostly in **Ring 3**, userland on x86, reducing (but not altogether removing) the need for ring transitions.

Here is a hypervisor implementation detail, that may provide further insight into how protection domains work—a virtualized guest operating system on x86 typically runs its kernel operations in **Ring 1**, leaving the more privileged **Ring 0** to the hypervisor. This doesn't matter to the guest.

The following figure illustrates the execution path of a network system call in a JVM running on a normal Linux operating system compared to doing the same in the JRockit VE kernel. The dashed vertical lines are the time axes.

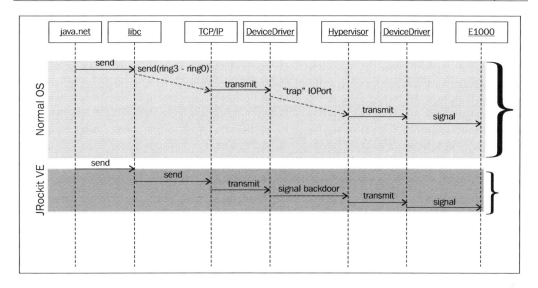

The system call starts with Java code calling a function in the `java.net` package. Control is then transferred gradually through the layers, down to the actual hardware, where the network driver executes assembly instructions. The dashed lines correspond to expensive privileged operations, such as ring changes, needing to take place. The overhead for doing the same thing in JRockit VE is vastly smaller.

Hopefully, this makes a case that virtualization overhead can be aggressively reduced if the OS is replaced with a more specialized layer. This is what gives JRockit VE a unique and attractive selling point. One of the biggest problems with implementing cloud computing, as discussed early in this chapter, is the performance loss incurred from going virtual. By replacing the operating system layer, JRockit VE can significantly reduce that overhead, when compared to traditional virtualization solutions.

Memory footprint

The JRockit VE kernel is a self-contained boot image that is just a few megabytes in size. This small amount of storage, except for a few configuration files and the JRE, is all the space in a JRockit VE-based virtual machine image not taken up by user code. A modern operating system, even a JeOS (Just enough OS) implementation, is on the order of several hundred megabytes in its simplest install.

The small size of a JRockit VE system and its kernel ensures that the amount of system memory in the virtual machine that can be used for running the actual Java application (i.e. resources available to the JVM) is maximized. This is most important on 32-bit setups, which still is a fairly common virtual machine representation in a cloud configuration.

Manageability

Manageability comes in two flavors—**offline manageability,** on the virtual machine image level, and **online manageability,** the ability to deploy and control a running virtual machine image in a cloud computing environment.

For an undeployed JRockit VE virtual machine image, all interaction with its "outside world" is handled by the Image Tool that is shipped with the JRockit VE product and its derived products, such as WLS on JRockit VE. Any aspect of a JRockit VE virtual machine image, file system, virtual machine configuration, enabled services, and so on, can be manipulated offline with the Image Tool in a hypervisor agnostic way.

The other very visible aspect of manageability is the virtual machine image concept. Given that a JRockit VE virtual machine image conforms to a known hypervisor format, it may be introduced into another resource management system, such as Oracle VM Manager.

Oracle VM Manager already exists as a product today. The typical use case is that it enables the administrator to work with several virtualized versions of Oracle Enterprise Linux. It requires little or no modification to work with other kinds of virtual appliances in virtual machine images—for example instances of WLS on JRockit VE, that are packaged on top of JRockit VE. To the management framework, one of these "WebLogic blobs" will look the same as any other virtualized guest. The ability to fit into existing virtualization management frameworks makes adoption problems for JRockit VE a non-issue. We have seamlessly removed the standard operating system layer from the virtual machine image.

Simplicity and security

It may not be a universal truth that security follows simplicity, but with JRockit VE we shall see that this is the case.

A full-fledged operating system is a complex beast. It needs to be, as it contains a jungle of system daemons and user applications such as web browsers and e-mail programs. It also has to provide a generic multi-tasking environment and enable multiple processes to co-exist. There are usually several entry points to a remote workstation running a standard OS, such as open ports for network services, login protocols, and so on.

As the kernel layer in JRockit VE provides only the bare necessities required to run a JVM, the inherent complexity of the system is orders of magnitude smaller. As mentioned, there is only one preinstalled service, sitting on top of the kernel, allowing remote access—a 100 percent pure Java SSH daemon. This service is also disabled by default. It needs to be explicitly enabled by the creator of a JRockit VE virtual machine image in order to work. With the low number of entry points from the outside world, no native code allowed, and the JVM handling verification of all potentially malicious Java code, security is by design much better than that which can be provided in a more complex environment.

Also, as previously mentioned, the "OS" itself, the JRockit VE kernel, can only run one process—the JVM. So, we have no process and resource separation problems that can make JRockit VE more insecure.

The JVM maintains the security of an executing Java application according to the Java Virtual Machine specification. Given that native code is banned, the sandboxed JVM model can fully protect us against buffer overruns and malicious code. No other memory protection is needed for the running Java program than the intrinsic one provided by the JVM. So, by excluding native code from our execution model, we get both simplicity and security at the same time.

A generic operating system also normally allows several users with different access control levels. This has to be supported down to the process and file system levels. The JRockit VE "OS" allows zero users. The only user is the implicit process owner of the JVM. Managing users is left to the Java application. The typical use case, running an application server, is ideal, as it usually contains an intrinsic implementation for user accounts and access rights. Outsourcing user access controls to the Java application server neither causes a restriction for our common use cases nor a security problem.

Configuring a generic operating system requires several utilities or configuration files. Configuring JRockit VE virtual machine images requires modifying and applying changes from just one configuration file that works auto-generated out of the box, or using an existing management framework.

Approximate number of	JRockit VE	JeOS	Linux
Config Files	1	100	1,000
Commands	10	500	3,000
Command/Kernel Params	100	10,000	50,000
Admin tools	1	200	500
Size (MB)	3(*)	200	1,000
Average ratio to JRockit VE	1	50	500

Consider the previous table that presents a very rough comparison of the complexity between a full-fledged OS (a server Linux distribution), a stripped down "Just Enough OS" Linux distribution (or JeOS), and an application running on JRockit VE. Keeping a small system secure is feasible, but it gets exponentially more difficult when size and complexity grows.

*We need to ship the JRE as well, but let us for the sake of argument consider it a userland application on the same level as the Java application. This is technically true.

Constraints and limitations of JRockit VE

The two major limitations of JRockit VE are lack of JNI support and lack of GUI.

As has been mentioned, the JRockit VE kernel supports only pure Java. This is because allowing arbitrary native code would obviously require massive security efforts and a more "complete" operating system. This is not too much of a problem, as these days most well-written Java applications for the server side are 100 percent pure Java and perform well on modern JVMs to boot. The lack of JNI support turns out to be a non-issue. While we still execute native code in the form of libraries that the JVM may need, this is native code known not to perform any dangerous or unimplemented operations.

JRockit VE can currently only export information through its console, not through a GUI. The console is limited to text output only, i.e. writes to `System.out` and `System.err`. Console output can also be redirected to log files in the local file systems or to NFS shares on the network. Applications with graphical user interfaces are consequently not supported. Again, for the server side this turns out not to be much of a problem.

A look ahead—can virtual be faster than real?

Performance potential doesn't just end with successfully removing or slimming down unnecessary layers. If we control the operating system layer and the JVM knows how to talk to it, several previously unavailable pieces of information can be propagated to the JVM, vastly extending the power of an adaptive runtime.

This section is more speculative in nature than the rest of the chapter. While not all of the techniques described herein have been proven feasible in the real world, they still form part of the basis of our belief that high performance virtualization has a bright future indeed.

Quality of hot code samples

One example of where performance potential can be had would be in the increased quality of samples for hot code. Recall from *Chapter 2, Adaptive Code Generation* that the more samples; the better the quality of code optimizations. When we run our own scheduler and completely control all threads in the system, such as is the case in the

JRockit VE kernel, the sampling overhead goes down dramatically. There is no longer a need to use expensive OS calls (and ring transitions) to halt all threads in order to find out where in Java their instruction pointers are. Compare this to using green threads for the thread implementation in the JVM, as introduced in Chapter 4. Starting and stopping green threads carries very little overhead as OS threads are not part of the equation. That way, the JRockit VE thread implementation has a lot in common with a green thread approach.

The quality of samples for JRockit VE is potentially comparable to hardware-based sampling, also discussed in the chapter on code generation. This helps the JVM make more informed optimization decisions and enables it to work with higher precision in the number of samples required for different levels of reoptimization.

Adaptive heap resizing

Another example of performance potential in the virtual stack would be enabling **adaptive heap resizing** for the JVM.

Most hypervisors support the concept of **ballooning**. Ballooning provides a way for the hypervisor and the guest to communicate about memory usage, without breaking the sandboxing between several guests running on one machine. This is typically implemented with a **balloon driver** showing up to the guest as a fake virtual device. This can be used by the hypervisor to hint to a guest that it needs more memory. This can be done by "inflating" the balloon driver, making it take up more memory. Through the balloon driver, the guest can efficiently get and interpret the message, "release some more memory, or I'll swap you" from the hypervisor, when memory is scarce and needs to be claimed for other guests.

Ballooning may also enable **overcommitment** of memory, i.e. the appearance that the guests together actually use more memory than is physically available to the hardware. This can be a powerful mechanism given that this leads to no actual swapping.

As the Java heap part of the total memory of the virtual machine is orders of magnitude larger than the native memory taken up by the JRockit VE kernel, it follows that the most efficient way to release or claim memory from the hypervisor is to shrink or grow the Java heap. If our hypervisor reports, via the balloon driver, that memory pressure is too high, the JVM should support shrinking its heap through an external API call ("external" meaning exported to the JRockit VE kernel from the JVM). Possibly, this needs to involve triggering a heap compaction first.

The other way around, if too much time is spent in GC, the JVM should ask the kernel if it is possible to claim more memory from the hypervisor. These "memory hint" library calls that are no-ops on platforms outside JRockit VE, are unique to JRockit and JRockit VE. They will be part of the platform abstraction layer that the JVM uses for the JRockit VE platform.

Traditional operating systems have no way of hinting to a process that it should release memory or use more. This opens a whole new chapter in adaptive memory management. JRockit VE is thus able to make sure that the running JVM (its single process) uses exactly the right amount of memory, returns unused memory quickly so other guests on the same hardware can claim it, and avoids swapping by dramatically reducing heap size if resources start to be scarce. This makes JRockit VE ideal for Java in a virtualized environment—it quickly adapts to changing situations and maximizes memory utilization even between different guests.

Inter-thread page protection

Removing a traditional operating system from the layer between the JVM and the hardware can also bring other, perhaps rather surprising, benefits.

Consider the standard OS concepts of threads versus processes. It is, by definition, the case that threads share the same virtual memory in a process. There is no inherent memory protection between threads in the same process. Different processes, however, cannot readily access each others' memory. Now, assume that instead, each thread could reserve memory that would be protected from other threads in the same process as well as from other processes. If a thread tried to access another process-local thread's protected memory with such a mechanism in place, a page fault could be generated. This is similar to when trying to access protected memory in a standard OS. This, more fine-grained, level of page protection is not available in any normal operating system. However, JRockit VE can easily implement it by changing the concept of what a thread is.

Implementing a quick and transparent process-local page protection scheme in the JVM is impossible in a standard operating system, but quite simple when the JVM is tightly integrated with an OS layer like JRockit VE kernel. Oracle has filed several patents on this technology.

To illustrate why this would be useful, we can come up with at least two use cases, where inter-thread (intra-process) page protection would be a very powerful feature for a Java platform.

Improved garbage collection

As we have already discussed in Chapter 3, there are plenty of benefits to thread local object allocation in Java, partly because we avoid repeatedly flushing out new Java objects to the heap, which requires synchronization.

Also recall that many objects in Java die young and can be kept in a nursery for added garbage collection throughput. However, it turns out that several Java applications also tend to exhibit a behavior where many objects are allocated locally in one thread, and then garbage collected before they are seen by (or made available to) other threads in the executing Java program.

It follows that if we had a low-overhead way of extending the thread local allocation areas to smaller self-contained **thread local heaps**, for objects that have not been seen by other threads yet, immense performance benefits might theoretically be gained. Trivially, a thread local heap could be garbage collected in a lock free manner—the problem is maintaining the contract that only thread local objects may exist inside it. If all objects were thread local, a complete latency-free and pauseless GC would be possible. Obviously, this is not the case. Thread local heaps could also be garbage collected independently of each other, which would further decrease latency.

Along with the thread local heaps, a **global heap** (as usual, taking up the largest part of the system memory) would exist for objects that can be seen by more than one thread at the same time. The global heap would be subject to standard garbage collection. Objects in the global heap would be allowed to point out objects in the thread local heaps as long as the GC is extended to keep track of any global to local references.

The main problem with this approach would be to detect if an object changes visibility. Any field store or field load involving a thread local object can make it visible to another thread, and consequently to the rest of the system. This would disqualify it from its thread local heap and it would have to be promoted to the global heap. For necessary simplicity, no two objects on different thread local heaps can be allowed to refer to each other.

In order to maintain this contract in a standard JVM, running on a standard OS, we would need some kind of expensive read and write barrier code each time we try to access a field in an object. The barrier code would check if the accessor is a different thread than the object creator. If this is the case, and if the object has not been seen by other threads before, it would have to be promoted to the common global heap. If the object is still thread local, that is just being accessed by its creating thread, it can still remain in the thread local heap.

The pseudocode for the barriers might look something like this:

```
//someone reads an object from "x.field"
void checkReadAccess(Object x) {
  int myTid = getThreadId();

  //if this object is thread local & belongs to another
  //thread, evacuate it to global heap
  if (!x.isOnGlobalHeap() && !x.internalTo(myTid)) {
    x.evacuateToGlobalHeap();
  }
}
```

```
//someone writes object "y" to "x.field"
void checkWriteAccess(Object x, Object y) {
  if (x.isOnGlobalHeap() && !y.isOnGlobalHeap()) {
    GC.registerGlobalToLocalReference(x, y);
  }
}
```

At least on a 64-bit machine, where address space is vast and readily available, a simple way to identify objects belonging to a particular thread local heap would be to use a few bits in the virtual address of an object to tag it with a thread ID. Read and write barriers would then be only a few short assembly instructions for the fast case—check that the object is still thread local. However, even if all accesses were thread local, the check would still incur a code overhead, and make use of precious registers. Each read and write barrier, i.e. each Java field access, would require the execution of extra native instructions. Naturally, the overhead for the slow case would be even more significant.

Research by Österdahl and others has proven that the barrier overhead makes it impractical to implement thread local garbage collection in a JVM running in a general purpose OS. However, if we had access to a page protection mechanism on a thread level instead of a process level, at least the read barrier would become extremely lightweight. Accessing an object on a thread local heap from a different thread could be made to trigger a fault that the system can trap. This would require no explicit barrier code.

Naturally, even with much more efficient read and write barriers, thread local GC would also increase the total performance overhead in applications where objects need to be frequently promoted to the global heap. The classic producer/consumer example, where objects created by one thread are continuously exported to another would be the simplest, completely inappropriate application for thread local GC.

However, hopefully, it turns out that in the same way that many applications lend themselves well to generational GC, many applications contain large numbers of thread local objects that are never exposed to the rest of the system before being garbage collected.

The approach described in this section seems nice, in that it fits well with the "gambling" approach used in many areas of an adaptive runtime—assume thread locality that is cheap, and take the penalty if proven wrong. Although this all sounds well and good, an industrial strength implementation of thread local garbage collection would be fairly complex, and not enough research has been done to determine if it would be of practical use.

Concurrent compaction

Another application of inter-thread memory protection would be for jobs that are hard to parallelize without massive amounts of synchronization. One example would be heap compaction in the garbage collector. Recall that compaction is an expensive operation as it involves working with objects whose references potentially span the entire heap. Compaction using several threads also requires synchronization to do an object trace, and thus is hard to parallelize properly. Even if we split the heap up into several parts and assign compaction responsibilities to different threads, continuous checks are needed when tracing references to see that one compacting thread doesn't interfere with the work of another.

A concurrent compaction operation would potentially be a lot easier and faster if the interference check was handled implicitly by inter-thread page protection. In the event that one compacting thread tried to interfere with the work of another, this could be communicated by a page protection fault rather than with an explicit check compiled into the GC code. Then the compaction algorithm would potentially require less synchronization.

Summary

This chapter briefly covered virtualization and hypervisors to provide a background for understanding the JRockit Virtual Edition product family. Virtualization is the practice of running software on emulated, virtualized, hardware, and may potentially increase the resource utilization of a machine park. Virtualization also typically comes with some overhead because of the hardware emulation. A virtualized piece of software, for example an operating system, is called a guest. The two most important types of virtualization are full virtualization, where the guest does not know it is virtualized and can run unmodified in the virtualized environment, and paravirtualization that requires the guest to use a communication layer with the underlying system.

The piece of code making it possible to run multiple guests on a single piece of hardware is called a hypervisor. Except for "faking" the hardware to the guest and handling context switching between guests, it can help provide services like device drivers. Hypervisors are either hosted, running as standard operating system applications, or native, installed on bare metal hardware.

JRockit Virtual Edition works by removing the need for a standard general purpose operating system layer in a virtual application stack. Thereby, it increases the performance of a virtualized system. JRockit Virtual Edition can be likened to an operating system that is only able to run a single process—the JVM. Having to provide only the functionality the JVM needs, JRockit VE is vastly simpler than any general purpose operating system. This provides both speed and security.

Offline manageability of virtualized software running on top of JRockit VE is handled by the Image Tool that is part of the JRockit VE product suite. Online manageability and deployment is handled by a hypervisor-specific management framework, such as Oracle VM Manager.

Finally, this chapter discussed how to potentially gain even more power and performance in virtualized Java environments, given the prerequisite that we completely control everything between the hypervisor and the Java application. Our longterm goal is to provide virtual environments for Java that actually perform better than physical ones. We believe this can be done.

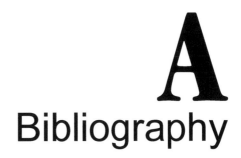

A
Bibliography

Abuaiadh, Diab, Yoav Ossia, Erez Petrank, and Uri Silbershtein. *An efficient parallel heap compaction algorithm*. ACM SIGPLAN Notices, 2004.

Adamson, Alan, David Dagastine, and Stefan Särne. *SPECjbb2005 – A year in the life of a benchmark*. 2007 SPEC Benchmark Workshop, SPEC, 2007.

Adl-Tabatabai, Ali-Reza, Richard L. Hudson, Mauricio J. Serrano, and Sreenivas Subramoney. *Prefetch injection based on hardware monitoring and object metadata*. ACM SIGPLAN Notices, 2004: 267-276.

Aho, Alfred, Ravi Sethi, and Jeffrey D. Ullman. *Compilers: Principles, Techniques, and Tools*. Addison Wesley, 1986.

Allen, Randy, and Ken Kennedy. *Optimizing Compilers for Modern Architectures: A Dependence-based Approach. 1st Edition*. Morgan Kaufmann, 2001.

Alpern, B, et al. *The Jalapeño virtual machine*. IBM Systems Journal (IBM) 39, no. 1 (2000): 211-238.

AMD Corporation. *AMD Virtualization*. `http://www.amd.com/us/products/technologies/virtualization/Pages/virtualization.aspx` (accessed December 31, 2009).

Apple Corporation. *Apple – Rosetta*. `http://www.apple.com/rosetta/` (accessed January 1, 2010).

Bacon, David F., Clement R. Attanasio, Han B. Lee, V.T. Rajan, and Stephen Smith. *Java without the coffee breaks: a nonintrusive multiprocessor garbage collector*. Proceedings of the ACM SIGPLAN 2001 conference on Programming language design and implementation, 2001: 92-103.

Bacon, David F., Perry Cheng, and V.T. Rajan. *A real-time garbage collector with low overhead and consistent utilization*. ACM SIGPLAN Notices, 2003: 285-298.

Bacon, David F., Ravi Konuru, Chet Murthy, and Mauricio Serrano. *Thin locks: featherweight synchronization for Java.* Proceedings of the ACM SIGPLAN 1998 conference on Programming language design and implementation, 1998: 258-268.

Bacon, David, et al. *The "Double-Checked Locking is Broken" Declaration.* http://www.cs.umd.edu/~pugh/java/memoryModel/DoubleCheckedLocking.html (accessed December 31, 2009).

Barabash, Katherine, Yoav Ossia, and Erez Petrank. *Mostly concurrent garbage collection revisited.* Proceedings of the 18th annual ACM SIGPLAN conference on Object-oriented programing, systems, languages, and applications, 2003: 255-268.

Bergamaschi, F, et al. *The Java Community Process(SM) Program - JSR:s Java Specification Requests – detail JSR# 174.* http://jcp.org/en/jsr/detail?id=174 (accessed January 1, 2010).

Blackburn, Stephen M., et al. *The DaCapo benchmarks: Java benchmarking development and analysis.* ACM SIGPLAN Notices, 2006: 169-190.

Blanchet, Bruno. *Escape analysis for Java™: Theory and practice.* ACM Transactions on Programming Languages and Systems (TOPLAS), 2003: 713-775.

Bloch, Joshua. *Effective Java. 2nd Edition.* Prentice Hall, 2008.

Bodik, Rastislav, Rajiv Gupta, and Vivek Sarkar. *ABCD: eliminating array bounds checks on demand.* Proceedings of the ACM SIGPLAN 2000 conference on Programming language design and implementation, 2000: 321-333.

Boehm, Hans-J., Alan J. Demers, and Scott Shenker. *Mostly parallel garbage collection.* ACM SIGPLAN Notices, 1991: 157-164.

Box, Don, and Chris Sells. *Essential .NET, Volume I: The Common Language Runtime.* Addison-Wesley Professional, 2002.

Chaitin, Gregory. *Register allocation and spilling via graph coloring.* ACM SIGPLAN Notices, 1982: 66-74.

Chaitin, Gregory J., Mark A. Auslander, K. Ashok Chandra, John Cocke, Martin E. Hopkins, and Peter W. Markstein. *Register allocation via coloring.* Computer Languages, 1981: 47-57.

Choi, Jong-Deok, Manish Gupta, Mauricio J. Serrano, Vugranam C. Sreedhar, and Samuel P. Midkiff. *Stack allocation and synchronization optimizations for Java using escape analysis.* ACM Transactions on Programming Languages and Systems (TOPLAS), 2003: 876-910.

Chynoweth, Michael, and Mary R. Lee. *Implementing Scalable Atomic Locks for Multi-Core Intel® EM64T and IA32 Architectures. Intel corporation.* November 9, 2009. `http://software.intel.com/en-us/articles/implementing-scalable-atomic-locks-for-multi-core-intel-em64t-and-ia32-architectures/` (accessed January 31, 2010).

Cooper, Keith, and Linda Torczon. *Engineering a Compiler. 1st Edition.* Morgan Kaufmann, 2003.

Cormen, Thomas H., Charles E. Leiserson, Ronald R. Rivest, and Clifford Stein. *Introduction to Algorithms.* McGraw-Hill, 2003.

Cox, J. Stan, Aaron Quirk, Derik Inglis, Nikoli Grcevski, and Piyush Agarwal. *IBM® WebSphere® Application Server WAS V7 64-bit performance – Introducing WebSphere Compressed Reference Technology.* IBM. IBM. November 14, 2008. `ftp://public.dhe.ibm.com/software/webserver/appserv/was/WAS_V7_64-bit_performance.pdf` (accessed January 31, 2010).

Cytron, Ron, Jeanne Ferrante, Barry K. Rosen, Mark N. Wegman, and Kenneth Zadeck. *Efficiently computing static single assignment form and the control dependence graph.* ACM Transactions on Programming Languages and Systems (TOPLAS), 1991: 451-490.

The DaCapo Research Group. *DaCapo Benchmarks Home Page.* `http://dacapobench.org/` (accessed January 1, 2010).

Dahlstedt, Joakim, and Peter Lönnebring. *System and method for using native code interpretation to move threads to a safe state in a runtime environment.* USA Patent 7,080,374. July 18, 2006.

Deneau, Tom. *How JVMs use Escape Analysis to Improve Application Performance.* AMD Corporation. 2008. `http://developer.amd.com/documentation/articles/pages/01302008_jvm.aspx` (accessed December 31, 2009).

Dibble, P, et al. *The Java Community Process(SM) Program – JSRs: Java Specification Requests – detail JSR# 1. 2006.* `http://jcp.org/en/jsr/detail?id=1` (accessed December 31, 2009).

Dice, David. *Biased Locking in HotSpot.* August 18, 2006. `http://blogs.sun.com/dave/entry/biased_locking_in_hotspot` (accessed December 31, 2009).

Dice, David, Mark Moir, and William Scherer. *Quickly Reacquirable Locks.* 2006.

Domani, Tamar, Gal Goldshtein, Elliot K. Kolodner, Ethan Lewis, Erez Petrank, and Dafna Sheinwald. *Thread-local heaps for Java.* Proceedings of the 3rd international symposium on Memory management. Berlin, Germany: ACM, 2002. 76-87.

Eclipse. PDE. http://www.eclipse.org/pde/ (accessed April 20, 2010).

Fink, Stephen J., and Feng Qian. *Design, implementation and evaluation of adaptive recompilation with on-stack replacement.* ACM International Conference Proceeding Series, 2003: 241-252.

Goetz, Brian. *Java theory and practice: Fixing the Java Memory Model, Part 1.* http://www.ibm.com/developerworks/library/j-jtp03304/ (accessed December 31, 2009).

Goetz, Brian, Tim Peierls, Joshua Bloch, Joseph Bowbeer, David Holmes, and Doug Lea. *Java Concurrency in Practice.* Addison-Wesley, 2006.

Gosling, James, Bill Joy, Guy Steele, and Gilad Bracha. *The Java™ Language Specification. 3rd Edition.* Addison-Wesley, 2005.

Gough, John. *Compiling for the .NET Common Language Runtime (CLR).* Prentice Hall, 2001.

Grove, David. *Ramblings on Object Models.* January 11, 2006. http://moxie.sourceforge.net/meetings/20060111/grove-ngvm.pdf (accessed January 10, 2010).

von Hagen, William. *The Definitive Guide to GCC. 2nd Edition.* Apress, 2006.

Hirt, Marcus. Marcus Hirt's Oracle Blog. Oracle Corporation. http://blogs.oracle.com/hirt (accessed April 20, 2010).

Hirt, Marcus. *Oracle JRockit Mission Control Overview.* Oracle. 2008. http://www.oracle.com/technology/products/jrockit/pdf/missioncontrol_whitepaper_june08.pdf (accessed April 20, 2010).

Hyde, Paul. *Java Thread Programming. 1st Edition.* Sams, 1999.

Intel Corporation. *Intel® 64 and IA-32 Architecture Software Developer's Manuals.* http://www.intel.com/products/processor/manuals/ (accessed January 1, 2010).

— *Intel® Itanium® Processor Family - Technical Documents.* http://www.intel.com/design/itanium/documentation.htm (accessed January 1, 2010).

— Intel(R) VTune — Intel® Software Network.
`http://software.intel.com/en-us/intel-vtune/` (accessed January 1, 2010).

— Virtualization technologies from Intel.
`http://www.intel.com/technology/virtualization/`
(accessed December 31, 2009).

Jones, Richard, and Rafael D. Lins. *Garbage Collection: Algorithms for Automatic Dynamic Memory Management.* Wiley, 1996.

Kawahito, Motohiro, Hideaki Komatsu, and Toshio Nakatani. *Effective sign extension elimination for Java.* ACM Transactions on Programming Languages and Systems (TOPLAS), 2006: 106-133.

Kotzmann, Thomas, Christian Wimmer, Hanspeter Mössenböck, Thomas Rodriguez, Kenneth Russell, and David Cox. *Design of the Java HotSpot™ client compiler for Java 6.* ACM Transactions on Architecture and Code Optimization (TACO), 2008.

KVM. `http://www.linux-kvm.org/page/Main_Page` (accessed January 1, 2010).

Lagergren, Marcus. *Experience Talk — "QA Infrastructure — Meeting commercial robustness criteria".* January 11, 2006.
`http://moxie.sourceforge.net/meetings/20060111/lagergren-ngvm.pdf`
(accessed December 31, 2009).

Lagergren, Marcus. *System and method for iterative code optimization using adaptive size metrics.* USA Patent 7,610,580. 2009.

Lea, Doug. *Concurrent Programming in Java™: Design Principles and Patterns. 2nd Edition.* Prentice Hall, 1999.

Lea, Doug. *The JSR-133 Cookbook for Compiler Writers. 2008.*
`http://g.oswego.edu/dl/jmm/cookbook.html` (accessed December 31, 2009).

Lindholm, Tim, and Frank Yellin. *The Java™ Virtual Machine Specification. 2nd Edition.* Prentice Hall, 1999.

Low, Douglas. *Java Control Flow Obfuscation.* Master's Thesis, University of Auckland, Auckland, 1998.

Lueh, Guei-Yuan, Thomas Gross, and Ali-Reza Adl-Tabatabai. *Fusion-based register allocation.* ACM Transactions on Programming Languages and Systems (TOPLAS), 2000: 431-470.

Lueh, Guei-Yuan, Thomas Gross, and Ali-Reza Adl-Tabatabai. *Global Register Allocation Based on Graph Fusion.* Lecture Notes in Computer Science, 1996: 246-265.

Manson, Jeremy, and Brian Goetz. *JSR 133 (Java Memory Model) FAQ. 2004.*
http://www.cs.umd.edu/users/pugh/java/memoryModel/jsr-133-faq.html
(accessed December 31, 2009).

Manson, Jeremy, William Pugh, and Sarita V. Adve. *The Java memory model.*
Proceedings of the 32nd ACM SIGPLAN-SIGACT symposium on Principles of
programming languages, 2005: 378-391.

Microsoft Corporation. *Microsoft: Hyper-V Server Homepage.*
http://www.microsoft.com/hyper-v-server/ (accessed January 1, 2010).

Muchnick, Steven. *Advanced Compiler Design and Implementation. 1st Edition.* Morgan
Kaufmann, 1997.

Nicholas, Ethan. *Understanding Weak References | Java.net.*
http://weblogs.java.net/blog/2006/05/04/understanding-weak-references
(accessed December 31, 2009).

Nolan, Godfrey. *Decompiling Java. 1st Edition.* Apress, 2004.

Oaks, Scott, and Henry Wong. *Java Threads. 3rd Edition.* O'Reilly, 2004.

Öhrström, Fredrik. Fredrik Öhrström's blog. Oracle Corporation. December 2009.
http://blogs.oracle.com/ohrstrom/ (accessed December 31, 2009).

Oracle Corporation. *Deterministic Garbage Collection: Unleash the Power of Java with
Oracle JRockit Real Time.* Oracle Corporation. 2008.
http://www.oracle.com/appserver/docs/jrockit-deterministic-garbage-
whitepaper.pdf.

— *Oracle JRockit.* http://www.oracle.com/technology/products/jrockit/index.
html (accessed December 31, 2009).

— *Oracle JRockit Webdocs.* http://download.oracle.com/docs/cd/E13150_01/
jrockit_jvm/jrockit/webdocs/index.html (accessed December 31, 2009).

— *Oracle VM | Oracle Virtualization.* http://www.oracle.com/virtualization/
(accessed January 1, 2010).

Ossia, Yoav, Ori Ben-Yitzakh, Irit Goft, Elliot K. Kolodner, Victor Leikehman, and
Avi Owshanko. *A parallel, incremental and concurrent GC for servers.* ACM SIGPLAN
Notices, 2002: 129-140.

Österdahl, Henrik. *A Thread-Local Heap Management System for a JVM using Read- and Write-Barriers.* Master's Thesis, Stockholm, Sweden: Royal Institute of Technology, 2005.

Parallels. http://www.parallels.com (accessed February 20, 2010).

Printezis, Tony, and David Detlefs. *A generational mostly-concurrent garbage collector.* ACM SIGPLAN Notices, 2001: 143-154.

Pugh, William. *The Java Memory Model.* http://www.cs.umd.edu/~pugh/java/memoryModel/ (accessed December 31, 2009).

Pugh, W, et al. *The Java Community Process(SM) Program – JSR:s Java Specification Requests – detail JSR# 133. 2004.* http://jcp.org/en/jsr/detail?id=133 (accessed December 31, 2009).

Ravenbrook Corporation. *The Memory Management Glossary. Ravenbrook.* December 04, 2001. http://www.memorymanagement.org/glossary/ (accessed December 31, 2009).

Rivest, Ron R. *RFC 1321 (rfc1321) – The MD5 Message-Digest Algorithm. 1992.* http://www.faqs.org/rfcs/rfc1321.html (accessed December 31, 2009).

Rose, J, et al. *The Java Community Process(SM) Program – JSR:s: Java Specification Requests – detail JSR# 292. 2009.* http://jcp.org/en/jsr/detail?id=292 (accessed December 31, 2009).

Ruf, Erik. *Effective Synchronization Removal for Java.* ACM SIGPLAN Notices, 2000: 208-218.

Shiv, Kumar, Ravi Iyer, Chris Newburn, Joakim Dahlstedt, Marcus Lagergren, and Olof Lindholm. *Impact of JIT/JVM Optimizations on Java Application Performance.* Proceedings of the Seventh Workshop on Interaction between Compilers and Computer Architectures. ACM, 2003. 5.

Siegwart, David, and Martin Hirzel. *Improving locality with parallel hierarchical copying GC.* Proceedings of the 5th international symposium on Memory management. Ottawa, Ontario, CA: ACM, 2006. 52-63.

sipstone.org. *SIP Stone – Benchmarking SIP Server Performance.* http://www.sipstone.org (accessed January 1, 2010).

SPARC International. *SPARC Architecture Manual Version 9.* Edited by David L. Weaver and Tom Germond. Prentice Hall, 1993.

Spec Corporation. *SPECjAppServer2004.*
`http://www.spec.org/jAppServer2004/` (accessed January 1, 2010).

— *SPECjbb2005.* `http://www.spec.org/jbb2005/` (accessed January 1, 2010).

— *SPECjEnterprise2010.* 2010.
`http://www.spec.org/jEnterprise2010` (accessed February 13, 2010).

— *SPECjvm2008.* `http://www.spec.org/jvm2008` (accessed January 1, 2010).

Sun Microsystems. *Java HotSpot Garbage Collection.*
`http://java.sun.com/javase/technologies/hotspot/gc/g1_intro.jsp`
(accessed December 31, 2009).

Ubuntu Server Edition JeOS | Ubuntu.
`http://www.ubuntu.com/products/whatisubuntu/serveredition/jeos`
(accessed January 1, 2010).

Ungar, David. *Generation Scavenging: A non-disruptive high performance storage
reclamation algorithm.* ACM SIGPLAN Notices, May 1984: 157-167.

VirtualBox. `http://www.virtualbox.org/` (accessed January 1, 2010).

VMware corporation. `http://www.vmware.com/` (accessed January 1, 2010).

Wikipedia. *Double-checked locking — Wikipedia, the free encyclopedia.*
`http://en.wikipedia.org/wiki/Double-checked_locking`
(accessed December 31, 2009).

— *JAD (JAva Decompiler) — Wikipedia, the free encyclopedia.*
`http://en.wikipedia.org/wiki/JAD_(JAva_Decompiler)`
(accessed December 31, 2009).

— *Just enough operating system — Wikipedia, the free encyclopedia.*
`http://en.wikipedia.org/wiki/Just_enough_operating_system`
(accessed January 1, 2010).

— *Non-Uniform Memory Access — Wikipedia, the free encyclopedia.*
`http://en.wikipedia.org/wiki/Non-Uniform_Memory_Access`
(accessed December 31, 2009).

— *Page (computer memory) — Wikipedia, the free encyclopedia.*
`http://en.wikipedia.org/wiki/Huge_pages#Huge_pages`
(accessed January 1, 2010).

— *Virtual memory — Wikipedia, the free encyclopedia.*
`http://en.wikipedia.org/wiki/Virtual_memory`
(accessed February 20, 2010).

— Virtualization — Wikipedia, the free encyclopedia.
`http://en.wikipedia.org/wiki/Virtualization`
(accessed January 1, 2010).

XenSource. `http://www.xen.org/` (accessed January 1, 2010).

Zorn, Benjamin. *Barrier Methods for Garbage Collection.* University of Colorado at Boulder, 1990.

Glossary

Abstract syntax tree

An Abstract Syntax Tree (AST) is a representation that the compiler frontend can derive from code, provided that it is structured and unobfuscated. Each node in the AST represents a high-level language construct, such as a loop or an assignment. The AST contains no cycles.

Java bytecode is unstructured and can express more than Java source code, sometimes making it impossible to use it to derive an AST. Thus, the JRockit IR representations are always graphs instead of trees.

See also *IR*.

Access file

In JMX, an access file specifies the access rights of different roles. It is normally located in JROCKIT_HOME/jre/lib/management/jmxremote.access.

See also *Password file* and *JMX*.

Adaptive code generation

Adaptive code generation is the practice of generating code in an adaptive environment, such as just in time or as part of mixed mode interpretation. Typically, this involves reoptimizing code for performance using runtime feedback. A Java Virtual Machine can be an adaptive environment for code generation while a statically compiled system cannot.

See also *JIT compilation* and *Mixed mode interpretation*.

Adaptive memory management

Automatic memory management is the concept of using some kind of runtime memory management, such as a garbage collector. Adaptive memory management, the way the term is used in this book, extends this further by using runtime feedback to control the behavior of the garbage collector for optimum performance.

Agent

In this book, "agent" either refers to the JMX agent or the flight recorder engine depending on context.

See also *JMX* and *JRockit Flight Recorder*.

Ahead-of-time compilation

Usually, ahead-of-time compilation is the process of compiling all or several methods in a system way before they are to be executed. An example would be a C++ compiler that generates a binary executable.

See also *JIT compilation*.

Allocation profiling

This is a JRockit Management Console feature that allows the user to view in real-time how much memory the different threads in an application are allocating. There are also allocation profiling events in the JRockit Flight Recorder, allowing the user to view things like the amount of allocation per thread and allocation histograms on a per-type basis.

AST

See *Abstract syntax tree*.

Atomic instructions

An atomic instruction is guaranteed to be either fully executed or not executed at all, with respect to any consumer of its result. Compared to a normal instruction, which may be executed out-of-order and with weaker memory semantics depending on hardware model, an atomic instruction is usually orders of magnitude slower to execute. An example of a common atomic instruction on many CPU architectures is compare and swap.

See also *compare and swap*.

Automatic memory management

For our purposes, automatic memory management is the concept of using a garbage collector in a runtime system.

Balloon driver

In a virtual environment, the hypervisor can sometimes use a mechanism called a balloon driver, in the form of a virtual device driver, to implicitly communicate the amount of memory available in the outside system to the guest. This way hints that a guest should release memory or risk being swapped out, can be delivered across the virtualization abstraction barrier.

See *Virtualization, Guest, Hypervisor.*

Basic block

A basic block is the smallest control flow unit in an intermediate representation of a compiler. Typically, the basic block contains zero or more instructions and has the characteristic that if one of the instructions in the basic block is executed, the others are guaranteed to be executed as well.

See also *Control flow graph.*

Benchmark driver

A benchmark driver is usually a machine or collection of machines that injects load into a benchmark, but its work is not measured as part of the actual transaction time of the main operation in the benchmark.

Biased locking

See *Lazy unlocking.*

Bytecode

Bytecode is a platform-independent binary representation of source code. In Java, the format of compiled Java is known as Java bytecode. Java bytecode consists of operations that are one byte in length, together with their operands of variable size. Bytecode is less structured than Java source code, in that it can use arbitrary `gotos` and other constructs not available in Java source code. Consequently, it can also express more programs than Java source code.

Bytecode interpretation

Bytecode interpretation is the process of executing a program in bytecode form by emulating the bytecode instructions on a virtual execution stack, along with the current state of the VM, such as contents of local variables. Interpreted bytecodes get to execution faster than if bytecode has to be compiled to native code first, but runtime performance is very poor.

Call profiling

Call profiling typically involves inserting invocation counters in the JIT code to figure out how often a method call is executed, or inserting code that helps to compute a call graph. The collected profiling information is used to aid various code optimizations, for example to help pick better inlining candidates.

See also *Adaptive code generation* and *JIT compilation*.

Card

For our purposes, typically, a structure representing a section of the heap. The entire heap is represented by a number of cards—the card table. The card table is used in generational GC to determine which parts of the old space are dirtied, that is, may have references pointing back to the young space.

See also *Write barrier* and *Generational garbage collection*.

Card Table

See *Card*.

CAS

See *Compare and swap*.

Class block

A class block is JRockit-specific terminology referring to the piece of type information that has to be pointed out by each object header.

See also *Object header*.

Class garbage collection

Class garbage collection is the process of getting rid of class information in the JVM. This happens if a class has been unloaded and no `java.lang.ClassLoader` or piece of code references the class or its methods anymore.

Client-side template

JRockit Mission Control client-side templates are in Java property file format. They are used to control the event settings of a recording. The templates are fully resolved, that is they do not contain wildcards. The templates are also versioned.

See also *Event settings* and *Server-side template*.

Cloud

A cloud is a somewhat fuzzy concept describing a large amount of (possibly virtualized) distributed computing power on which applications can be deployed. Instead of a fixed number of "beige boxes" of different varieties, a collection of servers may be viewed as one large resource pool of computing power.

See also *Virtualization*.

Code generation queue

The code generation queue is JRockit-specific terminology for the ordered code generation requests that need to be executed by the JVM in order to keep a Java program running. The queue is consumed by one or several code generator threads depending on configuration.

See also *Optimization queue*.

Color

For our purposes, a color is an identifying characteristic of a node in either register allocation or in tracing GC algorithms.

In a graph coloring register allocator, variables in use at the same time are represented as adjoining nodes in a graph. The problem of assigning a limited number of registers to a potentially very large set of virtual variables can be reduced to coloring this graph so that no adjoining nodes have the same color. The number of available colors in this case equals the number of available physical registers.

Color can also refer to node characteristics in the search graph in a tracing GC. Mark and sweep typically uses a set of colors to identify which parts of the object graph have been traversed in a GC.

See also *Register allocation* and *Tracing garbage collection*.

Compaction

Compaction is a method to reduce heap fragmentation. Through compaction, objects are moved to form contiguous "live regions" of heap space, so that the case where there are plenty of small "holes" of free space disappears. Full heap compaction is hard to do without stopping the execution of a concurrently running Java program.

See also *Fragmentation*.

Compare and swap

This is a common atomic instruction that exists on many CPU architectures. (x86: `cmpxchg`, SPARC: `cas`). It compares a value in memory with a value in a register, and if they match, overwrites the value in memory with a third value. If successful, the operation sets a status flag that can be used for branching. This can be used to efficiently implement spinlocks.

See also *Atomic instruction* and *Spinlock*.

Compressed references

For our purposes, compressed references refer to an implementation of the Java object model where references to objects in the executing application are smaller than system-wide pointers. For example, if a heap is less than 4 GB on a 64-bit machine, it can still be fully addressed by 32 bits, making it unnecessary to use 64 bits for each object reference in the runtime. This generally creates less overhead loading and dereferencing pointers to Java objects and can provide significant speedups to a program.

See also *Reference compression* and *Reference decompression*.

Concurrent garbage collection

Concurrent GC is a term used in this book to refer to any kind of garbage collection that can largely take place at the same time as a Java program is executing.

See also *Parallel garbage collection*.

Conservative garbage collection

This is the approach of treating everything that looks like an object pointer as an actual object pointer in the GC, avoiding the need to store metainfo about object liveness. The downside to this approach is that it is slow, because extra checks are needed. For example, we trivially know that 17 is not a pointer, since it is outside the heap space, but 0x471148 might well be an object, if it is in the heap range, but could equally well be a constant. Conservative GC also potentially suffers from unintentional object retention if a constant happens to point to an object on the heap. It also severely limits the ability to move objects in memory.

See also *Exact garbage collection*, *Livemap*, and *Safepoint*.

Constant pool

The constant pool is the section of a Java .class file where constants such as strings and large integers are stored for all methods in the class.

Continuous JRA

The concept name for JRockit Flight Recorder was "continuous JRA" during its early development.

See also *JRockit Flight Recorder*.

Control flow graph

A Control Flow Graph (CFG), is a program description that shows the possible paths through a program as a graph (usually with nodes being basic blocks). An edge between nodes in a control flow graph is some kind of jump, for example a goto, a conditional jump, a table switch, or just a fallthrough.

See also *Basic block*.

CPU profiling

CPU profiling is a feature that can be enabled in the JRockit Management Console. It makes CPU usage information available on a per-thread basis.

Critical section

A critical section is a piece of code that can only be executed by one thread at a time. Locks (such as a synchronized block) around the critical section are used to implement this.

Dead code

Code that exists in a program but will never be executed is dead. If the compiler can prove this, it usually removes the dead code from the compiled program.

Deadlock

If two threads are blocked, each holding part of a resource and each needing the other part of the resource to unblock, a deadlock has occurred. In this situation, none of the threads will ever wake up, since they are both blocked waiting for the rest of the resource to become available. While always fatal, a deadlock, at least when the locks involved are fat, consumes no CPU cycles.

See also *Fat lock* and *Livelock*.

Deadlock detection

Deadlock detection is a feature in the JRockit Management Console. It can be used for detecting deadlocked threads.

See also *Deadlock*.

Design mode

Design mode is an unsupported mode of running the JRockit Flight Recorder client. It allows direct access to the tools used to build the user interface. Design mode can be used to customize the GUI, make additions to it, and to export the changes as plug-ins that can be shared with others.

See also *Run mode*.

Deterministic garbage collection

This book uses the term deterministic GC to refer to the low latency garbage collector that comes as part of the JRockit Real Time product.

See also *Latency* and *Soft real-time*.

Diagnostic command

Diagnostic commands can be sent to the JRockit JVM using JRCMD, the `DiagnosticCommand` MBean and/or JMAPI.

See also *JRCMD* and *JMAPI*.

Double-checked locking

Double-checked locking is the attempt to avoid lock acquisition overhead by first checking the locking criterion in an unsafe manner before taking the lock. This is strongly discouraged, since it may behave differently, or not work at all, across memory models.

See also *Java memory model*.

Driver

See *Benchmark driver*.

Editor

A fundamental concept in the Rich Client Platform, the editor normally occupies the central part of the RCP application and provides the central view of the data opened.

See also *Rich client platform*.

Escape analysis

Escape analysis is a code optimization that determines how wide the scope for a particular object is, and potentially removes that object. If it can be proven that an object only exists in a finite scope and doesn't "escape" from it, for example by being passed as a parameter to method calls within the scope, the object need not be allocated and can be represented as its fields as local variables instead. This saves allocation overhead. This is equivalent to allocating an object on the stack instead of on the heap in languages like C++.

Event

In the JRA latency analysis tool and in JRockit Flight Recorder, an event is a set of data associated with a point in time. Some events also have a duration, that is an end time as well as a start time. An event also has an event type describing the event.

See also *Event type*.

Event attribute

An event contains a number of named values. Each of these named values is called an attribute. Event attributes are also referred to as event fields.

See also *Event*.

Event field

See *Event attribute*.

Event settings

Event settings control which event types to record, and other properties such as what threshold to use and whether or not to record stacktraces and thread information.

See also *Client-side template* and *Server-side template*.

Event type

An event type describes a type of event in JRockit Flight Recorder. The event type contains information about the different event fields and other metadata such as the event path, name and description. The relationship between event types and events can be thought of as the relationship between classes and instances.

Exact garbage collection

This is the opposite of conservative garbage collection. In exact garbage collection, the runtime needs to provide enough metadata so that it is known which registers and positions on the local stack frames contain object pointers. Then the garbage collector doesn't need to guess if a pointer-like value really is a pointer or not, trading some memory overhead for the metainfo for faster and more complete GC execution.

See also *Conservative garbage collection*.

Exact profiling

Exact profiling means instrumenting code to get exact profiling results, such as timing every single method invocation or counting every single method call in an application. This typically incurs runtime overhead.

See also *Sample-based profiling*.

Extension point

In Eclipse Equinox (OSGi) terminology, an extension point defines a way that another plug-in can contribute functionality. For example, there is an extension point in the JRockit Management Console that allows third-party plug-ins to implement new tabs. An entity that contributes to an extension point is called an extension.

Fairness

When all threads in a system receive an equal share of the time quantas in which to execute, they are said to be scheduled fairly. This may not necessarily be an attractive property, since frequent context switches incur overhead. However, in many cases, it is important that thread spread for processing is evenly distributed.

Fat lock

A fat lock is a more intelligent, and consequently more complex, lock implementation than a thin lock. The implementation usually involves putting threads to sleep when they are waiting for the lock and keeping a priority queue of candidates who want the lock. Fat locks are more optimal for frequently contended locks or locks that are held for a long time, since they are less CPU-intensive.

See also *Thin lock*.

Fragmentation

Fragmentation is the degradation in allocation behavior and available allocation space that is caused by lots of small heap "holes" where objects have been previously garbage collected. If the heap is full of holes and all of them are fairly small, it might be the case that there is no place to put a freshly allocated larger object, even if the total amount of free space is a significant part of the total heap size. Fragmentation is one of the hardest problems to solve concurrently and efficiently in modern garbage collectors. It is always addressed with some kind of compaction.

See also *Compaction*.

Free list

The free list is the structure that the runtime uses to keep track of available heap space. Typically, the free list points to holes in the heap where new objects can be allocated. The free list keeps track of the holes in a manner that can range from a simple linked list to more priority and size-based approaches. Each time a new object goes on the heap, the free list is used to find a hole of free space where it fits.

See also *Fragmentation*.

Full virtualization

Full virtualization is the practice of using a virtual machine that looks like physical hardware to a guest, and requires no modification of the guest in question.

See also *Virtualization* and *Guest*.

GC heuristic

A GC heuristic is a set of rules determining how the settings for the garbage collector should look. Examples of heuristics are `throughput` and `pausetime`.

See also *GC strategy*.

GC pause ratio

The term GC pause ratio is used in JRockit Mission Control to refer to the total time quota between running application code and stopping the world in the garbage collector. Note that the application runtime is wall clock time and may include latencies such as swapping to disk.

GC strategy

In the JRockit garbage collector, especially in versions prior to R27, this refers to the GC behavior used to best fulfill a heuristic. In JMAPI the strategy is defined as the triple: nursery (on/off), mark phase behavior (parallel/concurrent) and sweep phase behavior (parallel/concurrent).

See *GC heuristic*, *Parallel garbage collection*, and *Concurrent garbage collection*.

Generation

A generation is a part of the total heap. Typically, objects are placed in a particular generation depending on their age (time since they were created).

See also *Heap* and *Generational garbage collection*.

Generational garbage collection

Generational GC is the practice of splitting the heap into two or more regions, or generations. Objects are allocated in a "young generation" or "nursery" that is typically smaller than the main part of the heap. The nursery is frequently garbage collected, and because of its small size, this is quicker than garbage collecting the "old space". Given that most objects are temporary in nature and die young, generational GC is a good memory management optimization. However, generational GC usually adds some kind of overhead for write barriers, which are needed to keep track of references from the old space to the nursery during nursery GC.

See also *Nursery*, *Old space*, *Young space*, and *Write barrier*.

Graph coloring

Graph coloring is an algorithm used in register allocation for computing register assignments. Variables in use (live) at the same time are treated as connected nodes in a graph. The register allocator tries to color the graph using as few colors as possible, so that no adjoining nodes have the same color. If the number of colors used at any given point exceeds the number of available physical registers in the machine, spill code needs to be generated. Graph coloring is NP-hard but can be approximated in quadratic time, still making it one of the most computationally intensive algorithms in a code generation pipeline.

See also *Color*, *Register allocation*, *Graph fusion*, and *Spilling*.

Graph fusion

Graph fusion is an extended variant of graph coloring. The IR is split into sub-regions by some heuristic (typically hotness). The regions are then graph-colored independently and fused afterwards. This process needs to produce shuffle code on the edges between the regions, so that the register assignments of one region map to those of another. If the hotness criteria are good enough, so that the algorithm can start with the hottest parts of the code, this becomes a powerful algorithm. This is because it has the property that less spill code/shuffle code is generated at nodes that are processed early.

See also *Color*, *Register allocation*, *Graph coloring*, and *Spilling*.

Green threads

Green threads is the practice of using one instance of an underlying thread representation (such as an OS thread) to represent several threads of a higher abstraction layer (such as `java.lang.Threads`). While this is simple and fast for uncomplicated applications, there are plenty of problems with this approach. The most serious one has to do with handling threads and the acquisition of locks. In native code, where no control can be exerted over the threads, or when threads are waiting for I/O, deadlocks can occur. If the need arises to put a green thread to sleep, usually the entire OS thread below it has to go to sleep as well, trapping all other green threads in that particular OS thread.

See also *NxM threads*.

Guard page

A guard page is a special page in memory that has its OS-level page protection bit set. Thus, trying to dereference the page will throw an exception. This is used, for example, as a mechanism to detect stack overflows by keeping guard pages at the end of the stack. It can also be used for implementing safepoints, by protecting a previously unprotected guard page that is dereferenced from the generated code at a given safepoint. This makes the runtime throw an exception the next time that safepoint is reached, and control can be halted in a structured manner.

See also *Safepoint* and *Livemap*.

Guest

A self-contained system, such as an operating system, that runs on top of a hypervisor is referred to as a guest. Several guests can run on top of one hypervisor, but this setup is normally not visible to the guests, who, in the case of full virtualization, each believe themselves to be running directly on physical hardware.

See also *Virtualization* and *Hypervisor*.

Hard real-time

The qualifier "hard" in "hard real-time" is used to refer to environments with real-time requirements that require exact control over latencies. This is often not necessary for a Java server-side application, where soft real-time demands, i.e. a quality of service levels of latencies rather than explicit control over the GC typically is enough.

See also *Soft real-time*.

Hardware prefetching

Hardware prefetching is prefetching implemented in the underlying hardware, typically when a CPU heuristically tries to prefetch appropriate data before it is accessed, without interaction from the running program.

See also *Prefetching* and *Software prefetching*.

Heap

For our purposes, the heap is the space in memory reserved for Java objects in the Java Virtual Machine.

See also *Native memory*.

HIR

HIR stands for High Level Intermediate Representation. In JRockit, this is what the bytecode first turns into, when generating native code from bytecode. JRockit HIR is a directed control flow graph with basic blocks as nodes. Each basic block contains zero or more operations, which in turn may use other operations as operands. JRockit HIR is, like Java, completely platform-independent.

See also *MIR*, *LIR*, *IR*, *Register allocation*, and *Native code*.

Hosted hypervisor

A hosted hypervisor is a hypervisor that runs as a user application in an existing operating system.

See also *Hypervisor*.

Hypervisor

A hypervisor is a piece of software that enables multiple operating systems, also known as guests, to run concurrently on a physical machine, providing some degree of physical hardware abstraction to each of the guests.

See also *Virtualization*, *Guest*, *Native hypervisor*, and *Hosted hypervisor*.

Inlining

Inlining is a code optimization that saves call overhead by copying callee code into a caller. Done right, this is a very powerful mechanism. However, if inlining is done overoptimistically or for too many cold calls, problems such as instruction cache misses will arise.

Intermediate representation

Intermediate Representation (IR) is the format that a compiler uses to represent code internally. Typically, this is neither the compiled language, nor the native code, but something more generic in between. An IR format should lend itself well to optimization and transforms. In JRockit, the intermediate representation has several tiers, the top tiers looking more like Java code, and the bottom tiers looking more like native code. This is a fairly standard approach.

See also *HIR*, *MIR*, *LIR*, *Register allocation*, and *Native code*.

Internal pointer

For our purposes, an internal pointer is a Java object reference that has been offset so that it points *into* an object rather than to the actual object header where the object starts in memory. While this construct needs to be treated specially by the garbage collector, it is useful when generating high-performance code, to implement things like array traversal. Internal pointers are also necessary on platforms with limited addressing modes, such as IA-64.

IR

See *Intermediate representation*.

Invocation counters

Invocation counters are an instrumentation mechanism for the detection of hot code. Typically, an invocation counter is implemented as a piece of code, compiled into a method header, that increments a value in memory. Thus, each invocation of the method will lead to the counter being incremented. An adaptive runtime can regularly scan the counters to see if they have reached threshold values, which would qualify the method for reoptimization. Invocation counters are quite a coarse tool for hotspot detection and should probably be combined with some other mechanism, for example thread sampling.

See also *Exact profiling* and *Thread sampling*.

Java bytecode

See *Bytecode*.

Java Memory Model

Since Java is a platform-independent language, care has to be taken when executing the same Java program on different CPU architectures. If bytecode loads and stores were simply mapped to native loads and stores, the semantics of the Java program would change between platforms, usually because some platforms impose stronger memory ordering than others.

In order to guarantee that memory operations in Java are interpreted the same way on different architectures, a Java Memory Model exists. It specifies the semantics of memory accesses in Java. When Java first came out, this model was rather broken, but was later made consistent, through the work of JSR-133.

See also *JSR-133*.

JFR

See *JRockit Flight Recorder*.

JIT compilation

JIT compilation stands for Just In Time Compilation. This is the process of compiling a method to native code only just before it is to be executed for the first time.

See also *Static compilation* and *Ahead-of-time compilation*.

JMAPI

JMAPI stands for the JRockit Management API. This is a proprietary JVM management API, used to monitor the JVM and modify its behavior at run time. It was the very first JVM management API in existence, well before any standardization had taken place in this area. JMAPI was partially deprecated in JRockit R28 and will be phased out and replaced by JMXMAPI.

See also *JMXMAPI*.

JMX

Java Management Extensions (JMX) is a standard for monitoring and managing Java applications.

See also *MBean*.

JMXMAPI

JSR-174 introduced a standardized, JMX-based, management API for JVMs. The JRockit specific extensions to that API are known internally as the JMXMAPI. It is a set of MBeans that expose JRockit-specific behavior that is used by JRockit Mission Control. In JRockit, JMXMAPI has been around since R27, where it superseded the JSR-174 implementation from R26. JMXMAPI is not yet officially supported and has so far changed with every major release of JRockit.

See also *JMX*, *JSR-174*, and *MBean*.

JRA

See *JRockit Runtime Analyzer*.

JRCMD

JRCMD is a small command-line utility distributed with the JRockit runtime. It is used to send diagnostic commands to locally running instances of JRockit. JRCMD can be found in the `JROCKIT_HOME/bin` folder. The name JRCMD is short for JRockit CoMmanD.

See also *Diagnostic command*.

JRMC

See *JRockit Mission Control*.

JRockit

JRockit is the umbrella name for a number of different technologies aimed at improving the runtime performance and manageability of Java applications. The JRockit JVM is the flagship product under the JRockit brand. Other products that are included under the JRockit brand are JRockit Virtual Edition, JRockit Real Time, and JRockit Mission Control.

JRockit Flight Recorder

JRockit Flight Recorder (JFR) is the main profiling and diagnostics tool in JRockit R28/JRockit Mission Control 4.0 and later. The flight recorder can continuously record profiling data both in memory buffers and to disk.

JRockit Memory Leak Detector

The JRockit Memory Leak Detector (also known as Memleak) is the memory leak detection and cause analysis tool in the JRockit Mission Control tools suite. The memory leak detector can also be used for other kinds of more general heap analysis.

JRockit Mission Control

JRockit Mission Control (JRMC) is the JRockit tools and manageability suite. It can be used to manage, monitor, and profile applications running on the JRockit JVM. It also includes a tool for tracking down memory leaks.

See also *JRockit Memory Leak Detector*, *JRockit Runtime Analyzer*, and *JRockit Flight Recorder*.

JRockit Runtime Analyzer

The JRockit Runtime Analyzer (JRA) is the main profiling tool in JRockit R27 and earlier versions. Since R27.3, JRA also contains a powerful latency analyzer. This is useful for understanding why a program is idle at certain points during its runtime. The JRockit Runtime Analyzer was superseded by JRockit Flight Recorder in JRockit R28.

See also *JRockit Flight Recorder*.

JSR

A JSR is a Java Specification Request. The Java language and its APIs are subject to change by means of a semi-open process, called the Java Community Process. Whenever a change is to be implemented to the Java standard, it is described in a JSR and subject to a community process with votes. Things like the new Java Memory Model (JSR-133) and support for dynamic languages (JSR-292) are examples of well-known JSRs.

JSR-133

JSR-133 is the now-completed JSR that aimed to solve the initial problems with the Java Memory Model.

See also *JSR* and *Java Memory Model*.

JSR-174

JSR-174 was created to improve and standardize monitoring and management of the Java runtime. JSR-174 resulted in the `java.lang.management` package and the platform MBean server. The JSR is now completed and is implemented in Java 5.0 and later.

See also *JSR, MBean server*.

JSR-292

JSR-292 proposes modifications to the Java language and the bytecode specification in order to better support compiling dynamic languages (for example Ruby) to bytecode and executing them in a JVM.

See also *JSR*.

JVM Browser

The tree view to the left in JRockit Mission Control is called the JVM Browser. It shows the JVMs that Mission Control can connect to.

See also *JRockit Mission Control*.

Keystore

A keystore is used in public key cryptography. It contains both public and private keys and is protected by a passphrase.

See also *Truststore*.

Lane

A lane is a track in the JRockit Flight Recorder **Events | Graph** tab. JRockit Flight Recorder places all event types with the same parent in the same lane. Thus, it is a good idea to ensure that the events of event types under the same parent in the event path do not overlap in time in the same thread.

See also *Event*.

Large pages

Large pages is a mechanism available in all modern operating systems. With large pages, a virtual address page is increased from the order of several kilobytes to the order of several megabytes. The benefit is that virtual address translation gets sped up, since there are less misses in the translation lookaside buffer. The downside is that the size of the smallest addressable unit increases dramatically, which may cause native memory fragmentation.

See also *Native memory*.

Latency

Latency is the cost of performing a transaction, not useful to the transaction itself. This can be, for example, code generation costs and memory management costs in the VM, required for a transaction in a Java application to complete. Unpredictable latencies cause trouble, since it is hard to determine load levels over time. Sometimes, it is better to pay for predictable latencies with lower total throughput.

See also *Stopping the world, Deterministic garbage collection, Concurrent garbage collection,* and *Parallel garbage collection.*

Latency threshold

Timed events in JRockit Flight Recorder have a threshold setting. If the duration of the event is lower than this threshold, it will not be recorded.

See also *JRockit Flight Recorder.*

Lazy unlocking

Lazy unlocking is also sometimes known as biased locking. This is an optimization of lock behavior that works if the assumption is valid that many locks are thread local, albeit possibly frequently taken and released. In lazy unlocking, the runtime gambles that locks are likely to remain thread local. When a lock is released for the first time, the runtime may choose not to unlock it, treating the unlock as a no-op. When the lock is later reacquired by the same thread, that lock also becomes a no-op. The worst case is, of course, if another thread tries to acquire the lazy locked monitor. In that case, it needs to be converted to a normal lock or forcefully unlocked to preserve semantics. Consequently, locks that are "ping ponging" back and forth, repeatedly being acquired and released by different threads are ill-suited for lazy unlocking.

A lazy unlocking implementation typically contains various heuristics to make it perform more optimally in a changing environment, for example, by banning its application on certain objects or certain object types that have too frequently needed to be forcefully unlocked.

LIR

LIR stands for Low Level Intermediate Representation. This is the lowest tier of the JRockit internal representation of Java code. LIR contains constructs like hardware registers and hardware-specific addressing modes. LIR may or may not be register-allocated. Register-allocated LIR maps directly to native code for the current platform.

See also *HIR, MIR, Register allocation, Native code,* and *IR.*

Livelock

When two threads actively compete to acquire an entire resource, where both already hold parts of it without releasing it, we get a livelock. A livelock costs CPU time since the threads competing for the resource do not sleep, but rather make repeated failed attempts to acquire the resource.

See also *Deadlock*.

Livemap

A livemap is a piece of compiler-generated metainfo. It keeps track of which registers and positions on a local stack frame contain objects at a given program point. This is used for exact garbage collection.

See also *Exact garbage collection*.

Live object

An object that is in the root set or referred to by other live objects is live. The terms "live" and "in use" are used interchangeably. A live object may not be garbage collected.

See also *Root set*.

Live set

Live set usually refers to the space in memory that live objects are occupying on the heap.

See also *Live object*.

Live Set + Fragmentation

In effect, this is the amount of heap space that is "in use". This term is used in JRockit Mission Control and determines the lower boundary of the amount of heap memory required to run an application at all.

Lock deflation

Lock deflation is the practice of, possibly heuristically and based on runtime feedback, turning a fat lock into a thin lock. Normally, this is done because a lock previously flagged as contended isn't anymore.

See also *Lock inflation*, *Fat lock*, and *Thin lock*.

Lock fusion

Lock fusion is the process of having the code generator turn two lock/unlock regions that use the same monitor, into a wider one. This is optimal if just a small amount of side-effect-free code exists between them. Lock fusion is one way of reducing the overhead from many frequent acquisitions and releases of a particular monitor. Lazy unlocking is another.

See also *Lazy unlocking*.

Lock inflation

Lock inflation is the practice of, possibly heuristically and based on runtime feedback, turning a thin lock into a fat lock. Normally, this is done because a lock previously thought to be uncontended isn't anymore.

See also *Lock deflation, Fat lock,* and *Thin lock.*

Lock pairing

In Java bytecode, there no implicit way of keeping track of which particular `monitorenter` instruction(s) (locks) are paired with which particular `monitorexit` instruction(s) (unlocks), even though this is explicit and undeniable in Java source code. In order to perform some lock operations quickly and in order to support, for example lazy unlocking and recursive locking with low overhead, it is a good idea to let the code generator try to figure out which locks correspond to which unlocks. This is done in JRockit and is referred to as lock pairing. Lock pairing involves associating lock and unlock instructions with a "lock token", uniquely identifying the lock/unlock pair.

See also *Lazy unlocking, Recursive locking,* and *Lock token.*

Lock token

A lock token is a unique token associated with a lock/unlock pair (or tuple), as determined by lock pairing. Typically, a lock token consists of the object pointer to the Java monitor object with a few extra bits of information at the least significant byte, keeping track of how this monitor is currently locked. Examples of information that is stored can be "thin locked", "fat locked", or "locked recursively". The lock token can also flag the lock or unlock instruction as "unmatched" if it isn't possible to determine where the other half of the lock/unlock tuple is. This is unusual but possible, due to the nature of Java bytecode, and makes for slower synchronization than with paired lock tokens.

See also *Lock pairing.*

Lock word

The lock word is the bits in an object header that contain lock acquisition information about the particular object. In JRockit some GC information resides here as well.

See also *Object header*.

Mark and sweep

Mark and sweep is a tracing garbage collector algorithm that follows live object references in order to establish a live set. Then it removes all untraversed objects that are known not to be live after all references have been traced. The phases of mark and sweep can be parallelized with varying degrees of efficiency. Mark and sweep is the basis of virtually all garbage collectors in commercial JVMs today.

See also *Tracing garbage collection*.

Master password

The master password is used to encrypt and decrypt the passwords stored in JRockit Mission Control.

MBean

MBeans are part of the instrumentation-level JMX specification. An MBean is a managed bean—a Java object representing a resource to be managed. An MBean has attributes that can be read, operations that can be invoked, and notifications that can be emitted.

See, for example, the J2SE management documentation for more information on MBeans at `http://java.sun.com/j2se/1.5.0/docs/guide/management/overview.html#mbeans`.

MBean server

The MBean server is a core component of the JMX infrastructure, managing the life cycle of MBeans and exposing them to consumers through connectors.

See also *JMX* and *MBean*.

MD5

MD5 is a well-known hash function.

Memleak

Memleak is short for the JRockit Memory Leak Detector included in JRockit Mission Control.

See also *JRockit Memory Leak Detector*.

Memory Model

See *Java memory model*.

Method garbage collection

Method garbage collection is also known as garbage collection of code throughout this book. This refers to the process of getting rid of code buffers full of native code that is no longer in use, for example since the methods in question have been reoptimized or regenerated due to invalidated assumptions.

Micro benchmark

A micro benchmark has a small and well-understood workload. Micro benchmarks can be used for testing performance improvements or for performance regression testing.

MIR

MIR stands for Middle Level Intermediate Representation. In JRockit, this is what the bytecode turns into before most platform-independent optimizations are applied. MIR is a directed control flow graph with basic blocks as nodes. Each basic block contains zero or more operations that may only use variables as operands. This is similar to "three address code", the main IR form for most classic compilers. JRockit MIR is, like Java, completely platform-independent.

See also *HIR*, *LIR*, *Register allocation*, *Native code*, and *IR*.

Mixed mode interpretation

Mixed mode interpretation is the act of using bytecode interpretation to execute most parts of a Java program in a JVM, but with added firepower from a JIT compiler. The compiler optimizes methods that the runtime knows are hot, i.e. called frequently or where the program spends large amounts of its time.

See also *Bytecode interpretation*, *Java bytecode*, and *JIT compilation*.

Monitor

A monitor is a class object or a generic instance object that can be used for synchronization. This means using it as the constraining resource when several threads want to access a critical section.

See also *Critical section*.

Name mangling

Name mangling is a bytecode obfuscation technique that replaces names of methods and fields in compiled code with auto generated, less meaningful ones, to prevent an adversary from decompiling the program.

See also *Obfuscation*.

Native code

Native code, in this book, is used interchangeably to mean either assembly language or machine code. Native code is the specific language of a particular hardware architecture, such as x86.

Native hypervisor

A native hypervisor is a hypervisor that installs directly on bare metal hardware.

See also *Hypervisor*.

Native memory

Native memory, the way the term is used in this book, means the parts of memory used by the runtime for purposes other than Java heap. This can be space for code buffers or system memory that is "malloced" when the runtime needs to acquire space for internal data structures.

See also *Heap*.

Native threads

Native threads (sometimes referred to as OS threads) is the thread implementation provided by a particular platform or operating system. One example is POSIX threads on Linux.

Non-contiguous heaps

This is the practice of keeping the Java heap in several non-adjacent chunks of system memory. Non-contiguous heaps require additional bookkeeping, but can vastly increase the amount of available heap space in environments where, for example, the operating system resides in the middle of the address space. This is mostly relevant on 32-bit architectures where the amount of address space is limited.

NxM threads

NxM threads are a variant of green threads, where several native threads (n) contain several green threads (m). This implementation fares a little better than green threads when it comes to issues like deadlocks and blocking I/O, but it is generally not improvement enough to be used in modern commercial JVM environments.

See also *Green threads*.

NUMA

NUMA stands for Non-Uniform Memory Architecture and is a relatively new concept in computer hardware. In order to save bus bandwidth, a NUMA configuration divides the responsibility for parts of the physical address space between several CPUs. A memory operation on a CPU's own part of memory is faster than a memory operation on a different CPU's part of memory which has to be marshalled one or more hops across the bus to the other CPU.

NUMA presents a challenge for adaptive memory management, since object placement on the heap placement becomes much more of an issue.

Nursery

See *Young space*.

Obfuscation

Java code obfuscation is the act of deliberately modifying bytecode so that it will be harder to reverse engineer. Changing names (name mangling) is not harmful to performance, but may of course still cause problems for debuggers. Changing control flow to use constructs not available in Java source code, however, may confuse or break JIT compilers and optimizers. This should be avoided.

See also *Name mangling*.

Object header

In a JVM, each object needs to keep track of some meta info, such as its class, its GC state and if it is used as a monitor in a lock operation. This information is referenced so frequently that it makes little sense to store it anywhere other than in the header of the object itself, accessible by dereferencing the object pointer. Typically, an object header contains lock state, garbage collection state, and type information.

See also *Lock word* and *Class block*.

Object pooling

Object pooling is the practice of avoiding allocation overhead by not allowing objects to be garbage collected. Typically, this is done by having the program reuse objects instead of allocating new ones. This is accomplished by keeping dead object references in a pool to prevent them from being garbage collected. Object pooling is generally discouraged since it interferes with GC heuristics and will make short-lived objects seem like long-lived ones to the memory system.

Old space

In generational GC, the main part of the heap, where objects are placed after being evacuated from the young space(s) when they grow too old, is called the old space.

On-stack replacement

On-stack replacement is the process of switching out code while it is being executed, and replacing it with new code (possibly because of optimization or invalidation). JRockit does not support on-stack replacement. Rather, it waits until the method in question has finished executing until exchanging it for new code. This can lead to some surprising behavior in badly written benchmarks, but turns out to be not much of an issue in "the real world".

Operative set

The operative set is a user-defined set of events in JRockit Mission Control. It is mainly used to filter and to carry the results of a search from one tab to another. The operative set is also used when finding events related to each other through event attributes with a relational key.

See also *Relational key*.

Optimization queue

The optimization queue is JRockit-specific terminology for the queue of code generation requests that need to be executed by the JVM in order to generate new (and better) code for hot methods. The queue is consumed by one to several code optimizer threads, depending on configuration.

See also *Code generation queue.*

Out of the box behavior

Starting a program with default or no extra configuration should ideally be the only thing required in an adaptive runtime. Runtime feedback should provide the system with whatever extra information it needs, making it possible for it to achieve a steady state, optimum behavior, and correct heap size without user intervention. This is sadly enough not always the case in the real world, so good out of the box behavior is a hot research topic for JVMs.

Overprovisioning

Overprovisioning is the practice of deploying applications on more hardware than strictly needed, in order to be able to handle usage spikes.

OS threads

See *Native threads.*

Page protection

Page protection is the practice of making a page in virtual memory unreadable or non-executable (if it contains code). Accessing the page in the forbidden manner triggers an exception. Page protection can be used for all manner of applications, such as detecting stack overflows, enabling cheap safepoints in Java code where threads can be halted, and for switching out old code that is no longer in use instead of executing it..

See also *Guard page* and *Safepoint.*

Parallel garbage collection

Parallel GC, in this book, is a term used to refer to any kind of garbage collection that tries to maximize throughput, without considering latency. This typically leads to unpredictable pauses, since garbage collection when a Java program is halted is algorithmically very much simpler and more parallelizable than when optimizing for low latencies.

See also *Latency, Deterministic garbage collection,* and *Concurrent garbage collection.*

Paravirtualization

Paravirtualization is virtualization where the guest needs to know about the underlying hypervisor, and typically uses an agreed-upon API to communicate with the hypervisor.

See also *Full virtualization* and *Virtualization*.

Password file

In JMX, the password file contains the definitions and passwords for different roles. It is normally located in `JROCKIT_HOME/jre/lib/management/jmxremote.password`.

See also *Access file*.

PDE

PDE is short for Plug-in Development Environment, an Eclipse IDE feature facilitating the development of Equinox (OSGi) plug-ins. The PDE provides wizards and templates for generating boilerplate code for new plug-ins, as well as extension points for adding new templates and wizards.

See also *Extension point*.

Perspective

A perspective is RCP terminology for a predefined configuration of views. For example, there is a JRockit Mission Control perspective with the views most commonly used from JRockit Mission Control. **Window | Reset Perspective** from the main menu can be used to revert to the default configuration.

See also *Rich client platform*.

Phantom References

See *Soft references*.

Prefetching

Prefetching is the act of retrieving memory into cache lines ahead of time, before the memory is to be accessed. While a prefetch is a slow operation, this doesn't necessarily matter if enough time (unrelated instructions to be executed) exists between the prefetch and the memory access in question. Then, the latency caused by the prefetch will be hidden, and the memory access will be orders of magnitude faster, since the memory is guaranteed to be in the cache upon access.

Prefetching can be done implicitly by the CPU (hardware prefetching) or explicitly by the programmer, by placing prefetch instructions in the code (software prefetching).

Software prefetching is often done heuristically by the compiler. In JRockit it is used, for example, to access TLA space for object allocation and in optimized code before large amounts of field accesses take place. Placing prefetch instructions in the wrong locations can be detrimental to performance.

See also *Thread local area*, *Hardware prefetching*, and *Software prefetching*.

Producer

In JRockit Flight Recorder terminology, a producer (or event producer) is an entity that provides a namespace and type definitions for events.

See *Event* and *Event type*.

Promotion

Promotion is the act of moving an object reference to a different, more permanent, area of memory. The term is used, for example, both for moving objects from a Thread Local Area (TLA) to the heap and from a younger generation to an older generation on the heap.

See also *Generational garbage collection* and *Thread local area*.

RCP

See *Rich client platform*.

Read barrier

A read barrier is usually a small piece of code generated by the compiler next to that of a field load. This might be needed for certain kinds of garbage collectors or, for example, to determine if an object that started out thread local is still thread local, or if the field load was executed by a different thread than the one who created the object.

See also *Write barrier*.

Real-time

For our purposes, "real-time" refers to the need to control latencies in a runtime environment, i.e. soft real-time.

See also *Soft real-time* and *Hard real-time*.

Recording agent

See *Recording engine*.

Recording engine

The recording engine is the part of JRockit Flight Recorder that is built into JRockit. It handles I/O, memory buffers, and provides an API for controlling the lifecycle of recordings. It is also known as the recording agent.

Recursive lock

Java permits a lock to be acquired multiple times before being unlocked. Consider, for example, the case where one synchronized method in an object inlines another. The synchronization mechanisms in the VM must handle this, and consequently keep some kind of flag or reference count in order to determine which lock or unlock is the "real" one and which should be treated as a no-op.

See also *Lock pairing* and *Lock token*.

Reference compression

Reference compression is the function that turns a native size reference into a smaller one in an environment where compressed references are used.

See also *Compressed references* and *Reference decompression*.

Reference counting

Reference counting is a method of garbage collection that works by keeping a reference count in each object, tracking the number of referrers to that particular object. Trivially, when there are zero referrers left, the object may be garbage collected. Reference counting is simple to implement but has the intrinsic weakness that cyclic data structures, where several objects have mutual references, can never be garbage collected.

See also *Tracing garbage collection*.

Reference decompression

Reference decompression is the function that turns a compressed reference back into its native form (unpacking the reference) in an environment where compressed references are used.

See also *Compressed references* and *Reference compression*.

Register allocation

Register allocation is the process of turning IR into a more platform-dependent representation by assigning hardware registers to virtual registers/variables. Normally, there exist fewer hardware registers than variables in the program, and if more registers than available have to be in use at the same time, the register allocator will have to "spill" some of them to memory (typically, the user stack). This adds execution overhead to the generated code since additional instructions are used for the spills. Optimal register allocation is a non-trivial and computationally intensive problem.

See also *Spilling*.

Relational key

The relational key is metadata for event type attributes, specifying a relationship between different event types. The value of the relational key for an event type attribute is in URI format. The value of the actual attribute is then used to link the events together.

Rich client platform

This is the Eclipse-based rich client application platform. The core of the Eclipse platform can be used to build applications other than IDEs, using technologies such as the Eclipse OSGi implementation Equinox and the Standard Widget Toolkit (SWT). The JRockit Mission Control client is built on Eclipse RCP.

Role

A role is part of the security framework in JMX for remote monitoring and management. A role is associated with access rights. To be functional, a role must have an entry in both the password and access files.

See also *JMX*, *Password file*, and *Access file*.

Rollforwarding

Rollforwarding is a mechanism used in older versions of JRockit (pre R28) to bring a halted thread to a safepoint by emulating the instructions that remain before the next safepoint, modifying the context of the stopped thread.

See also *Livemap* and *Safepoint*.

Root set

Any tracing garbage collector starts out with a set of objects that are reachable "from the beginning". This usually means the objects present in registers and on the local stack frame in the thread context of the Java threads that are stopped for garbage collection. The root set also contains global data, such as objects in static fields.

See also *Livemap* and *Tracing garbage collection.*

Run mode

Run mode is the default mode of running the JRockit Flight Recorder user interface.

See also *Design mode.*

Safepoint

A safepoint is a place in Java code where a Java thread may halt its execution. The safepoint contains information for the runtime that isn't available in other places, such as which registers contain objects (needed by the GC). The safepoint also guarantees that everything in the thread context is either an object, an internal pointer to an object or not an object. No intermediate states exist.

See also *Livemap.*

Samples

Samples are data collected over a period of time that, with enough resolution, accurately describe the behavior of a program, i.e. where the program spends its time. A fundamental building block for adaptive runtimes is a system that produces enough samples of high enough quality.

Sample-based profiling

Sample-based profiling is the practice of using a statistically representative subset of all possible data, or samples, to profile an application. If done right, this usually leads to much less profiling overhead and better information than alternative techniques.

See also *Exact profiling.*

Semaphore

A semaphore is a synchronization mechanism that provides functionality built on the semantics of `wait` and `notify`. Every object in Java is equipped with `wait` and `notify` methods.

Executing `wait` in a synchronized context tells the executing thread to go to sleep and wait to be woken up by a notification request. Executing `notify` in a synchronized context tells the scheduler to wake any other thread waiting on the monitor. `notifyAll` in Java does the same, but wakes up all waiting threads—whoever gets to the monitor first gets to execute, the rest must go back to sleep. `notifyAll` is generally safer to use since it avoids deadlocks better. Naturally, it comes with some additional overhead.

See also *Deadlock* and *Monitor*.

Server-side template

A server-side template is information in JSON format, used to control the event settings of a JRockit Flight Recorder recording.

See also *Event settings* and *Client-side template*.

Soft real-time

The qualifier "soft" in soft real-time is used to refer to real-time environments that require some kind of control over latencies, but not an exact bound for every pause. Typically, soft real-time involves specifying a quality of service level for latencies that is not to be exceeded. The JRockit Real Time garbage collection policies support this (deterministic GC).

See also *Hard real-time*.

Soft references

Soft references are Java object classes that are to be treated specially by the garbage collector. Besides from standard "strong" references, there are soft references, weak references, and phantom references, all of which provide different levels of reachability than a standard reference. Soft and weak references are allowed to be garbage collected if memory is scarce, and are typically referenced by a wrapper object. A wrapper object is normally a `Reference` instance. Thus, soft and weak references may automatically be removed from a wrapper object by the GC if no other references exist. Phantom references, never reachable from their wrapper objects, can be used to implement finalization with safer semantics.

Software prefetching

Software prefetching is prefetching implemented by explicitly placing prefetch instructions in program code.

See also *Hardware prefetching* and *Prefetching*.

Spilling

A register allocator needs to map a large number of variables to a smaller number of physical registers. If a larger number of variables are in use at the same time than the number of available registers, spilling needs to take place, i.e. some variables have to be moved to memory. Typically, they are moved to positions on the stack frame of the method that is being generated. Spill move instructions to and from memory are inserted at appropriate places in the code. Large amounts of spill code leads to performance loss.

See also *Register allocation* and *Atomic instructions*.

Spinlock

A spinlock is a small lock implementation that typically consists of an atomic check and a conditional jump, forming a small loop that burns CPU cycles as long as the lock is blocking thread execution. Spinlocks are a good and a simple way to implement uncontended locks that are known to be held for a short time only. For most other applications, spinlocks are suboptimal.

See also *Thin lock* and *Fat lock*.

SSA form

SSA (Single Static Assignment) form is a transform domain for intermediate code where each variable can be written to only once. This makes several optimizations and data flow analyses easier. The transform is possible since SSA form defines a join operator, Φ, that takes an arbitrary number of sources and one destination. The operator defines the destination to be "any of the source variables". Since Φ cannot be expressed as native code on any hardware architecture, SSA form has to be transformed back to normal form before code emission.

Static compilation

Static compilation refers to compilation in a static environment, typically before the program is run and no runtime feedback is available. Static compilation is the way languages like C++ are compiled, ahead of time. Static compilation has the advantage that whole program analyses are known to be true forever because the runtime cannot change the program adaptively and that compile time overhead may be large (since compile time doesn't impact total execution time). Thus, the compiler becomes more efficient. The disadvantage is that an adaptive runtime can provide far better information to base optimization decisions on and optimize for changing program behavior over time.

See also *Ahead-of-time compilation*, *Adaptive code generation*, and *JIT compilation*.

Stop and copy

Stop and copy is a tracing garbage collector technique that partitions the heap into two equally sized halves that are never in use at the same time. The tracing algorithm that computes the live set incrementally moves the live objects to the other heap half during garbage collection, providing the intrinsic property of compaction. After the GC, the other heap half, with the freshly moved objects, is used as the new heap. This algorithm is fairly simple to implement, but obviously wasteful of memory.

See also *Tracing garbage collection*, *Compaction*, and *Fragmentation*.

Stopping the world

Stopping the world refers to the need to halt a thread that is executing application code. This may be needed for internal runtime work. An example of such work is non-concurrent garbage collection. This is a major source of latency in an application. Another source of latency is the application itself when it does things other than execute code, such as waiting for I/O.

See also *Latency*.

Strong references

This is the standard object reference in Java. The qualifier "strong" is rarely used. If it is, this is just to contrast normal (strong) references to soft/weak references.

See also *Soft references*.

SWT

SWT stands for Standard Widget Toolkit. This is the user interface toolkit library used by the Eclipse RCP platform, and consequently also by JRockit Mission Control.

See also *RCP*.

Synthetic attribute

A synthetic attribute does not correspond to a real attribute in a JMX MBean. The synthetic attribute is a client-side construct in the JRockit Mission Control console.

See also *JMX* and *MBean*.

Tab group

A tab group is a set of tabs in the JRockit Mission Control GUI, grouped together.

See also *Tab group toolbar*.

Tab group toolbar

The tab group toolbar is to the left in the JRockit Mission Control Console, JRA, and JRockit Flight Recorder editors.

See also *Tab group*.

Thin lock

A thin lock is a small and simple lock implementation, designed to be optimal for locks that are never contended and quickly released. Thin locks are often implemented as spinlocks.

See also *Fat lock* and *Spinlock*.

Thread local allocation

Thread local allocation is the concept of first allocating new objects in a thread local area, and then promoting them to the heap en masse when the area is full or when otherwise optimal.

See also *Thread local area*.

Thread local area

A Thread Local Area (TLA) is a small thread local buffer used for allocation in the runtime. The use of TLAs may significantly decrease object allocation overhead, since allocating objects in the TLA requires no synchronization. When a thread local buffer is full, it has to be promoted to the ordinary heap.

Thread local heap

A thread local heap is an extension of the thread local area concept. GC can be implemented with several largish thread local heaps and a global heap. This is beneficial if most objects are temporary as well as thread local. In that case, they never need to be put on the global heap, which is subject to more synchronization. Usually, the cost of a thread local garbage collection policy is quite high for everything but quite specific applications. This is because both read barriers and write barriers are required to keep track of if an object is still thread local or if it has been exposed to other threads. There are however environments, such as in a specialized OS layer, where this overhead can be somewhat reduced.

See also *Generational garbage collection* and *Thread local area*.

Thread pooling

Thread pooling is the practice of keeping a number of threads alive in a resource pool and reusing them when they finish executing instead of allocating new threads. This may or may not be a good idea depending on the situation and underlying thread model.

Thread sampling

Thread sampling is a hotspot detection method that works by periodically examining where in a program the executing threads spend their time. Typically, threads are stopped and their instruction pointers are cross-referenced against a table of known methods/regions. Enough samples in a given method means that the method is hot and should be optimized. Thread sampling can, if the number of samples is large enough, also be used on a more fine-grained level, determining which code paths or regions inside a method are hotter than others.

Throughput

Throughput is usually a measurement of the average number of transaction units per time unit. No heed is usually taken to deviations in this value as long as the average is maximized.

See also *Latency* and *Parallel garbage collection*.

TLA

See *Thread local area*.

Tracing garbage collection

Tracing garbage collection is any GC technique that uses an algorithm to traverse object references on the heap, following them from one object to another. This is done in order to establish the set of live objects. After the trace, unreachable objects are known to be dead and can be garbage collected.

See also *Mark and sweep* and *Stop and copy*.

Trampoline

A trampoline is a mechanism used, for example, in JIT compilation without interpretation. A trampoline is usually a piece of native code placed in memory that "pretends" to be a fully compiled method. When the method is called, the trampoline is executed. The trampoline contains code that makes the called method generate itself and then dispatches control to the freshly generated code. Future calls to the trampoline are back patched to go directly to the real method. When no more calls are relayed through the trampoline, its code buffer can be reclaimed.

See also *Method garbage collection* and *JIT compilation*.

Trigger action

A trigger action is simply a custom or predefined action to take when a trigger rule is invoked in the JRockit Management Console.

See also *Trigger rule*.

Trigger condition

A trigger condition is what makes a trigger rule fire. It may contain an attribute value and a condition, for example "trigger when the CPU load is over 90% for two minutes".

See also *Trigger rule*.

Trigger constraint

A trigger constraint limits when a trigger rule may fire, for example only between 8 AM and 5 PM.

See also *Trigger rule*.

Trigger rule

A trigger rule in the Management Console consists of a trigger condition, a trigger action, and optionally, one or more trigger constraints.

See also *Trigger condition*, *Trigger action*, and *Trigger constraint*.

Truststore

The truststore is a repository for the certificates of trusted parties.

See also *Keystore*.

Virtualization

Virtualization is the process of running a guest (such as an operating system) on top of virtualized/emulated hardware through the use of a hypervisor. This enables the concurrent execution of several operating systems on one piece of physical hardware. Potentially, this makes machine resource usage more efficient. Virtualization is also used to turn a server room of physical machines into an abstract "computing cloud", accessible through some unifying management framework.

See also *Guest*, *Hypervisor*, *Full virtualization*, and *Paravirualization*.

Virtual machine image

For our purposes, a virtual machine image is a preinstalled application and a hardware description—a setup ready for virtualization. It typically consists of a hypervisor-specific configuration file and one or more disk images containing a pre-installed application to run. Sometimes, the virtual machine image is referred to as virtual image or virtual appliance.

See also *Virtualization*.

Volatile fields

A `volatile` qualifier on a field in Java imposes stricter memory semantics. Declaring a field volatile guarantees that all threads immediately see the same contents of the field after it has been written to.

See also *Java Memory Model*.

Warm up round

A benchmark warm up round executes a (possibly smaller) run of the main benchmark payload operation. This is used in benchmarking to give adaptive runtimes enough time to achieve a steady state and to eliminate deviation from the main measurements. The main measurements are done later, when warm up is complete.

Weak reference

See *Soft references*.

Write barrier

A write barrier is usually a small piece of code generated by the compiler next to that of a field store. This is needed when the semantics of a field store affect other parts of the system. For example, in generational GCs, it is common to use some kind of write barrier to flag which parts of the entire heap have been written to, or "dirtied". This is because the GC not only needs to trace references pointing from a young generation to the old generation, but the other way around as well. Trivially, there would be no performance benefit from generational GC if the entire old space had to be traversed for each nursery collection. Better instead to pay the price of a few extra instructions of write barrier code for each field store.

See also *Read barrier*, *Generational GC*, *Old space*, and *Young space*.

Young space

A young space is a partition (or several partitions) of the heap, typically orders of magnitude smaller than the entire heap, where new objects are allocated. The young space is garbage collected separately. This works well when there are plenty of temporary or short-lived objects, which is often the case. This is because the smaller young space can be garbage collected more frequently than the rest of the heap. If objects live longer than a preset amount of time, for example, if they survive one young space collection, they are promoted to another partition of the heap that is less frequently garbage collected.

In this book, the terms "young space" and "nursery" are used interchangeably.

See also *Generational garbage collection*.

Index

design mode. *See also* **run mode**

design mode 510

determininstic garbage collection. *See also* **latency**

determininstic garbage collection. *See also* **soft real-time,**

determininstic garbage collection 510

diagnostic commands. *See also* **JMAPI**

diagnostic commands. *See also* **JRCMD**

diagnostic commands 510

direct call 31

disk=[true|false] option 338

dispatch table 31

DMS 342

double-checked locking. *See also* **Java memory model** 511

double checked locking 160, 161

driver. *See* **benchmark driver**

dump_flightrecording command 410

duration events

    Garbage Collection event 334

E

ECID 352

editor. *See also* **rich client platform**

editor 511

Entry class 387

escape analysis 30, 511

event producers 335

events. *See also* **event type**

events

    about 334, 511

    duration events 334

    event producer 335

    event types 335

    instant events 335

    requestable events 335

    timed events 334

event attribute

event Field. *See* **event attribute**

event Field 511

event settings. *See also* **client-side template**

event settings. *See also* **server-side template**

event settings 512

event types 335, 512

exact garbage collection. *See also* **conservative garbage collection**

exact garbage collection 512

exact profiling. *See also* **sample-based profiling**

exact profiling 512

executing Java threads, halting

    conservative garbage collector 83

    exact garbage collector 83

    livemaps 84-86

Execution Context ID. *See* **ECID**

Experimental Update Site 246, 247

extension point 512

externalPercentage flag 198

F

fairness, 512

fat lock. *See also* **thin lock**

fat lock 513

false optimization

    object pooling, types 116

Flight Recorder. *See also* **JRockit Flight Recorder**

Flight Recorder

    client, extending 366

    enabling 336

    GUI builder, accessing 366, 368

    in design mode 368

    in JRockit Mission Control 340

    in run mode 368

    new group, adding 369

    Placement Path group 370

    properties tab group 370

    range selector, adding space to 371

    recording engine 337

Flight Recorder, in JRockit Mission Control

    about 340

    advanced wizard concept 345-348

    client-side templates 341

    Dump Recording dialog 344

    Flight Recorder Control view 340, 343

    interval of recording 345

    ast part of recording 345

    whole recording 345

forbid bit 157

fragmentation. *See* also compaction
fragmentation 75, 513
full virtualization. *See* also guest
full virtualization. *See* also virtualization
full virtualization 513

G

GadgetMaker class 161
garbage collection
  executing Java threads, halting 81
  generational garbage collections 88
  in JRockit 92
  low latency, optimizing for 91
  real-time 107
  reference counting 77
  throughput, optimizing for 91
  tracing 77
  tracing, techniques 77
  tracing techniques, mark and sweep 78, 80
  tracing techniques, stop and copy 80, 81
  write barriers 88, 89
garbage collection, in JRockit
  external compaction 95
  internal compaction 95
  nursery collections 93
  old collections 93
  permanent generations 94
generational garbage collections
  multi generation nurseries 88
GC heuristic. *See* also GC strategy
GC heuristic 513
GC pause ratio 514
GC strategy. *See* concurrent garbage
  collection
GC strategy. *See* parallel garbage collection
GC strategy. *See* also GC heuristic
GC strategy 514
generation. *See* also generational garbage
  collection
generation. *See* also heap
generation 514
generational garbage collection. *See* also
  Nursery
generational garbage collection. *See* also
  young space

generational garbage collection. *See* also
  write barrier
generational garbage collection 514
generic tuning
  compressed references 205
  large pages 206
getAreaFromRadius method 63
globalbuffersize=[size] option 338
graph coloring. *See* also spilling
graph coloring. *See* also graph fusion
graph coloring. *See* also register allocation
graph coloring. *See* also color
graph coloring 59, 514
graph fusion. *See* also spilling
graph fusion. *See* also graph coloring
graph fusion. *See* also register allocation
graph fusion. *See* also color
graph fusion. 59, 515
global heap 489
green threads. *See* also NxM threads
green threads 515
guard page. *See* also livemap
guard page. *See* also safepoint
guard page 515
guest. *See* also hypervisor
guest. *See* also virtualization
guest 515

H

hard real-time. *See* also soft real-time
hard real-time 516
hardware prefetching. *See also* prefetching
hardware prefetching. *See also* *software*
  prefetching.
hardware prefetching 516
heap. *See* also native memory
heap
  about 72, 516
  non-contibuous heap
  spliting, into memory addresses 75, 76
heap_diagnostics command 411- 415
heap management
  compaction 76
  fragmentation 75
  objects, allocating 74, 75

LIR. *See also* **IR**
LIR. *See also* **native code**
LIR 522
list_vmflags command 416, 417
livelock 126
live set. *See also* **live object**
live object. *See also* **deadlock**
live object 523
livemaps. *See also* **exact garbage collection**
livemaps
    about 48, 84, 85, 523
    rollforwarding 86
live set attribute 381
loadWebApp(...) method 356
local variables 21
lock coarsening. *See* **lock fusion**
lock deflation 153
lock fusion. *See* **lazy unlocking**
lock fusion 154
lock heuristics
    -XX:UseAdaptiveFatSpin, using 168
    controlling 168
lock inflation. *See also* **lock deflation**
lock inflation. *See also* **thin lock**
lock inflation. *See also* **fat lock**
lock inflation 152, 524
lock pairing. *See also* **lock token**
lock pairing. *See also* **recursive locking**
lock pairing. *See also* **lazy unlocking**
lock pairing 524
lockprofile_print command 167, 417, 418
lockprofile_reset command 167
lock profiling
    about 166
    enabling, -XX:UseLockProfiling used
        166, 167
    JRCMD, using 167
lock queue
    spinlock 141
lock token
lock token. *See also* **lock pairing**
lock token. *See also* **object header**
lock token 524
Low Level Intermediate Representation.
    See **LIR**
LIR 522

locks
    about 123
    examining, -Xverbose:locks used 162
    fairness 143
    lock word 143-145
locks, synchronization implementation
    fat locks 143
    thin locks 141
    thin locks, spin locks 141, 142
lock token 148, 149
lock word 124

M

malloc object 424
Management Console
    about 251
    Advanced tab group 276
    extension point 284
    form page 284
    General tab group 254-261
    General tab group, actions 256
    MBeans tab group 261
    Other group tab 283
    Other group tab, JConsole 283
    Runtime tab group 271
    using 253
Mark and sweep. *See* **tracing garbage
    collection**
master password 525
MBean
    about 23
    URL 23
MBean server. *See also* **MBean**
MBean server. *See also* **JMX**
MBean server 525
MD5 hash function 525
Memleak. *See also* **JRockit Memory Leak
    Detector**
Memory Model. *See* **Java memory model**
method garbage collection 23
micro benchmark 23
Middle Level Intermediate Representation.
    See **MIR**
MIR. *See also* **IR**
MIR. *See also* **native code**
MIR. *See also* **register allocation**

optimized code
  HIR 58
  LIR 59
  MIR 58
  overview 58
  working 60-63
oracle.ci.jit.count 454
oracle.ci.jit.timeTotal 454
oracle.ci.opt.count 454
oracle.ci.opt.timeTotal 454
Oracle Dynamic Monitoring System.
        See **DMS**
Oracle Enterprise Manager 252
oracle.rt.counterFrequency 454
Oracle WebLogic Diagnostics Framework.
        See **WLDF**
overprovisioning 317

P

page protection. *See* also **safepoint**
page protection. *See* also **guard page**
page protection 530
parallel garbage collection 530
password.properties file 244
password file. *See* also **access file**
password file 531
PDE. *See* also **extension point**
perspective. *See* also **rich client platform**
Phantom References. *See* **soft references**
prefetching. *See* also **software prefetching**
prefetching. *See* also **hardware prefetching**
prefetching. *See* also **Thread Lock Area**
prefetching 531
PDE 246, 285
PDE Integration Plug-in 284
performance issues, problems
  Java, not siver bullet 217
  live data in large amounts 216
  wrong heap size 216
perspective 229
PID 404
plain crashes 126
platform independence language
  benefit 20
Plug-in Development Environment. *See* **PDE**
pre-multiplier 261

print_class_summary command 419
print_codegen_list 420
print_memusage command 421-428
print_object_summary command 428, 431
print_properties command 431
print_threads command 432, 434
print_utf8pool command 434
print_vm_state command 434, 435
Process ID. *See* **PID**

R

reader/writer lock 131
real-time garbage collection
  hard real-time 107
  JRockit Real Time 108
  oft real-time 109
recording agent. *See* **recording engine**
recording engine
  about 335, 336
  configuring, options used 337, 338
  highly optimized time stamping of events,
        examples 336
  recording facility, examples 335
  stack traces, examples 335
  threshold, examples 335
recursive locking 153
redefineClass method
  example 450
register allocation 54
relational key
  about 351-353
  GCID, URL 351
renegade threads 150
repository=[dir] option 337
requestable events
  CPU Load Sample event 335
Reset to default button 256
Rockit Management Protocol. *See* **RMP**
RMP 446
rollforwarding
  advantage 86
  disadvantage 87
root set 77
runfinalization 436
run_optfile command 435
runsystemgc command 436

workbench
about 228
editors window 228
views window 228

X

XXcompaction:abortable flag 198
XXcompaction flag 197
XX:DisableOptsAfter=<time> 66
XXgcThreads option 201

Y

young space. *See* also generational garbage collection
young space 543

Thank you for buying
Oracle JRockit

About Packt Publishing

Packt, pronounced 'packed', published its first book "Mastering phpMyAdmin for Effective MySQL Management" in April 2004 and subsequently continued to specialize in publishing highly focused books on specific technologies and solutions.

Our books and publications share the experiences of your fellow IT professionals in adapting and customizing today's systems, applications, and frameworks. Our solution based books give you the knowledge and power to customize the software and technologies you're using to get the job done. Packt books are more specific and less general than the IT books you have seen in the past. Our unique business model allows us to bring you more focused information, giving you more of what you need to know, and less of what you don't.

Packt is a modern, yet unique publishing company, which focuses on producing quality, cutting-edge books for communities of developers, administrators, and newbies alike. For more information, please visit our website: www.packtpub.com.

About Packt Enterprise

In 2010, Packt launched two new brands, Packt Enterprise and Packt Open Source, in order to continue its focus on specialization. This book is part of the Packt Enterprise brand, home to books published on enterprise software – software created by major vendors, including (but not limited to) IBM, Microsoft and Oracle, often for use in other corporations. Its titles will offer information relevant to a range of users of this software, including administrators, developers, architects, and end users.

Writing for Packt

We welcome all inquiries from people who are interested in authoring. Book proposals should be sent to author@packtpub.com. If your book idea is still at an early stage and you would like to discuss it first before writing a formal book proposal, contact us; one of our commissioning editors will get in touch with you.

We're not just looking for published authors; if you have strong technical skills but no writing experience, our experienced editors can help you develop a writing career, or simply get some additional reward for your expertise.

Oracle SOA Suite Developer's Guide

ISBN: 978-1-847193-55-1   Paperback: 652 pages

Design and build Service-Oriented Architecture Solutions with the Oracle SOA Suite 10gR3

1. A hands-on guide to using and applying the Oracle SOA Suite in the delivery of real-world SOA applications.

2. Detailed coverage of the Oracle Service Bus, BPEL Process Manager, Web Service Manager, Rules, Human Workflow, and Business Activity Monitoring.

3. Master the best way to combine / use each of these different components in the implementation of a SOA solution.

Getting Started With Oracle SOA Suite 11g R1 – A Hands-On Tutorial

ISBN: 978-1-847199-78-2   Paperback: 482 pages

Fast track your SOA adoption – Build a service-oriented composite application in just hours!

1. Offers an accelerated learning path for the much anticipated Oracle SOA Suite 11g release

2. Beginning with a discussion of the evolution of SOA, this book sets the stage for your SOA learning experience

3. Includes a comprehensive overview of the Oracle SOA Suite 11g Product Architecture

JDBC 4.0 and Oracle JDeveloper for J2EE Development

ISBN: 978-1-847194-30-5   Paperback: 444 pages

A J2EE developer's guide to using Oracle JDeveloper's integrated database features to build data-driven applications

1. Develop your Java applications using JDBC and Oracle JDeveloper

2. Explore the new features of JDBC 4.0

3. Use JDBC and the data tools in Oracle JDeveloper

4. Configure JDBC with various application servers

5. Build data-driven applications quickly and easily

Oracle VM Manager 2.1.2

ISBN: 978-1-847197-12-2   Paperback: 244 pages

Manage a Flexible and Elastic Data Center with Oracle VM Manager

1. Learn quickly to install Oracle VM Manager and Oracle VM Servers

2. Learn to manage your Virtual Data Center using Oracle VM Manager

3. Import VMs from the Web, template, repositories, and other VM formats such as VMware

4. Learn powerful Xen Hypervisor utilities such as xm, xentop, and virsh

5. A practical hands-on book with step-by-step instructions

Please check **www.PacktPub.com** for information on our titles

Made in the USA
Lexington, KY
19 November 2010